STRUCTURE,
STYLE, and USAGE

STRUCTURE, STYLE, and USAGE
Rhetoric and Reasoning
Third Edition

HULON WILLIS
Bakersfield College

HOLT, RINEHART and WINSTON, INC.
New York   Chicago   San Francisco   Atlanta
Dallas   Montreal   Toronto   London   Sydney

For **PROFESSOR NORMAN L. THOMAS**

Friend, Philosophic Adversary, Mentor

Preface

The course called Freshman Composition varies rather widely from college to college and sometimes from instructor to instructor within one college. For example, one English department may ask its instructors to emphasize various aspects of language study, while another department may use as a chief text a collection of essays on politics, philosophy, the arts, contemporary issues, and so on. But the kind of writing most often asked for in Freshman Composition is, I think, exposition or a mixture of exposition and persuasion. Certainly many students may expect such theme assignments as this:

> Our college is considering establishing a Fairness Committee to evaluate student complaints about teachers. Write an essay explaining who you think should serve on such a committee and why, and what procedures you think the committee should follow in handling a complaint.

Assigned a topic of this kind, a student must know how to write in order to inform and convince. Presumably such topics are common in many courses in Freshman Composition because they give the student practice in the kind of writing that is called for by his college term papers and essay exams, and also practice in the kind of writing that undoubtedly will be required in his professional career. Because I believe there is great wisdom in this view of the purpose of Freshman Composition, this book is limited to a close explication of the rhetoric of exposition and persuasion.

My opening chapter is intended to introduce the student to the kind of writing he is to study (it gives him a brief overview of basic principles) and to the important key terminology that he will encounter over and over. The presentation will, I hope, also increase the student's interest in learning to write well.

Chapter 2, on logic and composition, gives a simple but thorough introduction to inductive and deductive logic and shows that most paragraphs in themes utilize one or the other of these kinds of reasoning. The student learns that one kind of paragraph has an inductive generalization as a topic sentence and is developed with specific details and examples intended to make the generalization convincing. He learns that another kind of paragraph has a deductive conclusion as its topic sentence, with the logical development of the paragraph being intended to demonstrate the validity of the minor premise on which the conclusion in the topic sentence is based (the major premise usually being assumed). (Chapter 4 on paragraph development is tied rather closely to this chapter on logic.)

Chapter 3 on organization is devoted mostly to a simple but, I think, ingenious and effective method of deriving a basic organization of main points for a whole paper. The method calls for the student to use a plural noun, either stated or implied in the theme topic, as a guide to suggest the main points that will serve as topic sentences for the three or four paragraphs in his theme. Though not always applicable, this method of planning a basic organization will serve the student well for most of his college writing. Experience has taught me that the plural-noun approach to organization is the lesson in Freshman Composition that most students value most. Appendix 2 on formal outlining may be used in conjunction with Chapter 3 or may be reserved for application to the research paper. The chapter closes with a student theme plus commentary.

Chapter 4 on paragraphing emphasizes the importance of full development, coherence, and unity. But further, it explains in simple terms how inductive and deductive paragraphs are developed. It includes many sample paragraphs from student themes, showing that most such paragraphs are developed either through illustration (the topic sentence being an inductive generalization) or through logical analysis (the topic sentence being a deductive conclusion). Only simple elements of logic are presented in this chapter (and in Chapter 2); advanced logical theory is rigorously avoided. A full student theme with commentary closes Chapter 4.

Chapter 5 on sentence composition extensively treats the sentence, both from a positive point of view on how to compose strong, well-formed sentences and from a negative point of view on how to avoid faulty or weak sentence structure. The chapter provides extensive material intended to make the student aware of and desirous of achieving a pleasing style. Certain aspects of transformational grammar are treated in the chapter to help the student achieve more syntactic maturity. Chapter 6 on diction also has extensive material designed to help the student achieve a more pleasing style.

Chapter 7 on conventional usage (along with Appendix 3, A Glossary of Usage) covers the whole range of problems in usage that appear in freshman papers. Classes may vary in their need for this chapter. My approach to conventional usage is liberal, but I do comment in appropriate places that instructors may justifiably ask their students for a particular usage, such as *everyone . . . his,* even though the times now allow, at least colloquially, the *everyone . . . their* construction. This chapter on usage can also serve as a reference handbook for the student to use on his own initiative.

Though the chapters proceed in order from the whole composition to word choice, instructors may take up the chapters in a different order —for example, the chapter on paragraphing before the chapter on organization. The only necessity, I think, is that Chapter 2 on logic be considered before Chapter 4 on paragraphing.

Exercises are scattered plentifully throughout the text. Probably no instructor can use all of them (unless he has a two-term course in composition), but I have deliberately tried to make more than enough material available.

There are pertinent and sufficient examples for almost every general statement about the nature of composition. In providing examples I have relied heavily on student writing on the theory that it is a more useful model for students than is professional writing. Thus I hope the students will especially benefit from the plentiful examples.

An *Instructor's Manual* containing solutions to the exercises is available free from the publisher.

I am grateful to the following persons, whose suggestions have, I am confident, made the third edition of *Structure, Style, and Usage* a better book than its predecessors: Richard Beal of Boston University; Marilyn Fisher and Karen Hattaway of San Jacinto College; John I. Hartley of El Camino College; and Joan Setzer of Lamar State College of Technology.

H.W.

Bakersfield, California
January 1973

Contents

Contents
(Detailed)

Table of Exercises

STRUCTURE,
STYLE, and USAGE

CHAPTER 1

Some First
Considerations

FORM AND PURPOSE IN WRITING

Writing is one of man's most complex activities. Its purposes and varieties are manifold. It may be designed to entertain, to inspire, to insult, to persuade, to inform, to deceive, to guide, to enlighten, to provoke action, to prevent action, and so on. It may be a one-sentence memorandum to the milkman or a volume of philosophic discourse; an indulgence in self-expression or a work of impersonal objectivity; a workaday report of simplicity and directness or a masterpiece of subtlety and suggestion. Its creation may be a source of pride and joy or of anxiety and frustration. Its content is subject to a fallible human scrutiny for inaccuracy and bias; its quality is subject to widely varying value judgments; its correctness depends on social conventions and prejudices as well as on the rules of grammar. Though an indispensable tool in the educational process, it often presents the greatest challenge to the student, for it is so various and complex that two people— especially an expert and a novice—may find difficulty in focusing on the same aspect of it in the same way at the same time. Thus composi-

1

tion is one of the most difficult college courses. But it may also be one of the most rewarding.

Even in its complexity the composition course cannot possibly consider all aspects of writing. Indeed, no course in writing, no matter how advanced, can do that. This opening chapter, therefore, will specify in general terms the boundaries of the composition course. Because any writing about writing must concern itself with **form** and **purpose** (which can be translated into *technique* and *meaning*), and because the form and purpose of most student writing fall into a rather narrow range, these first considerations need not be lengthy.

The Four Classical Forms of Discourse

As we have stated, writing takes many forms and fulfills many purposes. But early writers on the nature of writing—scholars called *rhetoricians*—identified four broad forms of discourse (or expression of ideas), each with its own general purpose. The term *rhetoric* was applied to their study of these forms of discourse, and in their studies rhetoricians analyzed techniques in writing (and formal speaking) such as figures of speech, rhythms, word choice, many aspects of sentence structure, and many aspects of arrangement of material both in paragraphs and in the whole composition. Though styles of writing have changed over the centuries, modern rhetoric, which may be defined as "the art of writing effectively so that the writer's purpose is fulfilled with clarity and with pleasure for the reader," is still largely concerned with word choice and many aspects of structure. Much of this text will be devoted to such rhetorical matters.

Though nowadays writing may be classified in various kinds of groupings—with such terms as *journalism, satire, polemics,* and so on— the traditional fourfold classification is still useful and sound as a point of departure for a course in composition or rhetoric. The first of the four classical forms of discourse is **exposition, or expository writing;** its purpose is to inform, explain, or clarify. The word comes from the same root as *expose,* which means "to uncover or place into the open." Thus exposition appeals chiefly to the understanding (rather than to the emotions) and deals chiefly with facts and ideas. It is, simply put, informative writing.

The second form of discourse is **argumentation,** the purpose of which is to persuade. Though emotional suasion often plays a role in argumentation, this form of discourse is in many ways similar to exposition in that it appeals to the understanding and deals with facts and ideas. It does, however, bring logic (discussed in Chapter 2) into play more than do the other forms of discourse. But the term *argumentation* is subject to misunderstanding, since it connotes disagreement, riled tempers, and combativeness, whereas discourse intended to persuade can be calm and quiet, moderate and objective, and not calculated to appeal primarily to the emotions. For this reason some modern rhetoricians make a distinction between argumentation and persuasion. Such a distinction is not necessary for our purposes; we will use only the term **persuasion** and consider it the second form of discourse.

The third form of discourse is **narration**, or **narrative writing**, which is storytelling, either fictional or factual. Its main purpose is to entertain, though passages of narration are often useful in both exposition and persuasion.

The last classical form of discourse is **description**, or **descriptive writing**, which is writing that tells how something looks, feels, tastes, smells, or sounds. It is the form of discourse least used by itself. It appears mostly in narrative writing to develop setting, and its general purpose is to delight and to clarify, but it also is often useful in exposition and persuasion (as we will see in Chapter 4).

The Student's Kind of Writing and Its Utility

Though professional writing is very broad and varied, the kinds of writing asked of college students are chiefly **exposition** and **persuasion.** True, most colleges and universities have newspapers, literary magazines, and courses in creative writing, but only a few students write in these areas, whereas the whole student body writes in composition courses and in such areas as history, sociology, psychology, anthropology, and political science. Because writing for these courses almost always calls upon the student to inform or convince his readers, the rhetorical techniques to be taught in this book are those that apply to exposition and persuasion. We will not, however, make any sharp distinction between the two, first, because they have much in common in their treatment of facts and ideas, and second, because many student papers combine both kinds of discourse. Thus in his writing the student will not say to himself, "Now I am writing exposition" and "Now I am writing persuasion." The two merge easily.

A study of the techniques of exposition and persuasion, then, is the best kind of training in writing that can be given to a college student. Those very few students who become professional writers will most likely direct their advanced study and training to the kinds of artful professional writing they are most interested in. However, the skills necessary for writing good exposition and persuasion are common to almost all kinds of writing, and thus the freshman course in composition is of value to students who will later take courses in imaginative and journalistic writing.

The techniques of writing exposition and persuasion have utility for the student in two broad respects. First, the ability to write clearly is one of the most important assets a college student can have. The students who can best write essay exams and term papers are the ones most likely to succeed in a wide variety of college courses. In fact there are few courses that do not require considerable writing; and such test questions as these confront students almost weekly:

Distinguish between the "big bang" and the "continuous creation" theories of the origin of the universe.

Discuss the chief themes in Emily Dickinson's poetry.

Refute Carstairs's theory that "genetic pools" rather than "social organization" account for group failures.

Define *irony*.

And almost every semester a student is faced with writing at least one term paper on such topics as

Henry David Thoreau's Philosophic Attitudes as Revealed in His *Journals*

An Evaluation of Mark Twain's Social Criticism

Current Scientific Attitudes toward ESP

The Exposure of the Piltdown Hoax

Students who can best write the exposition and persuasion called for in such questions and topics are the ones who graduate with honors. And the beginning course in composition or rhetoric can do much to prepare a student to handle such writing assignments.

Second, the composition course has utility in many professions that students train for in college. Our world is becoming increasingly verbal, and more and more jobs now require the writing of reports, analyses of market conditions, suggestions or arguments designed to influence company policy, evaluations of subordinate workers, and the like. Thus learning the techniques of writing orderly, clear exposition and persuasion can be of great value to the student after he leaves school and enters his profession.

But we should also stress that utility, important as it is, is not the only attribute of the composition course. Many students also derive self-satisfaction from their study of form and style in language, for they discover that they are developing an aspect of their talent for creativity. Students whose initial attitude in a composition course is negative often come to *like* to write because they like to express themselves. Some even start keeping journals in which they write daily. The exciting aspects of writing—for example, developing smoothness, vigor, clarity, and other such qualities—outweigh those dull aspects that have mostly to do with usage.

A BRIEF OVERVIEW OF BASIC PRINCIPLES

As a final preliminary we will summarize more specifically, but briefly, what this book is about, on the assumption that the student will feel more comfortable about his composition course if he understands the direction it will take.

Chapter 2 on **logic** is not concerned with rhetorical techniques as such, but with the kinds of logic that underlie much exposition and persuasion. The chapter shows how we get **generalizations**—such as "high property taxes do not guarantee high quality public services"— into our minds, and also how we (usually unconsciously) use generalizations to arrive at specific **conclusions** (or **deductions**)—such as "my teacher's prejudice caused me to fail." The chapter also examines in detail how we often misuse logic.

Chapter 3 on **organization** and Chapter 4 on **paragraph development** are the ones covered by the word *structure*. Chapter 3 discusses methods of developing a basic organization of **main points** for a paper and of giving proper **arrangement** to these points. It also covers methods of **opening** and **closing** papers.

Chapter 4 is devoted to the structure—or development—of paragraphs. It is meant to teach the student how to convert the main points of his basic organization into **topic sentences** and how to fully develop each topic sentence, either with **illustrative details** or **logical analysis** or with both. The chapter strongly stresses **coherence**—or the linking together of sentences—and **unity,** which is a matter of sticking closely to the subject matter of the paragraph's topic sentence. Chapter 4 is tied closely to the chapter on logic, showing that many paragraphs are developed on the basis of one or the other of the two broad kinds of logic.

Chapter 5 on **sentence composition** and Chapter 6 on **diction** (or word choice) are the ones covered by the word *style*. Many descriptive terms are used to characterize style in writing: lively, dull, fresh, leisurely, flowery, vivid, pretentious, unassuming, bumbling, colorful, drab, rambling, convoluted, simple, unctuous, and many others. Naturally, a beginning composition student cannot be expected to quickly develop an individualistic and charming style, but of necessity all writing has style of some sort; students should try to develop at least a style of clarity and simplicity.

One of the two chief conditioners of writing style is the kind of **sentence structure** the writer employs. Chapter 5 demonstrates that good style calls for **composed sentences,** not just structures thoughtlessly issued from the mind. The chapter includes methods for achieving **economy, clarity, vigor, rhythm,** and **variety** in sentences. It covers something of the **generating processes** that our minds use for creating sentences; study of these processes will help students develop **syntactic maturity,** that is, ability to use a greater range of sentence structures.

Word choice, covered in Chapter 6 on **diction,** is the second chief conditioner of writing style. The chapter considers **levels of diction** and their **appropriateness,** and gives instruction for choosing **precise** and **vigorous diction.** The student will discover that to develop a good style he must *choose* words just as he must *compose* sentences.

Chapter 7 is devoted to the word *usage* in the title. All of the rules covering **conventional usage** are given in this chapter, but the use of these rules may vary widely from student to student, according to individual language backgrounds.

Three appendixes—The Research Paper, Formal Outlining, and A Glossary of Usage—complete the book.

CHAPTER 2

Logic
in Composition

DEFINITION OF LOGIC

Since logic is important in both exposition and persuasion, we will consider here those aspects of it that have a bearing on themes, essay exams, and term papers. Though anyone can usefully study both formal and symbolic logic as separate subjects, we will confine our discussion to the elementary aspects of logic that affect such comments as these:

> The student demonstrators who were jailed got what they deserved.
> I pay daily attention to my horoscope. I got a job on a day it said was financially advantageous for me.

and

> Since Communists are atheists, they will not keep their treaties.

Our discussion of logic provides the needed apparatus for determining the way such assertions get into our minds and for evaluating the soundness of them. Hopefully, an understanding of this apparatus will help you write papers that are reasonably sound in their logic (it is impossible for anyone to make assertions that are always 100 percent valid).

The word *logic* comes from a Greek word meaning "reason," and logic may be defined as "the science of reasoning." **Reasoning** is the act of drawing a **conclusion** (or **inference**) from evidence or what one takes to be evidence. For example, if you see an ambulance going very fast with its siren at full blast, you have evidence to draw the conclusion (or inference) that a medical emergency is in progress. You have reasoned and thus used logic. Logic, then has to do with the association of ideas which, at least in the mind of the reasoner, have a bearing one on the other. Broadly speaking, there are two routes to drawing a conclusion; they will be discussed in the sections below on induction and deduction.

INDUCTION

Definition of Induction

Inductive logic is often defined as "reasoning from the specific to the general," a definition that needs much explanation. With induction a reasoner reaches a conclusion (a conclusion or inference being the end result of all reasoning). The inductive conclusion is *always* a **generalization,** that is, a statement that covers many specifics, such as "cars pollute the atmosphere," which applies to millions of individual cars. The conclusion you drew about the medical emergency is not a generalization but a **specific** (just one incident), and you did not reach it by inductive reasoning but by deductive reasoning (which we will discuss later).

An inductive generalization is reached only after several or many similar occurrences end with the same result, causing the observer to believe that in the future a similar occurrence will also end with the same result. The generalization is then made that "this kind of occurrence will end with this result." For example, a housewife might start noticing that everytime she uses a certain deodorizing spray in her kitchen she feels ill a few hours later. After enough of these specifics, she might draw the inductive conclusion that "use of this particular deodorizing spray makes me ill," a generalization that applies to all instances of her use of the spray. If she were of a scientific bent of mind, she might even experiment to be sure that her inductive conclusion is valid. (Many inductive conclusions are not valid, for people can misinterpret evidence.)

The inductive reasoner, then, starts with specifics and ends with a generalization that will in the future apply to similar specifics. Often the generalization helps the reasoner to avoid past mistakes; and of course other persons may pick up the generalization without having themselves to go through the process of inductive reasoning. For example, each housewife does not need to go through the process of learning that a bloated can of food is spoiled and not safe to eat, for that inductive conclusion was learned long ago and passed on to all housewives. But individuals do draw inductive conclusions of their own, and thus you should be cautious about making an inductive generalization until you have observed enough specifics to assure yourself that the generalization is probably sound. For example, if you observe one or two taxi drivers being surly to their passengers you should not immediately form the inductive generalization that all taxi drivers are surly to their passengers, for you would not have enough specifics to form such a sweeping generalization.

Inductions Arrived at Scientifically

Because science uses the inductive method, let us consider two examples of its use in science. The first example is one in which people arrived at a scientific induction without knowing that they were being scientific. Sometime during the history of man's domestication of animals someone noted that when a breeding pair were the finest of the herd the offspring were also the finest. Later, probably after some crude experimentation, the inductive generalization was arrived at that "selective breeding within a herd will produce the finest offspring." Thus a scientific induction was made. A contemporary result of this induction is that prize bulls sometimes sell for more than $50,000, the purchaser expecting the continued reliability of the inductive generalization.

Here is a second example: in the 1930s a Swiss chemist was surprised to note that a compound he had synthesized (later to be called DDT) killed an insect. He came to no immediate conclusion but instead began testing the compound on various kinds of insects, finding that it invariably killed certain species. Thus he soon could make the inductive generalization that his substance, used properly, would always kill insects of certain species. Some years after the first widespread use of DDT, some observers noted that it no longer killed insects of a certain species. They suspected that this species had changed so that it was now immune to DDT. Further scientific observations led to the inductive generalization that some insect species can develop immunity to DDT. Thus scientific observation and experimentation can lead to inductive generalizations (though such a generalization can be thought valid for a long time, only later to be discovered false because of misinterpretation of evidence).

Inductions Arrived at by Public Experience

But scientific observation and experimentation is not the only way that inductive generalizations are reached. Both the general public and individuals can draw inductive generalizations without being actually scientific. Go back to the example involving the ambulance: you concluded that a medical emergency was in progress, for the inductive generalization was in your mind that a speeding, siren-blasting ambulance means a medical emergency is in progress. This generalization is in the public mind at large and was formed only after enough specific occurrences led people to believe that such an occurrence in the future would have the same meaning. Those who made the original inductive generalization were not being consciously scientific in their method. They drifted naturally into the generalization and passed it on to others.

In the minds of the general public there are thousands of such inductive generalizations not reached by conscious scientific experimentation: that unprotected goods are often stolen; that children in the same family can vary widely in personality; that nylon socks will wear longer than cotton ones. Many such publicly held inductive generalizations are factual, but many are only assumptions. An **assumption** is a supposition or a belief that is taken for granted by some people but that has not been or cannot be conclusively proved. Usually such inductive assumptions are based on far too few specifics to be valid. For example, a surprising number of people hold the generalization that every national Democratic administration will get the nation into a war. Now this is an inductive generalization, not just a political lie, because specific instances led to it. Its believers point out that every Democratic administration since Woodrow Wilson's has had a war. Of course this evidence is not sufficient to establish a factual inductive generalization; it is merely an assumption that many people hold. On the other political hand, there are also a great many people who hold the generalization that every Republican administration will bring on a depression. They have even less evidence for a sound inductive generalization: the Great Depression of Hoover's administration (which was worldwide), a mild depression under Eisenhower, and a mild depression under Nixon.

In short, many people inductively generalize on many topics from just such meager evidence, and in many cases they do harm. Take, for example, generalizations about race. These are usually inductively arrived at in that a few specifics lead to the generalization. No one ever accused the whole race of American Indians of being cruel until he knew of a few specific cases of Indian cruelty. Then he made a false inductive leap to the broad generalization that all Indians are cruel, a belief that permeated the nineteenth century. But in fact, large numbers of Indians were extraordinarily gentle and compassionate, even in the face of white brutality. Because of the complexity of human beings, inductive generalizations involving people—and particularly minorities—should be accepted only with great caution; often no number of specific instances will justify a sweeping generalization. For instance, no one should ever inductively generalize (as has been done) that *all* Frenchmen are sexually immoral until he has evidence that every single Frenchman has been. But in some uncomplicated areas—such as, for example, irrigating with salt water—a very few specific instances are enough to establish a permanent sweeping inductive generalization.

Probability and Qualification in Inductions

In distinguishing between factual inductive generalizations and mere assumptions arrived at by induction, we should remember that a factor of **probability** can enter a generalization normally and reasonably assumed to be factual. For example, the generalization that a speeding, siren-blasting ambulance means a medical emergency is in progress can reasonably be taken as factual, and we all behave as though it is. Yet there is a possibility than an ambulance driver may simply be taking an easy way to get home in a hurry. Or, for another example, it is taken as a factual generalization by cat breeders that Burmese cat parents will produce Burmese kittens. Yet on very rare occasions a kitten identical to a Siamese will be born to Burmese parents. Thus inductive generalizations range from being 100 percent factual (burned oxygen and hydrogen will always produce water) to those that are for all practical purposes factual (the ambulance and the medical emergency) on to assumptions that may have some validity (Eskimos become drunkards when absorbed into white culture) and further on to assumptions that have no validity at all (study of the stars can forecast a person's future). Thus probability must be associated with induction.

In connection with probability, **qualification** also must come into play in a consideration of inductive generalizations. *To qualify* in logic is to limit or restrict, as by conditions or exceptions. Thus if an inductive generalization is stated so that it is restricted rather than sweeping, it may very well be acceptable, even when it relates to, say, a minority race or nationality. For example, if the above assertion were changed to "*some* Eskimos become drunkards when absorbed into white culture," the qualifying effect of *some* produces a valid generalization. Or, for another example, inductive reasoning has led to the quite sound generalization that *many* Scotsmen are stingy. The word *many* qualifies;

put *all* in its place and a questionable sweeping generalization results. Such qualifying words as *sometimes, often, under certain circumstances,* and the like are quite important in dealing with inductive generalizations.

Noninductive Generalizations

Not all generalizations that exist in an individual's mind or in the general public's mind have been inductively arrived at. For example, many millions of people believe the generalization that drinking alcohol incites God's displeasure. Specific, observable instances did not lead to this generalization. It was not reached inductively. The section on deduction that follows shortly treats of noninductive generalizations and the great complexity surrounding some assumptions.

Induction and Student Writing

But what about the student writer and inductive reasoning? All college students have in their minds many inductive generalizations that pertain to their own personal tastes and that can hardly be refuted (**refutation** is the act of destroying the logical basis of a conclusion or generalization). For example, a student might write

> Charlie Chaplin movies are childishly dull.
> I like baroque music better than hard rock.

or

> I get along better by giving in to my father than by rebelling against him.

Such generalizations are arrived at inductively, and often on the basis of just a few specifics. But since many people think of induction only in connection with scientific experimentation, some readers might not accept such generalizations about personal taste as inductive. But *any* generalization that is arrived at on the basis of a few or many specifics is inductive in origin, whether it is factual or a matter of personal taste, whether it is true or false, or even whether it is subject to proof or not. (We might even note that induction goes on in the brains of rats, pigeons, and the like when they learn to press a lever for a reward or to avoid an object to prevent pain.)

Students sometimes write themes based on inductive generalizations about their own personal tastes. For example, if assigned the topic "Desirable Teaching Methods in College," a student might have this topic sentence for one of the paragraphs in his theme:

> In teaching poetry, a professor succeeds best when he demonstrates the relationship between the various poetic devices utilized in the poem and the meaning of the poem.

In developing this paragraph the student would express the specifics (his experiences) that led him to accept the generalization of the topic sentence. He would assume that it would be true in the future teaching of poetry. Thus he would be using inductive logic because he would show that specific instances led to a generalization. But the generalization is one of personal taste or subjective belief and therefore not subject to refutation or disproof. On the same subject another student might have this topic sentence:

> In teaching poetry, a professor succeeds best by letting students read poems aloud and form their own conclusions about them.

Then he would cite specific instances which led him to accept that inductive generalization. The composition teacher might disagree with the student's conclusion, but could not fairly accuse him of faulty logic since the generalization concerns the student's personal tastes.

More important, in other kinds of papers students express inductive generalizations that do not concern personal tastes but concern issues subject at least to objective controversy or, less often, to actual proof. Usually the student expresses such an inductive generalization in the topic sentence of a paragraph, and develops the paragraph with **examples, details, specifics, instances,** or **illustrations** to support the generalization. For example, in a paper entitled "Some Student Gripes," a student wrote this paragraph:

> The Administration, too, pretends to take student opinion into consideration in policy making but actually does not. When we suggested that student evaluation of professors be put in their official files, the Administration did not act. Nor did they pay any attention to our advice that several quiet study centers be set up in places other than the library. The Student Council formally asked that a school-wide poll be taken as to what general education requirements should be mandatory for majors in Arts and Sciences, but no such poll was ever taken. In short, the Administration only pays lip service to the myth that student opinion counts here.

This paragraph illustrates typical use of inductive logic in student writing. The paragraph opens with a topic sentence that expresses a generalization. Then the writer gives three specifics to substantiate that generalization. There would undoubtedly be some administrators who would argue against the validity of the inductive generalization, but the student presented specifics that are quite convincing, and thus his composition teacher could justifiably praise his clear use of inductive reasoning. Though his point is not 100 percent *proved,* his logic is sound.

In Chapter 4 we will have more examples of the development of paragraphs through induction. The main point is that specific details or examples are used to substantiate a generalization.

EXERCISE 1. Analyzing Inductive Generalizations

DIRECTIONS: Decide which of the following generalizations you think came into being because of inductive reasoning, that is, because some people noted specific instances before they thought of the generalization. The others will be noninductive generalizations (which will be discussed in some detail later in the chapter). Comment on the validity of the inductive generalizations, considering probability and the frequent need for qualification of generalizations.

a. Like father, like son.
b. Mother love never fails.
c. When seat belts are widely used, traffic fatalities go down.
d. God punishes the wicked.
e. Fertilizer, judiciously used, increases crop yield.
f. When all citizens vote, better government is assured.
g. In any job hard work will make up for low intelligence.
h. Men are better drivers than women.
i. Democracy is the best form of government for the average citizen.
j. If discovered soon enough, most cancers can be cured.
k. Alcoholics have no will power.
l. Heavy smoking increases the likelihood of lung cancer.
m. Chastity before marriage assures a happier marriage.
n. Atheists will lie freely.
o. Peach trees flourish better in Georgia than in New Hampshire.
p. Blondes have more fun than brunettes.
q. Wealth doesn't bring happiness.
r. Eclipses of the sun can always be predicted.
s. Prayer works.
t. Some politicians in the future will take bribes.
u. Honesty is the best policy.
v. The more highly educated a person is, the more likely he is to vote for the most qualified candidate in an election.
w. Belief in Jesus Christ will bring salvation.
x. A soft answer turneth away wrath.

y. In much wisdom is much grief, and he who increaseth knowledge increaseth sorrow.

EXERCISE 2. Inductive Generalizations

DIRECTIONS: Try to think of five inductive generalizations that you personally have arrived at and have not just accepted from someone else. Evaluate their soundness. Try to avoid generalizations about mere personal taste, though you need not avoid generalizations about people.

DEDUCTION

Definition of Deduction

Deductive logic is the reverse of inductive logic. Recall that with induction we observe specific instances and then reach as a conclusion an inductive generalization that applies to those specifics already observed and presumably to all similar specifics expected in the future. Induction helps us categorize the multitude of specifics that overwhelm us every day so that we can deal with them in something of a rational way. For example, if cooks had to guess anew each time how much of a particular ingredient to put in a particular dish, we would be served many gastronomic failures. But professional cooks carry in their heads hundreds of inductive generalizations that have been arrived at by experience. In putting the generalizations to use in preparing specific dishes, cooks engage in the logical process of deduction. Deduction is often defined as "reasoning from the general to the specific," the opposite of induction, but a better definition is that deduction is "the application of a generalization to a specific instance in order to reach a conclusion." Note that the process has three parts. For example, a cook may hold the (1) **generalization** that one pinch of thyme is desirable for each serving in a casserole dish he often prepares; he applies that generalization to the (2) **specific** that this time his casserole will serve twelve; the (3) **deductive conclusion** he reaches is that he will use twelve pinches of thyme for this particular casserole. He has reversed the process of induction and produced a deduction.

The Prevalence and Complexity of Deductive Reasoning

The example just given may seem so absurdly simple that you might be asking yourself what in the world it has to do with writing exposition and persuasion. The answer is that the logical process the cook used, simple as it seems, is the very one that all of us use dozens of times a day to reach conclusions of both great simplicity and great complexity—and many of the complex ones may be false and harmful. For example, a father once made his young son hold his hands in a large bucket of live eels because "it would be good for his character." The son said years later that the incident had permanently warped one of his mental attitudes. Now the father had gone through the same logical deductive process that the cook had used. The (1) generalization the father held was that having to do something you fear will be good for your character; the (2) specific to which he applied this generalization was that his son would fear putting his hands among the eels; the (3) conclusion the father reached was that making his son put his hands among the eels would be good for his son's character. The father went through exactly the same logical process as the cook, the difference being that the father's conclusion was false because he started with an unsound (or at least unqualified) generalization. It is a common human trait to start with unsound generalizations in making deductions; that is one reason why an understanding of deduction will help you learn to write exposition and persuasion with sounder reasoning. Also, an understanding of deduction will give you a much deeper insight into the process of thinking itself.

Induction, then, is reasoning from the specific to the general, and deduction is reasoning from the general to the specific. In our daily lives we use deduction much more than we use induction. As individuals we don't often reach new inductive generalizations, and even when we do put a new one into our minds—such as that children with certain kinds of brain damage can learn better if given certain drugs—we simply accept it from the observations or experimentations of someone else. An individual can go for weeks or months without acquiring a new inductive generalization of his own. But with almost every decision we make or conclusion we come to we use deduction. We often are not even aware of the generalization that is the starting point of our deduction, but it is buried there in our minds.

Next we will examine a rather simple method for investigating our minds to see just what generalization (it may be inductive or noninductive) has been responsible for our reaching a certain conclusion. An understanding of this apparatus—though the technical terms are not of great importance—can often help us spot flaws in our reasoning.

The Syllogism

One important type of deduction is known as a **syllogism;** it is composed of three parts: the major premise, the minor premise, and the conclusion. A premise is a proposition that serves as grounds for argument. A proposition is a statement affirming or denying something so that it may be stated as true or false. The proposition, whether stated in the affirmative or negative, may or may not be true or may just be doubtful. For example,

> Pigs are greedy animals

is a proposition affirming an idea as true, and the proposition is true. But

> The moon causes insanity

is also a proposition, but undoubtedly is false. Such a proposition as

> Alcoholics have a genetic flaw

may or may not be true, or may be true in only certain cases; no one really knows. It is for some research people an assumption, a belief taken for granted but without definite proof. All such propositions as these can serve as premises in deductive logic.

Here is the structure of a syllogism with definitions rather than ideas filling the slots:

MAJOR PREMISE: A generalization that covers all, many, or some members of a category

MINOR PREMISE: Identification of an object, idea, or the like as a member of the category covered by the major premise

CONCLUSION: An idea that results from the application of the generalization of the major premise to the specific of the minor premise

Here is a simple example of a syllogism with its ideas:

MAJOR PREMISE: All cities are noisy.
MINOR PREMISE: New York is a city.
CONCLUSION: New York is noisy.

The major premise is a generalization applying to all cities. The minor premise is a specific that identifies a particular city. The conclusion is the inevitable outcome of putting these premises together. As you can see, if the premises are both true, the conclusion must be true.

We must emphasize, however, that if the major premise is limited (qualified) the conclusion must be limited. For example:

MAJOR PREMISE: Many cities are noisy.
MINOR PREMISE: New York is a city.
CONCLUSION: New York may be noisy.

The conclusion must be qualified (with *may*) because the major premise is limited (with *many*). We will return to this kind of qualification several times.

Our Unconscious Use of the Syllogism

We all reach many conclusions daily without consciously going through the apparatus of the syllogism. For example, here are two conclusions you might hear by themselves at any time:

Our heating bill will be up again this month.
Jimmy is going to fail his chemistry exam.

Though we don't realize it, we have operated the syllogism to arrive at such conclusions. Here is the way it functions:

MAJOR PREMISE: Any time the weather is very cold our heating bill goes up.
MINOR PREMISE: It was very cold this month.
CONCLUSION: Our heating bill will be up again.

and

MAJOR PREMISE: Anyone who doesn't study for his chemistry exam fails it.
MINOR PREMISE: Jimmy didn't study for his chemistry exam.
CONCLUSION: Jimmy will fail the exam.

Thus the syllogism, though we are usually not conscious of it, is at the basis of every conclusion we draw, or deduction we make. The premises are in our minds, though perhaps not consciously.

The Need to Examine Premises
in Deductive Reasoning

Of course the soundness of a conclusion we draw depends on whether or not our premises are true. Since the minor premise is a specific and often factual, it perhaps is more often than not true, though it is quite possible for a minor premise to be subject to debate or to be downright false. Major premises are often false, or else they so need to be qualified that their use in a syllogism is unwarranted. Thus in drawing conclusions we should be wary of our premises. For example, conclusions such as these sometimes appear in student papers:

We should withdraw from the Vietnam war because it is immoral.
Women's Lib should be outlawed because it is run by revolutionaries.

The syllogism for the first conclusion is this:

MAJOR PREMISE: The United States should withdraw from a war if that war is immoral.

MINOR PREMISE: The Vietnam war is immoral.

CONCLUSION: The United States should withdraw from the Vietnam war.

Now both the major and minor premises here, especially the minor, are subject to endless debate and thus the conclusion is one that may reasonably be disagreed with. If a person wrote a paper with the conclusion given, he would need to reason out both his major and minor premises. The difficulty is that they cannot be inductively proved, and thus in trying to establish their validity the writer would have to draw on his personal value system and personal inclinations. It he does so objectively and with some acceptable reasoning (which would include other deductions and possibly inductions), he should receive praise for his paper even though it could by no means *prove* his point. But if he only says he's right because he's right and that his opponents are therefore wrong, his paper cannot receive praise. An important point to emphasize here is that words like *immoral, better/best, beautiful,* and the like are **value words** and are not subject to proof. But that does not mean we should avoid them in dealing logically with issues.

Now consider the syllogism of the second conclusion above:

MAJOR PREMISE: Any organization run by revolutionaries should be outlawed.

MINOR PREMISE: Women's Lib is run by revolutionaries.

CONCLUSION: Women's Lib should be outlawed.

First, the major premise would be rejected by many solid citizens in our country, though others would accept it. But the minor premise is simply false if the word *revolutionaries* is taken in its accepted meaning of people who want to overthrow and destroy a national government. Thus a composition teacher would generally reject such reasoning in a student paper.

Qualification of Major Premises

Many major premises are sound if qualified. For example, almost everyone would accept this premise:

Many TV ads try to sell the public through use of half-truths.

The qualifying word *many* greatly lessens the value of the premise in reaching a conclusion, for if the major premise is qualified, the conclusion must be qualified too. Example:

MAJOR PREMISE: *Some* auto repair shops will try to sell you repairs you don't need.
MINOR PREMISE: McNamara's is an auto repair shop.
CONCLUSION: McNamara's *may* try to sell you repairs you don't need.

The qualifying *may* of the conclusion is demanded by the qualifying *some* of the major premise. Thus the conclusion is useful only to tell you to be wary of McNamara's (or any auto repair shop) until you have specifics to apply inductively to that one shop.

Many people fail to qualify such premises as these:

Football players make dumb students.
Independent grocers give better service than chain markets.
Policemen are bullies.
Politicians are opportunists.

Failure to qualify such premises often leads to false or harmful conclusions. When a generalization must be qualified, specifics or conclusions deriving from it must be judged on their own merit. For example, when a teacher learns he has a football player in class, he should not immediately assume the player will be a poor student. The teacher should wait to judge the individual case. So beware of syllogisms based on major premises that should be qualified but aren't.

Syllogistic Conclusions as Premises

The conclusion in a syllogism is in a sense a specific deriving from the generalization that is the major premise. But a conclusion may itself be a generalization that can serve as a major premise from which another conclusion may be drawn. For example, here is a syllogistic deduction many would agree with:

MAJOR PREMISE: Any government that restricts noncriminal personal freedom is evil.
MINOR PREMISE: Communism restricts noncriminal personal freedom.
CONCLUSION: Communism is evil.

The conclusion is a specific deriving from the generalization that is the major premise (other forms of government besides communism can also restrict freedom). But it is also a generalization that can serve as a major premise. Example:

MAJOR PREMISE: Communism is evil.
MINOR PREMISE: The government of Russia is communistic.
CONCLUSION: The government of Russia is evil.

This conclusion, too, could serve as a major premise (generalization); so there can be a long chain of syllogisms, with the conclusion of one serving as the major premise of the next.

Enthymemes

The syllogism is an interesting device to investigate, and you will be given some exercises to test your skill in ordering the three parts of a syllogism. Though there are many technical aspects of the syllogism that formal logicians deal with, they are not of consequence in our learning to better understand the reasoning processes in order to write sounder papers. For example, "distribution of terms" in the syllogism has technical names. Consider:

MAJOR PREMISE: All men are mortal.
MINOR PREMISE: Rover is mortal.
CONCLUSION: Rover is a man.

Rover presumably is a dog, and the syllogism is fouled up because its terms are not distributed right. But we need not go into all the technicalities of faulty construction in syllogisms. You can learn to inspect your logic more carefully with just the elementary principles presented in this chapter.

We should mention one technicality, however. Often a conclusion seems to be based on a two-part structure instead of the three-part syllogism. This kind of reasoning is known as an **enthymeme.** Here are two examples:

We should eat organically grown food because it is better for the health.

You should believe in Jesus Christ, for belief in Him will save you.

It seems as though the reasoning structure here is simply this:

PREMISE: Organically grown food is better for the health.
CONCLUSION: We should eat it.

and

PREMISE: Belief in Jesus Christ will save you.
CONCLUSION: You should believe in Him.

But in actuality a syllogism is involved if a specific is understood. Examples:

MAJOR PREMISE: Organically grown food is better for the health.
MINOR PREMISE: We want to eat food that is better for our health.
CONCLUSION: We should eat organically grown food.

and

MAJOR PREMISE: Belief in Jesus Christ will save you.
MINOR PREMISE: You want to be saved.
CONCLUSION: You should believe in Jesus Christ.

The syllogism must really be in the enthymeme, for it is possible that one does not want to eat food better for his health or does not want to be saved. Thus when there is a deductive conclusion there is a syllogism even though one of its parts may escape the reasoner.

In many enthymemes the third part of the syllogism is more apparent than in the above examples because there is a clear **implied assertion**. For example, in such an enthymeme as

Capitalism is desirable because it encourages free enterprise

the implied assertion is

Free enterprise is desirable,

and the syllogism is

MAJOR PREMISE: Free enterprise is desirable.
MINOR PREMISE: Capitalism encourages free enterprise.
CONCLUSION: Capitalism is desirable.

Or in

Contraceptives should not be given to unmarried coeds because that would encourage premarital sex,

the implied assertion is

Premarital sex is wrong,

and the syllogism is

MAJOR PREMISE: Premarital sex is wrong.
MINOR PREMISE: Contraceptives encourage premarital sex.
CONCLUSION: Contraceptives should not be given to unmarried coeds.

In considering some of the points we make in our thinking it might often be worthwhile to establish the actual syllogism so that possible weaknesses in logic might be spotted. But in writing your themes of exposition and persuasion you will seldom construct actual syllogisms—or even think about them.

Inductive and Noninductive Major Premises

Now, to further sharpen your ability to evaluate the validity of deductive conclusions, we will consider the sources and types of the major premises that we all base our conclusions on. So far, we have dealt mostly with inductive generalizations as major premises, and they probably make up the majority of premises we reason from. As we have seen, many of these are 100 percent proved, often through scientific experimentation. For example, the generalization

> Use of certain quantities of vitamin B_1 will help many plants survive transplantation

is now proved. Other sound inductive conclusions are simply products of general public observation but may on rare occasions not be valid. For example, the generalization

> Property values in a neighborhood go up when all utility lines are put underground

can usually be trusted, but a factor of probability does enter it. Many useful inductive generalizations, however, need considerable qualification. For example, the generalization

> Blacks make superb athletes

should be qualified to read

> Some (or many) blacks make superb athletes.

And we have been warned that some inductive generalizations (such as "witches can kill farm animals with magic") are wholly false because evidence has been misinterpreted. But though many inductive generalizations are only assumptions or need qualification or are even wholly false, the *only* kind of generalization that can actually be *proved* is the inductive conclusion. *No other kind of generalization can be proved.*

So, as we have seen, proved and nonproved inductive generalizations abound and serve as major premises for probably a majority of our deductions. But many generalizations that we use as major premises did not arise inductively and thus cannot be proved. A primary source of these is the **cultural value system,** or **social mores,** that a person grows up with. In primitive societies these generalizations are for the most part uniformly held by all members of the society. For example, among the Eskimos who have had little contact with white people, this generalization is held:

> A man should share his wife with any overnight male guest.

The primitive society as a whole simply accepts this cultural generalization.

But in a culture as diverse as ours, many conflicting cultural generalizations are held by various segments of the population. Here are some examples of cultural generalizations held by a part, but not the whole, of our population:

> Extramarital sex is wrong.
> The double standard for men is acceptable.
> Children should be reared with firm discipline.
> Children should be reared with as much freedom from discipline as possible.
> Cleanliness is a virtue.
> Too much washing will weaken a person.
> A college education is desirable.
> Drinking alcohol is wrong.
> Social drinking is acceptable.
> Minding one's own business is a virtue.
> Becoming involved with other people to help them is a virtue.

Thousands of such cultural generalizations do not have an inductive basis, though many people would maintain that they do. For example, those who hold the generalization that children should be reared with firm discipline would try to support their assertion with specifics. Sociologists, psychologists, and other such social scientists do try to experiment in order to find a sound inductive basis for accepting or rejecting cultural generalizations. But for the most part these generalizations remain noninductive, and human nature being so complex, most of them probably never can have a true inductive basis. Yet we use them constantly to draw conclusions. But it is not wrong to draw conclusions on the basis of nonprovable generalizations, for every individual and society must have a cultural value system with noninductive generalizations. In drawing our conclusions, however, we should try to be sensible and reasonably objective.

Closely allied to cultural generalizations are major premises growing out of **religion**; in fact, it is very hard to separate cultural from religious generalizations. For example, such a generalization as

> You should do unto others that which you would have them do unto you

is for many definitely a generalization from their religion. But it did not originate with Christianity and may just as well be considered a cultural generalization. On the other hand, such a generalization as

> Belief in Christ as the Son of God is necessary for salvation

is wholly a religious or theological generalization and is based on faith that is passed from one generation to the next, not on any inductive evidence.

Some people might maintain that some of their major premises simply come from **inner conviction,** which is not based in a specific religion or on a cultural system. A possible example is this:

> One should give more than justice to minorities to compensate for the oppression of them in the past.

But such a generalization probably has as much basis in the holder's cultural-ethical background as it does in his personal inner conviction.

Some people will also claim that **insight** (that is, understanding deriving from native intelligence) is the basis of some of their major premises. An example might be this:

> The criminally insane should be executed for the protection of society.

It is hard to know whether such a generalization stems from what the holder thinks is his special understanding or whether it is a kind of inner conviction (not really based on intelligence or understanding).

Probably many generalizations of this sort are due to one's **learning** (that is, reading in history, philosophy, science, and the like). More examples:

> One is wholly at the mercy of his heredity and environment. (from reading in science)
> Every man has a little divinity in him. (from reading in transcendental philosophy)
> The United States must continue to keep heavy troop concentrations in Europe and Asia. (from reading in military history)

Doubtless an individual's learning can give him many such noninductive premises which are not strictly cultural in origin (but note that they may be false even though based on learning or reading). Various kinds of conclusions can be drawn from premises like these. Note also that such premises may or may not have in them such value words as *must, wrong, desirable,* and so on.

In a society as diverse as ours, many **political major premises** also abound. Though an individual might think that his political premises are inductive because he can cite specifics to substantiate them, it is probable that most of our political premises are noninductive. Some examples:

> Communism is evil.
> Socialism is the best form of government for the common people.
> The government shouldn't give any able-bodied person a free living.
> The government should furnish a guaranteed annual income to every family.

Such premises probably can never have a truly inductive basis.

Even in our day and age **superstition** still provides many people with major premises. Examples:

> The proper study of the stars and planets can forecast the general tendency of one's life.
> Like produces like. (as in hexing)
> Bad luck occurs on Friday the 13th.
> A copper bracelet will ward off various pains.

Some people maintain that their superstitious premises are inductive, since they can cite specifics to substantiate them. For example, in the seventeenth century nearly everyone thought there were enough specific instances to show that witches can kill farm animals by magic. But those people had simply misinterpreted their specifics, just as modern-day readers of horoscopes and other holders of superstitions do.

Some major premises may be attributed to plain **common sense.** Possible examples:

> Rich people should not be exempt from taxes.
> Suffering animals with incurable ailments should be put out of their misery.
> A hard worker should be rewarded more than a slacker.

But even premises that seem to derive from common sense may be at least partially cultural and may not be universally accepted, human nature being so complex.

Thus though the boundaries of their separate categories may be blurred, many major premises do not have an inductive basis and can never have. Since they are unprovable, conclusions drawn from them are not necessarily sound and should be objectively examined. (Remember, too, that though an inductive generalization is the only kind that is provable, many of them have not been and often cannot be proved.) Yet it would be foolish indeed to say that no conclusion should be accepted unless the major premise it is based on can be proved. For example, it once happened that a composition instructor tried to tell a college coed that since the major premise "premarital sex is wrong" has no provable basis, no specific conclusion drawn from it can be valid. Whatever his intention, the instructor misused logic. The girl had a perfect right to her major premise: it was a part of her cultural value system, was not harmful to anyone, and the conclusions she drew from it were valid for her. Moral judgments seldom derive from provable major premises but from generalizations that are part of a cultural value system. And a person has a right to his cultural value system if it harms no one.

But though individuals have a right to hold unprovable cultural generalizations and to draw conclusions from them, many such generalizations are faulty and lead to faulty (and often harmful) conclusions. Also, as we have seen, faulty conclusions can be drawn from inductive generalizations that are not properly qualified. In short, all of us reason badly on many occasions. The section on logical fallacies later in this chapter will show how syllogisms and other reasoning processes often go wrong.

Deduction and Student Writing

But what about deduction and student writing? In much of your writing—themes, essay exams, and term papers—there will be paragraphs that involve deductive reasoning, just as at times there will be paragraphs that involve inductive reasoning. In a paragraph of inductive reasoning, the topic sentence is usually an inductive generalization and the paragraph is developed with specifics intended to substantiate that generalization. In a paragraph of deductive reasoning, the topic sentence will usually be an idea that would be the conclusion of a syllogism (that is, a deduction) if a syllogism were actually constructed. A major premise for the paragraph will usually be assumed and not stated. And the logical development of the paragraph will be an attempt to show that the minor premise (which may be implied or partially stated) is valid. Not all deductive paragraphs will follow this exact formula, but most will.

Here is an example of such a deductive paragraph from a student paper entitled "How to Cure Welfare Abuses":

> Another law should be passed requiring sterilization of every woman who has an illegitimate baby and goes on welfare because of that baby. Most first-time "offenders" who get welfare because of an illegitimate baby are young women, and, in view of their history, they are very unlikely to give up sex. Furthermore, they are not likely to get married because most men will steer clear of marriage (but not sex) with a woman who has an illegitimate child. So this kind of woman is very likely to continue sex without marriage and she will probably be careless about contraceptives. In fact, she might even want more bastards because she knows they will bring bigger welfare checks. I read of one woman in Chicago with six illegitimate children and a tax-free welfare check of $850 a month. The only way to prevent such abuse is to immediately sterilize a woman who goes on welfare because of an illegitimate baby.

The syllogism for the above paragraph is this:

MAJOR PREMISE: Public tax funds should not be used to support women who continue to have illegitimate babies.

MINOR PREMISE: Sterilization is the only method to prevent an unwed, welfare mother from continuing to have illegitimate babies.

CONCLUSION: A woman who goes on welfare because of an illegitimate baby should be sterilized immediately.

The major premise is simply assumed. It was so obvious to the writer that probably he did not even formulate an expression of it in his mind. The minor premise is partially but not formally stated in the last sentence. The logical development of the paragraph is intended to show the validity of the minor premise. The conclusion, which is (in different words) the topic sentence of the paragraph, is then inescapable if the premises are accepted. Of course, there are many who, though they might be forced to accept the minor premise, would reject the conclusion on the grounds that it is better to spend the welfare money than forcibly to sterilize a woman. They would, in effect, not accept the major premise.

It is not necessary for a writer to construct a syllogism in order to write a logically acceptable deductive paragraph, but an elementary understanding of logic undoubtedly improves his ability to write soundly and convincingly. In Chapter 4 on paragraph development you will find other examples of deductive development of paragraphs.

EXERCISE 3.   Creating Syllogisms

DIRECTIONS: By making up proper major and minor premises, create a syllogism for each of the following conclusions. In the premises you may use generalized phrases—such as "such and such conditions" or "of this sort"—but you should make the premises as clear as you can. An example is given in (a) to show the process.

a.   It will rain before nightfall.

Syllogism for (a)

MAJOR PREMISE: Any time the sky has this cloudy appearance, it will rain before nightfall.

MINOR PREMISE: The sky now has this cloudy appearance.

CONCLUSION: It will rain before nightfall.

b.   Even though she knows little, Hazel will get an A from Professor Davenport.

c. The electorate should turn down Senator Snort's bid for a third term.
d. The student body should have a representative on the college's Administrative Committee.
e. Grades in college should be abolished.
f. All college students should be required to take a course in the philosophy of science.
g. Billy should be expelled from our commune.
h. The Republicans should be removed from office.
i. I am going to run away from home.
j. Only students with very high GPA averages should receive scholarships.
k. Henry is a deadbeat.
l. Billy's character is being strengthened.
m. Rosnakoff should be deported from this country.
n. George is going to hell.
o. Workers should sabotage AMG assembly lines.
p. Nobody loves me.

EXERCISE 4. Identifying Major Premises and Creating Syllogisms

DIRECTIONS: Decide which of the conclusions in Exercise 3 can also serve as major premises. Make a syllogism with each one you select.

EXERCISE 5. Cultural Major Premises

DIRECTIONS: Write out five major premises commonly held that you think have a cultural or religious basis only and not an inductive basis. Prepare a syllogism with each of them.

EXERCISE 6. Inductive Major Premises

DIRECTIONS: Write out five major premises that you think are inductive generalizations which came about through public observation and not scientific experimentation. Prepare a syllogism with each of them.

EXERCISE 7. Conclusions and Their Premises

DIRECTIONS: From editorials in newspapers select five statements that seem to be conclusions. What major and minor premises do you think these conclusions derived from?

EXERCISE 8. **Qualification of Major Premises**

DIRECTIONS: Write out five major premises that you think many people hold without qualification but that should be qualified. How would you qualify them?

EXERCISE 9. **Enthymemes**

DIRECTIONS: Show what the full syllogism is in each of the following enthymemes. Comment on the validity of each.

a. We should read the Bible daily so our souls will be pure.
b. We must keep fully armed; otherwise the Russians will conquer us.
c. A boy should have a father because he needs a man to identify with.
d. Pretty girls are less moral than plain ones because more boys pay attention to pretty girls.
e. You shouldn't drink liquor because it harms your liver.

LOGICAL FALLACIES

A **fallacy** is an erroneous or unsound idea, belief, or conclusion. For example, the belief of some African tribesmen that an albino Negro possesses strong magic is undoubtedly a fallacy. But that fallacy is not due to faulty reasoning but merely to superstition. Many false beliefs, however, are due to the misuse of the reasoning processes, and these are called **logical fallacies.** We will examine ten of the most common ones. The first two have already been touched on in the sections on induction and deduction, but we will briefly repeat them here for the sake of clear organization. A study of these logical fallacies will help you spot faulty logic in your own writing.

Faulty Deduction

Perhaps the most common logical fallacy is the **faulty conclusion** of a syllogism that has a false or unqualified premise. Of course the reasoner usually will not consciously go through the syllogism, but it is nevertheless buried in his mind. Here are three typical conclusions that might be encountered in student writing:

Byron's poetry was weak because he was an immoral man.
Professor Turley is a poor teacher because he flunked more than 10 percent of his class.
Sending men to the moon is a waste of money.

The major premises that led to these conclusions are these:

> Poetry written by an immoral man is weak.
> A teacher who flunks more than 10 percent of his class is a poor teacher.
> Scientific exploration of the moon by man is unproductive.

Now these major premises are probably false or at least need qualification, and thus the conclusions drawn from them would be considered logical fallacies by most thinkers. When one examines the premises that lie back of his conclusions, he often catches himself indulging in faulty logic.

Overbroad Generalization or Insufficient Sampling

The logical fallacy of overbroad generalization might also be called **faulty induction,** for it occurs when one draws an inductive generalization on the basis of too few specifics. Sometimes a small sampling warrants an all-inclusive generalization; for example, if one went into the Pacific Ocean at a San Francisco beach once in June, once in July, and once in August and found the water cold each time, he could safely draw the inductive generalization that the Pacific Ocean at San Francisco is always cold in summer, for ocean temperatures change very slowly. Quite often, however, enough sampling to warrant a sweeping generalization is simply not available. Then the generalization needs to be qualified. For example, if one bought three Fiats in a row and got a "lemon" each time, he could draw the qualified generalization that *some* (or *many*) Fiats are lemons. But he could not make the sweeping generalization that *all* Fiats are lemons, for undoubtedly many or most of the millions of Fiats made are sound cars.

Here are some typical overbroad generalizations that one might find in student papers:

> Arabs are lazy.
> Jews will try to cheat you.
> Black Panthers are traitors.
> Blacks don't want school integration.
> Modern poetry is not comprehensible to anybody but a specialist.
> Philosophy texts aren't clear.
> Highway patrol officers don't obey traffic laws themselves.

If such generalizations are to be used at all, they should be qualified with such words as *some, many, a small percentage of,* and so on. Unqualified generalizations like these represent logical fallacies.

Either-Or Thinking

A logical fallacy closely allied to faulty induction or deduction is **either-or,** or **polarized, thinking.** Because some people refuse to see that complexity—often enormous complexity—enters into human problems, they want to reduce everything to black or white, right or wrong, good or bad, and so on. For example, in the Israeli-Arab dispute many people will say that the Israelis are 100 percent in the right because the Hebrews originally lived in Israel. Others will say the Arabs are 100 percent in the right because the Zionists took Israel away from them. Such either-or thinking vastly oversimplifies the problem.

Here are some other examples of either-or thinking that might appear in student papers:

> You must be either for freedom or against it.
> Nobody who favors busing to achieve school integration really believes in the American freedoms.
> If you're a Communist, you'll commit any crime to advance your cause.
> If you believe in a guaranteed annual income for all, you're a socialist.
> If you're not a Christian, you're not to be trusted.
> Abortion is murder.

As you can see, either-or thinking tries to reduce every problem to just two sides, when in reality complex problems almost always admit of several points of view. Polarized thinking often leads to bigotry and lack of tolerance and thus is harmful as well as illogical. Our Puritan forefathers were notorious for their polarized thinking about theology, with the result that they severely persecuted Quakers and other non-Puritans.

False Judgment of Causation

Inductive generalizations are often built on the observation of **cause and result.** For example, if a person notices that every time he eats crab meat he gets sick, he will quickly come to the conclusion that eating crab is the cause of his getting sick and will consequently draw the proper inductive generalization. But all of us frequently misjudge the cause of a particular result and thus commit a logical fallacy. Especially in things human is the determination of cause and result usually very difficult. If we are to be sound in our logic, it behooves us to be wary of ascribing simple causes to complex events.

A common false judgment of causation is the simple fallacy *post hoc, ergo propter hoc.* The phrase means "after this, therefore because of this." Many TV ads cunningly use this fallacy to promote huge sales of products that are unrelated to the results depicted. For example, many people are led to believe that an increase in their popularity—or even a serious romance—will follow their use of a certain mouthwash or toothpaste or whatever. They illogically reason that since romance came (in the ad) after use of the mouthwash it came because of the mouthwash. On a more complicated level, many school children have been taught that the assassination of Archduke Franz Ferdinand at Sarajevo in 1914 was the cause of World War I—*post hoc, ergo propter hoc.* But anything as complicated as that war always has a labyrinth of causes.

Simultaneity of occurrence also leads many people into the logical fallacy of false judgment of causation. For example, millions of people believe that large doses of vitamin C will cure a cold. They have a cold, they take vitamin C, the cold ends; thus the taking of vitamin C caused the cure. It never occurs to them that in a healthy person a cold runs its course rather quickly and that there is no cause and result factor in the simultaneity of taking vitamin C and having the cold run its course. The cold would have ended anyway. And when the cold doesn't end quickly even with the taking of vitamin C, these people conveniently rationalize that the cold this time was too strong for the vitamin C.

Misinterpretation of evidence lies back of most false judgments of causation. For example, all superstitious people accept as good evidence events that have nothing to do with the result at hand—as, for instance, one's believing that the mere mention that the car is running well will cause it to break down. Here are some examples of false judgments of causation that might be found in student papers:

Unemployment is rising because the Republicans are in office.
Our maintaining extensive armaments causes Russia to arm extensively.
A copper bracelet cured my ringworm.
I got a low grade because the teacher didn't like me.
My army boyfriend was not sent to fight because I prayed for him.
English is a required subject in college just so English teachers can have employment.

It's human nature to ascribe simple causes to events, but usually the real causes are much more complex.

False Analogy

An **analogy** is a comparison, and comparison and contrast are useful and interesting ways of developing paragraphs (see Chapter 4). But an analogy usually doesn't *prove* anything, and a downright **false analogy** can be misleading because of its faulty logic. For example, if a psychologist were to compare the functioning of the human brain to that of an electronic computer, he would greatly mislead his readers and give them false notions. There may be some respects in which a brain is like a computer, but the differences are much greater than the similarities, for a computer does not have emotions and religions and sets of cultural values. The analogy might have limited usefulness, but as a whole it is false and one should be wary of it.

Here are the beginnings of some false analogies that might appear in student papers. Presumably details would be given to flesh out the analogies.

> The president of a college should run his school as a general runs an army—through a chain of command with rigid discipline for the troops (teachers).
>
> Democracy is really not a workable form of government. A country is like a ship: If the captain had always to take a vote among his sailors, the ship would get nowhere.
>
> Since we are in a war, we should not change presidents. "Don't swap horses when crossing a stream."
>
> The Communist countries are just like a ghetto street gang, with a leader directing criminal activities.
>
> The F grade should not be abolished in college courses. When you enter a college course it's just like starting a game of marbles. You have to decide at the beginning whether you are playing for keeps.

Remember that analogies can be very useful in writing, but try to avoid those that are blatantly faulty in their logic.

Ignoring the Issue

Ignoring the issue (the Latin name is *ignoratio elenchi*) means arguing off the point or substituting another issue or simply sidetracking. For example, if in discussing whether Franklin D. Roosevelt was a good president you argue that he was a poor president because he drank, you have ignored the issue or sidetracked. Actually in argumentation it is very difficult for anyone to keep to the point, and thus the fallacy of *ignoratio elenchi* is common in student papers.

Here are some further examples that might appear in student papers:

> In an argument about whether farm laborers should be organized: "They are ignorant people."
>
> In an argument about whether U.S. troops should be kept in West Germany: "Russia doesn't keep troops in East Germany."
>
> In an argument about whether the F grade should be abolished in

college courses: "Poor teachers don't have their paychecks con-
fiscated."

In an argument about whether a convicted murderer should be paroled:
"He isn't a Christian."

It is very easy in an argument for one to become illogically sidetracked.
As you write papers of persuasion, try to stick to the point.

Justification by Side Issue

Many people try to justify their point of argument by bringing in a
side issue. In a sense, this fallacy involves arguing off the point too,
but it is somewhat different from the immediately preceding fallacy. A
common example of this fallacy is for a person to assume that his
wrong is justified because his opponent also has done a wrong. For
example, some people have justified the shooting of civilians by American
troops in the Vietnam war on the grounds that the North Vietnamese shot
civilians too. Admittedly, there is a plausibility about such an argument,
but on reflection you will see that such reasoning tries to justify by side
issue.

Here are some further examples of justification by side issue that
might appear in student writing:

Shoplifting at supermarkets is not wrong because supermarkets themselves use deceptive sales practices.

I don't hesitate to cheat in class because my school cheats by illegally
subsidizing athletes.

Southerners have a right to resist integration because Northerners really
practice segregation themselves.

The Red Chinese are really not to be blamed for political suppression.
Look at how we oppress our minorities.

Such side issues by no means justify the conclusions in these examples.
The reasoning is faulty.

Argument ad Hominem

The logical fallacy of **argument ad hominem,** too, is somewhat like
ignoring the issue. The phrase means argument against the man (instead
of against the issue). For example, when President Harry Truman proposed a far-reaching, liberal domestic program, conservatives immediately attacked the man rather than the issues. They accused
Truman of being high-tempered, vulgar, profane, and "little." They
were indulging in argument *ad hominem,* for even if Truman had been

all the things he was called, his domestic program might still have been a good one. If it was a bad one, it was not because Truman was high-tempered and cussed a little. Even today this *ad hominem* attack lives on, and Truman's image in the minds of many is of a little, irascible man in an office he couldn't handle, whereas many historians rate Truman as one of the six greatest presidents this country has had. But of course conservatives aren't the only ones who engage in argument *ad hominem*. When President Eisenhower proposed conservative policies, the liberals attacked him rather than the issues by calling him unintelligent, naive, shallow, and small-minded. The labels stuck so well that it is only now that Eisenhower is becoming recognized again as having been a man of high intellect.

It is in the area of politics—from the president right down to a town council—that arguments *ad hominem* most abound. It seems to be human nature for an opponent of a policy to ignore the real issues and to attack the man who sponsored the policy. There was even a case in which a southern Senator always referred to an opponent as "the Jewish Senator from New York." He intended the word *Jewish* to be disparaging, and thus attacked the man rather than his issues. If you write papers on politics be sure that you distinguish between a man's character and religion and the policies he espouses.

Unsound Appeal to Authority

A logical fallacy of only minimal occurrence is an **unsound appeal to authority.** True, the opinion of authorities is important in a discussion of issues of all kinds, for one man's opinion is not necessarily as good as another's. Any man has a *right* to his opinion, but that doesn't make his opinion equally as sound as all others. Thus in discussion of or argument about various issues, people frequently rely on an appeal to authority. Sound authority does lend credence to one's stand on an issue, but always remember that on basic issues the very place one finds most disagreement is among the experts. For example, until his dying day Einstein maintained a belief in scientific determinism, whereas the majority of his highly expert colleagues in physics believed in the physical principle of indeterminacy. Still, both Einstein and his philo-sophic opponents were authorities well worth appealing to in a discussion of the basic nature of the universe. In general, then, recognized expert authority is worth quoting in argumentation, even though it may not absolutely *prove* a point.

Rather frequently, however, a writer (or speaker) will quote as an authority someone who has no claim to expertness at all. For example, if you wanted to quote an authority on how to militarily overrun a neighboring country in surprise warfare, you might well quote Adolf Hitler, who was an expert in this field. But if you wanted to quote an authority on racial differences, Hitler would not do at all, for, though he had opinions, he was an ignorant, bigoted man in the matter of racial differences. A man should be widely recognized by educated people as an expert in his field before he is quoted to help prove a point.

Here are some examples of an unsound appeal to authority that might appear in student writing:

> Quoting a student body president on the subject of which college courses should be required for graduation.
> Quoting a movie star on how to make a marriage succeed.
> Quoting a self-made man on the value of a college education.
> Quoting a physical education teacher on the desirable teaching load of a composition teacher.
> Quoting an army general on how to run a large school system.
> Quoting a popular but not-well-educated governor on the value of a philosophy department in a state university.

The main lesson here is to understand that a person who has made himself an expert in one field is not by any means necessarily an authority in other fields. Fame or notoriety alone does not make a person an authority in any field that happens to come under discussion. When you appeal to an authority to make a point in an argument, be sure he is a bona fide expert in the field under discussion, not just someone who is well known.

Non Sequitur

The Latin words *non sequitur* mean "it does not follow." This fallacy, then, bases a conclusion on a premise that has little or nothing to do with the conclusion. It is, in fact, a fallacy quite similar to the faulty deduction, but it is given a separate category here because there is a more glaring gap between its conclusion and premise than in a faulty deduction. Though the conclusion in a *non sequitur* is illogical, it may beneath the surface have an element of apparently associative truth. For example, one might say, "Abie won't finish his novel. He's an alcoholic." The conclusion that Abie won't finish his novel does not follow from the premise that he is an alcoholic. In fact, of the six Americans (not including T.S. Eliot, who was really an English writer) who have won the Nobel Prize for Literature, four were alcoholics and a fifth drank heavily. So the statement above is a *non sequitur*. Nevertheless there is a faint tinge of logic in the statement since the speaker connects alcoholism with lack of performance. Usually there is a kind of ambivalence about *non sequiturs,* but in essence a *non sequitur* represents a flaw in logic, for its conclusion does not follow from its premise. Here are some *non sequiturs* that might appear in student writing:

> People don't work at the same rate of speed; therefore labor unions should be abolished.
>
> Alcohol is made from grain; therefore prohibitionists, to be logical, should not eat bread.
>
> General Motors is the biggest auto manufacturer in the world; therefore its cars are the best.
>
> Charlotte is beautiful. Won't she have adorable children?
>
> Our philosophy text is poorly organized. None of us will do well in the course.
>
> Mr. Crossly is highly educated. He will vote for the best candidate.
>
> Mr. Ondine kicks his dog. Imagine how he must mistreat his children.

As you can see, there is a kind of faint logic in these statements, but they are really *non sequiturs* because the conclusions do not follow from the premises.

EXERCISE 10.   Identifying Logical Fallacies

DIRECTIONS: Specify which kind of logical fallacy, if any, is inherent in the following statements. In some cases a statement may fit more than one logical fallacy.

a.   The first applicant was a black. He won't measure up to the job.
b.   Indians want money, not a continuation of their old culture
c.   The universe is just like a clock and is running down.
d.   You have to be a parent to know anything about children.
e.   Flournoy will make the highest GPA because he has the highest IQ.
f.   We're due for another big step toward socialism, since the Democrats got elected.
g.   Stores that have the most sales have the poorest quality merchandise.
h.   Socialism is all right, for it is just like a family sharing everything.
i.   You either believe in Jesus as the Son of God or you're a mental weakling.
j.   We don't need to fear China. There are Chinese colonies in this country.
k.   Students shouldn't rate teachers in public pamphlets. They haven't finished their college education yet.
l.   Sure we give athletes payments under the table. The big corporations give their executives stock options.

m. You either should show school spirit at ball games or else get out of college.

n. Kennedy was a Catholic. How could he be a fair-minded president?

o. My father went to Harvard, so naturally he's against labor unions.

p. Sure I'm going to vote Republican. Our university president does.

q. Watson and Company make poor TV sets. Ours had to have repairs within two months.

r. I did poorly on my first final exam. I should go out on a bender.

s. Everyone should get drunk once in a while. It purges him of bourgeois thought patterns.

t. Truck drivers bluff their way through traffic.

u. I'm not going to get involved in political work. I'm a virgin.

v. I had bad luck because I forgot to take my good-luck charm with me.

w. Yes, I did plagiarize my term paper, but that wasn't wrong because the teacher gave us too much work.

x. I drink Minute Maid orange juice. Bing Crosby says it's the best.

y. In social structure, a Communist society is just like a beehive.

z.   I never saw a moor,
    I never saw the sea;
    Yet know I how the heather looks
    And what a billow be.

    I never spoke with God,
    Nor visited in heaven;
    Yet certain am I of the spot
    As if the checks were given. —Emily Dickinson

Organization
of the Whole Paper

THE MEANING OF ORGANIZATION

Some of your compositions may be assigned on topics that require research, some on topics about which you already have information and opinions. Some may be narrowly limited for you; some you may need to limit further yourself. In any case, you can plan your whole paper only after you have a limited topic and after the raw materials are in your mind. We will assume that your mind is stocked with materials adequate for any sufficiently limited topic assigned to you. Now, to write successfully, you must plan, or organize, your whole paper before you actually begin composing sentences.

The word *organize* is composed of the suffix *ize,* which means "to make into," and the root *organ,* which originally meant "a whole instrument or machine made up of interdependent parts." To organize, then, means to make into a whole, or to arrange interdependent parts into a whole structure. And this is exactly what you do when you organize a piece of writing: you arrange parts so that they form a clearly constructed whole. The parts are the ideas and the linguistic structures that contain them.

Organization, of course, does not apply just to the whole paper. A good paragraph requires intricate organization, for its parts—the sentences—must be carefully arranged so that the reader may proceed smoothly and with understanding through an involved sequence of details and ideas. A good sentence, too, is intricately organized. In fact, a mature sentence may be more complex in structure than most short papers, the parts of a sentence variously being such constructions as subjects, verbs, objects, subjective complements, adjectives, adverbs, a wide variety of phrases and clauses, conjunctions, subordinators, transitional phrases, absolute phrases, and the like. In short, a mature sentence generally has more parts than a short paper has paragraphs, and the relationships of its parts are more complex than the relationships expressed between paragraphs in a paper. In this chapter we will be concerned only with the organization of the whole paper. Chapters 4 and 5 are devoted to the organization of paragraphs and sentences. Though in a sense the organization of a whole paper is less complex than that of a mature sentence, in all probability you need more training in organizing whole papers, for you have already unconsciously learned a great deal about organizing sentences.

The parts to be arranged in organizing a whole paper are the introduction, the conclusion, and all the main points or central ideas you develop in between. It is these main points that give structure to your paper, and you must know what they are before you begin writing. Your problem in organizing, then, is to think of the main points of your paper and to give them order and development.

Some writers can organize with what seems magical, or at least natural, ease. They arrange and develop their subject matter so that a reader can glide effortlessly through their sequence of ideas. Most of us, however, must work hard at organizing; and most students need instruction in how to go about planning a whole paper. In fact, many composition teachers—and teachers in other academic subjects, for that matter—think that the greatest weakness in their students' writing is failure to organize well.

Just as there are many kinds of writing (if we use a classification system other than the four classical forms of discourse), there are many approaches to organization. But good organization of the kind of exposition and persuasion that constitutes most college writing can be based on one simple method, which will be explained in detail in the next section.

A BASIC METHOD OF ORGANIZATION

The most useful method of organizing a short paper of exposition or persuasion is to divide the whole topic into equivalent main points, and there is a very simple procedure for identifying such main points.

But before we illustrate the basic method, we should give attention to the writing assignment as a whole.

Title, Topic, and Thesis Sentence

Writing assignments in the composition course are handled in various ways by different instructors. Sometimes the student is given simply a **title** to work with. For example, here are two titles once given in a freshman composition class (they were connected with reading assignments):

> That's My Tax Money You're Spending
> Your Credit Is Good

Such titles give the student very little to go on in preparing an organization for his paper; further, they do not give the reader much insight into what the paper will be about. A title, then, may be little more than a clever heading for a paper. If a student is to organize a full, well-thought-out paper, he must know much more about its subject matter than such a title tells. In effect, he must know what his **topic** is. A topic expresses the central point to be discussed in a paper or speech. The word *topic* is usually applied to a short piece of discourse; for example, one would say, "The topic of my theme (or speech) is such-and-such," but "The subject of this book is such-and-such."

Sometimes the student must derive his own topic from the title given him, but much more often the writing assignment is in the form of a topic, which gives the student some clues for planning an organization for his paper. He may be expected to supply a suitable title, but that would have little bearing on his organizing his subject matter. Suppose the two titles listed above had been given to the students as these topics:

> Discuss some of the ways in which your county government wastes tax monies.
> Discuss how the credit practices of merchants often lead the consumer into excessive buying.

Any number of clever titles might be used for these topics, but the subject matter for the papers, and hence the organization, is expressed in the limited topic. With the writing assignment stated as such a topic, students are in a much better position to organize. Further, these topics will produce a mixture of exposition and persuasion, as many writing assignments do. For example, in the first one the writer would present facts about his county government and would also try to convince his readers that his county government is inefficient. With such a topic, the writer does need to be careful with his logic but does not need to say

"Now I'm writing exposition. And now I'm writing persuasion." The two forms of discourse mix easily.

The first essential in writing a composition, then, is to get in mind a clear, limited topic, not a clever title. The reader may not be much enlightened by a title, but that doesn't matter if he reads the paper. The writer, however, *must have a limited, understandable topic to begin with if he is to organize his subject matter clearly.* Here are further examples of topics that might be given as assignments or that the student might derive for himself out of an assignment:

> Discuss the qualities that a successful Peace Corps member should have.
>
> What are the results of conformity in dress among teen-agers?
>
> Discuss why you think an unwed mother should or should not keep her baby.
>
> Why do some very bright pupils do poorly in school?
>
> Write an essay giving advice to college teachers.[1]

Topics stated in this fashion are easily organizable, as we will soon see.

In addition to focusing on a clear, limited topic rather than a vague title, a composition student prepares himself for sounder organization if he writes out a **thesis sentence** for his assignment. The thesis sentence may also be called the **controlling idea;** that is, it is a one-sentence summary of the main point of the whole paper. The thesis sentence sometimes may be little more than a refinement of the topic, but it helps the student organize his whole paper. Here are thesis sentences for a few topics already stated above:

> In this paper I will explain how my county government wastes tax monies in a number of unjustifiable ways.
>
> A member of the Peace Corps should have knowledge and skills that will be of practical use to him in his dealing with the the illiterates of an underdeveloped area.
>
> This essay gives advice to college teachers that will make them more aware of student problems.

These thesis sentences expand the topics slightly by expressing the *direction* the paper will take as its central idea is developed. For example, the third thesis sentence expresses the topic (advice to college teachers) and also what the writer hopes will be the result of the advice. Thus with a clear topic and a precise thesis sentence the student is ready to start organizing. His title may express the substance of his paper or it may be little more than an ornament. The topic must be stated specifically.

---

[1] This topic will be carried through this chapter to show the progress from topic to completed paper. The work, which is edited, is that of a good student.

Clues to the Discovery of Main Points

Whether the paper is to be exposition or persuasion or a mixture of the two, it is best organized around equivalent main points.[2] This is true of most theme topics in composition and essay questions in the various academic subject matter fields. As we will see later, other patterns of organization exist, but the student who can learn thoroughly the one basic method of organization explained in this section will have an excellent tool that will serve him well throughout college and later in professional life.

The clue to organization in a well-stated topic is an important **plural noun** *(stated or implied) that, in a sense, can be divided.* First we will consider topics with stated plural nouns. Here is one that might produce a mixture of exposition and persuasion:

> Discuss the social uses of a knowledge of art.

A thesis sentence for this topic might be this:

> This essay demonstrates that a knowledge of art has many social uses for the modern sophisticated citizen.

The plural noun in the topic is *uses.* In a sense it can be divided into several singular nouns: *This use, that use, another use,* and perhaps *another use.* Each one of these uses will be a main point for the whole paper. In organizing with this method, you must think clearly and sharply so that you can identify real, general uses that do not duplicate each other. As you think of separate, broad uses, you list them in scratch outline form, like this:

1. Gives one the means to belong to a special group
2. Helps one to adjust better in a complex society
3. Provides one with a means of enjoying himself when alone
4. Gives one topics of conversation

Now you have a basic organization for your paper: four main points that, with an introduction and conclusion, will form a whole. (The next section on expanding the working outline will illustrate how details can be assembled under these main points.)

Before you begin writing, however, you must give consideration to the **arrangement** of the four main points. Often in this equivalent main point kind of organization almost any arrangement of the points is satisfactory, but occasionally there will be reasons for preferring a certain order. For example, in the topic above you might very well

---

[2] This does not mean that each point will occupy the same amount of space in the paper but that each is an equal, independent part of the paper.

decide that point 2 about adjustment in society should come last be-cause it is perhaps the most important. (It is common for a writer to save his most important point for an emphatic ending to his paper.) You might then decide that point 4 should come first, point 1 second, and point 3 third. Another arrangement might appeal to another writer, but any writer should give thought to the order or arrangement of his points. This is a structural part of writing.

Here is another example of the process of organizing by equivalent main points:

TITLE: The Teen-Age Trap

TOPIC: Convince your peers of the <u>disadvantages</u> of teen-age mar-riages. (*plural noun underlined*)

THESIS SENTENCE: This essay will analyze the troubles that frequently arise in marriages when both partners are teen-agers.

MAIN POINTS:

1. Their personalities haven't matured, giving rise to growing con-flicts.
2. They usually have neither enough money nor the maturity to handle it efficiently.
3. They still have the urge to go in gangs and be intimate with other people.
4. They too often have babies before they are ready for them.

Now we have the parts that, with an introduction and conclusion, can be assembled into a whole structure. You might decide to take up the main points in the order of 1, 3, 4, and 2, for that seems a reasonable flow of the ideas, but in any event, when you have your main points clearly stated, deciding on the proper arrangement is not difficult.

It is very important, here, that you understand that the main points derived from the plural noun are generalities, not specifics. Each will form the topic sentence of a paragraph, which will be developed with details or logical analysis. For example, for the topic

Discuss the <u>habits</u> of a wild animal you know well,

you might have this as one main point:

1. Eating habits of the jackrabbit

This is a generality which can be developed with specifics. If, instead, you were to put down as a main point

1. Eats sagebrush,

you would have mentioned a specific only, not a general main point. In Chapter 4 on paragraphing we will discuss further the distinction between generalities and specifics. The important concept to master here is that before beginning to write you must plan or organize your paper by deciding what its main points will be and the order in which you will take them up.

The most practical approach to organizing an expository or persuasive paper, then, is to find in the well-stated topic a plural noun that can be divided into several singular units and then to jot down in scratch outline form the three or four main points or central ideas (generalities) that this noun suggests to you. Here are other common topics that illustrate how a stated plural noun can be a guide to organization:

> Discuss what you think are the chief personal values of your generation.
>
> The college student has many problems not encountered in high school. What are some of these problems and how can they be solved?
>
> Discuss the three or four most important lessons about life that one should have learned by the time he is eighteen.
>
> Analyze as precisely as you can some of the personality traits of someone you dislike.

Once you spot the important plural noun, organization becomes much easier.

Now we must take a rather long further step in understanding this process of organizing by equivalent main points. Many good theme topics and exam questions do not contain a stated plural noun such as *uses, ways, methods, habits, problems, lessons, values, advantages,* and so on. Most topics, however, will have an *implied* plural noun which will give you the same guidance in organization. First let's consider the topic already mentioned as the one we will carry through to the completed paper: "Write an essay giving advice to college teachers." Since there is no stated plural noun in this topic to guide us (*teachers* obviously is not a plural noun that will divide into main points), we must see if one is implied. The word *advice* seems to be the central noun in the topic, and we do use the phrase "pieces of advice." Thus *pieces* is just the kind of plural noun we are looking for to guide us in organizing. So, after writing his thesis sentence, the student should enumerate in scratch outline form the separate, general pieces of advice he is to give, and they will constitute his main points, or general ideas. Here is the scratch outline of main points that a good student planned for this topic:

1. To try to understand better the freshman's limited background
2. To state clearly rules about absences, late work, and no work
3. To review important material and to give frequent quizzes
4. To have more personal interviews

The student decided to take up the main points in the order given here (he may have thought of them in a different order). So his paper was planned. Writing the introduction, detailed paragraphs, and conclusion would come next, as we will see later.

Here is another topic without a stated plural noun to provide a clue to organization: "Every community has a personality, just as a human being has a personality. Write an essay about the personality of your home town." The key noun of this topic appears to be *personality,* but that word is apparently not divisible into several singular units. It doesn't take much thought, however, to see that the noun *personality* implies *traits* or *characteristics.* For a basic organization, then, you just need to think of three or four general traits of personality your home town has. You might produce a scratch outline like this:

1. Is stuffy and prudish
2. Is proud without sufficient reason
3. Is intolerant of eccentric behavior
4. Demands more than it is willing to give

With a fully developed paragraph of details about each of these general traits, you would produce a well-planned and effective essay.

A similar example is involved in this topic: "Discuss the meaning of the sentence, 'After all, I'm only human.'" On first glance it is not clear just how this topic can be divided into three or four main points. But if you are to write an effective paper on this topic, you must organize it. A little thought will lead you to the implied phrase *"characteristics* of being human," which can be divided into singular units: *this characteristic, that characteristic,* and so on. So you can prepare a simple and clear basic organization by thinking of three or four general characteristics of being human:

1. Human beings are subject to temptations
2. To making mistakes
3. To inconsistency
4. To imperfect reasoning

By examining the topic closely, you found an implied plural noun from which you could extract a basic organization of main points, points about which you could write detailed paragraphs.

The implied noun *reasons* is one of the most common in topics that do not have a stated plural noun. Suppose you were assigned the topic "Explain why Americans are less individualistic now than in the nineteenth century." The word *why* suggests *reasons,* and an organization of *reasons why* might take this form:

1. Our political structure has become much more centralized.
2. Mass production has replaced self-sufficiency.
3. Public and private education has become more uniform.
4. The frontier has disappeared.

Now you have a framework for your paper, but still must arrange. What is the best order for presenting these main points? No one arrangement is necessarily best, but probably you would decide that the point about the disappearance of the frontier should come first (after a suitable introduction to the paper). You would then see a connection between the disappearance of the frontier and the centralization of the political structure, and would put that point second. Next, you might decide that the point about education should follow, since politics has an effect on education. The point about mass production would then necessarily come last. And you would have arrived at a sensible arrangement or order of main points.

Here is one more example of a topic based on the implied noun *reasons* or *grounds*: "Attack or defend the view that the best way to preserve peace is to prepare for war." You might say, "I will defend this view on these *grounds*" or "I will attack this view for these *reasons*." In defending the view you might prepare this basic organization:

1. Because disarmament plans of the past have failed
2. Because modern weapons will surely be a deterrent to war
3. Because unilateral disarmament would incite aggression

You would still be faced with the task of writing well-developed paragraphs about these main points. *But a writer must have main points in mind before he can make any sort of adequate beginning. The importance of preparing a basic organization cannot be overemphasized.*

It should be clear now that organization is the first requirement of any extended piece of expository or persuasive writing, whether an English theme, an essay exam, a term paper, a technical report, a business report, or any similar piece. The simplest approach to such organization is to state the topic clearly and then to find a plural noun in the topic. If no such noun is apparent, there will usually be implied such phrases as "*reasons* why I believe . . . ," "*steps* that I will take . . . ," "*grounds* on which I will defend . . . ," "*ways* in which something can . . . ," or "*characteristics* of . . . ." The division of such a noun into singular units will give the main points on which to base an organization.

Expanding the Working Outline

Some writers are ready to begin writing as soon as they have organized their main points. Their minds quickly produce and order details for the main points without their having to expand their scratch outline. Other writers, however, need to think a while and to jot down the details or sequence of ideas they will use for each main point. This is simply expanding the scratch outline for the student's private use; it is not preparing a formal outline for the benefit of the reader. Appendix 2 treats in detail the preparation of a formal outline to be handed in with a paper. Usually such an outline accompanies only a rather lengthy paper. But the appendix on formal outlining can be studied at this juncture in connection with the scratch or working outline. Your instructor will make the decision.

Following are some examples of expanding the scratch outline after the main points have been decided on and arranged. First, the second point from the topic on the uses of a knowledge of art:

2. Helps one to adjust better in a complex society
   a. Our society is getting more complex and sophisticated.
   b. Art reflects this complexity.
   c. Thus if one understands art he understands society better.
   d. Example from Picasso
   e. Perhaps an example from pop art

This expansion illustrates the two broad kinds of ideas that usually develop a main point: (1) a logical sequence of ideas and (2) specific details and examples. Sometimes only the first kind is used for a main point and sometimes only the other; but quite often the two are mixed in the development of one main point, as in this example. The first three points in the expansion are ideas in a logical sequence; the last two are illustrative examples.

Here is another example of the expansion of the scratch outline, based on the third point of the topic about the personality of your home town:

3. Is intolerant of eccentric behavior
   a. Local paper writes editorials against long hair on boys.
   b. Peculiar looking people picked up by police for no reason (give example).
   c. Some restaurants turn away people in unusual dress.
   d. Police crack down on soapbox orators in the parks.

This expansion consists only of illustratives details without any logical sequence of ideas. The writer would probably use more than one sentence for each of the four details. *Note especially that the main point is a generality with the details as specifics under that generality.* In organizing, the writer jots down his generalities, or main points, first.

Now here is an example of expansion that uses a logical sequence of ideas only. The generality is point 3 of the topic that says the best way to preserve peace is to prepare for war.

    3. Because unilateral disarmament would incite aggression
        a. Throughout history unarmed or underarmed countries have been attacked.
        b. Things are no different today.
        c. Therefore if the U.S. were to disarm, Russia or China would probably attack.
        d. They would have nothing to lose.
        e. Thus keeping prepared for war will actually prevent war.

Each idea of this expansion grows out of the preceding one rather than being a specific detail by itself. Some writers would be able to develop their main idea as they write without having an expanded scratch outline, but others might prefer to jot down their notes before beginning to write.

Now as a final example of expanding the working outline we will give the full scratch outline that a student produced for the topic "Write an essay giving advice to college teachers," the topic which we are carrying to its completion.

    1. To try to understand better the freshman's limited background
        a. Most freshmen know little and are scared when they enter college.
        b. Professors tend to forget this.
        c. Professors often start courses with too much work and too little explanation.
        d. They use words students don't know.
        e. They make allusions to learning that students don't recognize.
        f. They should treat freshmen as adults but should realize that their educational experience is limited.
    2. To state clearly rules about absences, late work, and no work
        a. Professors often leave students in the dark about the ground rules of their courses.
        b. Sometimes they will seem not to care whether a student attends class and then will drop him for excessive absences.
        c. Sometimes they will refuse to accept a late paper without having said anything about it.
        d. Sometimes they will fail a student for not doing a piece of work when the student doesn't understand.
    3. To review important material and to give frequent quizzes
        a. Some professors think that a student will remember everything he hears or reads.

    b. Actually, most students need a lot of repetition.

    c. Students like to know how they are doing and don't like a grade based on a final exam only.

    d. So frequent quizzes should be given.

    e. The quizzes should be preparation for the final exam.

4. To have more personal interviews

    a. When a student is doing badly the professor should call him in.

    b. Often a man-to-man explanation will be effective when a lecture isn't.

    c. Students like to think their professor cares.

This student prepared a rather detailed scratch outline so that the writing of his paper went quickly and smoothly. One advantage of expanding the scratch outline in this way is that the writer has less thinking to do as he writes and can devote more attention to composing clear, well-formed sentences. At the end of this chapter we will see how this student turned his scratch outline into a finished paper.

OTHER PATTERNS OF ORGANIZATION

The basic method of organization we have just presented is the most serviceable one for most theme topics and essay exam questions, but organizational patterns other than that of equivalent main points abound. In journalistic reporting, organization is generally based on an initial statement of *who, what, when, where,* and *why,* with details and further explanation following; this kind of organization leads many people to read only the first part of news stories, since they get the essentials there. In narration a time element is implicit, and thus narrative organization is likely to be built around a sequence of events in time. In description a spatial element may dominate so that the organization is based on shifting viewpoints. And even in exposition organization by other than equivalent main points is possible, though usually main points of some sort are involved, and usually the piece of writing is longer than a theme or essay exam question. (In most pieces of pure persuasion the writer uses organization by equivalent main points, for he is giving the *reasons* why he thinks as he does.)

Suppose for example, you were writing a longish paper on

The history and current status of IQ testing.

The topic is clearly one of exposition, but it contains no stated or implied plural noun. Yet the paper must have organization, and main points will certainly assert themselves. You would probably start with a kind of narrative organization that would explain the development of IQ tests. You might, as a guide to your writing, jot down these points:

1. The first attempt at intelligence testing
2. Contributions made by early psychologists
3. Shifts in the definition of intelligence
4. Contributions made by later psychologists

Then you could shift from a narrative type of organization (the history of anything is written mostly with a narrative type of organization) to one that would assess the present status of IQ testing, with such main points as

5. The types of test now used
6. Psychologists' estimation of the validity of the tests
7. The question of whether IQ can be changed
8. The racial problem in IQ testing

As you can see, this is still organization by main points but is somewhat more complex than organization by equivalent main points derived from a plural noun.

For another example, suppose you were asked to write a paper on the question

How effectively can a person do his own religious thinking?

No stated or implied plural noun readily presents itself; still, you must formulate some plan for the paper. *Just writing at random will inevitably result in a poor paper.* Thus you try to think of points that can be made and an effective order for them. You might arrive at this plan:

1. The obvious fact that one's religion derives from the culture he grows up in (examples)
2. The equally obvious fact that some adults do change their religion, even radically (examples)
3. An investigation of what causes some people to be hidebound in their religion and others to be able to grow religiously
4. Conclusion that only an unindoctrinated person can do his own religious thinking effectively

Again, main points give structure to the expository paper, but they are not equivalent main points deriving from a plural noun.

Here is another topic that does not lend itself readily to an organization by equivalent main points suggested by a plural noun: "Discuss Thoreau's concept of passive resistance." But main points of some sort must give organization to such a topic of exposition. There are various possibilities, of which the following seems quite appropriate:

1. A definition of passive resistance as expressed by Thoreau
2. The political events that caused Thoreau to formulate his theory
3. Some modern instances of the use of passive resistance
4. An evaluation of the effectiveness of this political weapon

These are not equivalent main points suggested by a plural noun, but they are main points that can give structure to the whole paper.

Sometimes the organization of an expository paper consists of main points with each point growing out of the previous one. For example, suppose you were given this topic, mentioned earlier:

Explain why Americans are less individualistic now than in the nine-teenth century.

This might well be a topic with the implied plural noun *reasons* and thus you could organize it on the basis of equivalent main points. But you could also organize it around main points, with each growing out of the previous one. Your scratch outline, expanded, might look like this:

1. In the nineteenth century sharp increases in population created a demand for industrialization.
   a. Factories proliferated.
   b. People flocked to the cities.
   c. Crowded tenements abounded.
   d. Politics changed.
2. Which brought division of labor and an end to self-sufficiency.
   a. Factories had one person just endlessly perform one little task.
   b. Workmen could no longer feel pride in making a whole product.
   c. People became more dependent.
3. Which decreased the individual's sense of his own worth and purpose.
   a. The factory worker began to feel like a cog.
   b. Workmen lost their sense of identity with the whole community.
   c. Examples
4. Which led him into a social structure of conformity rather than individualism.
   a. Illustrations of this conformity and its results

Such an organization is somewhat similar to one of equivalent main points deriving from a plural noun but is really the result of a different kind of thought process in the writer's mind. The main lesson here is that when you are presented a topic to write on you must *search for a pattern of organization*. Most of the time you will be able to derive a few equivalent main points from a stated or implied plural noun. When that kind of pattern is not available, you have the harder task of planning some other pattern of main points. But the more practice you have in organizing on the basis of a plural noun, the more skilled you will become in planning other kinds of organization.

EXERCISE 11.   Preparing Basic Organizations for Theme Topics

DIRECTIONS: First identify the key plural noun (stated or implied) in each of the following topics that, when divided into singular units, will provide a basic organization. Then prepare a basic organization for two or more topics by writing out three or four main points suggested by the noun you choose to divide. Also write thesis sentences for five of these topics.

1. What improvements in practice could be made in American democracy?
2. What are some of the advantages of not being a well-adjusted person?
3. What are the characteristics of an ideal children's story?
4. If your college had to eliminate either intercollegiate sports or plays and concerts, which should it eliminate and why?
5. Discuss the merit of fining or jailing parents for crimes committed by their minor children.
6. Are there valid reasons why ours should be called the age of anxiety?
7. Is equality for women in the business and political world desirable?
8. How to avoid a divorce.
9. Some justifiable uses of lying.
10. Attack or defend the emphasis on athletics at the college level.
11. There is often controversy between teachers and parents over novels assigned in high school. Explain and evaluate the issues involved in such a controversy.
12. What specific measures do you think should be taken to conserve one important natural resource—soil, forest, wildlife, or water—that is being depleted in our country?
13. If you have visited a foreign country, discuss the advantages or disadvantages of living there over living in the United States.
14. It has been said that the quality of higher education would be improved if universities and colleges gave neither grades nor degrees. Defend or attack this statement.
15. Discuss the values and attitudes expressed in one comic strip, such as "Pogo."

EXERCISE 12.   **Organizing Answers to Essay Questions**

DIRECTIONS: The following are actual essay examination questions that were given to college students. Decide which plural noun (stated or implied) could guide the student in organizing an answer for each question. Of course you are not expected to give answers to these questions, but you should be able to suggest main points for one or two.

1. What are the critcisms that George Gaylord Simpson gave of the gladiatorial theories of evolution?
2. Discuss the methods used for measuring astronomical distances.
3. What are the significant contributions of the Saxon system of local government to the present British system?
4. What are the evidences of human habitation in the New World before 15,000 B.C.?
5. What are the principal differences between the American and British civil services?
6. Discuss the characteristics of polypeptides.
7. Discuss the functions of the Judicial Committee of the Privy Council.
8. What are the chief differences between Lamarckian and Darwinian theories of evolution?
9. What advantages did Lincoln have in the election of 1860?
10. What objections have been lodged against Hoyle's theory of continuous creation?
11. Discuss the factors of Russia's geographical position that might influence her foreign policy.
12. Describe the various approaches for dealing with problems of mental health.
13. Why did England develop free institutions so far in advance of the other countries of the world?
14. How did Lenin's "New Economic Policy" differ from the "War Communism" of 1917–1921?
15. Why is there a tendency for government to gradually increase its powers of control over the economy?
16. How does Parkinson lampoon modern bureaucracy? What particular features in bureaucracy deserve his criticism?
17. Discuss the techniques and themes of Hawthorne's short stories.
18. Contrast the philosophic outlooks of Robinson and Frost.
19. How does Romanticism differ from Neoclassicism?
20. Attack or defend the kind of poetry that is known as "modern."

INTRODUCTIONS AND CONCLUSIONS

The introduction and the conclusion of an expository or persuasive paper are parts of its organization because they are concerned with the structure of the paper rather than with the individual details or logical analysis that make up its subject matter. Thus, though both introductions and conclusions may be separate paragraphs, a discussion of them belongs in Chapter 3 on organization rather than in Chapter 4 on paragraph development.

Effective Introductions

Many students, judging from the time they spend composing an opening sentence, find the introduction of a theme the very hardest part to write. They often feel that if they can just get the paper underway, the rest will be easy. A good basic organization should make the rest of the paper easy to write—or at least not overwhelmingly difficult—but an introduction itself should not be the cause of aimless diddling while one waits for inspiration. Once their nature is understood, introductions are not difficult to compose.

The first purpose of an introduction in exposition or persuasion is **to lead the reader directly into the topic** at hand so that he will know at once the general nature of what he is about to read. This purpose is especially true of term papers, essay questions, and other kinds of college (as well as business and professional) writing, including most themes. The purpose, in short, is to clarify the topic, not to tease the reader or to hold him in suspense.

The clue to writing an introduction that fulfills this purpose, like the clue to a basic organization, is in the fully stated topic. *Before trying to write your opening sentence or sentences, examine your topic closely so that you can compose an introduction that tells the reader substantially what the topic tells you.* Of course you want your opening to sound smooth and literary, not blunt like a class assignment. But the substance of the topic and of the introduction should usually be similar. (Some variations will be noted below.)

First consider the topic and basic organization of the theme we are carrying through to completion:

TOPIC: Write an essay giving advice to college teachers.
BASIC ORGANIZATION:
1. To try to understand better the freshman's limited background
2. To state clearly rules about absences, late work, and no work

    3. To review important material and to give frequent quizzes

    4. To have more personal interviews

The basic organization provides the main points to be developed but does not suggest an introduction. That is suggested by the fully stated topic itself. This is the opening that a student wrote:

> Many college teachers exhibit deficiencies in teaching techniques that they could easily overcome if they just knew the truth of their students' impression of them. Yet students generally don't dare give them advice. At the risk of reprisals in the form of low grades I shall give my teachers advice which, if followed, will greatly improve their students' performance and will also increase their students' respect for them.

Note that the core of the topic—with an added stylistic flourish—is stated in the introduction. The reader is led directly into the subject matter of the paper. (This introduction is longer than usual for a short paper—see paragraphs below on length of openings.)

    Here are some other examples of short, direct introductions based on a close scrutiny of fully stated topics:

TOPIC: Discuss the social uses of a knowledge of art.

OPENING: A knowledge of art is not an airy, useless element in one's mental storehouse but has practical uses of considerable social value.

TOPIC: Discuss some of the ways in which your county government wastes tax monies.

OPENING: Though a high degree of economic efficiency cannot be expected in an organization with many disbursing departments and numerous near-autonomous department heads, the officials in my county government seem determined to waste more of the taxpayers' money than can be condoned by those most tolerant of human frailties.

TOPIC: Every community has a personality, just as a human being has a personality. Write an essay about the personality of your home town.

OPENING: As I sit in my dormitory room, lonely and homesick, I think not only of the human beings I left behind, but also of my home town itself. For now I see it as a personality, a whole being with many moods and odd behavioral patterns.

TOPIC: Defend the view that the best way to preserve peace is to prepare for war.

OPENING: Many good-willed people think that only an abolition of all

> armaments can preserve peace, but a realistic look at world politics convinces me that only readiness for war can give any assurance of peace.

These examples show how the core of a well-stated topic can be smoothly and appropriately expressed in the introduction to a short paper. *The clue to writing an introduction, like the clue to basic organization, is in the topic.* If you find a paper particularly hard to open, try restating the topic or stating it more fully. Then you can spot the core idea that you will want to work into your introduction.

Besides leading directly into the topic, an introduction should also **arouse the reader's interest** so that he will want to continue reading. There is a widespread misapprehension, however, about what arouses interest in expository or persuasive writing. Many writers have the impression that no matter what their topic, they must open with some gimmick—either suspenseful, shocking, or colorful—to capture the reader's interest. Then, after attracting him with artificial bait, they give him the information which, apparently, they feared he might not be interested in. In truth, however, it is the subject matter of the paper, not a cute gimmick, which arouses initial interest, and thus the second purpose of an introduction is to a considerable degree achieved by the first. A clear statement of the subject matter to follow will usually arouse the interest of those who can be interested. A cute or suspenseful or startling introduction is not only not necessary but often is offensive to a sophisticated readership, for it has the insincere ring of the come-on technique.

As examples of a phony or come-on technique, consider these two openings from articles in one of America's most famous expository magazines:

> He had no antennas, no green scales, not even a plastic helmet or a space suit. Yet I distinctly heard him say:
> "Telephone? Of course. My number is Craters of the Moon 2."
> —*National Geographic*

> About three o'clock in the morning something woke me, and I lay listening. Lizards rustled in the thatch of our hut, but it wasn't that. A strange rumbling came from somewhere out in the night.
> "Are you awake?" Jinx whispered softly.—*National Geographic*

Now these openings are not poorly written, but they try to capture reader interest in a phony way. You perhaps expect the first to continue as a science fiction story; the second might be a bedroom scene in a love story.

Actually, the articles that follow these openings are expository and contain factual information of considerable interest. The first is about volcanic formations in southern Idaho; the second is about a wild game preserve in Africa. The authors (or, more likely, editors) seemed to feel that because no one would be immediately interested in mere factual material, their openings needed folksy, human-interest angles and narrative gimmicks. As a result the articles became less interesting to those who simply wanted the absorbing information available instead of intimate insight into the personality of Jinx.

Now examine some openings of expository articles from other famous American magazines:

> The fishes, of which there are some 25,000 living species, are un-rivaled among the vertebrates in the ability to adapt to unpromising living conditions. They have managed to invade and occupy some of the earth's most extreme and inhospitable environments.—*Scientific American*

> In some areas of the world supernatural practitioners known as witch doctors, shamans, or medicine men still treat the ailing.—*Natural History*

Compare these openings with the two examples above. For people truly interested in the ideas involved, these are far more attractive openings than the narrative-descriptive ones involving moon men and Jinx.

Or note the simple, direct approach to his topic used by this author:

> For a long time I have had the urge to speak up about the mislead-ing impression the public is being given about cancer research—and for that matter, medical research in general.—*Harper's*.

This is just a direct, simple explanation of what the article following will be about; yet considerable interest is aroused. Here is another opening from the same magazine:

> Last year I was elected to the Kentucky legislature after paying off many of the citizens in my district with the money and whiskey they demanded in return for their votes. Many of the men who sit with me as legislators were elected in the same way.

This opening does have some shock value, but only as much as the subject warrants, and it does lead directly into the topic of the essay.

The foregoing, however, is not to be taken as a blanket con-demnation of all narrative-dramatic openings for expository or persuasive papers. When tastefully used, such openings can be effective, for story-telling can be a natural way to arouse reader interest. The following, for example, is an introduction used for an essay on euthanasia:

> On his way to the hospital a minister stops at a house near his church to say a word of personal sympathy to a couple sitting on the porch with their family doctor. Upstairs the man's mother is in bed, the victim of a series of small cerebral hemorrhages over the last eleven years. Her voice went two years ago and there is now no sign that she hears anything. Communication has ended. Says the son, with a complex question-asking glance at his wife, "My mother is already dead."
> —*Harper's*.

This is a narrative-dramatic opening in good taste. The writer was not too folksy or sentimental in his attempt to lead into his expository topic. The example he used suggests directly the subject matter of his essay; it is not an inconsequential detail nor an artificial gimmick designed to trap the reader. A narrative opening can be effective if it is tastefully used and is related directly to the core subject matter of the article. But you should avoid opening too many of your papers with this technique.

The mere statement of a topic is not in itself sufficient to arouse strong reader interest. In addition to this, an introduction (like the rest of the paper) should be **pleasingly phrased,** for good style as well as subject matter stimulates reader interest. A realization of the importance of style is probably the origin of the misconception that a catchy or unusual opening is needed to arouse reader interest. But in an introduction the core idea of the topic, not some cute or startling or insignificant detail, should be artfully and pleasingly phrased.

Compare the effectiveness of the following introductions:

TOPIC: Explain why 12- and 13-year-olds should not go steady.

OPENING AS MERE STATEMENT OF THE TOPIC: There are many reasons why 12- and 13-year-olds should not go steady.

GIMMICK OPENING: Have you as a parent ever experienced the terror of having a teen-age daughter in trouble?

OPENING AS STYLISTICALLY PLEASING STATEMENT OF THE TOPIC: On the junior high school campus and at private parties I have seen flushed pleasure on the faces of 12- and 13-year-old sweethearts; but I have also seen enough anxiety on the same faces to convince me that children this age should not go steady.

TOPIC: Discuss the reasons why superior high school students should not be separated into special classes.

OPENING AS MERE STATEMENT OF THE TOPIC: In this paper I will show why superior high school students should not be separated into special classes.

GIMMICK OPENING: It is 1979, and the once brilliant high school stu-

dent is jobless, broke, and wearing off a hangover in a cheap flop-
house. Why?

OPENING AS STYLISTICALLY PLEASING STATEMENT OF THE TOPIC:
Though when superficially considered the segregation of brilliant high
school students into special classes seems an obvious means of providing them with superior instruction, in actual practice this system
is seen to have many defects.

In these examples the first opening is too flat to be effective, the second
too bizarre. A direct but pleasingly phrased introduction is usually best
for a short paper.

In addition to expressing the topic in a pleasing fashion, an introduction should also **establish a proper tone** for the whole paper. One
weakness of the gimmick opening is that it establishes a wrong tone
for expository and persuasive writing. Since the primary purpose of
exposition and persuasion is to inform or convince, their tone should
be objective, quiet, reasonable, open-minded. The tone should suggest
to the reader that there is something to be learned or an important issue
to be explained or an interesting point of view to be considered. A
startling or extravagant tone adversely affects the informative nature of
exposition and persuasion. An overbearing, pompous, or overly assertive
tone brings the writer's open-mindedness into question. A smug or
smirking tone will alienate readers.

A personal tone need not be avoided in either an introduction
or the body of a paper; the pronoun *I* is not out of place even in the
highest level scholarly writing. But in exposition and persuasion the
personal tone should not lapse into diffuse impressionism. A tone of
amusement may also be utilized provided it does not mask the informative nature of the paper. In general, the tone should suit the subject
matter; it should not be excessively dramatic or assertive.

Compare the effectiveness of the following introductions:

TOPIC: Account for the wide appeal that personal advice columns have
in the United States.

OVERLY ASSERTIVE TONE: Nothing more clearly demonstrates the low-
level intelligence, taste, and social awareness of Americans than their
silly addiction to personal advice columns.

REASONABLE TONE: The wide appeal that personal advice columns have
in the United States is not due to one simple trait or flaw in human
nature, but to a variety of complex human traits, some of which may
even be praiseworthy.

TOPIC: It has been traditionally asserted that sports help develop good
character. What undesirable traits of character, if any, do they
develop? Why?

EXTRAVAGANT TONE: All the mouthing that coaches and P.E. teachers make about sports developing good character is a lot of baloney. Varsity sports teach all sorts of bad habits.

REASONABLE TONE: Though most people agree that varsity sports have much character-building potential, there is some evidence that bad traits of character may also result from athletic participation.

A moderate or reasonable tone is much more likely to attract reader interest than an extravagant tone, as these examples illustrate.

Length is another troublesome aspect of introductions. A general misapprehension is that a successful paper is built around an introduction-body-conclusion structure with each of the three sections given equal weight, or with at least a full paragraph for both introduction and conclusion. But the introduction and conclusion should not be equivalent in length to the subject matter of the paper. An introduction should be just long enough to announce the topic of the paper in an interest-arousing fashion, and that means a short introduction for most college writing assignments. An overlong introduction dissipates reader interest.

When a one- or two-sentence beginning is sufficient to get a paper underway, the introduction should not form a separate paragraph. Instead, it should be combined with the first paragraph, which will be a discussion of the first main point of the paper. Consider, for example, this topic and basic organization:

TOPIC: Discuss the *principles* underlying the campaign of nonviolent resistance that southern blacks are using to win their civil rights.

　　1. Belief in the sacredness and effectiveness of Christ's principles of returning good for evil and of nonviolence

　　2. Belief that right will triumph if publicly demonstrated

　　3. Belief that steadfastness of purpose will defeat the opposition in a struggle of wills

OPENING: The campaign of nonviolent resistance that southern blacks are using to win their civil rights is based on a few principles which sound idealistic in theory but which are surprisingly effective in practice. The chief of these is Christ's injunction to return good for evil and to resist not evil. . . . [continuation in the first paragraph of an explanation of this main point]

For this topic a one-sentence introduction is sufficient, and that sentence should be a part of the first main paragraph, not a separate paragraph. A brief separate introductory paragraph tends to give a paper a bad appearance.

Occasionally, however, even a short paper needs a separate introductory paragraph. When the introduction requires as many as two long or three ordinary sentences, they may be given separate status without damaging the appearance or structure of the paper. Consider, for example, this topic: "What criticisms would you make of the reading program in your most recent high school literature course?"

> OPENING: A reading program for high school seniors is difficult to organize, for not only are seniors in general in an in-between stage of development, but they also vary more widely than is thought in their individual maturity. If adult books are assigned, some students may be damaged psychologically; if childish books are assigned, most students will lose interest in literature. The problem is difficult to solve, but I believe that on the basis of my experience in Literature 12A I have some valid suggestions to make.

An introduction of this length necessarily needs separate paragraph status of its own. The more usual short introduction should not be separated from the first main paragraph.

There are several kinds of **stock openings** that students frequently use but should be warned against, for they often do not lead directly into the topic of the paper, they seldom set an appropriate tone, and they never arouse any reader interest at all. One of the most commonly used and inept of these is the **opening that depends on the title for its meaning.** An opening should not contain a pronoun or phrase that refers to the title; instead, a paper should begin just as though a title were not stated. Consider such openings as these:

> I have thought a good deal about this problem.
> This is something I have read a lot about.
> You can't play a winning game without knowing the odds.

With such introductions, the reader is sent immediately to the title to see what *this,* or *something,* or *game* means. Such openings do not directly announce the purpose of the paper, and they do not arouse any interest. You should make it a cardinal rule never to refer to your title in your opening sentence.

Another weak introduction that the unthinking writer often resorts to is the mere **repetition of the assignment.** In effect, he passes the buck in order to get started. Such openings as these are examples:

> The question has been asked, "Why are Americans so disliked in many foreign countries?"
> In this paper I will discuss the relationship between the sales of hydrogen peroxide and the marriage rate.
> I have been asked to write about my favorite ecdysiast.

It is true that such openings announce the topic of the paper, but they are stylistically so dull and routine that they do little to arouse interest.

The **apologetic opening** should also be avoided, for it has a wet-blanket effect just at the point that the reader's interest should be attracted. Here are some examples of these dull and flabby openings:

> I'm not much of an expert in cybernetics, but I will try to tell you something about that science.
>
> I haven't worked very long as a shoestring-tip stapler, but I think the work will be interesting.
>
> Why dictators can come to power is a very hard subject to write about.

An introduction, rather than being apologetic, should be sure-handed and give the impression that the writer has a good command of his subject.

The **"both sides" opening** is a stock introduction that some students rely on whenever they are faced with a topic that calls for them to choose one of two points of view. Such topics usually ask the writer to "discuss the advantages or disadvantages of" or "to attack or defend." Rather than taking a stand and composing a brisk, interesting introduction, many a student composes a wishy-washy beginning that pays homage to both sides. Here are two examples:

> There are both advantages and disadvantages in having an exceptionally beautiful wife.
>
> In some ways I think it would be best for our country to disarm unilaterally, but in other ways I don't think it would be a good idea.

Such openings are indecisive and lacking in vigor.

Direct quotations, including dictionary definitions, generally make weak openings. For the most part, they not only fail to lead directly into the topic but also give the impression that the writer could not use his own words to get started. Such weak openings are more likely to appear in long term papers than in short themes.

Finally, students tend to overuse **rhetorical questions** as introductions. The method itself is not necessarily ineffective, but two common weaknesses frequently attend its use. First, the question itself sounds like just a repetition of the assignment (which it often is). For example, consider these two openings:

> Can one trust his conscience to show him what is right?
>
> Is conformity to the thinking of the majority a safe road to happiness?

The reader seems to hear the instructor speaking rather than the writer. The second weakness is that the writer often fails to make a smooth transition between the question and the next sentence. Too often he resorts to a clumsy transition like this:

> Given time, will scientific advancements solve all human problems?
> This is a question that concerns us all.

Be wary about using a rhetorical question as an opening. Choose such
a method only if you are sure of its effectiveness, not because it is the
only way you can think of to get started.

Effective Conclusions

The conclusion is also a part of the structure, or organization, of a
paper. Like the introduction, it is often misunderstood. A long expository paper may justifiably have one or more separate concluding
paragraphs that summarize the whole substance of the paper. But a short
paper, such as a 500-word theme, should not have such a conclusion,
for in a short paper the points have been so recently made clear to the
reader that he does not need a summary of them. It doesn't make much
sense to write, say, three paragraphs explaining three main points and
then a fourth paragraph explaining the three points you have just made.

The conclusion of an ordinary theme usually should not be a
separate paragraph, but should be the last sentence of the final paragraph
of development, just as the introduction is often the first sentence of the
initial paragraph of development. Also like the introduction, the conclusion is a general rather than a specific statement, for it has to do with
the general idea of the whole paper, not with just one specific detail.
For example, suppose you have written a theme on this topic:

> Discuss the disadvantages of having an exceptionally beautiful wife.

At the end of the paragraph that makes your last point you could
conclude the paper with this general statement of summary:

> A beautiful wife, then, is a dream on the honeymoon, a showpiece for
> the first year of marriage, but often a cross to bear during routine
> married life.

Or suppose your topic was this:

> Discuss the challenges and rewards of some unusual job you have had.

Your concluding sentence, attached to your final main paragraph, might
be this:

> I may find my job monotonous later, but after two years I still find
> shoestring-tip stapling challenging and gratifying.

Or you might have written on this topic:

> Discuss the trials and tribulations of dieting to lose weight.

A satisfactory concluding sentence might be this:

> So I have decided that a man losing weight is a frustrated, irritable, hungry man.

Such concluding sentences should not be given separate paragraph status, for usually a one-sentence paragraph at the end of a paper gives it a bad appearance, just as a one-sentence opening paragraph usually appears structurally unsound.

In a paper designed to prove a point or reach a valid conclusion after an investigation of pertinent evidence, the conclusion will, of course, be a statement, long as is necessary, of the point proved or the conclusion reached. If the paper is short, say a theme of 500 to 1000 words, such a conclusion may be briefly stated as the concluding sentence of the final paragraph of development; or, if it takes as much as two long or three ordinary sentences, it may constitute a separate paragraph. If the paper is a longer term paper or research project, the conclusion will always be a separate paragraph or paragraphs following the final developmental paragraph. For example, consider this topic:

> Build a case for the existence of psychic phenomena.

The concluding paragraph might be this:

> In spite of the fraud and charlatanism surrounding psychic phenomena, the authetically documented evidence we have cited can only lead to the conclusion that phenomena beyond the explanation of contemporary physics and chemistry do exist. Whether, as Rhine thinks, these phenomena are supernatural, or whether, as Stevenson asserts, they will have an ultimate scientific explanation cannot yet be known. But that they exist cannot be doubted.

Whether a conclusion is a one-sentence addition to the final paragraph of development or a full paragraph of its own like this example, it is a part of the structure rather than of the development of a paper.

The concluding sentence or sentences of an expository or persuasive paper should be emphatic, though not bizarre or unduly startling. A piece of fiction may use a shock technique in its conclusion, but the tone of an expository conclusion should be consonant with the tone of the whole paper. An emphatic conclusion will leave the reader with the dominant (general) idea of the paper. It will not be concerned with some minor detail or triviality; nor will it suddenly bring in an afterthough or irrelevancy. For example, consider this topic:

> A bit of advice frequently heard on college campuses is, "Don't let your studies interfere with your education." Discuss the merits of this idea.

TRIVIAL ENDING: Oh yes, a college student might also learn something from conversing with a custodian.

GENERAL ENDING: Thus we can see that the vast complexity of college life means that the educational process is strongly active outside the classroom.

As the second example illustrates, a conclusion should be emphatic enough to make the whole purpose of the paper appear to be fulfilled. That is the reason the conclusion is a part of the paper's structure: it shows the wholeness of the paper and keeps it from appearing fragmentary or at loose ends.

Students are often advised to develop the most important point of a paper last so that the conclusion can be emphatic. But the final point of a paper is not the conclusion; it is a part of the development of the subject matter. The points of a paper should be developed in their most logical order, which may, indeed, mean that the most important comes last. But the conclusion is another thing, even if it consists of only one sentence, and it should carry its own emphatic note.

A good conclusion will have an air of finality about it: it will *sound* like an ending, just as an introduction sounds like a beginning. In narration, an air of finality is not hard to achieve, for a story has a natural ending. But in exposition and persuasion it often seems difficult to wrap up the topic and give the reader a sense of completion. If, however, you have prepared a basic organization for your paper, you will be able to discuss the last point as though it is the last, and this will naturally leave the reader with an impression that you have covered all the points that you intended to cover. Then you should add a sentence or sentences that, as illustrated above, state the general idea of the paper in the tone of a conclusion. This will leave the reader with a sense of completion.

In summary, then, the composition of an expository or persuasive paper is the building of a whole structure. The introduction starts the structure by expressing the core idea to be discussed. The so-called body of the structure consists of a detailed development of main points, which, in college writing, can be treated openly as main points and not concealed for esthetic purposes by subtle and subjective organizational modes. The conclusion shows that the structure is finished.

EXERCISE 13.   Plain and Fancy Introductions

DIRECTIONS: The following introductory statements came from expository articles published in well-known American magazines. Decide which are plain or direct openings and which are fancy or cute. Comment on the quality of each. One good approach in judging is to decide just on the basis of the opening whether you are about to read a factual article, a piece of fiction, or some human-interest piece of journalism. (All the articles **are** factual.)

1. Most people are unaware of how widespread smoking is and of the pattern it takes among American people.
2. Almost until the present turn in human affairs an expanding population has been equated with progress.
3. Hatless and feeling out of place in my city clothes, I squeezed my way through the Wild West mob.
4. The girl clerk in the Seattle bookstore was comely and seemed to be intelligent, which made it all the worse.
5. The behavior of monkeys and apes has always held great fascination for men.
6. A kind of dream world enveloped us, a blank white waste of sodden snow patterned with shallow lakes and swirling melt streams.
7. Man's knowledge of the nature and structure of stars rests on a complex interplay between observation and theory.
8. The lady wore a sunsuit, wedgies, and a bemused expression.
9. I am finishing an enjoyable meal with my wife Simone and a tableful of good companions in a snug lodge we have built in a remote and primitive part of the world.
10. The moment when it first becomes apparent that one's marriage was a mistake is the beginning of probably the longest, darkest period in the human lifetime.

EXERCISE 14. **Effective and Weak Introductions**

DIRECTIONS: Following are ten theme topics with introductory sentences. First decide which plural noun (stated or implied) in each topic would guide you in preparing a basic organization. Then explain why each of the introductions is or is not effective. Rewrite one or more of the openings that you consider unsatisfactory.

1. TOPIC: Should capital punishment be abolished?
   OPENING: This is something you hear a lot about nowadays. I think both sides have many good points, but I don't see much use for it.
2. TOPIC: Is TV chiefly an instrument of education or of escape?
   OPENING: It can be both, depending on how you look at it.

3. TOPIC: What are the virtues or defects of one imported car that you are familiar with?

   OPENING: Arunhrunhrunhrunh. (pause) Arunhrunhrunhrunh. (pause) Arunhrunhrunhrunh. (pause) "Confound this &G%$#@*¢ sardine can, anyway."

   Every morning at about the time my father should be leaving for work, the above noises jolt me out of a sound sleep.

4. TOPIC: What special markets and advertising techniques have been developed for the teen-age consumer?

   OPENING: I don't have much money to spend myself, but I look at all the advertisements in the best known teen-age magazines.

5. TOPIC: Explain the care and nurture of a commercially valuable plant, fish, or animal.

   OPENING: Since they are sensitive and delicate, Burmese cats require more attention and medical care than ordinary alley cats. Yet if a Burmese queen is properly managed, she can bring her owner several hundred dollars profit a year.

6. TOPIC: Discuss the contention that jazz has been America's most significant contribution to world culture.

   OPENING: It has been stated that jazz has been America's most significant contribution to world culture. In this paper I will support this contention.

7. TOPIC: What characteristics of Americans make us disliked in some foreign countries?

   OPENING: First, I think, because we are so selfish.

8. TOPIC: Do any other minority groups in the United States suffer as much discrimination as southern blacks?

   OPENING: A general assumption in European countries, and among many Americans too, is that racial discrimination in America is confined to southern blacks. A few months' residence in Brooklyn and Manhattan, however, will reveal to you other complex patterns of racial discrimination.

9. TOPIC: Why have so many new democratic governments in Asia and Africa recently been supplanted by military dictatorships?

   OPENING: I don't know anything about those countries, but I imagine it is because they were not ready for democracy.

10. TOPIC: What foreign country (besides Russia) has, in recent years, had the most influence on the United States in one particular field (for example, transportation, art, or politics)?

   OPENING: I would say France has had more influence on our movies than any other country. They sure seem to be getting Frenchy.

EXERCISE 15. **Writing Introductions**

DIRECTIONS: Following are five theme topics. First decide which stated or implied plural noun would guide you in preparing a basic organization for each topic. Then write a one- or two-sentence opening for at least three of the topics.

1. What do you consider the most important single course or activity that college offers? Why?
2. Explain and refute some common misconceptions about members of a particular racial, national, religious, or political group.
3. Should college grading standards be sufficiently high to eliminate students who do not have above-average intelligence?
4. Discuss some ways in which the social and economic status of migratory agricultural workers can be improved.
5. Discuss the reasons why the study of a foreign language should not be required of all junior high and high school students.

COHERENCE BETWEEN PARAGRAPHS

Coherence, a most important quality of all good writing, is usually discussed in connection with paragraph structure; and Chapter 4 on paragraph development devotes considerable attention to it. In the present chapter we will limit our discussion of coherence to the linkage of paragraph to paragraph in the whole paper, a linkage that is an element in the organization of the whole. When present, coherence between paragraphs helps make the writing integrated, consistent, and intelligible.

The word *coherence* comes from the Latin *co*, meaning "together," and *haerere*, meaning "to stick." Hence coherence literally means "a sticking together." In good writing, the paragraphs must stick together, and the sentences within a paragraph must also stick together. The sticking together requires proper **transition,** which means a smooth flow from one part to another. The three most common methods of transition for achieving coherence between paragraphs follow.

Transition between Paragraphs

One common method of transition is the use of **transitional words** or **phrases,** such as *also, another, but, and, next, finally, in addition to,* and *on the other hand.* When a word or phrase of this sort (there are dozens) appears at the beginning of one paragraph, it signals to the reader's mind a continuation of the thought of the previous paragraph, thus keeping the writing integrated and intelligible. Here is an example:

> Most writers of major articles are given at least a year to prepare their manuscripts; not until a month before the scheduled delivery of the article is the author prodded to produce it. Immediately upon receipt, the words are counted and payment is promptly made. This policy was instituted because of Yust's own experiences as a free-lance writer, when quick compensation, however small, often elated him more than a delayed check, however large.
>
> The <u>next</u> step for the manuscript is the Robot, where receipt is recorded and a note made of illustrations furnished or needed. Along the route, the copy is read by the specialist advisers for authenticity, then checked several times by editorial workers. . . .—Herman Kogan, "The Modern EB: How It Is Edited"

The transitional word *next* provides coherence between the paragraphs.

A second method of transition is the **repetition** near the beginning of one paragraph **of an important word** from the preceding paragraph. The repetition of the word (usually a noun) also signals a continuation of the thought of the previous paragraph. When the reader's mind encounters the signal, it recognizes familiar material and feels the coherent union of the two paragraphs. Here is an example:

> Since the Renaissance, with its consistent portrayal of Biblical themes, a misunderstanding of the role of art has arisen that has created great confusion in the public mind. The public has become convinced that art mirrors what should be, rather than what is. Thus the ideal, not the life around him, is considered the correct subject for the artist.
>
> <u>Yet</u> the <u>artist</u>, being a part of that life, reflects his surroundings regardless of the apparent subject of his paintings. When we see a Renaissance portrayal of the "Madonna and Child," we seldom stop to consider that the Madonna is usually clothed in the most sumptuous of Renaissance clothing, that her hair is done in the most sophisticated style of the day and that she is usually laden with jewelry. . . .—Leslie Judd Ahlander, "Washington Gallery Shows Pop Art"

Not only the transitional word *yet* but also the repetition of the word *artist* effects coherence between these two paragraphs.

A third method of transition, similar to the second, is the **use of a pronoun** near the beginning of one paragraph to refer to a noun or whole idea in the preceding paragraph. Such a pronoun, too, acts as a signal to keep the reader's mind focused on the writer's line of thought. It helps integrate the two paragraphs. Here is an example:

Mr. Gugghenheim's desire to leave to his city something other than just the conventional museum lives after him—if it can find sympathetic appreciation of his often expressed and now manifested desire. His choice of myself as his architect was based upon the assumption that "the rectilinear frame of reference" for the exhibition of a painting referred more to the frame than to the painting.

He also (and with my complete sympathy) declared that a painting should be seen as nearly as possible as the painter saw it—in the continuation of artificial light managed to suit the exhibitor, and the natural daylight in which in all probability it was painted. To accomplish this, the museum in which to see a painting in an atmosphere suited to inspire the beholder with its beauty—meant a new order of architecture for this purpose.

That is why I went to work for Mr. Guggenheim—to give him a building creating an atmosphere instead of a frame in which to show the painting—incoporating it as a feature of the structure of the edifice in such manner as to reveal its properties of color and design more freely—less constructed and restricted than the bolt-upright canvas on a perpendicular wall under electric light from above.—Frank Lloyd Wright, "The Solomon R. Guggenheim Memorial"

The pronoun *he* in the second paragraph and the pronoun *that* (which refers to a whole idea) in the third paragraph provide clear coherence.

There are other means of achieving coherence between paragraphs. Sometimes, for example, a paragraph will begin with words that did not appear in the previous paragraph but that pertain to ideas expressed in the previous paragraph. The reader's mind makes an instantaneous interpretation and coherence is achieved. But the large majority of paragraphs in exposition and persuasion use one or more of the above three methods. You should make a conscious effort to use these methods of transition in your own writing. They do a great deal to produce the qualities of smoothness and clarity.

EXERCISE 16. Analyzing Transitions between Paragraphs

DIRECTIONS: Choose any selection from your textbook of expository essays and identify the means of transition (transitional words, repeated key words, pronoun reference) that appear between all the paragraphs. Be prepared to explain how these transitional elements act as signals to keep the reader's mind focused on the writer's train of thought.

Transitional Paragraphs in Long Papers

In long papers whole paragraphs are sometimes used for transitional purposes. Such paragraphs are a part of the organizational structure of a paper rather than of its development because they are used just to connect ideas rather than to introduce new ones. Short papers seldom have a need for transitional paragraphs, but term papers and long reports often require them when a simple transitional element will not suffice.

A transitional paragraph, usually quite short, is most frequently used to summarize the ideas of one part of a paper in preparation for the beginning of another part. Thus it forms a transition between two large parts of a paper. The following one-sentence paragraph is an example from a term paper entitled "The First Battle of Bull Run":

> These skirmishes, however, were only a prelude to the savage battle that followed.

This transitional paragraph helped the reader see the preceding paragraphs as one unit and the succeeding ones as another. It was, in fact, both a concluding and an introductory statement and was helpful in making clear the overall organization of the paper.

Following is another example of a well-used transitional paragraph, from a term paper entitled "Some Oddities of Eighteenth-Century Medicine":

> Such fantastic remedies were, of course, just passing fads and were soon abandoned; but stranger fads were soon solemnly adopted by leading physicians.

This short transitional paragraph clearly signals a turn in thought. It ties up in a bundle for the reader one set of ideas and also prepares him for another. It does not introduce new material but serves as an organizational signal for the reader.

Brief one-sentence paragraphs like the above are likely to be ineffective at the beginning or end of a paper, but as transitional paragraphs within a paper they can be useful. They prevent an abrupt shift of ideas by forming transitions between groups of paragraphs, just as words like *therefore, also, however,* and *finally* form transitions between sentences or paragraphs. Transitional paragraphs, then, are signals that keep the reader from losing his train of thought in a long paper just as transitional phrases, repeated nouns, and pronoun reference keep him from losing his train of thought from paragraph to paragraph.

THE COMPLETED ORGANIZATION OF A THEME

The following student theme, which has been edited, illustrates all the essentials of organization discussed in this chapter.

TITLE: A Student's Plea

> The title is mostly an ornament. It does not reveal the content of the paper.

TOPIC: Write an essay giving advice to college teachers.

> The topic is clear and contains a clue to organization.

THESIS SENTENCE: This essay gives advice to college teachers that will make them more aware of student problems.

> The controlling idea of the paper is stated in one sentence.

BASIC ORGANIZATION:

1. To try to understand better the freshman's limited background
   a. Most freshmen know little and are scared when they enter college.
   b. Professors tend to forget this.
   c. Professors often start courses with too much work and too little explanation.
   d. They use words students don't know.
   e. They make allusions to learning that students don't recognize.
   f. They should treat freshmen as adults but should realize that their educational experience is limited.
2. To state clearly rules about absences, late work, and no work
   a. Professors often leave students in the dark about the ground rules of their courses.
   b. Sometimes they will seem not to care whether a student attends class and then will drop him for excessive absences.
   c. Sometimes they will refuse to accept a late paper without having said anything about it.

> The topic is divided into four main points. The working outline is expanded with the details that will build the paragraphs. Some of the details are a logical sequence of ideas; some are examples.

   d. Sometimes they will fail a student
      for not doing a piece of work when
      the student doesn't understand.
3. To review important material and to
   give frequent quizzes
   a. Some professors think that a student
      will remember everything he hears
      or reads.
   b. Actually, most students need a lot of
      repetition.
   c. Students like to know how they are
      doing and don't like a grade based
      on a final exam only.
   d. So frequent quizzes should be given.
   e. The quizzes should be preparation
      for the final exam.
4. To have more personal interviews
   a. When a student is doing badly the
      professor should call him in.
   b. Often a man-to-man explanation
      will be effective when a lecture isn't.
   c. Students like to think their pro-
      fessors care.

Many college teachers exhibit deficiencies in teaching techniques that they could easily overcome if they just knew the truth of their students' impression of them. Yet students generally don't dare give them advice. At the risk of reprisals in the form of low grades I shall give my teachers advice which, if followed, will greatly improve their students' performance and will also increase their students' respect for them.

The introduction, pleasingly phrased, leads directly into the topic. It is long enough to be a paragraph by itself.

An axiom in college teaching so simple that many teachers forget it is that the college teacher should understand the freshman's limited background. Though physiologically they are adults, most freshmen know very little and are scared when they enter college. Professors tend to forget their beginning students' academic limitations and start courses with too much work and too little explanation. They

The terms *college teaching* and *college teachers* provide transition from the opening paragraph. The first main point of the basic organization is expressed as a clear topic sentence. The details from the scratch outline are converted into good sentences.

casually use learned words that students don't know, and they make allusions to the world of learning that students don't recognize. Professors should treat freshmen as adults but should realize that their educational experience is limited.

Another axiom in college teaching should be that the professor make any special regulations for his classes clear to all students from the start, but all too often professors leave their students in the dark about the ground rules for their courses. Professors have been known to say nothing about attendance requirements and then without notice to drop a student for excessive absences. Other professors will be vague about the due date for term papers and then will refuse to accept "late" ones. Similarly, students have been failed for not turning in certain work when it has not been made clear to them that the work was required or that it could be made up. The absentminded professor, it seems, is a populous breed.

Some professors seem surprised to learn that students want review and frequent quizzes, but the better students want exactly that. A student cannot immediately absorb everything he hears or reads, as some professors seem to think; he needs a lot of repetition. Particularly before the final exam a professor should review the high points of the course. But the final exam should not be the only basis for the term grade. Students—most of them, anyway—like to know how they are doing and thus like frequent quizzes. And the professor should see to it that such quizzes are preparation for the final exam.

My final piece of advice to college teachers is for them to have more personal interviews with their students. Any student doing badly should be called in by his profesor, for often a man-to-man explanation will be effective when a lecture isn't. Too, a student is likely to put out a little more effort if he thinks his professor

Transition—that is, coherence between paragraphs—is accomplished by the use of *another* and by word repetition. The second main point is converted into a smooth topic sentence.

The repetition of *professors* provides sufficient transition. The third main point is embodied in a topic sentence.

Clear transition is effected with the word *final*, and a topic sentence is created out of the fourth main point.

A simple note of finality is sounded in the last sentence, which remains cares. In fact, that is what this paper of advice amounts to: it urges the college teacher to care for his students' educational welfare.

a part of the last paragraph. The conclusion is strong and effective.

Though of course it cannot be accounted the equal of professional writing, this student theme is smoothly and clearly written. Its paragraphs and sentences are well constructed, but indispensable to its smoothness was the writer's formulation of a basic organization, his effective composition of an introduction and conclusion, and his achievement· of clear transitions between paragraphs. His paper has excellent structure.

Paragraph Development

THE WIDE RANGE IN PARAGRAPH STRUCTURE

In the earliest days of writing by alphabet, neither spaces, marks of punctuation, nor paragraph indentations were used. All of the letters were placed together with no indication to the reader where a word, sentence, or paragraph began. Gradually writers began to space groups of letters to set off single words and to use marks of punctuation to indicate units of words. The most important development in punctuation was, of course, the use of the period to signify the end of a full unit of thought. Later, writers began to use the symbol ¶ in the margin to mark the beginning of a unit of writing larger than one sentence. Gradually the use of the symbol ¶ declined and in its place writers began to indent a line to show the beginning of a unit larger than a sentence. Such units became known as paragraphs, for the symbol ¶ stood for the word *paragraphus* (medieval Latin), which in English means "to write beside."

Thus indented units of writing are known as paragraphs, and the only all-inclusive definition of the word *paragraph* is that it is a unit of writing that begins with an indentation (or is given separation by double spacing). This of course means that widely varying structures are called paragraphs. In journalistic writing—especially news reporting—often each sentence is indented as a paragraph, and seldom are more than two or three sentences not so marked. There are several reasons for this. First, news reporters think that many of their readers have such a short span of attention that they must be given frequents breaks in the flow of writing. Second, the news column is usually so narrow that even one sentence may take a half-dozen or more lines and thus look to be of paragraph length. A half-column of news reporting indented as one paragraph would look odd. And then the news information itself is such that one or two sentences often do form a unit. Here is a sample of journalistic paragraphing:

> WASHINGTON—A unanimous Supreme Court Monday voided any law that establishes an arbitrary preference for men over women.
>
> The decision by Chief Justice Warren E. Burger for the first time extended to women equal protection of the laws guaranteed by the 14th Amendment to the Constitution.
>
> Reaction by some advocates of outlawing sex discrimination was only lukewarm, however. They contended that the ruling established a less broad precedent than they had hoped for and that a proposed "equal rights" amendment to the Constitution still was needed.
>
> The decision struck down an Idaho probate code requirement that when a man and woman are equally entitled to administer a dead person's estate, the position must go to the man.
>
> "To give a mandatory preference to members of either sex over members of the other," merely to avoid hearings on conflicting claims, "is to make the very kind of arbitrary legislative choice forbidden by the equal protection clause," the court held.—from the Los Angeles *Times*

In college writing, as we will see, such short paragraphs are usually a grave weakness.

In narration, paragraph structure can range from one word to a length of two printed pages, or more. In dialogue each new speech is given paragraph indentation, so that even a word like "No" can be indented as a paragraph. On the other hand some writers of fiction, such as William Faulkner or Marcel Proust, may continue description, interior monologue, and even action for literally pages as one paragraph. There is no reasonably limited definition for a paragraph of narration, except that it is an indented unit.

Even long articles and books of exposition, as modern authors write them, are often rather loose in their paragraph structure. Seldom does the reader find in them the "ideal" textbook paragraph, with an easily identifiable topic sentence followed by detailed development. Instead, modern writers usually begin a new paragraph every 125 to 250 words. They take care, however, always to start a new indentation where there is a perceptible shift in ideas, thus in essence building each of their paragraphs around one central idea. Here is a sample[1] of typical modern paragraphing:

Since light has a finite velocity the astronomer can never hope to see the universe as it actually exists today. Far from being a handicap, however, the finite velocity of light enables him to peer back in time as far as his instruments and ingenuity can carry him. If he can correctly interpret the complex messages coded in electromagnetic radiation of various wavelengths, he may be able to piece together the evolution of the universe back virtually to the moment of creation. According to prevailing theory, that moment was some 10 billion years ago, when the total mass of the universe exploded out of a small volume, giving rise to the myriad of galaxies, radio galaxies and quasars (starlike objects more luminous than galaxies) whose existence has been slowly revealed during the past half-century.

Optical observations have shed little light on the evolution of ordinary galaxies because even with the most powerful optical telescopes such galaxies cannot be studied in detail if they are much farther away than one or two billion light-years. The astronomer sees them as they looked one or two billion years ago, when they were already perhaps eight or nine billion years old. Quasars, on the other hand, provide a direct glimpse of the universe as it existed eight or nine billion years ago, only one or two billion years after the "big bang" that presumably started it all.

Some 50 years ago the first large telescopes had shown that the light from distant galaxies is shifted toward the red end of the spectrum; the more distant the galaxy, the greater its red shift and the higher its velocity of recession. Like raisins in an expanding cosmic pudding, all the galaxies are receding from one another. From the observed velocities of recession one can compute that some 10 billion years ago all the matter in the universe was jammed into a tiny volume of space.

The term quasar, a contraction of "quasi-stellar radio source," was originally applied only to the starlike counterparts of certain strong radio sources whose optical spectra exhibit red shifts much larger than those of galaxies. Before long, however, a class of quasi-stellar objects was discovered with large red shifts that have little or no emission at radio wavelengths. "Quasar" is now commonly applied to starlike objects with large red shifts regardless of their radio emissivity.

We should emphasize that these paragraphs are from a long piece of exposition, not a short school composition that will make three or four main points. But there is unity and discreteness in these paragraphs even though they are not exactly like the paragraphs to be discussed in the next section. The authors of this excellently written article probably cut their teeth on the "ideal" student paragraph and then developed more sophistication as they became professionals.

DESIRABLE PARAGRAPH STRUCTURE IN STUDENT WRITING

Though in the whole world of writing there is wide variety in paragraphing, the kind of writing that students do in themes and essay exam questions usually calls for a rather limited kind of paragraph structure. The reason for this is that in most of his writing the student develops **main points,** and it is the main point that gives his paragraph its structure. In this context a desirable paragraph is one that has a main point expressed in a topic sentence, followed by development of this main point, with illustrative details or a logical sequence of ideas or both.

Topic Sentences

In Chapter 3 we saw that most student writing assignments, especially themes and essay exam questions, can be organized on the basis of equivalent main points derived from a plural noun, stated or implied, in the fully stated topic. Here is an example from a student paper:

TOPIC: Write an essay convincing Victorian-minded people that sex education in the elementary schools is desirable.

IMPLIED PLURAL NOUN: Reasons (why it is desirable)

THESIS SENTENCE: This paper expresses the chief reasons why pupils in the late elementary grades and in junior high school should be given sex education.

MAIN POINTS:

1. Makes them see sex as just one part of an integrated life
2. Keeps them from picking up false ideas in back alleys
3. Reduces their chances of developing complexes about sex
4. Helps close the generation gap

The main points in such a basic organization are themselves topics in the sense that each expresses a general concept that will be the subject or the central idea of one paragraph (or perhaps two; see page 90). In the paper itself each of these central ideas or main points should be expressed as the **topic sentence** of a paragraph, for a topic sentence is one that states the central idea (or topic or subject) of a paragraph. In student writing the topic sentence should be stated explicitly, at or near the beginning of the paragraph, so that the reader's mind will be prepared to understand what follows. His mind first focuses on the general statement in the topic sentence and then shifts easily to the details or analyses that explain the general statement. Thus the topic sentence is an aid to clarity; if the details or analyses were given without the unifying topic sentence, the reader might become confused.

Here are the opening and the topic sentences a student prepared for the above writing assignment:

OPENING: Many Victorian-minded and neurotically prudish people today fulminate against sex education in the schools, but they are misguided, for sex education in grades four through eight can be very helpful in producing well adjusted teen-agers and adults.

FIRST TOPIC SENTENCE (which was kept in the same paragraph as the opening):   Perhaps the most valuable result of such education is that it helps young people see sex as just one part of an integrated life, not a separate, hidden, sinful part of man's existence.

SECOND TOPIC SENTENCE: Sex education for young people is useful, too, in that it keeps them from acquiring false information in back alleys and latrines.

THIRD TOPIC SENTENCE: Furthermore, if young people learn about sex naturally they are far less likely to be scared of it when they become mature.

FOURTH TOPIC SENTENCE: Finally, if children and young teens are taught to accept sex naturally they are more likely to be open with their parents and to close the generation gap.

Each of these four sentences in effect states a topic, which was given paragraph development in the completed paper. Note that each topic sentence contains a transitional element to produce coherence: in the first, *such* relates to the introduction; in the second, *too* provides transition; in the third, *furthermore;* and in the fourth, *finally.*

Here are some more topic sentences culled from student papers:

In spite of their superstitious basis, a few old folk remedies have some therapeutic value.

Worn piston rings, however, are not the only cause of excessive oil consumption in automobile engines.

Basketball calls for more stamina in its players than football does.

In addition, medicine men have to be shrewd psychologists.

Secondly, a church should be a social as well as a religious organization in order to help its congregation adjust to a changing world.

Learning to compose such explicit topic sentences from the main points of a basic organization is excellent training, and you will find it of great aid in giving your paragraphs the development they need if your finished paper is to be praiseworthy. However, you should remember that good paragraphs can be composed without explicit topic sentences, as the paragraphs from *Scientific American* quoted earlier attest. Note, too, that most of the real-life topic sentences above have a transitional word or phrase to link them to preceding paragraphs, thus effecting coherence in the whole paper.

Though usually a topic sentence comes first in a paragraph, sometimes transitional or introductory material may open a paragraph, thus deferring the expression of the topic sentence. Here is an example from a student paper entitled "The Advantages of Early Marriage":

> There is one other advantage of early marriages that, so far as I know, has never been mentioned before. It is the reverse side of a coin frequently used to discourage early marriage. It is this: *if a person avoids an early marriage because he wants to observe many potential mates before he chooses, he may miss the very person he should have married by not taking her when he had the chance.* [The paragraph continued with an explanation of this general idea.]

The first two sentences of this paragraph are preparation for the italicized topic sentence. They form a transition between this paragraph and the preceding one, thus serving as an introduction to the paragraph. The topic sentence, though not first, comes immediately before the true development of the paragraph topic.

EXERCISE 17.   **Writing Topic Sentences**

DIRECTIONS: Each of the following topics has its basic organization stated in scratch outline form. Write a clear and full topic sentence for each of the main points. Phrase each topic sentence as though it were the opening sentence of its paragraph. Provide transition in the second and third topic sentences for each proposed theme.

1. TOPIC: Discuss some of the ways in which poetry differs from prose.
   a. Rhythm more pronounced and regular than in prose
   b. Meaning more concentrated—few words deliver much meaning
   c. More use of devices for melody and tone—sounds more carefully chosen than in prose
2. TOPIC: Discuss some of the advantages of living in a fraternity (or sorority) house.
   a. More social contacts in living quarters—built-in friends
   b. More social prestige on campus—access to affairs
   c. Study help and study aids available
3. TOPIC: Discuss some of the personal benefits resulting from military training.

    a. Instills discipline—good for later life
    b. Gives contact with wide variety of people and their customs
    c. Involves practical instruction in care of equipment, improvising, roughing it, and so forth

4. TOPIC: Discuss some of the evils of inflation.
    a. Harms old people living on pensions, savings, annuities
    b. Costs always outrun wages, harming workers
    c. Makes planning for the future hard for everyone

5. TOPIC: Discuss some of the evils of censorship
    a. Censors themselves can't be infallible—bad mistakes possible
    b. Censors would have to change—new ones might disagree with old
    c. Better to have some bad ideas than to kill good ones

Sentences of Restatement or Clarification

The topic sentence of a paragraph is a generality, which will be developed with specific details or logical analysis. Very frequently such a generality is given further clarification in a **sentence of restatement** that follows the topic sentence. For example, here are the opening two sentences in a paragraph from a student paper entitled "Keeping Up with First Graders":

> There is a tendency for six-year-olds to seek freedom and to resent it at the same time. *One impulse in them drives them to rebellion; another causes them to seek constant discipline and security.* For example, . . .

The first sentence is the topic sentence, the italicized sentence one of restatement. The sentence of restatement does not really add a *new* idea to the paragraph but clarifies and amplifies the ideas already stated in the topic sentence. Indeed, such sentences may be called **sentences of clarification** rather than of restatement. They expand the topic sentence somewhat, present its general idea from a different point of view, and further prepare the reader to understand the detailed development that will follow. In the example above the "seek freedom" and "resent [freedom]" of the topic sentence are repeated in the "drives them to rebellion" and the "to seek . . . discipline" of the sentence of restatement.

Here are two other examples of sentences of restatement or clarification. First, one from a student paper entitled "The Nonethical Uses of Religion":

> In addition to being a moral anchor, religion also gives one a sense of security. *If one believes in a personal God, he believes he will be taken care of.* In times of stress, for example, . . .

The italicized sentence of restatement clarifies the opening topic sentence by reinforcing its generality. The "sense of security" in the topic sentence is repeated in the "be taken care of" in the second sentence. The restatement really does not add a new idea. And here is the second example, from a paper entitled "Thoreau's Concept of Civil Disobedience":

> In "Civil Disobedience" Thoreau was not advising his readers to do as they pleased but to follow their consciences. *Act according to what you think is right, he is saying, not according to what the law says.* His premise is that . . . .

This italicized sentence of restatement not only clarifies and emphasizes but also amplifies the topic sentence by bringing in the idea of the law.

Sometimes two sentences of restatement or clarification follow a topic sentence. Here is an example from a student paper entitled "The Need to Abolish the Grade of F":

> Another reason for abolishing the F grade in college is that many students are in college not because they really want to be there but because our society has conditioned them to believe that they should be there. *Students of all social and intellectual levels hear about college throughout their years in elementary and high school, until they just naturally think that they must go to college. They are led to believe that no decent job will be open to them if they are not college graduates.* But . . . .

The two italicized sentences clarify, amplify, and emphasize the topic sentence by restating in different terms the idea of the topic sentence. The functions, then, of sentences of restatement are to clarify and emphasize the generality of the topic sentence by presenting it in different words and from a different viewpoint, and perhaps to amplify it by introducing a new but closely related idea. But remember that not all topic sentences require a following sentence of restatement.

Occasionally a student will compose what superficially appears to be a sentence of restatement but what really is a sentence of mere padding. Such a sentence usually sounds like a second beginning of the paragraph. Here is an example from a paper entitled "The Necessity of Education":

> Schooling will help a child to develop and to learn about life. *Schooling is one of the most important factors in a young person's life. . . .*

Omit the first sentence and the paragraph still has an opening topic sentence; omit the second and nothing is missed. The italicized sentence does not clarify or amplify the topic sentence. Instead, the repetition is distracting, boring, and meaningless. Be careful not to confuse useless repetition with useful restatement.

A sentence of restatement is also frequently used to end a paragraph. Such a sentence serves not only to further clarify and perhaps amplify the topic sentence but also to give the paragraph a sense of completion. *Since a paragraph is a unit of composition, it should sound as though it has a beginning and an ending. A well-written topic sentence will sound like a beginning; a good sentence of restatement will sound like a conclusion.* Here is an example from a student paper entitled "A Common Theme in Comic Strips":

> Another common type of cartoon, and one of the most disgusting, might be called "the tolerated brat." This is the cartoon that shows a young child annoying his neighbors or his school teacher without being punished or reprimanded by his parents—indeed, seemingly without his parents realizing how detestably he has behaved. The tone of these cartoons is one of amused tolerance of naughty behavior. Probably the best known of this type is the "Dennis the Menace" series. Dennis can make his neighborhood unbearable without drawing a stiffer sentence than a few minutes' incarceration in a corner. Cartoons of this sort perform an injustice to suburban living, for their widespread publication tends to leave the impression that parents cannot, or should not, discipline their children in the interest of pleasanter living in the suburbs. *"The tolerated brat" is a despicable cartoon topic, for its confusion of cuteness and nastiness in children is chipping away at child control and discipline in the suburbs.*

The italicized sentence of restatement does not add new details to the paragraph but restates or summarizes in different words the central idea of the paragraph. It serves both as an instrument of clarity and as a stylistic device to prevent an abrupt ending of the paragraph. It might be called the **clincher sentence** of the paragraph, for it rounds out the whole. Such a final sentence of restatement might seem to be a topic sentence if no clear topic sentence opens a paragraph, but in that case there is an *implied* topic sentence and the final sentence is really one of restatement. A real topic sentence never comes last in a paragraph, for the reader should not have to wait until the end of a paragraph to find out what general idea he has been reading about. The clincher sentence is one of restatement.

EXERCISE 18. Distinguishing between Useful Restatement and Useless Repetition

Directions: In some of the following items the second sentence is one of useful restatement and perhaps amplification;

in others the second sentence is just distracting repetition. Divide the items by number into the two groups and be prepared to explain how restatement clarifies and amplifies and how mere repetition is just padding.

1. To prevent federal aid to public education from becoming a liability, we must be careful to prevent federal control of education. We can keep federal aid from being harmful only if we keep the government from running things.

2. To prevent federal aid to public education from becoming a liability, we must be careful to prevent federal control of education. Only through constant vigilance can we prevent the danger of federal interference in our school programs.

3. To maintain a steady rate of progress, we need both liberals and conservatives in politics. With a proper balance between liberalism and conservatism there will be the proper degree of stability to promote progress.

4. To maintain a steady rate of progress, we need both liberals and conservatives in politics. We must have both liberalism and conservatism if we are to progress steadily.

5. The professional military mind is usually an unimaginative mind and thus is dangerous in politics. Discipline in the military calling is so strict that it quells the imagination needed in political activity.

6. The professional military mind is usually an unimaginative mind and thus is dangerous in politics. Generals and colonels aren't very imaginative and thus may be dangerous in politics.

7. The federal government must take steps to prevent water pollution if our country is not to perish for lack of pure water. Only an effort by an organization as large as the federal government can coordinate a program to combat pollution.

8. The federal government must take steps to prevent water pollution if our country is not to perish for lack of pure water. If the federal government doesn't do something we will soon be without pure water.

9. To progress with the times, churches must conduct themselves more as social institutions. Churches can keep up only if they become more social.

10. To progress with the times, churches must conduct themselves more as social institutions. There is much broader awareness now of social conditions, and churches must participate in converting this awareness to progress.

11. One important source of humor is incongruity. People laugh when a turn of events reveals a sudden shift from the dignified to the ridiculous or from the urbane to the rustic.

12. A question often asked today is whether marijuana should be legalized. Many people wonder whether it would be good to legalize marijuana.
13. In crime detection, the first step is to look for a motive. Only after they understand why the crime was committed can the police begin to search for suspects.
14. The automobile affects the life of the young adult more than he realizes. Consciously or unconsciously, he is both servant and master to his car.
15. World crises have often been the result of individual whim. When the powerful act on impulse, the delicate structure of political stability trembles.

EXERCISE 19. Creating Sentences of Restatement

DIRECTIONS: Following are five topic sentences. Try to compose for each a second sentence of useful restatement.

1. One should not judge the worth of an individual on the basis of his mode of dress.
2. High grades in school do not necessarily indicate brilliance.
3. In raising a family the mother and the father play different roles.
4. Prohibition of sexual experimentation, drinking, and even the use of mild drugs is not a satisfactory way to steer teen-agers into maturity.
5. Intercollegiate athletics give students a chance to abate their aggressive tendencies.

Paragraph Length

Students are often concerned not only with how long a composition should be but also with how long each paragraph in it should be. If a student will master the simple mode of preparing a basic organization of main points derived from a plural noun stated or implied in the topic, he will solve the problem of paragraph length. Since the "ideal" paragraph is a unit of composition built around one central idea, a basic organization of main points will determine how a paper is to be divided into paragraphs. Each main point will be developed into one paragraph (with the exception noted later); *two main points should never be incorporated into one paragraph.* For example, here is the basic organization a student prepared for a short paper on "Artificialities in Present-Day Education":

1. Students are required to learn some material before they use it.
2. Classroom situations do not imitate real life.

3. Fragmentation of subject matter prevents integration of knowledge.

After a suitable opening (which, being short, was a part of the first paragraph), the student planned, tentatively at least, to develop one paragraph for each of his main points—three paragraphs for the whole paper. Since most students do not give particularly extensive development to their main points, the plan of one paragraph for one main point works out for most themes. Here (with the introduction to his theme) is the student's paragraph for the first main point above:

> Today's school children are handicapped because of several harmful artificialities in their educational program. One of these artificialities is that the children are required to learn some material before they have any use for it. In primitive societies children are not taught tribal skills until the time comes for them to use the skills. Thus they very happily learn their lessons. But children in our complex society often resent their lessons because they see no connection between them and the life they lead. For example, many pupils are taught some of the principles of our democracy long before they are to participate in it, and they see no value in the teaching. This kind of teaching in a vacuum often leads to discipline problems and a general scorn for school on the part of many children.

This paragraph has 135 words, a very good length for a paragraph in a student theme. A good rule of thumb for student writing is not to have a paragraph of less than 75 words nor more than 200. That length fits well with the modern fashion in paragraphing for articles of exposition or persuasion.

If, as often happens, a good main point in the basic organization of a theme requires more than 200 words for suitable development, no real harm is done if the paragraph runs to as much as 300 words; however, since current reading practice calls for fairly frequent pauses, such a long paragraph should be divided into two indentations. Almost without exception a long paragraph will have a **natural breaking place** —that is, a shift in content or emphasis of the paragraph's subject matter—that allows for a second indentation. This break into two parts—two indented paragraphs—is actually a convenience for the reader. The development that the student writer gave to the third main point in the basic organization was rather lengthy, and he properly used two indentations. Here is his work:

> A third conspicuous and harmful artificiality in modern education is the fragmentation of subject matter. This means the division of knowledge into separate subjects, such as geography, economics, history, gov-

ernment, literature, biology, and so on. The high school student sits, patiently or obstreperously, for 40 or 50 minutes in one classroom listening (if the teacher is lucky) to discourse on one subject only. Then he goes to another classroom, which is a different world with entirely different subject matter. The student's mind is always having to shift gears, if it doesn't just stay in neutral. Life of course is not divided into small separate categories, but is one continuous whole. Therefore, since education is for life, it also should be one continuous whole and not divided into little fragments taught separately.

When a student goes from a class in geography to one in economics and then to one in history, he is likely to think that these are totally separate categories of human knowledge or endeavor, whereas they are really so closely bound up with each other that they cannot be separated without some distortion of truth. You can't, for instance, have history without geography and economics; therefore geography, economics, and history should be taught together. This principle holds true for most other subjects as well. How, for example, can biology be taught without the use of chemistry, physics, and mathematics? Students, then, should be taught integrated rather than fragmented courses. In this way they would perceive human knowledge and activities as a whole rather than as separate fragments. Thus their education would be for life.

These two paragraphs represent the development of one main point with one topic sentence, but the division of the main point into two indentations is a justifiable convenience for the reader. Because the writer chose a natural breaking point in what could have been one paragraph, the reader feels no gap at all when he begins reading the second indentation.

To summarize: In writing a theme, you should tentatively plan to devote one paragraph to each main point in the basic organization; by no means should you combine two main points into one paragraph. The average length of your paragraphs should be about 125 words—from one-half to three-quarters of a handwritten page. A paragraph of fewer than 75 words is usually undeveloped (see Paragraph Fragments below), and one of more than 200 words is usually fatiguing or confusing to the reader. If your development of a main point runs over 200 words you may divide it into two indentations, *provided a natural breaking point is available.* Such a divided main point will still have only one topic sentence.

So far in this chapter we have been discussing the organization and paragraph structure of theme topics without referring to Chapter 2 on logic in composition. Because more about logic will appear in our discussion of modes of paragraph development, you should have at least the concepts of induction and deduction firmly in mind as you study the rest of the present chapter. But let's pause briefly here to consider the logic in the student paragraphs that we have just examined.

Consider the first main point in the basic organization on page 90 and its paragraph of development. The student's logic here is part inductive and part deductive. The premises that children "resent their lessons because they see no connection between them and the life they lead" and that "This . . . leads to discipline problems" were arrived at by induction. The writer has heard many pupils complain about school and ask, "Why do I have to learn that?" He also has seen or heard of discipline problems and believes that these occur because the children are not interested in what they are supposed to learn. Thus he draws the inductive conclusion (specifics led to it) that children resent school because they are required to learn material before they have any use for it. Is his inductive conclusion correct? As is so frequently the case, 100 percent certainty is not possible. Probably various children resent school for various reasons. But his line of reasoning is convincing and thus is acceptable since he qualifies with the words *often* (twice) and *many*.

But there is also a deduction implied in the paragraph: "Our schools are harming children by teaching them material before they have use for it." The deduction is based on this syllogism:

MAJOR PREMISE: Teaching people material before they have use for it is harmful.

MINOR PREMISE: Our schools teach children material before they have use for it.

CONCLUSION: Our schools are therefore harming our children.

The minor premise was arrived at inductively, but the noninductive major premise is questionable, and thus the deductive conclusion is not necessarily warranted. It could easily be that children would be harmed even more if they were not taught material before they use it. Schools might have fewer discipline problems if our writer's implied reforms were followed, but the society of adults might have more problems. The writer by no means has proved his point.

The implied conclusion in the student's second main point also is based on a syllogism:

MAJOR PREMISE: Any educational plan that does not imitate real life will be unsuccessful.

MINOR PREMISE: The classroom situations in our schools do not imitate real life.

CONCLUSION: Our present classroom situations are not successful in educating our children.

The minor premise of this syllogism was perhaps inductively arrived at by observation of specific classrooms. But the major premise is simply an assumption without foundation, and therefore the conclusion is suspect.

In the third paragraph of the theme a few of the details are based on induction and perhaps can't be questioned, but the deductive conclusion of the paragraph is another matter. Its syllogism is as follows:

MAJOR PREMISE: Teaching knowledge in separate, fragmented categories results in poor education.

MINOR PREMISE: Our schools teach subjects in a fragmented way.

CONCLUSION: Our schools give poor education.

The inductive minor premise cannot be doubted, but the major premise is a debatable assumption with no inductive basis at all. Hence the conclusion is not justifiable. There is nothing to show that fragmented knowledge may not later be synthesized in the minds of students.

It will be instructive for you to examine the logic of some of your own themes in this way.

Paragraph Fragments

An indented unit of writing that does not meet the requirements specified in the previous section is usually a **paragraph fragment.** True, in some kinds of writing a very short paragraph is acceptable, but usually not in themes, essay examinations, and term papers. The notorious sentence fragment receives much attention in grammar and composition texts, but the paragraph fragment is more common and a more serious weakness in student writing.

One kind of paragraph fragment results from **excessive indentations.** Apparently many students absorb their understanding of paragraph structure from reports in newspapers, indenting every sentence or two. Excessive indentation makes for disjointedness and severely weakens the kind of writing most often done in college. Here is an example:

Some paragraphs are weakened because of the useless repetition of an idea that has already been made sufficiently clear.

A paragraph, like a sentence, should be terse and direct rather than wordy and roundabout. Usually repetition in a paragraph occurs because a writer has trouble thinking of what should come next.

Being unable to continue his train of thought, he resorts to a rewriting of his previous sentences in order to fill out his paragraph.

> Repetition for emphasis can be justified, but useless repetition is a serious weakness.

These four indentations belong to the main point, in the first sentence, that useless repetition of an idea can weaken a paragraph. Because only 88 words are used to develop the central idea, the idea need not be divided into two or more indentations for the convenience of the reader. In fact, the excessive indentation distracts the reader. To cure—or to avoid—this kind of paragraph fragment the writer should prepare a basic outline of main points and then devote one paragraph only to each main point, unless the content for one main point is extensive enough to call for two indentations.

A more serious kind of paragraph fragment is the **undeveloped paragraph.** When a topic sentence (generality) is presented with little or no development, the result is a paragraph fragment, which seriously weakens the whole paper. Here is an undeveloped paragraph from a student paper entitled "My Choice for President":

> In his travels Mr. X helped foreign relations. He has also stopped foolish wastefulness of foreign aid.

This is a doubly damaging paragraph fragment, for it contains two topic sentences with no development of either. The reader has a right to know *how,* in the writer's opinion, Mr. X helped foreign relations and *how* he stopped wastefulness of foreign aid. A mere statement of generalities is not convincing—details are needed. The logic of such statements cannot even be examined, for we haven't the specifics that led to the writer's inductive conclusions.

Here is another example, from a student paper on "The Advantages of Local Control of Public Education":

> A local school board knows better how to spend the money. They know what the schools need.

At least this indentation has only one topic sentence, but that topic sentence receives almost no development. The reader wants to know *why* the local school board knows so much. It is not even clear whether the writer, if forced, would have developed his paragraph inductively or deductively. His mere word is not enough to convince the reader of the soundness of the generality. Surely the paragraph fragments presented here are far more serious weaknesses than the much-criticized sentence fragment.

Usually a casual glance at a paper will tell whether or not it has paragraph fragments. Departure from the dicta expressed in the section above on paragraph length usually produces paragraph fragments.

TWO BROAD MODES
OF PARAGRAPH DEVELOPMENT

As we mentioned earlier in this chapter, there is wide variety in paragraph structure in the whole world of writing. But in the kind of exposition and persuasion that constitutes most college writing, paragraphs usually have a rather limited and definite kind of structure. Each paragraph begins with a topic sentence, which is a generality calling for development. Broadly speaking, there are two modes of developing a paragraph topic: (1) development through **illustration** and (2) development through **logical analysis** or **explanation.** Of course both methods may be evident in a single paragraph. The first method makes use of inductive logic (specifics lead to the conclusion), and the second makes use of deductive logic (a syllogism is implied). These two broad modes of development have various subclassifications, of which we will discuss the most common and useful.

Development through Illustration

Accumulation of Specific Details.   One of the most common, simple, and effective means of paragraph development is the use of an **accumulation of specific details** and **supporting data** to make the generality (topic sentence) more believable, interesting, and explicit. This method makes use of inductive logic in that enough specifics are accumulated to arrive at an inductive conclusion, which is usually the paragraph's topic sentence.

As a first example, we will consider the following paragraph fragment from a student paper entitled "The Differences between the Sexes":

> The two sexes also want different kinds of achievements. Women are satisfied with achieving less. Men have higher goals.

This example is a paragraph fragment because the topic sentence has no development. The second and third sentences do provide a little useful restatement, but specific details are needed to give the topic sentence inductive support. As written, the paragraph gives the reader no reason to believe its topic sentence, and just the flat statement of the topic is not interesting. Here is the work of another student, one among several given the task of making a real paragraph out of the fragment:

> Another major difference between the sexes is that they want different kinds of achievements. Men have higher goals than women. Whether these different attitudes are cultural or are inborn is not known, but they are there. A woman's goals are likely to be concerned with the here and now. She wants to redecorate the living room now and will

think about how to pay the bill later. A man is more likely to look to the future. He says, "Let's increase our percentage of savings for a while and then we'll think about what to do with the house." Small accomplishments, such as hand-making a dress, will delight a woman, but a man is dissatisfied unless he can achieve major successes, such as making a killing on the stock market. And for ultimate goals, a woman usually wants a home, love, and security, whereas a man, at least secretly, desires adventure and sex. Indeed, a man and woman's goals are often so different that they seem to speak of different species rather than just of different sexes.

Apparently this student had never heard of Women's Lib, but he did develop an adequate paragraph. He has good sentences of restatement and clarification after his topic sentence, and also he ends with a clincher sentence—a restatement that provides a good conclusion to the paragraph. His specific details might not *prove* his opening inductive conclusion, but they are presented in a convincing manner and at least give support to the topic sentence. And he does qualify somewhat with the phrase *more likely* and the word *usually*. The paragraph's development is good even if one disagrees with the ideas.

Here is another paragraph fragment, from a student paper entitled "A Successful First Date":

Good manners are an asset to any girl. Properly introducing your date to your parents is only one of many opportunities that good manners have to shine.

The one supporting detail in this paragraph fragment does not sufficiently develop the paragraph topic and does not make it interesting. The phrase "only one of many" should have told the student that she must give more details to build a full paragraph. Here is a student revision of the fragment:

Good manners are one of a girl's best assets when she is on a first date. Boys don't look just at figures but also at behavior. Introducing your date to your parents, for example, is a simple act of politeness that will put everybody at ease. Allowing your date to order for you will give him a feeling of importance and manliness. Listening politely and not dominating the conversation will give your date and your friends a pleasing sense of your agreeableness. Thanking your date for a pleasant evening is only common courtesy but will help ensure his calling you again. Good manners, indeed, are no bar to vivacity and contribute greatly to a successful first date.

The second sentence clarifies and emphasizes the topic sentence, and the clincher sentence or final sentence of restatement gives the paragraph a good conclusion. The specific details in between inductively support the idea "one of a girl's best assets" and make the paragraph topic more believable.

As a final example of paragraph development through an accumulation of details, here is a student's answer to the essay exam question "In one succinct paragraph demonstrate that Poe uses romantic or nonrealistic techniques in his tales":

> Poe's tales of psychological horror and terror are nonrealistic in their techniques. He often uses plot events that are completely impossible. In "Ligeia," for example, he has the spirit of a dead woman take over the body of another woman who is at the point of death. Also Poe's characters are usually given nonrealistic, highly romanticized development. They are always "ultra" in whatever characteristic is mentioned. Ligeia, for example, is more beautiful than any other woman and also more learned. Roderick Usher is more sensitive than any other man has ever been. Finally, Poe's settings are almost always weird, wild, and very uncommonplace. He sets his stories in "some decaying city on the Rhine," or on a dreary, deserted moor, or in dank catacombs. Certainly Poe's tales are ultraromantic in techniques.

This student writer found his training in the techniques of expository composition very useful in his writing of essay exams. Here he showed skill in composing a clear topic sentence and in developing its paragraph with an accumulation of specific details to prove the inductive conclusion of the topic sentence. Notice also that he knows how to make his last sentence *sound* like the conclusion of the paragraph.

In the kind of paragraph development illustrated in the three foregoing examples, the specific details make the paragraph topic believable and interesting. Also, the specific details are each independently related to the paragraph topic, not to each other. Therefore no set arrangement of the details is mandatory. Sometimes almost any order will do, but the good writer will give some thought to arranging details in a natural, effective order.

EXERCISE 20.   Developing Paragraphs with Specific Details

DIRECTIONS: Following are three topic sentences that can be developed with specific details. Write a full paragraph for one of them, doing these things: (1) composing one or more sentences of restatement or clarification to follow the topic sentence; (2) citing three to five specific details that will make the topic sentence believable; and (3) composing a final clincher sentence (restatement) that will sound like a conclusion to the paragraph.

1. I find that I adjust my language usage according to the kind of social situation I am in.
2. Psychologists report that everybody is dishonest at some time or other.
3. Student involvement in establishing college general policy leads to a better educational environment.

Extended Examples.   The use of one **extended example** to develop a paragraph topic is in a sense a variation of the use of an accumulation of specific details. Instead of giving support to the inductive conclusion (or topic sentence) with three to five specific details, the writer makes the paragraph topic believable and interesting with one *long* detail. For an extended example is just one long detail.

To understand better this method of paragraph development, consider the following paragraph fragment from a student paper entitled "Why Bright Students Fail":

> Another reason why intelligent college students sometimes fail is that the teachers often don't try to understand the student's problems. They don't seem to care.

The topic sentence is an inductive conclusion, but the reader is given no evidence to cause him to believe it. And without evidence in the form of details or examples, the fragment is singularly uninteresting. Given the task of inventing an extended example with which to develop this paragraph topic, one imaginative student produced the following:

> Another reason why intelligent college students sometimes fail is that their instructors don't try to understand their problems. For example, there is a brilliant lawyer in my home town who, even with an IQ of 140, flunked out of Torts University as a freshman. He had been compelled, because of illness, to enter college two weeks late, and in each of his classes the major assignments had already been made. Being somewhat shy, he was afraid to ask his professors what he needed to do to catch up, and so he drifted around without being sure just what was expected of him. Not a single professor even spoke to him personally. Consequently he never did get oriented and received an F in every subject for the first semester. He left Torts discouraged, but entered Blackstone University the next fall and established an outstanding record. Torts U. could have had the honor of being his alma mater if a professor or two had just spoken to a bewildered boy.

Note several points here. First, the topic sentence is not followed by a sentence of restatement or clarification, for one isn't needed. Also the final sentence is not, strictly speaking, one of restatement, but it does give the paragraph a conclusion. Next, the writer used only one example to support the inductive conclusion that is his topic sentence, and normally one instance is not enough to prove a generality. But the one example is sufficient to make the paragraph topic believable as well as interesting, and, after all, the writer was not trying to produce a scientific sociological report. Finally, note that the extended example is narration, for it tells a little story. Remember that in the opening chapter we said that spots of narration are often used in expository or persuasive papers.

Here is a second example of paragraph development through the use of one extended example, from an essay exam answer to the question "Show in one solid paragraph that Edgar Allan Poe had an analytical mind." The student could have drawn on his knowledge of Poe's "tales of ratiocination" to answer this question, but he remembered a story about Poe and used it instead.

> Most people think of Poe as rather crazy, but actually he had a very analytical mind. This is clearly illustrated by an incident that occurred in Richmond, Virginia, in 1836. There was an exhibition of an automatic chess player, called "The Grand Turk," that had been deceiving audiences in Europe and America since 1783. A stuffed figure of a Turk sat at a big desk on which was a chessboard and played against all comers, usually winning. People were allowed to examine the mass of machinery inside the desk, and all were convinced that a machine was playing chess. Poe observed one performance and immediately wrote a brilliant essay giving seventeen reasons why the machine was a fraud and why there had to be a concealed chess player. His first point was that the Grand Turk waited as long as he had to for his opponent to make a move. A machine, said Poe, could not do that. His second point was that there was no method by which a machine could sense what play an opponent made nor sense the location of all the chess pieces. And he gave fifteen more logical reasons why the machine was a fraud. The machine was then exposed as a fraud after decades of fooling audiences. Poe analyzed the situation.

This paragraph, too, uses just one example—a long detail—to support the inductive conclusion that is the topic sentence, but the one example is sufficient to make the paragraph generality believable and interesting. The comments made about the first sample paragraph of this section also apply here.

EXERCISE 21. Developing Paragraphs with Extended Examples

DIRECTIONS: Following are three topic sentences that can be developed with extended examples. Choose one and develop it with one convincing extended example that you simply make up.

You don't necessarily need to use restatement, but do give your paragraph a suitable conclusion.

1. Often a writer who attracted little attention in his own lifetime becomes famous after his death.
2. If a human being becomes overexcited by a sense of fear or urgency, he can often perform superhuman feats of strength.
3. Participating in student government may be worth as much as taking a class.

Comparison and Contrast.   A third method of using illustration to develop a paragraph topic is the use of examples that employ **comparison** or **contrast.** The accumulation of details and extended examples in the sample paragraphs above are used as simple evidence to make the paragraph topic believable and interesting. An example involving comparison or contrast serves the same purpose and is often used also to clarify a topic sentence that might not be fully clear to the reader. The idea is to compare or contrast the not-fully-clear generality with something the reader is fully familiar with, thus making the generality understandable. Therefore a comparison often—though not always—performs a dual function.

As a prelude to a sample of comparison, consider this paragraph fragment, from a paper entitled "The Care and Nurture of Honey Bees":

> Another problem facing a beekeeper is getting to know a newly arrived hive and getting it to know him. This is a delicate problem that calls for know-how. It takes a lot of tact.

This is not only an incomplete but also a dull paragraph. The mere statement of a generality in abstract terms is seldom interesting or convincing. A concrete example, however, can make the generality more believable and the paragraph more pleasing.

The writer of this fragment was given a strong hint as to the kind of example employing comparison that he could use to develop the fragment and was also encouraged to compose a stronger opening. He produced this far more attractive paragraph:

> Another problem facing a beekeeper is getting to know a newly arrived hive and getting it to know him, a delicate problem that calls for much tact. The hive of bees is a unit in itself with its own personality; no strange bees are allowed in it and none of its bees would venture into another hive. The keeper, too, is an individual personality. How shall the two personalities become familiar? The process is something like that of a young man becoming acquainted with a sensitive,

slightly suspicious young lady. First he must let her know of his presence without getting too close or jarring her sensitivity. After she becomes aware of him, he will venture a very polite social call to her
vicinity, say in a library, but still without getting close enough to touch
her. Doubtless he will then go through a few characteristic actions so
that she can identify him as a distinct individual. After two or three
gentle approaches of this sort, he will become a little bolder and will
engage her in polite social talk, or, in the case of the bees, in a little
amiable cleaning of the hive or other close activity among the cloud
of bees at the hive's mouth. Soon the two will be familiar with each
other and chatting gaily like old acquaintances.

This extended example not only supports the generality in the topic
sentence but also serves to clarify it. "Getting to know a hive of bees"
is not an idea that many people would understand fully, and thus making
the example a comparison gives the reader a familiar activity to apply
to the paragraph topic. The reader's understanding and enjoyment are
both increased.

The comparison of two things or events that are dissimilar but have
some common point of identity, as in the above sample paragraph, is
called an *analogy,* particularly if the comparison is rather short. Thus
often a short analogy can be used in conjunction with another method
to develop a paragraph fully. Here is an example *not* written by a
student:

Most composition textbooks illustrate the various modes of paragraph development with selections chosen from the writings of the best
professional authors. These sample paragraphs are skillfully written and
illustrate all the subtleties, refinements, and complexities of first-rate
writing. And indeed they should, for they were written by first-rate
authors. "There!" the textbook author says to the student. "That is how
to write a real paragraph!" The student, however, feels a little baffled.
He does not understand how to achieve such subtleties, refinements, and
complexities. In fact, he cannot even recognize most of them. He is a
beginner, not a professional. *The textbook author has, in effect, acted
like the piano teacher who ripped off a Chopin mazurka and then said
to her beginning pupil," There. That's the way to do it. Now you try it."*

The last, italicized sentences in this paragraph express an analogy. It
draws a parallel between two situations that have some similar attributes
in order to make clearer the particular situation under discussion. In this
case, the analogy clearly says that a composition student must learn
some fundamentals before trying to achieve professional complexities.
Note also that this paragraph does not have a stated topic sentence.
One could be something like this: "Some composition textbooks urge
students to imitate writing that is too complex for them to imitate as

beginners." Observing this admonition, we repeat that students should practice composing a topic sentence for each of their paragraphs.

Contrast as well as comparison can be employed in an example, both serving the same purpose. Here is a sample paragraph a student wrote for the topic "What differences do you see between your ideal of womanhood and your father's?"

> For another point, it is clear to me that my father thinks a woman's greatest asset is her looks—particularly her figure—, whereas to me it is her mind and spiritual outlook. This may not seem like a truthful evaluation of the two generations, but I think it is. From what I have read, the difference is somewhat like the difference in attitude between the two generations about their cars. I am told that in the thirties and forties a man thought of his car as a mistress. He loved to see it shine. He liked to feel it as he polished it. He used fur pieces as seat covers. He often gave it a female name. The case is quite different with me and, I think, my generation. I am quite willing for someone else's hands to feel my car as it is polished. I don't dress it up at all and would never give it a female name. Instead, I like its performance and road-ability. I want it to have power and smooth acceleration. I want its suspension system and torsion bars to make it road-worthy under the most difficult driving conditions. In short, I like its "mind" and "spirit," just as I do those of a woman. My father is welcome to "looks" in his women and his cars.

The extended example that develops this paragraph employs both comparison and contrast: attitudes toward women are compared with attitudes toward cars, and one person's attitudes toward cars is contrasted with another's. As a result, the paragraph topic is made more understandable and interesting. We might note here that comparison is used more often than contrast in paragraph development.

EXERCISE 22.   Developing Paragraphs with Comparison or Contrast

DIRECTIONS: Following are three topic sentences. Select one and develop a paragraph for it using an example that employs comparison or contrast.

1. Mr. X's party takes better care of the poor and oppressed in our nation than does Mr. Y's party.
2. Manipulating a teacher for your own advantage requires more than just brains.
3. Life in a dormitory can be very unpleasant.

Narration and Description in Paragraph Development.   In discussing the four classical forms of discourse in Chapter 1, we said that spots of **narration** and **description** can be useful in exposition and persuasion. Here is an example of a student's rhetorical use of narration in a paper of persuasion entitled "The Need for Short-Term Marriage Contracts":

> Another reason why marriage should be on a short-term contractual basis is that people can undergo surprising changes in values and attitudes, especially between the ages of eighteen to twenty-five. For example, at age twenty my brother married a girl, also twenty, who seemed ideally suited to his values and interests. For a couple of years they partied and lived it up with no strife between them. But then my brother's mind began to change rather rapidly and surprisingly. He was introduced to a book on comparative anthropology and this led to other reading. He began to see nothing but foolishness in TV, most movies, and empty partying. He tried to talk to his wife about newly-learned ideas, but couldn't. She started looking for someone who would play the old good-times games. Well, the result was catastrophe. An original three-year contract would have provided for an unexpected and 180-degree turn in my brother's values.

The student used a little story as an example with which to illustrate his topic sentence, and the spot of narration adeptly aided him in fulfilling his purpose—to convince.

And here is an example of a student's use of description as a clarifying aid in writing exposition. The title of the paper was "Nature's Variety in Caring for the Newborn."

> The baby quail differs from most other baby birds in that it is hatched precocious—that is, advanced in development and almost ready to take care of itself. Most other birds are completely helpless at hatching. The baby robin, for example, is hardly more than a mouth and stomach. Wobbling uncertainly, it opens its mouth 90 degrees and screams its hunger. It gulps its parent's offering, pushes its mates, continues screaming, and looks as though it is in the last throes of an anguished death. The baby quail, on the other hand, is almost from the beginning coordinated and agile. It is well-shaped, downy, and beguiling. And its pleasant chirp is music compared to the baby robin's screaming.

This student writer's purpose was to inform the reader about the differences between precocial and altricial birds, and he found some descriptive bits ideal rhetorically for his purpose. The description clarifies and also delights. For a scientific report, the student would have been more matter-of-fact, depending on expository illustration. But in his freshman theme he felt he could show his rhetorical skill by utilizing description.

Development through Logical Analysis or Explanation

In the above sections we have seen how paragraph topics can be developed with illustrations. In such development, the topic sentence is an inductive conclusion and the details and examples serve as specifics to convince the reader of the validity of the induction. This is really the same kind of thought process as that in which you tell someone that burning a mixture of hydrogen and oxygen always produces water and then prove your point by burning some hydrogen and oxygen a few times. An important difference, of course, is that the generalities (topic sentences) in the kind of paragraphs we have seen often cannot be fully proved, and thus the details and examples can serve only to convince, not to present scientific proof. In addition, the details and examples make the paragraph interesting.

But not all paragraph topics are best developed with illustrations. Many call for development through **logical analysis** or **explanation.** In such development, the relationships of the sentences to each other is different from that of sentences used in development through illustration. In the latter case the writer can consciously select details as to number and appropriateness, may order them in an arbitrary way, and on revision may decide to drop a detail or to add another, or both, since the details and examples are usually related to the topic sentence and not just to each other. In logical development, however, many if not most of the sentences are closely related to—or grow out of—the previous sentences, not to just the topic sentence, and thus a step-by-step progression of logic is necessary. It is important that a writer not skip a step in the logical development of a paragraph. We will examine four common variations of this broad pattern of development.

Logical Sequence of Ideas.   Like development through illustration, development through a **logical sequence of ideas** is intended to convince the reader that the topic sentence is valid. But the mode of convincing is different. Instead of giving details and examples, the writer shows the reasoning that led him to believe his paragraph topic, and the topic sentence is a deductive rather than an inductive conclusion, as will be shown below. We will not get deeply involved with the structure of logic in such a paragraph, but it is important that you understand that in using such development you are not presenting individual examples but are proceeding from idea to idea.

Again let's start our examples with a paragraph fragment, from a paper entitled "Regulation or Fraud":

> It is necessary that we have government regulations to protect the consumer against inferior goods and fraudulent advertising. The public can't protect itself.

The topic is stated, but the reasoning that led the student to believe it is absent. After much coaching in how to develop a line of reasoning, the student produced this revision:

> We must have governmental regulations to protect the consumer against inferior goods and fraudulent advertising, for he cannot protect himself. Everyday the average consumer uses dozens of products and is bombarded by hundreds of ads. He is so overwhelmed by the variety of material appurtenances in his life that he has only time to use them, not time to shop for them carefully in order to secure good quality. Furthermore, he seldom has the kind of education that will guide him in selecting quality even if he has sufficient shopping time. In the case of products that should last for years, the consumer can suffer badly if he has an inferior product foisted off on him. It is clear, too, that the consumer does not have the time, nor usually the education, to properly evaluate the endless ads that surround him. The scientific allusions alone now used in advertising are enough to baffle the ordinary consumer. Under such circumstances, then, must not modern society provide itself with regulatory agencies that will try to control the flow of inferior goods and false advertising?

The sentences that develop this paragraph are not separate examples but are logically related ideas. The writer is deducing his conclusion—which is stated at both the beginning and end of the paragraph—not arriving at an inductive conclusion.

The syllogism for the paragraph is this:

MAJOR PREMISE: Consumers should be protected from inferior goods and fraudulent advertising.

MINOR PREMISE: Only governmental agencies can protect consumers from inferior goods and fraudulent advertising.

CONCLUSION: We should have governmental agencies to protect consumers.

The major premise is not explicitly stated in the paragraph. The writer just naturally assumes it to be true. It is a noninductive premise that probably derives from plain common sense (see page 26). The minor premise derives from the sequence of ideas that develop the paragraph. And thus, if the major and minor premises are true, the conclusion inevitably follows. Of course some people might argue that neither of the premises is true. They might say that the consumer should not *be* protected, but should protect himself. Also they might argue that business, not governmental, agencies can best protect the consumer. Nevertheless, this well-developed student paragraph would sound convincing to most readers.

The next example of paragraph development through a logical sequence of ideas is the fourth revision of a student paragraph:

> In our present society governmental action to provide jobs is necessary unless we are to have widespread unemployment and economic distress. A new industrial revolution is now taking place with the result that fewer and fewer production workers are needed. Therefore in the manufacturing industries large numbers of workers are being laid off. Even when the demand for goods picks up, these workers will not be rehired, for automated machinery will allow the factories to increase production without adding new workers. What are the millions of unemployed to do? It is a mistake to assume that the private companies will find jobs for them, for each company is relatively small and must think of its own profit. Consequently, a superorganization—namely, the federal government—must plan new ways to use these surplus workers so that all can have a chance to make a living through useful work. Only the government is big enough to do such planning and to see that in the process of transition from production to service jobs large numbers of workers do not face grave economic distress.

The deductive conclusion is stated in the topic sentence, which is followed by a logical sequence of ideas expressing the writer's reasoning. The syllogism for the paragraph is this:

MAJOR PREMISE: All workers should have employment.
MINOR PREMISE: Only the federal government can plan the economy so all workers can have jobs.
CONCLUSION: The federal government should plan the economy so all workers can have jobs.

Again, the major premise is not stated but implied and is a noninductive conclusion that the writer assumes. Some people might not accept that premise as true. The logical sequence of ideas that develop the paragraph imply the minor premise, and many people would probably reject that premise too. Thus the conclusion is one that not everybody would accept. This is likely to be the case with any paragraph a student develops with a logical sequence of ideas. Still, the writer of the above paragraph did a good job of developing it.

Our final example of development through a logical sequence of ideas is a paragraph from a paper prompted by a bitter community fight over academic freedom:

> Also the Volunteer Civic Council's demand that Professor X be fired should be met. Everybody knows he is a communist and a pervert and

will harm students. As a communist he will secretly indoctrinate students, who aren't capable of protecting themselves. The students then will pass on their atheism and evil political beliefs to their friends, and eventually the whole city will be corrupted. Though his perversion hasn't been proved, everybody knows he is one, and that just makes his communism worse. He ought to be kicked out of the college tomorrow.

This remarkable—not to say bizarre—paragraph has the same kind of development illustrated above, but its logic is even more intriguing. Its base syllogism is this:

MAJOR PREMISE: Any professor who harms students by indoctrinating them with communism should be fired.

MINOR PREMISE: Professor X harms students by indoctrinating them with communism.

CONCLUSION: Professor X should be fired.

The major premise, which is only implied in the paragraph, would probably be accepted by most Americans, though some would question whether indoctrination in communism is harmful. But it is the minor premise—which derives from the paragraph's logical (or illogical) sequence of ideas—that would be rejected by most people, who then of course would not accept the conclusion, which (as is often the case in such paragraphs) is stated in the topic sentence. The reason for rejecting the minor premise is that the logic in the paragraph is extremely suspect. The "everybody knows" is a typical propagandistic phrase and is obviously false. The assertion that since Professor X is a communist and pervert he will harm students is a *non sequitur,* as is the assertion that he will secretly indoctrinate students. The claim that students can't protect themselves is an overbroad generalization, as is the claim that they will infect others to the point of corrupting the city. The assumption that students of a communistic professor will become atheists is a *non sequitur* of the first order. The assertion that his perversion (which seems quite unlikely to exist) will just make his communism worse is a wild false judgment of causation. And, finally, the student's disregard of due process in the final sentence is in a sense an unsound appeal to authority (that of the Volunteer Civic Council). The paragraph's logical sequence of ideas is not very logical.

Developing a paragraph topic with a series of logically related sentences is one of the hardest methods to learn. It calls for a line of reasoning, and most people have trouble pursuing a line of reasoning for any length of time. But once you understand that your topic sentence is a deductive (not inductive) conclusion and that you must show why you believe it is true, you should be able to develop a reasonably full and convincing paragraph—that is, if you take care with your logic.

EXERCISE 23.   Developing Paragraphs with a Logical Sequence of Ideas

DIRECTIONS: Following are three topic sentences that can be developed with a logical sequence of ideas. Choose one and develop as full a paragraph as you can by giving the line of reasoning that leads you to accept the idea in the topic sentence.

1. Education and property qualifications for voting would be very wrong.
2. High school students should be allowed to read books that ultraconservative people think are obscene.
3. In all levels of education it is best not to put superior students in one class and average students in another.

Cause and Result.   In such paragraphs of logical analysis as those above, a major premise is usually just assumed and not stated. For example, if the major premise were

> Any court system that does not provide speedy and undoubted justice should be reformed,

the sentences of logical analysis would try to justify the minor premise, such as

> The adversary trial system does not provide speedy and undoubted justice.

The topic sentence of the paragraph would state the conclusion, such as

> Our adversary trial system should be reformed.

A paragraph of this kind is one of persuasion, intended to convince its readers.

In a paragraph developed through a **cause-and-result relationship,** the logical analysis is not necessarily persuasion but often is just explanation that shows why a certain situation (the result) exists. In such a paragraph the result, such as

> Big-city governments are in desperate financial straits,

is the topic sentence, and the paragraph development shows the cause of this result. Usually the result is an accepted fact. But often a "result" open to debate, such as

> The United States is now far on the road to socialism,

can be a topic sentence, with the "cause" sentence being intended to convince as well as explain. Thus in this method of development, the result (topic sentence) is a deductive conclusion, but usually it is one about which there would be no argument. For example, the syllogism for the first "result" above is this:

MAJOR PREMISE: Any big-city government that cannot provide its citizens with needed services and welfare is in desperate financial straits.

MINOR PREMISE: None of our big-city governments can provide these services.

CONCLUSION: Big-city governments are in desperate financial straits.

The "cause" part of this paragraph, if it were written, would demonstrate the minor premise. Thus obviously this particular method of paragraph development is quite similar to the method of development through a logical sequence of ideas.

Here is a revised paragraph of cause-and-result, from a paper entitled "School Conflicts":

No doubt the chief cause of this kind of school rivalry [intense rivalry between two high schools] stems from a natural desire among young people to engage in competitive activities. A teen-ager feels good when it is demonstrated that he or a group he belongs to is superior to a rival. Consequently, even in an activity as innocent as a ball game the desire to win is very strong on both sides, particularly if the teams "belong" to teen-agers. This natural individual drive becomes accentuated when large numbers of individuals are thrown together at one time with the same competitive desire. The result is apt to be an extension of the competitive feeling beyond the mere game itself. In fact, little fracases are apt to break out. After this sort of thing has happened two or three years in a row, a "tradition" of rivalry is apt to grow up between two schools. Thus there exist many established, permanent, intense school rivalries. It all goes back to the natural human desire for competition.

The result is the topic sentence and the cause is contained in the sentences of development. Notice particularly how the sentences of logical analysis grow out of each other: "Consequently, . . ."; "This natural . . . drive . . ."; "The result is . . ."; "In fact, . . ."; "After this sort . . ."; and "Thus . . .". A line of reasoning is used to develop the cause. The syllogism for the paragraph is this:

MAJOR PREMISE: A natural desire among young people for competition can result in rivalry.

MINOR PREMISE: This natural desire for competition is accentuated in high schools.

CONCLUSION: Intense rivalry between high schools is due to a natural desire for competition.

Few people would reject these premises and therefore most would accept the conclusion. Thus the paragraph is really one of explanation rather than persuasion.

Here is another paragraph developed through a cause-and-result relationship. It is an answer to the essay exam question "Show in one succinct paragraph why the Puritan theocracy in colonial New England died."

> The Puritan theocracy in New England, which flourished mightily from the 1620s to the 1690s, was virtually dead by 1750. The Puritans, who were very intolerant in regard to theology, tried to keep out people of other faiths, but as the migrations increased, numerous non-Puritans, including Quakers, came to New England. This diluted the Puritan hegemony and weakened the power of the Puritan clergy. Also the leading Puritans, especially Cotton Mather, became positively psychotic about their theology, to the point that the ordinary people were literally scared to death by the harsh Calvinistic tenets of predestination, election, and the depravity of man. The pendulum had to swing, and many turned in revulsion from these tenets. Also the Puritans' hanging of twenty witches in 1692 brought further revulsion, so that Puritanism declined rapidly thereafter and was virtually gone by 1750.

This paragraph is pure exposition with no persuasion in it, but its development is one of stating a result in the topic sentence and then giving the cause of that result. In fact, notice that three causes are given: the migration in of other faiths, the revulsion against Calvinism, and the revulsion against hanging the witches. Often more than one cause is given in a cause-and-result development. If the student had been writing a longer answer, he would have developed a full paragraph for each of the causes.

EXERCISE 24.   Developing Paragraphs through a Cause-and-Result Relationship

DIRECTIONS: Following are three topic sentences that can be developed as cause and result. Choose one and write a full paragraph showing the cause of the situation stated in the topic sentence.

1. Students today are more idealistic than they were in the 1950s.
2. Professor X is very popular with his students.
3. Prisons do not rehabilitate prisoners.

Steps in a Process.   The "How to . . ." theme, such as "How to Overhaul a Car Engine" and "How to Study When in Love," is a common assignment in composition classes. Sometimes one specific process occupies the whole theme, so that in effect one topic sentence serves three or four paragraphs. The above two titles might be examples of this kind of theme topic. Sometimes, however, such a theme will call for three or four topic sentences, each of which will have its own development. A possible example is "How to Avoid a Divorce." Here is a basic organization for this topic:

1. Equable distribution of money
2. Shared interests in sports and social life
3. Sensitivity to feelings and changes in mood

Each of these three main points would form a topic sentence and each topic sentence would be developed with sentences that would show "how to . . .." The whole theme would be on a "how to . . ." topic and so would each paragraph.

In this kind of paragraph the reader is carried through a series of steps that show how the process is performed. Each sentence of development usually grows out of the previous one so that logical analysis or explanation, not individual examples, forms the basis of development (though of course an example might also be included in the development). The question "how?" rather than "why?" or "what?" is asked about the topic sentence and then answered. Here is a paragraph from a paper entitled "How to Train Dogs." Each paragraph in the paper showed the steps in the process of training dogs for particular purposes.

> Dogs can also be taught to protect young children. The first step the trainer takes in this part of the dog's education is to make the dog aware that the child is helpless. He does this by letting the dog see him rescue the child from various difficulties. Next he tries waiting until the last moment to rescue the child, thus giving the dog a chance to perform the rescue himself. The intelligent dog will soon catch on and will begin to take a possessive interest in the child. Then the trainer undertakes to teach the dog various dangerous situations that confront the child, such as those involving the streets, high places, stray animals, and loose objects. With such training an adaptable dog will soon become a better protector than the child's own mother.

Note that the topic sentence demands an answer to the question "how?" The sentences of development then carry the reader step by step through the process. The whole paragraph is pure exposition since it simply explains and does not try to convince. Still, the sentences come logically in a sequence and cannot be presented in any other order. Note that the words *the first step, next,* and *then* link the steps together.

Here is another example of this mode of paragraph development, from a paper entitled "How to Deceive Your Professor." The student gave three ways, each being a process by itself. Here is the third:

> A most artful way to deceive your professor is to ask him to refer you to extra outside readings and then to pretend you have read them. Of course you have already given the impression of being attentive in class and taking notes. Now after class one day you ask for titles of additional articles and books. Every professor will happily cooperate. Of course you only take a quick look at the suggested reading, making a few isolated notes, such as that B. F. Skinner is a behaviorist. Then you watch for your chance in class. At an opportune moment you raise your hand and ask, "Don't you think Spencer Klaw's analysis of Skinner's behaviorism is too simplified. That is, I mean . . . ," and you drop in a couple more terms. Of course your professor doesn't remember anything about Klaw's writings, and you are home free without having read more than the opening paragraph of an article. Doubtless your professor will give you a grade higher than you deserve.

Note that the steps which explain the topic sentence must have a set order: (1) asking for the reading list; (2) taking a quick look at an item and making a note; (3) taking an opportunity in class to deceive the professor; and (4) benefiting from your deception. Note also that the writer used an example to illustrate one of the steps in his process. Examples are often useful in themes or paragraphs that explain steps in a process.

EXERCISE 25. Developing Paragraphs through Steps in a Process

DIRECTIONS: Following is a "how to . . ." theme topic with a basic organization of three main points. Choose one of the points, compose a topic sentence for it, and then develop the paragraph through steps in a process. Use one or more examples if you can.

TOPIC: How to Cheat Your Way through Life
BASIC ORGANIZATION:
1. Learn to pick the brains of others in school and at work.
2. Learn to make others think you are doing them a favor when they are doing you one.
3. Learn to be gracious in letting your family and friends pay when you should pay.

Extended Definition.   One of the most common writing assignments given college students is to define a term, principle, or concept. According to the term to be defined and the desires of the instructor, a definition may consist of only one sentence or a paragraph or a paper of several paragraphs. We will limit our discussion to definitions of paragraph length, for if you learn to handle a definition of this length, you will be able to write longer or shorter ones. The basic method of developing a paragraph of definition utilizes a logical sequence of ideas, but examples may be used also.

Two common pitfalls in writing extended definitions are (1) defining a concept in terms of itself and (2) omitting relevant aspects of the concept so that only a vague half-picture of its meaning is delivered. The following paragraph fragment from a student's answer to the essay exam question "Discuss the principles of outlining" illustrates both weaknesses:

> Another principle of good outlining is parallelism of structure in headings. The headings should be parallel in the way they are constructed. This holds true for headings on various levels.

Note that the student defined the concept "parallelism of structure" in terms of itself. This is like a dictionary's definition of *opsonification* as "the act of opsonifying." Who knows any more than he did? Worse yet, the third sentence gives none of the relevant aspects of the concept needed for a full, clear definition. Following a **plan of four steps** will produce clear, meaningful definitions.

The first step is one of **classification.** It calls for the fitting of the term to be defined into a larger classification that it belongs to and differentiating it from other terms in that larger classification. The sentence that accomplishes this dual function will be the topic sentence of the paragraph of definition. Here are two examples:

> A Petrarchan sonnet is a poetic form consisting of fourteen lines of iambic pentameter.
>
> DNA is a nucleic acid that gives instructions as to what kinds of proteins are to be manufactured in different cells.

In the first, *Petrarchan sonnet* is classified as a "poetic form" and is differentiated from other poetic forms. In the second, *DNA* is classified as a nucleic acid and in differentiated from other molecules in being described as carrying genetic information. Both examples can be topic sentences of developed paragraphs.

The second step in the four-part plan of extended definition is to identify the **special characteristics** of the term being described and to arrange them in a logical order. This will be the chief development of the paragraph, and the order in which the characteristics are presented will determine the organization of the paragraph. Here is an example:

> A Petrarchan sonnet is a poetic form consisting of fourteen lines of iambic pentameter. Its rime scheme is *a b b a a b b a c d e c d e.* The

first eight lines, which present some kind of proposition or raise a question, are called the octave. The last six lines, which solve the problem of the octave, are called the sestet. The turn between the octave and sestet is called the volta. Most often the subject matter of the Petrarchan sonnet is love. It differs from the Shakespearean sonnet in its rime scheme and in the fact that the latter has three quatrains, rather than an octave and sestet, and a closing couplet which comments epigrammatically on the quatrains.

Now the term is classified and has its special characteristics enumerated and organized. Note that contrast is employed at the end of the definition to clarify further the term's special characteristics. Comparison and contrast can be very useful in extended definitions.

The third step in the process of extended definition is not always necessary. It is to give a **limited definition of any special term** appearing in the definition. Here is an example:

A Petrarchan sonnet is a poetic form consisting of fourteen lines of iambic pentameter. A line of iambic pentameter is composed of five iambs, with an iamb being a metrical foot consisting of an unaccented syllable followed by an accented syllable. . . .

In an extended definition any special term that the reader might not understand should be given a limited definition.

The fourth step in the four-part plan is also not always necessary. It is to give a **specific example** to illustrate the definition; in the definition above a Petrarchan sonnet could be included as an example. Here is another extended definition using all four steps:

Hyperbole is a figure of speech which makes the writer's meaning clear through overstatement. A figure of speech is any phrase or statement which on the surface is literally false but which beneath the surface expresses a truth. For example, Macbeth's "Life is a tale told by an idiot" is literally false but expresses a truth for Macbeth. As a figure of speech, hyperbole states an exaggeration, or tells more than the truth, in order to deliver the writer's meaning. For instance, when Robert Burns wrote

And I will luve thee still, my dear,
    Till a' the seas gang dry,

he exaggerated mightily to make his point. The figure of speech in the second line is hyperbole.

This extended definition of *hyperbole* follows the four-step plan: (1) *Hyperbole* is classified as a figure of speech and is differentiated from other terms in that classification. (2) The special characteristics of hyperbole, which are few, are expressed, chiefly in sentence 4. (3) The term *figure of speech* is given limited definition. And (4) a general example of a figure of speech and an example of hyperbole are given. This plan for writing definitions is well suited to both paragraph and theme writing.

EXERCISE 26. Writing Extended Definitions

DIRECTIONS: Following are twelve terms. Choose one and write a full paragraph defining it.

puppy love	Unitarianism
true love	a know-it-all
a square	a school grind
a farce (play)	a bash
jazz	sedimentary rock
Bohr atom	pop art

Use of Anecdote and Allusion in Paragraph Development

An **anecdote** or an **allusion,** like an example, can often be used to make a paragraph more interesting and fuller in its development. An anecdote is a brief story or joke; an allusion is a reference to some past occurrence or piece of literature. Generally, neither an anecdote nor an allusion will, by itself, be sufficient to effect full development of a paragraph's central idea; a single anecdote or allusion may, however, be a significant addition to a paragraph that has been partially developed by some other method.

Here is an example of the use of an anecdote:

> Another common misconception is that short men are not only physically but also mentally inferior. Even people intelligent enough to read William Faulkner's novels are often surprised to learn that he was just over five feet tall; they marvel that such a short man could have written such great books. And no doubt there are millions of Americans who would sleep less soundly if they knew that our most important naval commander is only sixty-six inches tall. Actually, there is not a bit of anthropological evidence to show that there is any correlation between height and intelligence. Long legs may enhance basketball skill, but not intellectual powers. *When Abraham Lincoln, , renowned for his height and his genius, was asked how long a man's legs should be, he replied, "I've always felt they should be long enough to reach the ground."*

The last, italicized sentence of this example paragraph is an anecdote, a witty little story. It does not add new information, but it increases the paragraph's clarity and interest. It also serves as a good conclusion to the paragraph.

An allusion serves the same purpose in a paragraph as an anecdote —to enliven it and increase its clarity. Here is an example:

> Though it can never be proved, it seems to me that the greatest baseball players were active in the 1920s. Everyone knows of Babe Ruth's record of sixty home runs in 154 games. Few know that he was also one of the greatest pitchers before he went to the outfield. Everyone also knows how Grover Cleveland Alexander saved the 1926 World Series after going on a binge the night before, when he thought his chores for the Series were over. When Walter Johnson was at his fastest, it was hard for a batter even to see the ball. Once when he was in his prime, Johnson faced a pretty good hitter who had just come into the American League. After the umpire had called the second straight strike, the batter started back to his dugout. "Wait," said the umpire. "You have another strike." "I don't want it," replied the batter. *Truly, there were giants in the earth in those days.*

This paragraph utilizes both an anecdote and an allusion to improve its development. The material just before the last, italicized sentence is an anecdote. The italicized sentence is an allusion, a reference to a familiar quotation from the Bible. Both help develop the paragraph, and the allusion gives the paragraph a good conclusion.

An anecdote or allusion may be used in paragraphs with almost any kind of development. The first example paragraph above is developed with both examples and explanations. The second one is developed only with examples. But even in a paragraph with rather rigid logical development an anecdote or allusion is not necessarily out of place. In general, a writer should use only allusions that will be familiar to his readers.

Basic Organization and Paragraph Development

A paragraph is a separate unit of composition with its own self-contained structure, but all the paragraphs of a paper merge together to form a longer unified structure. Therefore a writer should not begin building an individual paragraph until he has a plan for all the paragraphs of his paper. In college exposition such a plan is usually a basic organization that establishes the main points of the proposed paper. Only after he has the whole structure of his paper in mind should a writer begin considering the modes of paragraph development that he will utilize.

Suppose, for example, that in an economics class you were asked to write an essay exam on this question: "Discuss some of the promotional gimmicks used by supermarkets to increase sales." First you would analyze your topic for clues to organization; the plural noun *gimmicks* would of course suggest that you give your paper structure by discussing from two to four different groupings of gimmicks. Your basic organization might take this form:

1. Contests, drawings, and other something-for-nothing lures
2. Displays designed to induce impulse buying
3. Various kinds of bogus sales and loss-leader promotions

Note the necessity of stating generalities to give a framework to your paper; just a catalogue of individual details would give you no design for paragraph composition.

With three paragraph topics clearly in mind, you would be ready to compose an introduction and then to undertake paragraph development. Only after getting the detailed paragraph composition underway would you decide whether or not one of the main points should receive two or more paragraph indentations for the convenience of the reader. So far as paragraph development itself is concerned, you would first plan to have three paragraphs plus a suitable introduction and conclusion.

At this point you should ask yourself whether your paragraphs will be essentially illustrative or logical in development—whether you will state a generality and then support it through details, examples, anecdotes, allusions, or comparisons or whether you will state a generality (or proposition) and then demonstrate its validity through logical analysis, cause-and-result relationship, steps in a process, or definition. Your decision will be determined by the kind of paragraph topics you have established in your basic organization. The three main points for the above essay question rather clearly call for development through illustration. After your introduction you would write a topic sentence to the effect that supermarkets use various kinds of contests and drawings to lure customers. Then you would develop your paragraph topic with illustrative details and examples. Whether you used two or more indentations would depend on the extensiveness of your answer. And so with the other two points. The general points (to be stated as topic sentences) are necessary to give focus to the details that build the paragraphs.

For another example, suppose that in a psychology class you were given this essay question: "Discuss some of the reasons why human beings are so likely to rationalize their motivations." First you would look for the clue to organization contained in your topic, and the plural noun *reasons* would be your guide. Your basic organization might be this:

1. Because of a desire to conceal their selfishness and egotism
2. Because of a desire to conceal their irrationality and limited problem-solving abilities
3. Because of a desire to feel important and admired

Now you would be ready to compose an introduction and to begin paragraph development.

On inspecting these paragraph topics, you would see that a logical development seems most appropriate. Not only examples but logical explanation is called for. Thus in dealing with the first point you probably would develop the idea that there is a conflict between human selfishness and the social demand for the appearance of unselfishness and that, consequently, people rationalize when they explain why they behave as they do. A pattern of cause-and-result relationship would underlie your paragraph development.

As a final example, suppose that in a literature class you were given the question "Discuss the main influences on the growth of naturalism in American literature." In analyzing your topic, you would see that the plural noun *influences* suggests that you give your paper structure by discussing in order several major influences. Your basic organization might take this form:

1. The influence of nineteenth-century deterministic science
2. The influence of the deteriorating economic and social scene
3. The influence of the naturalistic movement in French literature

Only with such paragraph topics in mind would you be ready to compose an introduction and undertake paragraph development.

Human thought being as complex as it is, you will of course find that often both illustration and logical analysis must contribute to paragraph development. For example, in developing the first of these three paragraph topics for the above essay question, you would probably use definition to explain deterministic science, a cause-and-result relationship to show how this science influenced philosophy and thus literature, and some specific examples of authors and books that exhibit this influence. You would perhaps use more than one indentation even though according to your basic organization you would be composing one paragraph.

PARAGRAPH UNITY

A successful paragraph must be not only complete in its development, but also unified in its content. As we have seen, a paragraph is a **unit** of composition because it develops just one central idea. Its unity is evident when each of its sentences pertains to its one central idea.

When even one sentence in a paragraph is off its topic, the paragraph has lost its unity.

Actually, however, **disunity** is not an especially common weakness in student writing. Underdevelopment of paragraphs is far more common and far more destructive (see the section on paragraph fragments earlier in this chapter). Paragraph disunity does occur, however, when (1) a detail is included that is not related to the topic sentence or central idea and (2) when a second topic sentence or main point is introduced into a paragraph indentation.

Here is an example of the first kind of disunity, from a student paper entitled "Building Good Will in a Small Business":

> Another way to build good will in a small business is to always keep only first-rate goods for your customers. In a small business, most of your sales will be to repeat-customers whom you know. All you have to do to lose one of them is to sell him one piece of inferior merchandise. It's true that other stores with cheaper items will draw off some of your trade, but as the buyers learn that the cheaper items are not good, they will come back to you and pay the higher prices that you have to charge for good merchandise. *To encourage your customers to come back you should once in a while give them a little extra without extra cost, such as a little more than a pound of nails.*

The detail in the last, italicized sentence doesn't relate to the paragraph's topic sentence. It belongs to some other main point, such as "Creating good will by making each customer think he is of special importance." The out-of-place detail creates disunity. If a writer has very clearly in mind what his paragraph topic is and has thought about its development, he is not likely to include out-of-place details.

Sometimes disunity can occur when none of the details of a paragraph, rather than just one detail, relate to the topic sentence. For example, here is the opening of a student theme about the oceans (the student was to specify his own limited topic):

> The ocean has always been a provider. Britain has been saved several times from invasion by the water which surrounds her. Today people can be found at anytime during the year on one of the beaches of the world, enjoying the sun and the water. . . .

It isn't clear whether the student intended the first sentence to be an introduction to the theme or a topic sentence for one paragraph (with no introduction for the theme). But in any case there is flagrant disunity in this paragraph. The word *provider* implies tangible resources, such as food and minerals, whereas the following two sentences have nothing to do with such resources. The student had read a little about the oceans but made no attempt to plan his paper. Consequently the structure, at least of this paragraph, collapsed because of disunity.

More common in student writing is paragraph disunity caused by the mixing of two main points in one paragraph indentation. Here is an example from a student paper entitled "The American Scene as Reflected in Comic Strips":

> "Pogo" has a lot of political satire in it. The cowbirds represent communists and are satirized. Also it makes fun of election methods. "Li'l Abner" also has some political satire. It also makes fun of other comic strips too in its "Fearless Fosdick" sequences. They imitate "Dick Tracy."

This pseudo paragraph is mixed and therefore lacking in unity. The student should either have written one paragraph about "Pogo" and another about "Li'l Abner," or one paragraph about political satire in comics and another about other kinds of satire in comics. But even worse than the disunity is the lack of development of any of the possible main points. With the mixture of two main points the indented unit perhaps gives the appearance of being long enough to make a real paragraph, but if the two points are separated each will obviously be a paragraph fragment. And the fragmentation is worse than the disunity. The student probably failed to plan a basic organization of main points for his paper and certainly gave no thought to development of main points.

Here is another example of paragraph disunity due to a mixture of main points, from a student paper entitled "Let's Integrate All Schools":

> By denying federal aid to segregated schools, we can promote integration. It is morally wrong for tax money to be used to maintain segregation. The South is not the only area that practices segregation, and integration should be nationwide. Money is the biggest factor. When a school sees that its source of money is drying up, it will quickly integrate in order to keep its money. We can't keep private white schools from springing up all over, as they have in the South. But if we deny federal funds to segregated schools we will speed integration.

This paragraph, too, is disunified because two main points are mixed in it: (1) the idea of denying federal funds to segregated schools and (2) the idea of the need for integration throughout the nation. Each of these central ideas warrants a full paragraph of development, but each is only skimpily developed. The student writer's eye probably told him that he had a full paragraph, but his mind failed to tell him that he had both disunity and incompleteness in his paragraph. If he had carefully planned a basic organization of main points, he would not have mixed his paragraph topics in this way.

PARAGRAPH COHERENCE

The Meaning and Importance of Coherence

The sections above have illustrated two important principles of paragraph development: **completeness** and **unity.** A third is **coherence.** Chapter 3 explained that coherence literally means "a sticking together of parts," which in writing means the sticking together of paragraphs and sentences. It helps make writing integrated, consistent, and intelligible. Coherence in the whole paper is achieved when there is a clear **transition,** or link, between paragraphs. Similarly, a paragraph is coherent when its sentences are all closely joined to each other.

Coherence in a paragraph is different from unity in that unity pertains to the actual relationship between the sentences, whereas coherence pertains to the **verbal expression** of that relationship. Of course a real relationship between sentences must exist if coherence is to be achieved, but coherence can be lacking even when the real relationship is there. The following three sentences illustrate this fact of language:

> Automation can provide worldwide abundance for all people. If I were directing industrial expansion, I would reduce the rate of changeover to automated production. Unemployment is just as much a problem as is a scarcity of goods.

A real relationship exists between these sentences, and the reader—if he tries hard—can perceive that relationship. But the reader also experiences a momentary hesitation in reading the sentences and feels a kind of disjointedness between them. This is so because the "glue" to provide coherence is missing. The relationship between the sentences needs to be **expressed.** Note the improved intelligibility of the sentences when a verbal means of transition is added to the sentences:

> Automation can provide worldwide abundance for all people. *But* if I were directing industrial expansion, I would reduce the rate of changeover to automated production, *for* unemployment is just as much a problem as is a scarcity of goods.

The connectives *but* and *for* express the relationship between the sentences and thus effect coherence. The good writer gives great attention to achieving such coherence in his paragraphs.

Some students might think that such a weakness as omitted transitions is not common in college writing. But student writers *do* frequently fail to achieve coherence between their sentences. For example, here is the opening of a paper entitled "A Dog's Life":

> I believe it is quite a privilege to be part of the highest form of animal life. If I had to be any other animal I would be a dog.

If the connective *but* is placed between these two sentences, their relationship springs to life. But without the *but* the two sentences seem on first reading to be disjointed and clashing, for they lack coherence.

And here are the two opening sentences from a student paper entitled "A Special Use of the Dictionary":

> A dictionary is a little known source of pleasant reading. Besides definitions there are etymologies, usage labels, subject labels, geographical and biographical information, and so on.

The *there are* construction in the second sentence does not refer to *dictionary* and thus does not cause its sentence to "stick to" the preceding one; that is, there is lack of coherence between the two sentences. Note the great improvement when a verbal means of expressing the relationship between the two sentences is used:

> A dictionary is a little known source of pleasant reading. In *it* one may find not only definitions but also etymologies, usage labels, subject labels, geographical and biographical information, and other interesting data.

The pronoun *it*, referring to *dictionary*, is the verbal means of achieving coherence here, and it greatly improves the quality of the writing.

Coherence in a paragraph is important because it helps the reader follow smoothly and rapidly the writer's train of thought. When coherence is lacking, there is an abruptness and disjointedness between sentences that hinders the reader or stops him altogether. Therefore a writer must give thought not only to the relationship between his sentences but also to the *way* each sentence is linked to the previous one. We will illustrate the four primary methods of achieving coherence.

Transitional Words and Phrases

The simplest and most easily recognizable method of achieving coherence between sentences (and between parts of compound sentences too) is the use of **transitional words** and **phrases**. There are many of these in English used solely to connect related ideas. The simple **coordinating conjunctions,** such as *and, but,* and *for,* form one set of them. Another set is comprised of the so-called **conjunctive adverbs,** which include such common connectives as *however, therefore, nevertheless, consequently, thus,* and *moreover.* And a third set may just be called **connective,** or **transitional, phrases,** such as *for example, in addition to,* *of course, after all, on the other hand,* and *at the same time.* A subset to this group is the **enumerators,** such as *first, second, next,* and *finally.* All told, there are dozens of these connectives and transitional phrases. Their sole task is to express a relationship between ideas—sometimes between clauses of compound sentences, sometimes between sentences, and sometimes between paragraphs. No writer should underestimate the great importance in discourse of these connectives. The noted English author Samuel Taylor Coleridge went so far as to say that "a good writer may be known by his pertinent use of connectives." And another great English writer, Thomas de Quincy, said "All fluent and effective composition depends on the connectives."

Though there are dozens of connectives and transitional phrases in English, only a few kinds of relationship between ideas are expressed, chiefly **cause-and-result, contrast, time,** and **accumulation.** For example, the general relationship of contrast (which includes opposition, contradiction, paradox, qualification, and concession) is expressed by *but, however, yet, nevertheless, still, on the other hand, on the contrary, not, in contrast,* and perhaps others. But these vary slightly in their suggestive meanings and in their explicitness, and thus usually one will seem most appropriate for a particular sentence.

To appreciate the usefulness of transitional elements in achieving coherence, first read the following paragraph without connective words:

> Many educators suggest that we should turn to history and philosophy in order to solve the problems of our time. Historians are in disagreement even about what happened in the past. They are hopelessly confused about why historical trends occur. Philosophers have been and still are in muddled confusion. None of them agrees with any others. Educators can't agree in their choice of philosophers whom we should listen to. In the midst of such confusion, does it not seem wise to work with new ideas?

Though an average reader can follow this paragraph if he tries, he does have to try harder than he should. He experiences a certain disjointedness, which puts an increased demand on his ability to understand. Now read the same paragraph with the connectives added:

> Many educators suggest that we should turn to history and philosophy in order to solve the problems of our time. *But* historians themselves are in disagreement even about what happened in the past, *and* they are hopelessly confused about why historical trends occur. Philosophers, *too,* have been and still are in muddled confusion. None of them, *at any rate,* agrees with any others. *Furthermore,* educators themselves can't agree in their choice of philosophers whom we should listen to. In the midst of such confusion, *then,* does it not seem wise to work with new ideas?

No additional meaning has been added to the paragraph, but the meaning already there is much more accessible because of the integrating effect of the connectives. Smoothness displaces the disjointedness. Note particularly that *but* (as well as *and*) can be used *very* effectively to begin a sentence, or a paragraph, for that matter. But incredibly, some students still report that they have been taught not to begin a sentence with *and* or *but*. Such a "rule" has never been valid. Also note that connectives are often stylistically best placed within instead of at the beginning of a sentence.

A final comment about the use of transitional words and phrases to achieve coherence is that the enumerators—*first, second, third, . . . finally*—need not at all be avoided within a paragraph to present examples or at the beginning of paragraphs to introduce the paper's main points. Such an obvious means of transition is fully acceptable, but it should not be overused.

Repetition of Key Words

Coherence between sentences may also be effected through the **repetition** in a sentence **of an important word,** usually a noun, that appears in the previous sentence. The repetition of the word signals to the reader's mind that a train of thought is being continued. With such a signal, the reader is able to progress smoothly with his reading. If no signal of any kind is present, he stumbles or is made to pause needlessly.

To understand how repetition of important words can provide coherence in a paragraph, first note the disjointedness between these sentences:

> Politics is a suitable profession only for men with agile minds. Since problems shift suddenly and rapidly, one must be able to alter his mode of thinking quickly to meet new and unforeseen situations.

The absence of a signal in the second sentence to connect it with the first causes the reader to be left with a vagueness or indefiniteness in his understanding. Now note how coherence is effected through the repetition of a key word:

> Politics is a suitable profession only for men with agile minds. Since the problems of politics shift suddenly and rapidly, a politician must be able to alter his mode of thinking quickly to suit new and unforeseen situations.

The words *politics* and *politician* in the second sentence are positive signals that help the reader's mind respond with rapid comprehension. They provide transition between the sentences and thus effect coherence.

Here is another example of the coherent value of word repetition:

> Language may be called *the* universal requisite of culture. Transmission of ideas is necessary.

The reader's mind feels a jolt as he tries to relate the two sentences. Now note again how word repetition provides coherence:

> Language may be called *the* universal requisite of culture. For culture to continue, transmission of ideas is necessary, and they can be transmitted only with language.

Though the second sentence is now longer, it really contains no information not implied in the defective example. But the repetition of *culture* and *language* makes the relationship between the sentences crystal clear. The extra words do not constitute the flaw of wordiness. They are necessary to effect coherence.

Now here is an example of a whole paragraph being made coherent through word repetition:

> The smallest insects are made up of a very large number of *cells*. An ant or a gnat, for example, is composed of hundreds of thousands of *cells*. Furthermore, the *cells* in these small creatures are widely differentiated in structure and function. Even a mite has skeletal, digestive, and nervous organs composed of many specialized *cells*. The *cellular* structure of such small creatures cannot be seen by the naked eye, but it is nonetheless miraculously complex.

Note that the noun *cells* appears in each sentence except the last; and even in that sentence the adjective *cellular* is in fact a continued repetition. The repetition is not useless or awkward; instead it produces coherence by forging a close linkage between the sentences.

A variation of word repetition that effects coherence in the same way as repetition is also illustrated in the above example paragraph. The phrase *smallest insects* appears in the first sentence. Then in the following sentences the words *ant, gnat, small creatures,* and *mite* are in a sense a kind of repetition of the opening key phrase. The use of a word not identical to but closely related to one in a previous sentence also has a coherent effect in that it provides a signal that keeps the reader's mind oriented to the flow of ideas.

Pronoun Reference

In the example paragraph above, the word *cells* was repeated because the use of a pronoun would have been awkward or impossible. But quite frequently, of course, a pronoun can be used in the place of a noun. When a pronoun in one sentence refers to a noun in the preceding sentence, it serves as a signal for the reader's mind just as a repeated word does. Hence **pronoun reference** is a common method of achieving coherence between sentences.

To understand better the usefulness of this method of transition, first note the unclear connection between these sentences:

> The president of the school board rejected the lay committee's recommendation. Shortsightedness and prejudice were evident.

There is no specific signal in the second sentence to carry the reader's train of thought along smoothly. Coherence is lacking. Now note how the inclusion of a specific means of transition makes for smoothness between the sentences and expresses their logic clearly:

> The president of the school board rejected the lay committee's recommendation. He recognized its shortsightedness and its prejudiced point of view.

The pronouns *he* and *its* in the second sentence are the signals that enable the reader's mind to follow the train of thought rapidly and with full comprehension. The two sentences are now coherent.

Here is a full paragraph that further illustrates the use of pronoun reference to achieve coherence:

> The novel *Elmer Gantry* by Sinclair Lewis is one of the most controversial pieces of fiction ever published in America. It is a satiric attack on hypocrisy and humbug in the American clergy. Its author maintained that he was not attacking religion, but only those who misused religion. He cited proof that some clergymen are corrupt and showed that he had respect for those who were not. But many religious groups believed he was attacking religion in general. They, in turn, were merciless in their attacks on him.

Note how each sentence is tied to the preceding one through pronoun reference. There is an invisible thread running from *Lewis* to the final *him* and holding the sentences together. The paragraph, of course, has other coherent elements, too.

Now suppose the paragraph were to be written in this way:

> The novel *Elmer Gantry* by Sinclair Lewis is one of the most controversial pieces of fiction ever published in America. Hypocrisy and humbug in the American clergy are the subject of a satiric attack. Religion was not actually attacked, but only those who misused religion. Proof has been cited that some clergymen are corrupt and that there is respect for those who are not. Many religious groups believed religion was attacked. Lewis was mercilessly attacked.

In this rewriting, the meaning of the original paragraph is not wholly obscured, but its smoothness and definiteness have certainly been drastically weakened through the absence of specific transitional signals, such as pronouns. The result is rough and indefinite—in a word, incoherent—writing.

Clear Movement of Ideas

At least one of the above three methods of achieving paragraph coherence—transitional words and phrases, word repetition, and pronoun reference—appears in the large majority of sentences in good exposition and persuasion. But coherence can be achieved without them through a **clear movement of ideas.** Of course the above methods help produce clear movement, for coherence makes for clear movement, but it can be achieved without the verbal expression of transition. Here is an example:

> Money may not be the root of *all* evil. A lust for power has led many political leaders to commit horrendous crimes. Sexual psychotics rape and murder. Disturbed children and adolescents sometimes destroy their families' property or even their families. Child abuse is extremely widespread in this country—so much so that some colleges offer courses in the legal and social aspects of it. Teachers sometimes mentally torture pupils just to satisfy their vindictiveness. No, money is just the root of *some* evil.

None of our first three methods of achieving coherence is present in this paragraph, except between the first and last sentences, and yet the movement is so clear that full coherence is effected. The reason for this is that both a **pattern of thought** and a **pattern of sentence structure** are set up to lead the reader smoothly through the paragraph. Such means of effecting coherence is somewhat more sophisticated than effecting it through verbal expression.

EXERCISE 27.   Improving Paragraph Coherence with Transitional Words

DIRECTIONS: The following paragraphs lack coherence because of the absence of transitional words and phrases. Indicate transitional words and phrases that will provide coherence between sentences. Some sentences may not need additional words.

1.   (1) One of the most important qualities for a politician to possess is imagination. (2) It seems that most politicians are singularly unimaginative. (3) Some have such one-track minds that they never vary from

a set line of thought and procedure. (4) Our current mayor still spends hours a week on arithmetical checkup on employees even though the city now owns a computer. (5) He seems to fail to see that the city's political problems change. (6) He is likely soon to be out of a job unless he applies more imagination to his work.

2.   (1) Most people have three misconceptions about the nature of rules of grammar. (2) They feel that an arbitrary rule makes an expression correct or incorrect, whereas, it is custom only that makes correctness. (3) They think that only whole words are involved in grammatical constructions, whereas parts of words—or morphemes—play an important grammatical role. (4) The verb parts *ing, en, ed, s,* and so forth are important grammatical entities. (5) They seem to assume that all languages have similar grammatical systems, which is of course far from the truth. (6) Estonian has twelve cases, whereas Latin has only five. (7) There are innumerable differences between grammatical systems. (8) We see that the general public is much misinformed about grammar.

3.   (1) My professor of Comparative Religion maintains that religious truths are relative. (2) It seems to me that many points of religious belief must be absolute. (3) How can polytheism and monotheism both be true? (4) Consider the idea of afterlife. (5) How can it both exist and not exist? (6) It seems to me that the idea of relativism can be overvalued.

4.   (1) Political liberals condemn the "go slow" tactics of conservatives on the grounds that the liberal ideas of the past have become the conservative ideas of today. (2) The liberals feel that they represent the advanced thought that leads to progress and that the conservatives represent the stagnant thought that prevents progress. (3) This line of argument oversimplifies the true nature of progress. (4) An equally important idea to remember is that not every liberal idea of the past has proved to be of value. (5) Conservatives should receive as much praise for killing unsound ideas as the liberals receive for nurturing good ideas.

5.   (1) Space enthusiasts urge that billions of dollars be spent on moon travel on the assumption that valuable minerals might be mined there and transported to the earth. (2) These enthusiasts are grossly ignorant of the costs that would be involved in such mineral extraction and transportation. (3) There is not a single mineral known that could ever be profitably mined on the moon and shipped to earth. (4) Regardless of how cheaply we can learn to manufacture rocket fuel, we will always have to pay hundreds of dollars a pound (in terms of current purchas-

ing power) to get any substance from the moon to the earth. (5) The cost of outfitting and shipping miners to work on the airless and alternately boiling and freezing surface of the moon will always be thousands of dollars an hour. (6) We can be pretty sure that no known substance —diamonds, gold, uranium, platinum—can ever be profitably brought from the moon in commercial quantities. (7) As for substances now unknown, who can say?

EXERCISE 28. Identifying Transitional Devices

DIRECTIONS: In the following paragraphs indicate the transitional words and phrases, repeated words, and pronoun references that link each sentence with the preceding one. Be prepared to explain how each word or phrase you select helps provide coherence in the paragraph.

1.   "Ideas need the backing of institutions and firm social approval if they are to result in practical application. Yet I see pharisaic temples being built everywhere in psychiatry; pick up our journals and you will see meetings listed almost every week of the year and pages filled with abstracts of papers presented at them. These demand precious time in attendance and reading, and such time is squandered all too readily these days. Who of us, even scanting sleep, can keep up with this monthly tidal wave of minute or repetitive studies? And who among us doesn't smile or shrug, as he skims the pages, and suddenly leap with hunger at the lonely monograph that really says something? As psychiatrists we need to be in touch not only with our patients but with the entire range of human activity. We need time to see a play or read a poem, yet daily we sit tied to our chairs, listening and talking for hours on end. While this is surely a problem for all professions, it is particularly deadening for one which deals so intimately with people and which requires that its members themselves be alive and alert."—Robert Coles, "A Young Psychiatrist Looks at His Profession."

2.   "Many students of discrimination are aware that the victim often reacts in ways as undesirable as the action of the aggressor. Less attention is paid to this because it is easier to excuse a defendent than an offender, and because they assume that once the aggression stops the victim's reactions will stop too. But I doubt if this is of real service to the persecuted. His main interest is that the persecution cease. But that is less apt to happen if he lacks a real understanding of the phenomenon of persecution, in which victim and persecutor are inseparably interlocked."—Bruno Bettelheim, "A Victim."

3.   "Grammarians have arrived at some basic principles of their science, three of which are fundamental to this discussion. The first is that a language constitutes a set of behavior patterns common to the members of a given community. It is a part of what the anthropologists call the culture of the community. Actually it has complex and intimate relationships with other phases of culture such as myth and ritual. But for purposes of study it may be dealt with as a separate set of phenomena that can be objectively described and analyzed like any other universe of facts. Specifically, its phenomena can be observed, recorded, classified, and compared; and general laws of their behavior can be made by the same inductive process that is used to produce the 'laws' of physics, chemistry, and the other sciences."—W. Nelson Francis, "Revolution in Grammar."

4.   "Memory is a word which has a variety of meanings. The kind that I am concerned with at the moment is the recollection of past occurrences. This is so notoriously fallible that every experimenter makes a record of the result of his experiment at the earliest possible moment: he considers the inference from written words to past events less likely to be mistaken than the direct beliefs which constitute memory. But some time, though perhaps only a few seconds, must elapse between the observation and the making of the record, unless the record is so fragmentary that memory is needed to interpret it. Thus we do not escape from the need of trusting memory to some degree. Moreover, without memory we should not think of interpreting records as applying to the past because we should not know that there was any past. Now, apart from arguments as to the proved fallibility of memory, there is one awkward consideration which the skeptic may urge. Remembering, which occurs now, cannot possibly—he may say—prove that what is remembered occurred at some other time, because the world might have sprung into being five minutes ago, exactly as it then was, full of acts of remembering which were entirely misleading. Opponents of Darwin, such as Edmund Gosse's father, urged a very similar argument against evolution. The world, they said, was created in 4004 B.C., complete with fossils, which were inserted to try our faith. The world was created suddenly, but was made such as it would have been if it had evolved. There is no logical impossibility about this view. And similarly there is no logical impossibility in the view that the world was created five minutes ago, complete with memories and records. This may seem an improbable hypothesis, but it is not logically refutable."—Russell, *An Outline of Philosophy*.

5.   "Since, then, it is necessary for a prince to understand how to make good use of the conduct of animals, he should select among them the

fox and the lion, because the lion cannot protect himself from traps, and the fox cannot protect himself from the wolves. So the prince needs to be a fox that he may know to deal with traps, and a lion that he may frighten the wolves. Those who act like the lion alone do not understand their business. A prudent ruler, therefore, cannot and should not observe faith when such observance is to his disadvantage and the causes that made him give his promise have vanished. If men were all good, this advice would not be good, but since men are wicked and do not keep their promises to you, you likewise do not have to keep yours to them. Lawful reasons to excuse his failure to keep them will never be lacking to a prince. It would be possible to give innumerable modern examples of this and to show many treaties and promises that have been made null and void by the faithlessness of princes. And the prince who has best known how to act as a fox has come out best. But one who has this capacity must understand how to keep it covered, and be a skillful pretender and dissembler. Men are so simple and so subject to present needs that he who deceives in this way will always find those who will let themselves be deceived."—Machiavelli, *The Prince*.

A COMPLETED THEME

To conclude our chapter on paragraph development we will reproduce a revised student theme and will comment on the quality of its paragraphing and the validity of its logic.

TOPIC: Write an essay convincing your peers of either the desirability or the harm of abolishing the D and F grades in college courses.

TITLE: The Need for Retaining the Grades of D and F

THESIS SENTENCE: This paper will analyze the reasons why abolishing the grades of D and F in college would harm the educational process.

BASIC ORGANIZATION:

1. The resulting decline in student effort
2. A general decline in the meaningfulness of other grades
3. Failure to prepare students for the competitive life that comes after college
4. Distortion of information for employers

The Need for Retaining
the Grades of D and F

There currently is a movement underway in college circles to eliminate the grades of D and F. The proponents of this system say only the respectable grades of A, B, and C should be used. Students who do not earn one of these

The introduction is long enough to be a paragraph by itself. It leads directly into the topic.

grades would get either an NC (no credit) or a W (withdrawn) on their transcript. I believe this movement spells danger for the educational process.

If the threat of an F or D is removed, many, if not most, students will reduce their effort. "What have I got to lose?" they will say. Students are in most courses because the courses are required, not because the students are really interested. And it is human nature to be lazy if one is allowed to be. Thus, without the threat of failure or a low grade, many students would just coast along, waiting to see what will happen. They will rationalize by saying, "Oh, well, I can always try again." In college courses as in other fields of endeavor, both the carrot and the stick are necessary.

If the D and F are dropped, the other traditional grades may lose some of their meaningfulness. The grades of A, B, and C have partially derived their traditional meaning through contrast with D's and F's. With that contrast gone, students, parents, and teachers are likely to lose some of their respect for higher grades, especially since teachers would tend to give C's even when they weren't earned. In fact, dropping the D and F would give great impetus to the monstrous movement to abolish all grades except Credit and No Credit. Presumably there is a correlation between grades and the amount learned. This correlation should be maintained —for the benefit of good students if for no other reason.

Another reason why the D and F grades should be retained is that their presence helps prepare students for the competitive life they will lead after college. If young people do not see that degrees of success and also failure exist in the real world, they will not be prepared for the real world. If the D and F are dropped, I can just hear future ex-students crying, "Why didn't they tell us?" Schooling should be preparation for life.

A clear topic sentence is composed.

The paragraph topic is well developed with sentences of logical analysis.

Coherence is effected with transitional words and word repetition.

A clincher sentence, or restatement, closes the paragraph.

A second clear topic sentence is composed.

Again, logical development growing out of the topic sentence creates a full paragraph. The writer gives the reasons why he believes in the topic sentence.

Good coherence is maintained.

There is no clincher sentence for this paragraph, but it has a good conclusion.

A transitional word relates the third topic sentence to the preceding paragraphs.

The second sentence is one of restatement and clarification.

This paragraph is satisfactory, but not as fully developed as the others.

Finally, without the low grades on a transcript an employer is at a disadvantage when trying to decide whom to hire. Traditionally, the better students have either gotten the better jobs or have been hired first. Industry seems to think this system has worked well. The proposals now going around threaten this system, and I doubt that an equally good one can be found. Dropping the D and F, in my opinion, will harm both students and the public.

A transitional word prepares the reader for the fourth topic sentence and also for the conclusion of the paper.

The coherence is excellent. For example, the words *hire, jobs,* and *industry* provide clear transition.

A single sentence of restatement provides a good conclusion for the whole paper.

Though this student wrote a well-developed, coherent, convincing paper, his logic might be questioned. The syllogism for his first main paragraph is this:

MAJOR PREMISE: If students are not faced with a threat of failure or a low grade, they will not put out much effort.
MINOR PREMISE: Eliminating the grades of D and F in college will remove the threat of failure or low grades for students.
CONCLUSION: Students will reduce their effort if D's and F's are eliminated.

The student's major premise may be faulty. There is no inductive evidence that the threat of failure spurs student effort. The major premise is a mere assumption without an inductive basis. Thus the conclusion is questionable.

The syllogism for the second main paragraph is this:

MAJOR PREMISE: The meaningfulness of the grades A, B, and C is partially due to their contrast with D's and F's.
MINOR PREMISE: Elimination of D's and F's will remove the contrast.
CONCLUSION: Elimination of D's and F's will reduce the meaningfulness of A's, B's, and C's.

On the surface this major premise seems quite valid, and thus the conclusion seems valid. But one might argue that A's, B's, and C's get most of their meaningfulness in ways other than a contrast with D's and F's. However, the student has struck a good blow here.

The syllogism for the third main paragraph is this:

MAJOR PREMISE: School should prepare students for the competitive life after school.

MINOR PREMISE: The presence of low and failing grades in school
                  prepares students for the competitive life.
CONCLUSION: Low and failing grades should be retained to prepare
                  students for the competitive life.

Many people would object to both the major and minor premises here.
The major premise is a mere asumption that can have no inductive basis.
It is open to endless argument. Also there probably is no inductive
evidence for the minor premise. Remember that though most minor
premises are specifics and truthful, not all are. This one is questionable.
Therefore the conclusion might be rejected by many.

The syllogism for the final paragraph is this:

MAJOR PREMISE: The presence of D and F grades on a transcript helps
                  industry have a good basis for hiring practices.
MINOR PREMISE: We want industry to have a good basis for hiring
                  practices.
CONCLUSION: We should retain the grades of D and F.

Many people would object to this logic. They might say that an applicant's
school record is only one of many bases for industry's hiring practices.
Thus the major premise is at least weakened. Furthermore, some would
extend the logical argument by saying industry can easily find a substitute for school grades as a basis of judgment. Thus many would reject
the conclusion.

This student's logic, then, can easily be attacked, but that is the
case with almost all arguments not based on inductive major premises
that have been 100 percent proven. At least this student did his job
of writing quite well.

CHAPTER 5

Sentence Composition

COMPOSED SENTENCES AND STYLE

The good writer **composes** his sentences; he does not let them just happen. It is true that much of the arrangement within a sentence is automatic because of the writer's subconscious knowledge of the syntax of his native language. For example, such constructions as

> one of the most highly valued skills

and

> who engineered the escape from prison

automatically arrange themselves, as do many short sentences, because of the writer's natural command of the structure of his language. But the *kind* of sentence written is subject to choice. For example, a writer might choose to compose this sentence:

> The element carbon, which has an amazing capacity to form chainlike molecules of enormous size, is found in all organic compounds and therefore in some fossils.

Or he might have reason to think this version stylistically more desirable in a particular context:

> Carbon, an element found in all organic compounds and thus in some fossils, has an amazing capacity to form chainlike molecules of enormous size.

He would have exercised choice as to the *kind* of sentence desired. Or he might have written (not composed) this sentence:

> Carbon is an element and is found in all organic compounds and in some fossils and has an amazing capacity to form chainlike molecules of enormous size.

In the last case he would have just let his sentence issue thoughtlessly from his mind.

The good writer composes, both in his head as he writes and by revision as he rereads what he has written. To compose well, he must have **syntactic maturity**—that is, a command of the wide variety in sentence structure that exists in the world of good writing. There are considerable differences between the sentence structure of good exposition and persuasion and the sentence structure of most ordinary, casual conversation. Thus good writing must be learned apart from oral language, even though there are, of course, many similarities between speech and writing. Ordinary chatter may be likened to simple arithmetic: one can do it in his head with little forethought. Good writing may be likened to more advanced math: with pencil and paper and forethought one can solve problems far more complicated than those of simple arithmetic. The student writer usually has pen and paper and time and thus has the tools with which to learn to compose sentences.

Here is an example from a student paper of what might be called noncomposed sentences, sentences that are equivalent only to the simplest arithmetic:

> I didn't think Governor X's tax reform was good. It seems to help only the rich. I know our taxes didn't go down, but I think some fat cats' taxes did. I think the reform should have done more for the little fellow.

This writer depended wholly on the kind of sentence structure he uses in his everyday conversation. He did no composing at all. The sentences just leaked from his mind. If the student had composed his sentences instead of just letting them happen, he might have written a passage like this:

> Governor X's tax reform was, in my opinion, not really a reform at all, for it seems to have helped only the rich. My family, which has

only a modest income, received no tax reduction from the reform, but I understand from editorials that many so-called fat cats did receive tax reductions. It seems to me that if reform really was to be effected it should have benefited the little fellow.

This rewriting of the passage, though ordinary and of no great merit, sounds more like writing, for it makes use of the kind of sentence structure that appears in good writing but not often in casual conversation. The sentences are composed, not just tossed out without forethought. The style of the passage might be described as serviceable or workmanlike.

In learning to compose better sentences, you would do well to pay close attention to the sentences in the textbooks and magazines you read. By reading carefully you will pick up the rhythms (actually the sentence structure) of good writing and will be able to apply them to your own composing. You need not know the grammatical structure of the sentences; you just need to get a feel for them—to establish their patterns in your mind. As long as any student depends on the syntax of his spoken sentences only, he will not learn to write well. A satisfactory style requires *composed* sentences.

Composing must of course go on in the head, but if a writer has time he can also compose on his paper as he writes his first draft. He can make a false start, spot it, and begin again. He can change structure after a sentence is underway. To illustrate this composing process here is a sample from the work of a young student. First we will look at the finished passage handed to the teacher:

> Every individual has a set of values which motivates him, and frequently he assumes that his values are the only "good" ones. He knows that other individuals have different beliefs and desires, but he is positive that, if made aware of the soundness of his, everyone else would adopt them, forgetting their own. One often finds it difficult to see how important other things can be to other people.

Now we will see the composing process that produced this finished product with its smooth, pleasing style:

> ~~There are many motives for the actions of men.~~
> ~~Each individual has~~
> ~~Mankind~~
> ~~M~~ Every individual has a set of values which motivates him, and frequently he assumes that his ~~set~~ values are ~~the only ones that count are important~~ the only ~~really~~ "good" ones. He knows that other individuals have ~~their own belie~~ different beliefs and desires, but he ~~assumes that~~ is ~~sure~~ positive that, if made aware of the ~~real im~~ soundness of his

~~valu set values,~~ everyone else would ~~forget their own and adopt his~~ adopt them, forgetting their own. ~~An individual~~ One ~~can~~ often finds it difficult to see how important ~~something can~~ other things can be to other people.

This is perhaps an extreme example of composing on paper; many people would be able to do more of it in their heads so that the rough draft would look a little cleaner. But the important thing is that a composing process must go on if a piece of writing is to have a satisfactory style.

In addition to composing in his head and on paper as he writes, a writer, if he has time, often revises after he has his whole composition completed. This kind of revision is a continuation of the composing process in that sentences are changed to produce greater clarity and a more pleasing style. As a writer revises, he tests each of his sentences for smoothness and clarity, in effect judging the quality of his original composing. When he finds weaknesses, he recomposes. Thus his *composed* sentences largely dictate the quality of his style.

SENTENCE ECONOMY

A common enemy of strength and clarity in sentences is **wordiness,** which creates a flabby style that both obscures clarity and reduces reader interest. Thus the good writer seeks **economy of expression,** not only for its contribution to clarity but also for the terseness and conciseness that it contributes to style (almost all experienced readers like a tight style). Economy of expression, however, is not as easy to achieve as beginning writers might assume. Most good writers have to think about the composition of each of their sentences to make them economical. And when revising, most writers find that they need to reduce rather than increase their wordage—unless, of course, a whole new idea is being added.

As a beginning college writer you cannot be expected to make every sentence a model of economical expression, but there are three specific kinds of wordiness that you can learn to avoid, at least to a degree. We will devote the next three sections to the modes of avoiding these kinds of wordiness. Also, as you become more experienced in writing, you will, like all good writers, come to rely on your ear to tell you that your phrasing is economical.

Recasting Sentences with Piled-up Constituents

Length and wordiness are not the same in sentence composition. A long sentence can be tight and free of excess wordage, and a comparatively short one can include useless words. But length in presenting *one idea* is often a source of wordiness. Such wordiness is usually due to a **piling up of several constituents** (phrases and clauses) when one or two better chosen constituents will express the same idea more economically and clearly. Here is an example of recasting a sentence for more economy. First, consider the wordy sentence:

> A flabby, verbose sentence, if not downright unclear, often has a narcotic effect / on the reader / so that he fails to see / the clarity that is there.

By the time a reader finishes this sentence he is as limp as it is. With its use of four constituents (marked with slashes) to express one idea, the sentence itself is flabby and verbose. Recasting can produce a tight sentence with no loss of meaning:

> A flabby, verbose sentence, if not downright unclear, will drug its reader into inattention.

Now two sentence constituents do the full work of the four in the wordy sentence, producing a stronger, clearer sentence. The good writer depends on his ear to warn him of excess sentence constituents; grammatical analysis of such structures is of no use in eliminating wordiness.

Here are some other examples of wordiness due to a piling up of sentence constituents, which are marked off with slashes. An economical revision follows each example. Reading the two versions of each aloud will illustrate the striking difference in style between wordiness and economical phrasing.

> Parody is a type of writing / that imitates another piece of writing / by copying some of the characteristics / of that piece of writing / and making fun of it.
>
> A parody ridicules an original piece of writing by humorously imitating some of its techniques.

> An unwanted guest may be ecouraged to leave / when he seems reluctant to leave / by letting him know / that you have a difficult job to do / that he may be able to help you with.
>
> You may encourage an unwanted guest to leave by hinting that he may help you with some difficult work.

> Our age is called the age of anxiety / because of all the tensions / that everyone feels / about the possibility of a war / that might destroy us all completely.
>
> Ours is an age of anxiety because the fear of total war breeds tensions in us all.

A beginning writer is likely to accept uncritically wordy sentences of the puffed-up variety just illustrated, because in our casual conversation we make little if any effort to be concise in our phrasing. We usually utter thoughts as they come into our minds, and our listeners accept whatever structures we use without demanding economy of phrasing. (In listening to a formal speech, an audience becomes more critical of wordy meandering.) But the experienced reader of good articles and books demands that the writing be tight; if it isn't he may simply stop reading it. Thus the beginning writer should try to cultivate a critical ear that will reject clumsy, piled-up phrasing that ruins economy of expression. He can do this because, in most writing situations, he has time to listen with his mind's ear to the sound of his sentences.

Reducing Uselessly Long Sentence Constituents

Another kind of wordiness is due to the choice of a **uselessly long sentence constituent** in expressing one idea. The three broad kinds of sentence constituents are clauses, phrases, and single words. Clauses tend to be longer than phrases, and phrases are longer than single words. Thus if a longer constituent is used when a shorter one will express the same idea just as clearly, wordiness results. Consider these two sentences:

The professor dismissed the student in a tactful way.
The professor tactfully dismissed the student.

The phrase *in a tactful way* and the word *tactfully* are identical in meaning, but the word is shorter and thus the second sentence has more economical phrasing. In general, then, it is best to choose the shortest constituent that will make your meaning fully clear. But since writing is so complicated, longer constituents can often be preferable, and you should not spend too much time trying to find the briefest expression possible for your ideas. Do not pretend that you are composing telegrams. However, always *listen* to your phrasing to see that it is smooth and clear and not noticeably wordy.

Here are more examples of how a beginning writer can make his sentences more economical by choosing the shorter constituent. First a wordy sentence is given, and then an economical revision.

A student who works hard will make a favorable impression on his teacher.
A hardworking student will favorably impress his teacher.

The biography of Mark Twain which was written by Dixon Wecter is both accurate and definitive.

Dixon Wecter's biography of Mark Twain is both accurate and definitive.

A student who is earnest will set aside a specific study period for each course that he is taking.

An earnest student will set aside a specific study period for each of his courses.

The committee chairman acted in a selfish way when he rejected the suggestion that had been proposed by the secretary.

The committee chairman acted selfishly when he rejected the secretary's suggestion.

The second version of each sentence is stylistically more desirable because of its greater economy. In the first example, the clause *who works hard* is replaced by the briefer adjective *hardworking,* and the long predicate *will make a favorable impression on his teacher* is shortened to the smoother *will favorably impress his teacher;* both changes make for a tighter sentence. The other examples have similar grammatical changes that reduce wordage without omitting meaning. Again, grammatical analysis is not necessary in order to reduce wordiness, but a critical ear is an asset.

Eliminating Deadwood

In the previous two sections we have shown how to reduce wordiness by recasting sentences. Sometimes, however, wordiness can be eliminated simply by dropping a sentence constituent, not by recasting the sentence. Wordiness of this sort is known as **deadwood,** because the offending words and phrases can be cut out with no loss of life in the sentence. Deadwood is also known by three other imposing terms: *redundancy, tautology,* and *pleonasm.* Good dictionaries use these words as synonyms for each other, but some authorities see slight differences in their meanings. Though they can be used just to mean the presence of useless words, both *tautology* and *pleonasm* are sometimes used to mean the expression of the same meaning twice. By this definition, the italicized words in the following examples are tautological or pleonastic:

He is writing his *own* autobiography.
She is a widow *woman.*
I received a *free* gift.
I thought that if he won *that* I would ignore him.

Redundancy, a much more commonly used term, can mean the expression of the same meaning twice or simply inclusion of words that add nothing to the desired meaning. Examples:

I suspect *that there is* no one *who* completely understands Einstein.
Most of my friends *consist of those who* are star athletes.

Even though they do not just repeat the meaning of another word,
the italicized words in these sentences are redundant because they can be
omitted with no loss of meaning. They could also be called tautological or
pleonastic. They are also deadwood.

Here are other examples of deadwood:

Repeat that *back over once again*, please.
I won't enroll in calculus because *of the fact that* I would fail it.
The Dean proposed a *new* innovation.
John is *equally* as bright as Bill.
Admiralty Island, *which is* located in Southeastern Alaska, is being
    deforested *of its trees*.
A government should express the will of the people *it governs*.
We live in a rapidly changing era *of time*.
She will *continue to* remain faithful.
You should recast that sentence *in different words*.
Her whisperings were audible *to the ear*.

The italicized words can be omitted without a recasting of the sentences
or a loss of meaning. Probably most educated people would apply the
word *redundant* to them.

Now a word of caution against making a game of brevity. A
writer can go too far in trying to compress his meaning into fewer words.
Full clarity and smoothness of phrasing are more important than
economy of expression, especially if that economy diminishes clarity or
smoothness. For example, one dictum in a manuscript for a composition
text was stated in this way:

When you can leave a word out, always leave it out.

Obviously the word *always* itself can be omitted from this sentence
with no loss of meaning. The author violated his own rule. However,
the sentence (if one really wanted to write it) sounds better with the
always; it does not sound wordy at all. In contrast to the above dictum,
Mark Twain once wrote

But tautology cannot scare me, anyway. Conversation would be intol-
erably stiff and formal without it; and a mild form of it can limber up
even printed matter without doing it serious damage. Some folks are
so afraid of a little repetition that they make their meaning vague, when
they could just as well make it clear, if only their ogre were out of
the way.—*The Atlantic Monthly* (June 1880).

This is a very good quotation with which to temper advice on the value of economy of expression.

EXERCISE   29.   **Eliminating Wordiness**

DIRECTIONS: Each of the following sentences is too wordy for good exposition. Eliminate the wordiness in each by either recasting to achieve terseness, reducing clauses or phrases to shorter constituents, or omitting deadwood.

1. Two characteristics which are necessary for success in salesmanship are aggressiveness and tact.
2. You must consciously look at your sentences to see if words or phrases can be left out because they are useless.
3. A car that is old is often more expensive to own than one which is new.
4. Your logic apparently seems contradictory.
5. Because I had had a disagreement with Professor McCall, I was in a state of anxiety about my grade in Political Science.
6. In order to be impartial in his judging, the judge studied both sides of the issues that were involved before he gave his verdict in the case.
7. She received my call to her on the telephone in a courteous manner.
8. The visiting minister spoke in a vague way that was not very clear to the congregation that was listening.
9. He won each and every prize that his school had to offer.
10. Many college instructors in composition classes where writing is taught teach students rules that contradict the rules that they were taught in their high school English classes.
11. In a state of nervousness, he advanced to the podium.
12. In my opinion I believe that parents who have children who are destructive should have to pay for the damage that their children do.
13. C. P. Snow, who is an Englishman, precipitated the debate about the two cultures, which are the humanistic and the scientific.
14. Two essential traits necessary for a successful politician are the ability to remember names that he hears and the knack of appearing to be interested in individuals.
15. A professor who is learned is more likely to gain his students' respect than one who takes a friendly stand but is superficial.
16. The process of developing color photos is a much less complicated process now than it was twenty years ago, when it was a very complicated process.
17. With a great deal of sadness, we left the cemetery.
18. Many students study for courses they are taking by reading notes that other students in the same course have taken from class lectures.

19. In a less conspicuous way, I followed John to the dormitory where we students lived.

20. A citizen who is conscientious will study the issues that are involved in an election before going to the polls to vote on them.

SENTENCE VIGOR

Individual sentences can be muscular and vigorous like brisk ale or watery and weak like cheap strawberry punch. The tongue tests the strength of liquids; the ear tests the vigor of sentences. Good writers listen with their mind's ear to the sound of their sentences in order to achieve such qualities of style as **vigor.** Wordiness, as we have seen, usually reduces sentence vigor and emphasis. There are other commonly used weak constructions that diminish sentence vigor. In the following six sections we will discuss methods of increasing sentence vigor by avoiding such constructions.

The Active Voice

Generally, more sentence vigor is produced by the **active voice** than by the **passive voice.** Here is the difference in construction between the two voices:

ACTIVE VOICE: Paul kissed Susan.
PASSIVE VOICE: Susan was kissed by Paul.

The ear of anyone somewhat skilled in language tells him that the active voice possesses more sentence vigor, partly because it requires fewer words and partly because the idea of action is accentuated. Also an active-voice sentence may be more vigorous because the most important word in the sentence is the subject. Example:

ACTIVE VOICE: The beauty queen turned down many requests for dates.
PASSIVE VOICE: Many requests for dates were turned down by the beauty queen.

Because in these sentences *queen* is a more important word than *requests,* for vigor and emphasis it should be placed in the dominant, subject position in the active voice.

Here are other examples of the greater strength of the active over the passive voice. Each first sentence is passive, with its more vigorous active-voice version following.

The food was devoured by the hungry immigrants.
The hungry immigrants devoured the food.

The game was played hard by the evenly matched teams.
The evenly matched teams played the game hard.

The little republic of Erewhon was bailed out again by our government.
Our government again bailed out the little republic of Erewhon.

Little notice was given the girls by the visiting team.
The visiting team gave the girls little notice.

True, the difference between each pair of sentences is not great, but an excessive use of the passive voice in an extended piece of writing can noticeably weaken sentence vigor.

We should say, however, that often a passive-voice sentence is acceptable or even necessary because the doer of the action in the sentence is not known or is unimportant. (In the active voice, the doer of the action is the subject.) Examples:

Much corn is grown in Iowa because of the excellent growing conditions.
The victim was murdered in a particularly vicious fashion.

In the first sentence, the farmers do the growing, but the writer doesn't consider that an important fact to include. In the second, the murderer is not known, and thus the news reporter leaves him out. The phrases *by the farmers* and *by the murderer* could be placed at the end of the sentences but are unnecessary or even undesirable.

In general, if the *by* phrase is not needed, a passive-voice sentence is fully acceptable; if the *by* phrase is needed, the sentence should probably be written in the active voice for greater vigor.

Effective Placement of Subordinate Constructions

Word order can greatly affect sentence vigor, but there are so many subtle aspects of word order in long English sentences that it is impossible for us to codify all of them for study. We will consider only two simple aspects of word order, one in this section and one in the next.

One kind of word order that affects sentence vigor is the **placement of a subordinate construction at the end of a sentence,** where it may be weak, instead of at the beginning or in the middle of the sentence, where it will more likely be strong. Consider these two sentences:

I worked unsuccessfully for two hours at trying to land the marlin,
   not being experienced in deep-sea fishing.
Not being experienced in deep-sea fishing, I worked unsuccessfully for
   two hours at trying to land the marlin.

The second version is decidedly more vigorous because the italicized subordinate construction is placed at the beginning of the sentence rather than at the end. Usually the kind of word order exhibited in the revised example produces more sentence vigor, for a minor idea is disposed of first.

Here are other examples of achieving increased sentence vigor by shifting tagged-on subordinate constructions to the beginning of the sentence:

We might have lost the Revolutionary War *if France had not come to our aid.*

If France had not come to our aid, we might have lost the Revolutionary War.

Grant allowed corruption to enter his administration, *not being a strong president.*

Not being a strong president, Grant allowed corruption to enter his administration.

In the 1920s too many people bought stocks on margin. The stock market collapsed, *as a result.*

In the 1920s too many people bought stocks on margin. As a result, the stock market collapsed.

President Truman was wise to implement the Marshall Plan, *in my opinion.*

In my opinion, President Truman was wise to implement the Marshall Plan.

The experienced writer usually depends on his ear to guide him in proper placement of such subordinate constructions.

Proper Placement of Modifiers

Another aspect of word order that affects sentence vigor and emphasis is the **placement of modifiers** of all sorts, not just the placement of a subordinate clause or phrase at the end of a sentence. In the latter case, meaning may be fully clear but the sentence may lack vigor. In misplacement of modifiers clarity may be obscured or an absurd construction may result. Generally (with the notable exception of some adverbs) a word or phrase modifier should, for sentence vigor and clarity, be placed near the word it modifies. If the modifier is not properly placed, the sentence structure is likely to be loose and weak. For example, consider these two sentences:

A lecture was scheduled on choosing marriage partners wisely *during the third period.*

A lecture was scheduled during the third period on choosing marriage partners wisely.

The italicized modifier in the first version is misplaced because it seems to modify the verb *choosing* when it should modify *was scheduled,* as it does in the revision. True, all readers would eventually understand the faulty version, but its absurdity kills any vigor or tightness the sentence might have.

Here are other examples of misplaced modifiers (they are italicized) with proper revisions:

> This simple operation can be learned by anyone who has had high school algebra *in eight hours.*
>
> This simple operation can be learned in eight hours by anyone who has had high school algebra.

> A mother wants to know what her daughter's plans are *for her own satisfaction.*
>
> For her own satisfaction, a mother wants to know what her daughter's plans are.

> People worry from the time they get up until they go to bed *about many things.*
>
> People worry about many things from the time they get up until they go to bed.

Such misplaced modifiers are common in student writing and do much to reduce sentence vigor. To revise such sentences for proper placement of modifiers does not require grammatical analysis. The writer's ear, if he will listen carefully to his sentences, will help him place modifiers properly for sentence clarity and vigor.

Proper Subordination of Ideas

Sentence constituents can be coordinated, or one can be subordinated to another. **Coordination** means that the constituents are given equal rank. They are usually joined by **coordinating conjunctions** (such as *and, but,* and *or*) or (if independent clauses) by **conjunctive adverbs** (such as *therefore, however, nevertheless,* and *so*). **Subordination** means that one constituent is not equal to the constituent it is related to but modifies it. There are many kinds of constituents that can be subordinate, but we will be concerned only with subordinate clauses, which are introduced either by **subordinating conjunctions** (such as *because, though, when,* and *so that*) or by **relative pronouns** (*who, whom, whose, which,* and *that*). The reason for our limitation is that the only common enemy of proper subordination is faulty coordination, which is remedied by converting one of the coordinate clauses into a subordinate clause.

Here is an example of how sentence vigor can be weakened by faulty coordination:

> FAULTY COORDINATION: We seniors set up an advertising campaign and it helped us pay for our yearbook.

EFFECTIVE SUBORDINATION: We seniors set up an advertising campaign which helped us pay for our year book.

Almost anyone's ear will tell him that the second example is more vigorous. The first sentence sounds childish for the reason that the second clause is not equal to the first; it should be made subordinate for effective delivery of ideas.

Here are other examples of the increased vigor that proper subordination brings:

FAULTY COORDINATION: Dean Collins prepared a new school calendar, and it calls for longer exam periods.

EFFECTIVE SUBORDINATION: Dean Collins prepared a new school calendar that calls for longer final exam periods.

FAULTY COORDINATION: I read an article by Paul Pundit in *The Reporter*, and it said that by 1980 the United States and Russia would form an alliance against China.

EFFECTIVE SUBORDINATION: I read an article by Paul Pundit in *The Reporter* which said that by 1980 the United States and Russia would form an alliance against China.

WEAK COORDINATION: The Floor Leader knew the bill would not pass at that time, so he postponed the vote.

EFFECTIVE SUBORDINATION: Since he knew the bill would not pass at that time, the Floor Leader postponed the vote.

WEAK COORDINATION: Earnings on school bonds are not taxable, so I invested my money in our local bond issue.

EFFECTIVE SUBORDINATION: Since earnings on school bonds are not taxable, I invested my money in our local bond issue.

Note that both *faulty* and *weak* coordination are listed in the examples. The differences between weak coordination and more effective subordination can be very subtle. The commonest source of weak coordination, however, is an excessive use of the connective *so*. Though fully acceptable in ordinary conversation, the connective *so* tends to weaken sentence vigor in writing. Usually instead of using *so* to coordinate two clauses, a writer should make his first clause subordinate by introducing it with *since* or *because* (see examples three and four above).

Recasting Chopped-up Sentences

A sentence broken into many short phrases and clauses usually lacks vigor since it prevents the reader from maintaining a sustained pace in his reading. Here is an example from a student paper:

> For many years, since the birth of our country, the schools of the
> South, and some in the North also, have welcomed, heartily, any
> American (except those in black skin) into their doors.

The student's attempt at irony is praiseworthy, but his sentence is so
chopped up that the reader cannot get properly launched in his reading.
With a little more attention to the *composing* process, the student could
have produced this sentence:

> For many years the schools of the South have welcomed any American
> (except those in black skin) into their doors.

In this version no important meaning is lost, the irony is accentuated,
and sentence vigor is increased.

Here is another chopped-up sentence from a student paper:

> In this period of our lives, as the United States stands, almost alone,
> defending itself against communism, we feel the urge, in our anxiety,
> to be conservative.

The reader himself feels chopped to pieces as he reads the sentence. Just
minor revision will produce a stronger, tighter sentence:

> In this period of our lives, as the United States stands almost alone in
> resisting communism, we feel the anxious urge to be conservative.

If the student had tested his original sentence with his mind's ear, he
would have realized the need for eliminating the chopped-up quality of
the sentence in order to increase its vigor.

Recasting Overloaded Sentences

Another enemy of vigor is the overloaded sentence. This is the
kind of sentence into which a writer crams too many ideas without giving
due consideration to the relationship between them. A long sentence
is not necessarily limp and weak if all of its parts are closely related and
logically fitted to each other. But a long sentence without these qualities
is invariably overloaded and weak. Here is an example:

> College entrance tests seem to be holy writ to counsellors, for they
> take the scores to be immutable evidence of a student's ability, and they
> aren't always, and so when some other data might give the counsellor
> a better understanding of the student's capacity, he'll only say, "But
> your score was so and so," whereas I know that a student can make an
> entirely different score on a different day, which I did once.

This sentence has no sustained vigor, for there is too much looseness
between its parts. It rambles too much.

Here is a revision:

Counsellors seem to think of college entrance tests as holy writ, for they take the scores to be immutable evidence of a student's ability. Thus when some other data might give the counsellor a better understanding of a student's capacity, he'll only say, "But your score was so and so." But I know from experience that an individual's score on a test one day may vary widely from his score on the same test on another day. Thus I believe that test scores should not be thought of as iron-clad evidence of one's ability.

Now the rambling, loose quality has been eliminated with the separation of the ideas into four sentences. The resulting tightness greatly improves the vigor of the writing.

The comments about sentence vigor in the last six sections have all related to sentence structure. We have advised student writers (1) to prefer the active over the passive voice, (2) to avoid using subordinate constructions as tag-ends of sentences, (3) to place modifiers in a clear position, (4) to avoid faulty or weak coordination, (5) to avoid chopping up a sentence into a series of small units, and (6) to avoid rambling, overloaded sentences. Choice of words is also important in composing strong sentences. Chapter 6 on diction will treat this aspect of composition.

EXERCISE 30. Improving Sentence Vigor

DIRECTIONS: Write a more vigorous and concise version of each of the following sentences.

1. Some unfavorable criticism is beginning to be written about Hemingway by the critics.
2. My sociology professor has just published a new book, and it is about the effects of divorce on children.
3. Secretary Burrows made a policy speech about Sikkim though he had been warned by the President to avoid commenting on the Sikkim-China fracas.
4. A new industrial revolution is coming. Its new machinery is not mechanical. It is electronic. The principle of the gear and cam is still valid. But the electronic impulse does new and more wonderful things. The giant electronic brains are the basis of the new revolution. They seem to become more marvelous every month.
5. Our professor brought in a guest lecturer and he talked about the religious beliefs of the Australian aborigines.

6. Today's new highways are much superior to those of twenty years ago chiefly because the development of huge earth-moving machines, which were pioneered by a man named Le Tourneau, who had his plant in Toccoa, Georgia, has allowed engineers to plan roads with no short or sharp curves or steep grades because they can simply cut huge gaps through mountains and make small hills level so that the road bed can be straight with only a small degree of rise or fall.

7. When they are potted, my grandparents like African violets.

8. I was chatting with my girl friend when my father came home on the telephone.

9. In these modern times, when crises develop daily, the political authorities, who are often uneducated, make many decisions, and also appointments, that intensify rather than relieve pressures, much to our unrest.

10. Is a mentally ill person of today treated better than one of the past by society?

11. We had to walk about twelve blocks to our appointment in the rain.

12. Many experimental books were written by William Faulkner, and the general reading public has been puzzled by most of them.

13. Our relations with Russia could be improved if more tourists from each country would visit the other, which would give everybody better understanding, in my opinion.

14. To vote right, or at least intelligently, in national elections, and some local ones, too, you must not only know the candidates, that is, how they stand on issues, but also the views of the two parties, for the parties, being strong organizations, often dominate the candidates.

15. We had been warned that a storm was brewing, so we took the large boat which would be able to weather high gales.

SENTENCE RHYTHM

All language has rhythm, the source of which lies in the varying stresses that we give to individual syllables. Stress in language is the degree of loudness in pronouncing syllables. Even when we are reading, the stress of syllables is silently recorded in our minds, and we thereby feel the rhythm of the phrases. There are four degrees of stress, but for the sake of simplicity we usually speak only of accented (stressed) and unaccented (unstressed) syllables. When studying poetry, students are often asked to mark off the pattern of accented and unaccented syllables, as in the lines by Housman on the following page. The rhythm of this poetry is due to the poet's special arrangement of accented and unaccented syllables.

Obviously, there can be enormous variety in the sequence of accented and unaccented syllables, especially since there are really four

> "Ter/ence, this/ is stu/pid stuff:
> You eat/ your vic/tuals fast/ enough;
> There can't/ be much/ amiss,/ 'tis clear,
> To see/ the rate/ you drink/ your beer.
> But, oh,/ good Lord,/ the verse/ you make,
> It gives/ a chap/ the bel/lyache."[1]

degrees of stress. Poets consciously manipulate this variety to produce their poetic rhythm, but prose writers generally let the accents fall where they will. Nevertheless, the mere presence of various degrees of stress creates rhythm of some sort in all writing. And while a pleasing rhythm is perhaps more important in imaginative writing, good writers of exposition make it a practice to listen to their sentences to avoid harsh, awkward, or limp rhythm and to achieve some degree of smoothness.

Following are a few well-known prose quotations that illustrate the power of strong rhythm:

> I returned, and saw under the sun, that the race is not to the swift, nor the battle to the strong, neither yet bread to the wise, nor yet riches to men of understanding, nor yet favor to men of skill; but time and chance happeneth to them all.—Ecclesiastes
>
> In much wisdom is much grief, and he who increaseth knowledge increaseth sorrow.—Ecclesiastes
>
> The sun never shone on a cause of greather worth. 'Tis not the affair of a city, a county, a province, or a kingdom, but of a continent. —Tom Paine, *Common Sense*
>
> A foolish consistency is the hobgoblin of little minds.—Emerson, *Self-Reliance*
>
> Under a government which imprisons any unjustly, the true place for a just man is also a prison.—Thoreau, *Civil Disobedience*

The stirring quality of these famous quotations is due partly to their powerful rhythm. If they were rewritten in a humdrum fashion, much of their power would disappear. In fact, a noted English author wrote a paraphrase of the first quotation above from Ecclesiastes to show how the elimination of its rhythm and other qualities of vigor would ruin the original. Here is his paraphrase:

> Objective consideration of contemporary phenomena compels the conclusion that success or failure in competitive activities exhibits no tendency to be commensurate with innate capacity, but that a con-

---

[1] From " 'Terence, this is stupid stuff:' " from "A Shropshire Lad"—Authorized Edition—from *Complete Poems* by A. E. Housman. Copyright © 1959 by Holt, Rinehart and Winston, Inc. Reprinted by permission of Holt, Rinehart and Winston, Inc.

siderable element of the unpredictable must invariably be taken into account.—George Orwell, *Politics and the English Language*

Though Orwell was not mainly concerned with the rhythm of the original, his paraphrase does illustrate the sad effect of marring the rhythm of an excellent sentence. The student writer need not—in fact, should not— try to give poetic rhythm to his expository writing, but he should use his mind's ear to avoid awkwardness and limpness. Rhythm and smoothness are very closely allied to sentence vigor, and thus when a writer achieves vigor he also achieves satisfactory rhythm.

SENTENCE VARIETY

A concise, vigorous, rhythmic sentence is a creation to be proud of. But unfortunately you cannot learn just one sentence pattern embodying these qualities and then use it over and over. In the first place, a wide variety of sentences is necessary to express different kinds of meaning. Furthermore, a sequence of unvarying sentences becomes monotonous and destroys vigor. Though repetition of sentence structure can often be used effectively, each sentence is, nevertheless, a separate challenge and must develop its own vigor wtihout aimlessly imitating that of the preceding sentence.

To achieve smooth qualities in writing, you must effect some variation in your sentences both in kind and length. Wholly unvarying structure in the sentences of a paragraph produces dull writing even if each separate sentence is vigorous and smooth. Here is an example:

When you travel in a foreign country, you should imitate the customs and habits of the natives. When you see a native use strange table manners, you should observe closely so you can learn them. If you find that all the gentlemen of the street are dressed formally, you should dress in that fashion. If, on the other hand, the natives dress in sport clothes, you should also wear them. Even if a custom seems repugnant to you, you should still practice it. For example, if in rural France you find men and women using the same rest room together, you should use it too unabashed.

Such unrelieved repetition of one sentence pattern eventually becomes monotonous, regardless of the quality of the individual sentences.

Now note the improvement to be gained through varying sentence structure:

When you travel in a foreign country, you should imitate the customs and habits of the natives. On your day of arrival, you might begin by closely observing table manners, which are sure to differ from yours.

> By the second or third day, you should be eating like a native. You may also quickly learn to imitate the habits of dress in your host country, and soon you should not be so gauche as to be seen in the wrong kind of clothes. Even if a custom seems repugnant to you, you should still be courteous and brave enough to practice it. For example, in rural France you might find men and women using the same rest room together. With a little will power you can behave as though intimate bathrooms are the rage in your own country.

Even the most unperceptive reader will respond more readily to this paragraph than to the monotonous first one, for his sense of rhythm receives more satisfaction from it. You may often want to repeat sentence structure for special effects, but you should avoid having four or five similar sentences in sequence.

When used in sequence, sentences of the same length also become monotonous and lose vigor. In the faulty paragraph above, the sentences are not only similar in construction but also in length. This is usually the case in a paragraph without sentence variety, for sentences of similar patterns are often of about the same length. The most common and offensive kind of repetition of sentence length, however, is the use of a sequence of short, choppy sentences. Here is an example:

> Most of modern man's illnesses are psychosomatic. This means that the mind makes the body sick. These illnesses affect all parts of the body. The most common of them occur in the digestive system. But the circulatory organs are also affected. Liver and diabetic troubles can also be psychosomatic. According to some doctors even obesity has a similar origin. And of course most headaches are psychosomatic.

A short, compact sentence has many uses in expository writing, but seldom can more than two of them appear in sequence without sounding childishly monotonous.

Now note the improved vigor gained through injecting sentence variety into the above paragraph:

> Most of modern man's illnesses are psychosomatic, which means that the mind makes the body sick. These illnesses affect all parts of the body. The most common of them occur in the digestive system, but diseases of the circulatory organs, the liver, and the pancreas can also be psychosomatic. Even obesity, according to some doctors, can be caused by the mind's effect on the body. And of course most headaches are psychsomatic.

Two short sentences are effectively used in this revised paragraph. But they are separated and thus do not set up a monotonous pattern of rhythm.

GENERATING SENTENCES

There are only about a dozen basic patterns in English sentences, but from these few patterns an infinity of different sentences can be composed. In this section we will briefly examine the processes by which our minds can **generate** endless numbers of sentences that no one else has ever before uttered or written in exactly the same way. We will confine ourselves to the nontechnical aspects of these processes and to aspects that will be of practical use to students trying to improve their writing. On an advanced level of linguistic scholarship there are many highly technical theories about generative grammar.

The Sentence Core and Its Generating Process

Every regular sentence[2], no matter how long, has a **sentence core** or **nucleus,** which is an independent clause with a subject and predicate. (Compound sentences have two or more cores.) Sometimes even in the most learned writing a sentence is just a core or nucleus, without expansion constituents set off by commas or other marks of punctuation. Here are some examples, with the subjects and predicates separated by slashes:

Television / teaches children much about the world of knowledge.
Children / learn much about the world of knowledge from television.
Children / are taught much about the world of knowledge by television.
Much about the world of knowledge / is taught children by television.

Several matters are to be noted here. First, we have considered such independent clauses to be sentence cores or nucleuses even though each contains more than an absolute core. For example, in the first version, *Television / teaches / children / much* is the absolute core of subject-verb-indirect object-direct object, and *about the world of knowledge* is a kind of expansion. However, for the purpose of studying composition (and not grammatical analysis) such self-contained independent clauses without additional large constituents (usually set off by punctuation) are best thought of as sentence cores.

Second, all four sentences say exactly the same thing but were obviously generated differently in the writer's mind. Once one of the sentences was underway, the rules of English structure pretty well dictated the remaining course of the sentence, though there could be

---

[2] We will not consider request sentences, which have no subject, or questions, or various kinds of utterances that many linguists call sentences but that do not have a subject-predicate combination.

some variations. For example, sentence two could read either . . . *learn much about . . . from . . .* or *learn from television much about.* . . . The processes in the mind that account for such small variations in structures are completely unknown. However, the experienced writer will often know that such small variations are possible and might revise his original to produce better sentence vigor or clarity.

But what is the **generating process** that dictates how the sentences are to begin? Linguists understand very little about such processes, but one important point is clear. If the sentence is not the first in a piece of discourse, what has gone before may generate the beginning of the sentence under study. For example, if a writer is composing a passage about television, with *television* as the key word, then his mind is ready to begin the generation of the first sentence above with the key word *television* from the previous sentences. But if the piece of discourse is about children, then the writer's mind is ready to use the key word *children* to begin generation of the second sentence above or (less likely on the part of a good writer) the third sentence (which is a rather awkward passive-voice sentence). However, as every composition teacher knows, a consistent generation of sentences such as that described for the first two examples above does not necessarily occur in the writing of even rather good students. Some writers, whether or not their central subject matter was television or children, might very well generate the fourth example sentence above and thus produce some inconsistency in the structure of their writing.

In general, then, little can be said about the generation of sentence cores. In generating them, the mind obeys rules of grammar (usually), and the rules of grammar can be codified, but what sets the generating process in motion and what causes the slight variations that make most sentences unique are not very clear.

Generating Sentences with Expansions

In good writing of most kinds, the majority of the sentences will be composed of more than a sentence core or nucleus. They will have in addition large constituents, or **sentence expansions,** which contain full ideas that could be expressed in sentence cores. In such sentences great variety in structure is possible with little, if any, change in meaning. Here are some examples:

> Usually, faulty predication occurs in rather complicated sentences, for in short, simple sentences the error is often too apparent to escape detection.
> Since in short, simple sentences the error of faulty predication is often

too apparent to escape detection, it usually occurs only in rather complicated sentences.

Faulty predication, which is usually easily detectable in short, simple
sentences, occurs most often in rather complicated sentences.

And we could go on and on.

What are the generating processes behind such **complex sentences,**
which have never been composed before? Obviously, such huge complexity is involved that linguists and psychologists probably can never
know in great detail just how the generating processes work in the brain.
But in some way the brain understands X number of closely related ideas
that could be sentence cores, initiates an expression of these ideas—
perhaps on the basis of what has just gone before or perhaps on some
other, unknown basis—and continues with a generation of structures that
will include the X number of ideas, at least one of which will be a sentence core. That's quite an order for the brain, but it obviously goes
through a generating process something like that. Here is an example.
A news reporter had these ideas of sentence-core nature in mind:

Politicians like Sandman have dominated the state Senate for the last
half-century.

Politicians like Sandman are strongly opposed by the city newspapers.

Politicians like Sandman represent the southern, rural counties.

Politicians like Sandman seem to have a stronger grip than ever on the
state's legislative processes.

The generating mechanism in the reporter's brain allowed the reporter
to initiate and continue generating this sentence:

Though strongly opposed by the city newspapers, politicians like Sandman, representing the southern, rural counties, have dominated the
state Senate for the last half-century and seem to have a stronger
grip than ever on the state's legislative processes.

The generating process that allowed the reporter to produce this complex sentence is so complicated that no other writer with the same
information would have composed an identical sentence. For it is true
that most sentences in good writing are unique. Thus it might seem idle
for us to talk about the sentence-generating processes in a composition
text.

But we can make two important and useful points. First, the
methods set forth earlier for improving sentence economy, vigor, and
clarity are as useful in composing complex sentences as in composing
sentence cores. You can utilize these methods in your mind as you
thinks about your subject matter, or you can utilize them as you revise
your written work by listening to your sentences and checking for

clarity, conciseness, and vigor. Understanding the generating processes is not necessary for success in the composing and revising processes. The composing process, though closely related to the generating processes, is really an area of its own. The composing process is, in part at least, artistic, whereas the generating processes presumably are mechanical.

The second important point is that through elementary study of the generating processes you can expand greatly the kinds of complex sentences that you can compose. Learning better to handle the chief sentence expansions does make use of the generating processes, at least unconsciously, and will greatly help you gain a more mature command of the infinitely variable English sentence, which Winston Churchill called "a noble thing." One of the chief weaknesses in student writing is that most students depend on the kind of simple sentence structures that make up their casual conversation rather than on the more complex kinds of structures that appear in good writing. Our next sections will provide elementary instruction in learning to use more effectively the major sentence expansions which contain ideas that could be expressed as sentence cores.

Types of Sentence Expansions

In explaining the nature of the major sentence expansions that are used in generating complex sentences, we must use some common grammatical terms. But in learning the lessons to follow, you need not be overly concerned about grammatical labels. For example, if you are asked to generate a sentence with an appositive phrase but instead produce one with the same meaning but with an adjective clause rather than an appositive, you can feel that you have done your work effectively. *No good writer thinks about grammatical terms as he writes,* but the kind of minimum grammatical study to follow can help you become a better writer.

Compound Constituents.   One of the most common means of generating sentences of more than core value is the use of **compound constituents.** Compounding means the joining of two or more constituents that are grammatically alike. Almost any kind of sentence constituent can be compounded, but the compounding of subjects and predicates is all we need to consider in our study of composition. First we will consider an example of compounded subjects. Suppose a writer has the following information in mind and composes these sentence cores:

CORE: The professor who made the assignment was abused by the local press.

CORE: The student who performed the assignment was abused by the local press.

CORE: The Dean who supported the professor was abused by the local press.

The generating process allows the writer to compound the subjects so that he composes one strong sentence (the subjects are italicized):

EXPANSION: *The professor who made the assignment, the student who performed it,* and *the Dean who supported the professor* were all abused by the local press.

Both economy and vigor are the results of compounding these large constituents.

But what is the generating process that produces such compound constituents from two or more underlying sentence cores? **Transformational grammar** is the leading kind of generative grammar, and the transformational theorists say that every sentence of any complexity is a **transform** of two or more **kernel sentences,** which are the simplest possible. (We are using the term *sentence core* to mean a regular independent clause, not a kernel sentence.) Various kinds of transformations, in this view, are responsible for the completed complex sentence. In producing sentences with compound constituents, as in the above example with three subjects, a **deletion transformation** occurs. In other words, parts of a series of sentence cores are deleted in the mind so that compound constituents may be utilized. We give extremely elementary explanation here solely to get into your mind the idea that a complex sentence is the result of some kind of transformation of sentence cores. You need not be particularly concerned with the terminology; we are concentrating wholly on composition, not on grammar.

Whole predicates, too, can be compounded to reduce the number of sentence cores. Example:

CORE: The committee interrogated three witnesses.

CORE: The committee pondered the evidence given.

CORE: The committee decided to recommend replacement of the Dean of Students.

The generating process, using a deletion transformation, permits compounding of the predicates (which are italicized):

EXPANSION: The committee *interrogated three witnesses, pondered the evidence given,* and *decided to recommend replacement of the Dean of Students.*

Through a very simple grammatical process, such compounding of large constituents can greatly affect stylistic qualities in writing. We should note here (it will be demonstrated later) that the kinds of sentence expansions illustrated in the following pages—such as appositives and adjective clauses—can also be compounded.

Under the heading of compound constituents we will also consider **compounded sentence cores,** which are simply the familiar compound sentences. Two or more sentence cores closely related are often compounded with a coordinating connective either between them or shifted to the interior of the second sentence core (sentence cores always being independent clauses). Here are two of examples:

> In 1936 only two independent countries were left on the African political map, *and* these two were not democratic.
> The camel may be the "ship of the desert"; the Sahara Desert, *nevertheless*, is a greater obstacle to travel than the Mediterranean Sea.

Such compounding is also possible with just a semicolon and no connective between the sentence cores. Also, of course, other kinds of sentence expansions can occur in such compound sentences, as we will see later.

EXERCISE 31. **Generating Compound Constituents**

DIRECTIONS: As a very simple exercise to prepare for more complicated ones to come, form a single sentence out of each set of the following sentence cores by compounding either subjects or predicates.

1. a. The women reporters for the local newspapers stalked out of the press conference.
   b. The demonstrators for Women's Lib stalked out of the press conference.
   c. A few liberal politicians stalked out of the press conference.
2. a. The Senator's assistant scrambles for the file bearing upon the conversation.
   b. The Senator's assistant places it in front of his boss's eye.
   c. The Senator's assistant offers up key information in urgent whispers.
3. a. The Dean of Students openly quarreled with the President.
   b. The Dean of Administration openly quarreled with the President.
4. a. The burglar carefully jimmied the window open.
   b. The burglar silently climbed into the kitchen.
   c. The burglar came face to face with a shotgun.

Appositive Phrases.   A very useful sentence expansion common in professional writing but surprisingly uncommon in student writing is the

appositive phrase. Basically, an appositive is a repeater, being used most often to further identify a noun or to tell what the noun is. It is said to be *in apposition* to that noun. It is usually a noun phrase but can be a verb phrase or noun clause. An appositive can also be in apposition to the whole idea of a sentence core instead of to a single noun. It is a useful expansion because it contains the information for a whole sentence core but expresses that information more economically. Since it expresses the idea of a sentence core without part of the core being stated, the appositive is also the result of a deletion transformation.

Here are some examples of how the generating process can utilize an appositive phrase to produce mature sentence structure (the appositive phrases are italicized):

CORE: The whale is a completely naked mammal.
CORE: The whale is adapted by blubber to living in polar waters.
EXPANSION: The whale, *a completely naked mammal*, is adapted by blubber to living in polar waters.

CORE: John Wilkinson is a skillful translator of science fiction.
CORE: John Wilkinson is himself a scientist.
EXPANSION: John Wilkinson, *a skillful translator of science fiction*, is himself a scientist.

The writer's brain contains the two sentence cores, but its generating process allows it to express one of them as an appositive phrase and so produce better sentence vigor and economy. Note that with a form of the verb *to be* between the appositive and the noun it is in apposition to, a regular sentence core is formed.

Here is an infinitive (verb) phrase used as an appositive:

His greatest wish—*to be governor*—was never realized.

Here is a present-participial (verb) phrase functioning as an appositive:

The candidate's biggest mistake—*ignoring the black vote*—cost him the election.

Here is a noun clause used as an appositive:

The belief *that Maytubby was guilty* was widespread.

And here is an appositive in apposition to the whole idea of a sentence core:

He ate like a pig, *an indication of his low-class upbringing*.

The sentence core for this appositive is this:

His eating like a pig was an indication of his low-class upbringing.

A deletion transformation produced the appositive.

Sometimes appositives are introduced by *such as* or *or*:

Unusual skin markings may indicate congenital brain abnormalities, such as *mental deficiency and epilepsy.*

Most mammals have long, sensitive vibrissae, or *whiskers,* around the muzzle.

In such constructions, *such as* and *or* are known as **appositive conjunctions.**

If an appositive is not needed to identify the noun it is in apposition to but just gives additional information about that noun, it is nonrestrictive and is set off by commas or dashes. Here is an example:

They seemed uninterested in my chief concern—*how to balance the budget.*

The adjective *chief* identifies the noun *concern,* and thus the appositive is nonrestrictive and is set off, in this instance by a dash. If an appositive is necessary to identify the noun it is in apposition to, it is restrictive and is not set off by punctuation. Here is an example:

The suggestion *that we invest in stocks* was rejected.

The appositive is needed to identify the noun *suggestion* and thus is restrictive.

The more practice a writer gives his generating processes in producing sentences with appositive expansions, the more mature his style will become. We will skip other minor aspects of appositive constructions that are of interest in grammatical analysis, not in composition.

EXERCISE 32. **Generating Appositive Phrases**

DIRECTIONS: Convert each of the following sets of sentence cores into one sentence with an appositive phrase. In two of the sets use compound constituents as well. In one, use a compound sentence (two sentence cores) with an appositive in only one of them.

1. a. At about three months hair starts to form on the fetus's head.
   b. The fetus's head is the part of the body that develops first.
2. a. Man is in many ways built like his furrier relatives.
   b. Man's furrier relatives are the gorilla, the orangutan, and the chimpanzee.
3. a. The first fact established was all the police had to go on.

b. The first fact established was enough to give the police a clue.

c. The first fact established was that the burglar had been a female.

4. a. Ecology is the study of the mutual relationships between organisms and their environment.

b. Ecology is required for a degree in forestry.

c. Ecology is recommended for a degree in mining.

5. a. The theory of relativity maintains that space is curved.

b. The theory of relativity is a concept that most of us find hard to understand.

6. a. Deliberate entrapment may be unconstitutional.

b. Deliberate entrapment accounts for a large percentage of narcotics arrests.

c. Deliberate entrapment is a technique often used by vice squads.

Adjective Clauses.   Another sentence expansion that is a transformation of a sentence core is the **adjective clause.** As its name implies, it usually modifies a noun or pronoun in a sentence core or in another sentence expansion, but it may also modify the whole idea of a sentence core or expansion. It is introduced by a relative pronoun (*who, whom, whose, which,* and *that*) that has as its antecedent the noun the adjective clause modifies. If the antecedent of the relative pronoun is substituted for the pronoun, a regular sentence core results. Thus a **substitution transformation** is used in generating an adjective clause.

Here are two examples of how the generating process can transform a sentence core into an adjective clause (the adjective clauses are italicized):

CORE: New Mexicans have to travel hundreds of miles to find a lake.

CORE: The lake then by Eastern standards is likely to be a puddle.

EXPANSION: New Mexicans have to travel hundreds of miles to find a lake, *which then by Eastern standards is likely to be a puddle.*

CORE: Urban renewal has brought into view multitudes of people.

CORE: These multitudes of people are in themselves walking slums.

EXPANSION: Urban renewal has brought into view multitudes of people *who are in themselves walking slums.*

In the first example the relative pronoun *which* has *lake* as its antecedent; in the second, *who* has *people* as its antecedent. The generating process has converted sentence cores into expansions, with a better style resulting.

If the relative pronoun is a direct object in its own adjective clause, it may be omitted. Here is an example:

CORE: We felt as though we were crossing a desert.

CORE: No white man had seen (that desert) before.

EXPANSION: We felt as though we were crossing a desert *no white man had seen before.*

An understood *that* (or *which*), which is the direct object of *had seen,* introduces the adjective clause and has *desert* as its antecedent.

Here is an example of an adjective clause modifying a whole idea in a sentence core rather than a single noun:

CORE: Our troops planned to attack after dark.

CORE: Attacking after dark seemed the best strategy.

EXPANSION: Our troops planned to attack after dark, *which seemed the best strategy.*

The relative pronoun *which* does not have a specific noun but the whole idea in the sentence core as its antecedent. Such a sentence is entirely acceptable provided it is not ambiguous.

When an adjective clause is not necessary to identify the noun it modifies but just gives additional information about the noun, it is nonrestrictive and is set off by a comma or commas. Here is an example:

Mr. Cruxton, *whom the local press opposed*, won the election.

Since Mr. Cruxton is identified by name, the adjective clause gives additional information about him and is nonrestrictive. When an adjective clause is necessary to identify the noun it modifies, it is restrictive and is not set off by commas. Here is an example:

The Board was composed of citizens *whose selfless dedication to duty was evident.*

The adjective clause is needed to identify the citizens meant and thus is restrictive.

EXERCISE 33. **Generating Adjective Clauses**

DIRECTIONS: Make one sentence out of each of the following sets of sentence cores, having one adjective clause in each. If you can also use compound constituents or appositive phrases, do so, but in each case generate just one sentence. Certain minor revisions in wording may be necessary.

1. a. We shall need certain governmental institutions.
   b. These governmental institutions will replace a host of local governments.
   c. These governmental institutions will replace various private enterprises.

2. a. Mr. Banner was elected to be *Yonko.*
   b. *Yonko* is the chief of the OIA.
   c. Mr. Banner has founded several organizations.
3. a. Longo was a captain.
   b. Longo's sense of self-possession never deserted him.
   c. Longo's vanity was never crushed.
4. a. New Mexico is mostly a beautiful wilderness.
   b. New Mexico is unlike California.
   c. California's history has largely been erased by developers.
5. a. I inspected a jagged chunk of the plane's propeller.
   b. My host had carried the chunk down from the mountain side.
6. a. The Cannes festivals have given art movies opportunities.
   b. Art movies would not otherwise have had these opportunities.

Adjective Phrases.   Often an adjective phrase functions as a part of a sentence core. For example, in

John was *happy about his scholarship,*

the italicized adjective phrase is an indispensable part of the sentence core, not an expansion of the sort we are studying.

But **adjective phrases** often function as sentence expansions that have been transformed from sentence cores. Through the deletion transformation, the generating process produces more mature sentence structure. Each adjective phrase has an adjective as its headword and the whole phrase modifies a noun in a sentence core or in another sentence expansion. With the noun it modifies and a form of the verb *to be,* the phrase will form a sentence core. Here are two examples of the generating process producing an adjective-phrase expansion out of a sentence core (the adjective phrases are italicized):

CORE: Henry let the used-car salesman fleece him.
CORE: Henry was not old enough to know his own mind.
EXPANSION: *Not old enough to know his own mind,* Henry let the used-car salesman fleece him.

CORE: The Captain was happy to have brought his men back safely.
CORE: The Captain reported the results of his patrol.
EXPANSION: The Captain, *happy to have brought his men back safely,* reported the results of his patrol.

The adjective headwords in the two complex sentences are *old* and *happy.* Note that the adjective phrase in conjunction with the noun it modifies and a form of *to be* (second core in the first example and first core in the second example) makes a full sentence core. Through deletion, the generating process permits its transformation into a sentence expansion.

Because adjective-phrase expansions such as those illustrated above are usually nonrestrictive, they are set off by commas. But restrictive adjective phrases do occur, as in this sentence:

The girl *green with envy* is in reality rich herself.

The italicized adjective phrase is needed to identify which girl the sentence is talking about; hence it is not set off by commas. But in general, adjective-phrase expansions cause few problems in punctuation.

When an *ed* word, such as *excited* or *printed,* is the headword in an expansion like those above, it is an adjective only if it can be modified by *very.* Otherwise it is a verb. For example, in such a sentence as

Henrietta, *very excited about her approaching wedding,* said she was going to New York "to get her torso ready,"

the italicized constituent is an adjective phrase. But in such a sentence as

The term *tejano* is derogatory, *intended to conjure up an image of a vicious cowhand,*

the *intended* in the italicized phrase cannot be modified by *very* and is a verb, not an adjective, and the whole constituent is a verb phrase.[3] This kind of verb phrase will be considered later, but the grammatical distinction between the two kinds of phrases is of no importance in the study of composition.

EXERCISE 34. **Generating Adjective Phrases**

DIRECTIONS: Compose one sentence out of each of the following sets of sentence cores, having one adjective phrase in each. If a set also calls for an appositive phrase or an adjective clause or compound constituents, use them.

1. a. The sunrise was beautiful to behold.
   b. The sunrise filled us with hope.
   c. Hope had almost left us.
2. a. We got sick when we visited Samoa.
   b. We were unused to the native foods.
   c. Samoa is the most lovely island in the South Pacific.

---

[3] The phrase is a verb phrase by form only. By function, it is an adjectival phrase because it modifies the noun *tejano.* Such a grammatical distinction need not trouble the composition student.

3. a. My blood pressure was high for a man of my age.
   b. My blood pressure caused the doctor to order other clinical tests.
   c. None of the clinical tests showed me to have a disease.
4. a. The revolutionaries were blind to their opportunity.
   b. The revolutionaries actually divulged some of their secrets to the plainclothesmen.
   c. The plainclothesmen had been waiting for such information.
5. a. Sergeant Miller was bloody from several grenade wounds.
   b. Sergeant Miller was ordered back to base camp by Lieutenant Vedo.
   c. Lieutenant Vedo was his immediate superior.
6. a. The novel was full of titillative passages.
   b. The novel sold well to spinsters.

Verb Phrases.   Three kinds of verb phrases function as sentence expansions and are the end result of a deletion or a deletion plus verb-form-change transformation of sentence cores. The transformations themselves are very complicated, but the composition student can work with the expansions without extensive grammatical knowledge. We should say, however, that the phrases are verb phrases by form only. By function they most frequently are adjectivals and occasionally (especially the infinitive phrase) adverbials.

The first of the three verb-phrase expansions is the **infinitive phrase** (the infinitive being a verb stem preceded by *to,* such as *to see*). Infinitives and infinitive phrases perform many functions in our language, but we will concern ourselves only with those that are quite clearly expansions in the sense that we have been using the term. Here are two examples (the infinitive phrases are in italics):

CORE: The candidate wanted to increase his chances of election.
CORE: The candidate went into the ghettos to talk to groups and individuals.
EXPANSION: *To increase his chances of election,* the candidate went into the ghettos to talk to groups and individuals.

CORE: The kidnap victim wanted to attract passersby.
CORE: The kidnap victim threw notes written on toilet paper through the window grill.
EXPANSION: *To attract passersby*, the kidnap victim threw notes written on toilet paper through the window grill.

The first core in each example shows how the expansions are deletion transformations of whole sentence cores. When infinitive-phrase expansions come first in a sentence, they are set off by commas, but when they come last (which is less often) they usually are not set off by commas.

The second verb-phrase expansion, the **present-participial phrase,** is the one most commonly used (the present participle being the *ing* form of a verb, such as *seeing*). Present participles and present-participial phrases perform many functions in our language, but, again, we will be concerned only with those that are clearly expansions in the sense that we have been using the term. The generating process transforms a regular sentence core to produce this expansion. Here are two examples (the present-participial phrases are italicized):

> CORE: Nine conservative Congressmen spoke before two hundred businessmen.
>
> CORE: Nine conservative Congressmen charged that the Urban Renewal Act is "taxing the needy to benefit the greedy."
>
> EXPANSION: Nine conservative Congressmen, *speaking before two hundred businessmen*, charged that the Urban Renewal Act is "taxing the needy to benefit the greedy."

> CORE: The Committee underestimated the scope of their task.
>
> CORE: The Committee oversold the Urban Renewal program as a cure-all for city problems.
>
> EXPANSION: *Underestimating the scope of their task*, the Committee oversold the Urban Renewal program as a cure-all for city problems.

As the first cores in both examples show, the expansions are deletion plus verb-form-change transformations of full sentence cores. The generating process in structures like these is very complex, but it admirably provides for sentence economy and vigor.

In the two examples above, the present-participial phrases are nonrestrictive because they are not needed to identify the nouns they modify; thus they are set off by commas. But a present-participial phrase can be restrictive—needed to identify its noun—and then is not set off by commas. Example:

> CORE: The car was driven by a deputy sheriff.
>
> CORE: The car was carrying the criminals.
>
> EXPANSION: The car *carrying the criminals* was driven by a deputy sheriff.

In the complex sentence the present-participial phrase is needed to identify the noun *car* and is restrictive. But present-participial expansions cause little trouble in punctuation.

The third kind of verb-phrase expansion is the **past-participial phrase** (the past participle being the *ed* form in regular verbs, such as *talked,* and various forms in irregular verbs, such as *seen* and *blown*). Of course the past participle functions in many ways in our language, but we will consider it only in the kind of sentence expansions we have been studying. The past-participial phrase expansion is a deletion transformation of a sentence core and provides for sentence economy and vigor. Here are two examples (the past-participial phrases are italicized):

CORE: The corpse was battered beyond recognition.

CORE: The corpse was thought to have been a member of the Sherbull gang.

EXPANSION: The corpse, *battered beyond recognition*, was thought to have been a member of the Sherbull gang.

CORE: A condensation of the book was published in the *Reader's Digest*.

CORE: A condensation of the book emphasized the increase of crime in our cities.

EXPANSION: A condensation of the book, *published in the Reader's Digest*, emphasized the increase of crime in our cities.

The first cores in each of the examples show how the expansions are deletion transformations of whole sentence cores. These two examples are nonrestrictive and are set off by commas. But past-participial expansions can be restrictive. Example:

CORE: The phrase was not in the original.

CORE: The phrase was printed in italics.

EXPANSION: The phrase *printed in italics* was not in the original.

In the expansion, the restrictive past-participial phrase is needed to identify the noun *phrase* and thus is not set off by commas. But as with present-participial expansions, past-participial expansions cause little trouble in punctuation.

Both present- and past-participial expansions can be introduced by connective words that express the relationship between the expansion and the sentence core it goes with. Here are two examples:

CORE: Senator Fuzee used up some of his political capital.

CORE: Senator Fuzee managed to get his bill passed.

EXPANSION: *By using up some of his political capital*, Senator Fuzee managed to get his bill passed.

CORE: The car's engine was run at excessive speeds.

CORE: The car's engine showed no signs of breakdown.

EXPANSION: *Though run at excessive speeds*, the car's engine showed no signs of breakdown.

In example one, the connective *by* shows a cause-and-result relationship; in example two, the connective *though* shows a relationship of contrast.

As illustrated, the present- and past-participial expansions in each complex sentence are deletion plus **addition** transformations of whole sentence cores and are used to generate economical and vigorous sentences. (The additions here are the connectives *by* and *though*.)

EXERCISE 35. **Generating Verb Phrases**

DIRECTIONS: Convert each of the following sets of sentence cores into one sentence with at least one verb-phrase expansion. Also include other kinds of expansions that you have studied if they are called for.

1. a. The dog was barking furiously.
   b. The dog dashed at the animal warden.
   c. The animal warden was an enemy the dog didn't recognize.
2. a. The win pacified the alumni.
   b. The win ended a twelve-game losing streak.
   c. The alumni were about to fire the coach.
3. a. The President wanted to secure sufficient funds for expansion.
   b. The President made the business community feel their future was at stake.
   c. The President was a very smooth PR man.
4. a. Little John Charney was taken quickly to Dr. Forney.
   b. Dr. Forney was coincidentally the owner of the dog.
   c. Little John Charney was bitten severely by a vicious dog.
5. a. Americans are the richest people in the world.
   b. Americans are letting 98 percent of their mentally disturbed children slip through their fingers.
   c. Americans condemn the disturbed children to lives of futility and anguish.
6. a. A juvenile judge deals day in and day out with delinquents.
   b. A juvenile judge has an excellent opportunity to spot mentally disturbed youngsters.
   c. Some of these mentally disturbed youngsters should be given psychiatric care.
7. a. The professor canceled his final exam.
   b. The professor thereby endeared himself to his students.
8. a. The skull fragment was clearly a great fossil discovery.
   b. But the skull fragment was cracked in several places.
9. a. Mr. Cobb found out that Mr. Blanks was bankrupt.
   b. Mr. Cobb found this out after signing the partnership contract.
10. a. But the rare book was perfectly preserved.
    b. The rare book brought a low price.

Adverb Clauses.   The final kind of sentence expansion that we will study is quite different from those already discussed. In those discussed, the generating process transforms a complete sentence core into a sentence expansion that carries the meaning of a sentence core but not all of its words. This can happen because the sentence expansion draws some meaning from the sentence core it goes with. To refresh you memory, here is an example:

CORE: Three months later Corby was in a Brooklyn police station.

CORE: Corby was confessing to a horrendous catalogue of sex crimes.

EXPANSION: Three months later Corby was in a Brooklyn police station, *confessing to a horrendous catalogue of sex crimes.*

The italicized sentence expansion contains the meaning of a full sentence core because it takes the meaning of *Corby* from the core in the whole complex sentence. The transformation that produced the expansion called for deletion of words, as most of the expansions we have studied do. The only exception is the adjective clause, which calls for the substitution of a relative pronoun for the noun that would make the dependent clause a full sentence core that could stand by itself.

The **adverb clause**[4] is different from the expansions discussed above in that the generating process does not transform its sentence core by either deletion or substitution. Instead, an **addition transformation** is responsible for the adverb clause. What happens is that a **subordinating conjunction** is added to a whole sentence core, which then, as an adverb clause, is attached to a regular sentence core or sentence expansion to form a complex sentence. The subordinating conjunction both keeps the clause from standing by itself as a sentence core and also expresses a relationship between the adverb clause and the sentence core or sentence expansion it is attached to.

Eight kinds of relationships are expressed by the subordinating conjunctions that introduce adverb clauses. **Cause-and-result** is expressed by the subordinating conjunctions *because, inasmuch as, in that, now that, since, so that, so . . . that,* and *as* (colloquially). Following is an example. There is no need to show cores and expansions since nothing but the subordinating conjunction (italicized here) is added to or deleted from the sentence core in the adverb clause.

Since the election is over, we can now forget our differences for another four years.

---

[4] The construction is called an adverb clause because early grammarians thought it modified, usually, the verb of the main sentence core. But in reality the adverb clause most often functions as a sentence modifier in that it usually modifies a whole sentence core, not just the verb in the sentence core. But these grammatical distinctions are of no importance to the student of composition.

Two sentence cores are involved:

> The election is over.
> We can now forget our differences for another four years.

The subordinating conjunction *since* not only makes one core a dependent clause but also expresses the relationship between the two cores. If you will tinker with this complex sentence, you will see that other of the listed subordinating conjunctions will express the same relationship. For example, this sentence gives the same meaning:

> *Inasmuch as* the election is over, we can now forget our differences for another four years.

Usually, however, one of the group will sound best, and presumably the generating process (or maybe it is the composing process) is at work selecting the most appropriate conjunction.

The relationship of **contrast** is expressed by *although, though, whereas, while, however,* and *no matter how.* Example:

> *Although* he expected to lose the election, Casey won by a margin of 1 percent.

The last two listed conjunctions cannot operate in this sentence, but, with tinkering, the others can. The last two conjunctions express contrast in this way:

> *However* much you protest, I will eventually marry you.

The conjunction *no matter how* will express the same contrast here. (*However* as a conjunctive adverb is a coordinating connective.)

The relationship of **condition** is expressed by *if, in case, unless,* and *provided (that).* Example:

> *If* we get a 90 percent voter turn out, we can win the election.

The other three listed conjunctions can function in this sentence, though the generating process must adjust to them. For example, the sentence core must be made negative if *unless* is used:

> *Unless* we get a 90 percent voter turn out, we can*not* win the election.

The relationship of **manner** or **method** is expressed by *as, as if, as though,* and *like* (usually colloquial). Example:

> Casey conducted his campaign *as* a gentleman should.

Not all of the conjunctions listed will function in the same sentence, but all do express manner or method.

The relationship of **purpose** is expressed by *so that, so* (colloquially), and *in order that.* Example:

So that he could win the election, Casey learned to converse with Spanish-speaking voters.

All three of the listed conjunctions will function here.

A **time** relationship is expressed by *after, as, as soon as, before, since, once, until, when,* and *while.* Obviously most of these must be used in sentences of different meanings, according to the time meant. Some of these, especially *when* and *after,* often express a cause-and-result relationship as well as time. Example:

When the earthquake struck, people rushed from their homes.

The idea in the adverb clause is the cause and that in the sentence core is the result. The time element of simultaneity is also expressed.

A **place** relationship is expressed by *where* and *wherever.* Example:

I'll follow you *wherever* you go.

The adverb clause could open the sentence rather than close it.

A relationship of **comparison** is expressed by *as . . . as, more . . . than* and *more than, less . . . than* and *less than,* and the comparative form of an adjective or adverb (for example, *noisier*) followed by *than.* Examples:

Paula is *as* compassionate *as* you (are compassionate).
Reginald arrived earli*er than* Rufus (arrived).

The constituents in parentheses are usually just understood in such sentences of comparison.

Punctuation of sentences containing adverb clauses is not subject to definite rules. When the adverb clause come first, many writers always set it off with a comma. But many other equally skillful writers will not use a comma if the adverb clause is comparatively short. If the adverb clause comes last in a sentence, a comma should separate it only if there is a distinct voice pause between it and the first part of the sentence. Similarly, if an adverb clause comes in the middle of a sentence, it should be separated by commas only if there is a distinct voice pause before and after it. Here are examples of these suggestions for punctuation:

When the campaign became dirty because of unsubstantiated accusations, Johnson declared that until the election he would not again refer personally to his opponent. (Fairly long opening adverb clause set off by a comma.)

After the election was over Norwell took a two-week vacation. (Short opening adverb clause not set off. A comma after *over* would not be wrong.)

I refused to continue to work, *since it was clear my employer had no funds*. (Final adverb clause set off because of a distinct voice pause between it and the sentence core.)

I objected to the proposal *because it would bankrupt the club*. (Final adverb clause not set off because there is no voice pause between it and the sentence core.)

In the very early morning, *when most people are in bed*, I like to roam the streets. (Internal adverb clause set off on both sides because of distinct voice pauses.)

I looked up *when the bell rang* and saw that the clock was ten minutes slow. (Internal adverb clause not set off because there are no distinct pauses.)

This is as close a guide as can be given to the punctuation of adverb clauses.

Because noun clauses only rarely function as the kind of sentence expansion we have been discussing, we are not including a section on them. Most noun clauses are basic parts of sentence cores (that is, subjects or objects).

EXERCISE 36.   **Generating Adverb Clauses**

DIRECTIONS: Convert each of the following pairs of sentence cores into one sentence core with one adverb clause. So that you may focus on the relationship between the two clauses expressed in the subordinating conjunction, we have not put additional sentence expansions in these exercises. Use one of the subordinating conjunctions to introduce each adverb clause and be prepared to tell the relationship it expresses.

1. a. Pornography is seldom of much importance.
   b. Pornography may be of considerable interest.
2. a. In common practice no clear distinction is made between pornography and obscenity.
   b. I am offering for convenience a definition in which the single word *pornography* is stretched to include most of obscenity.
3. a. There is a special problem raised by realism.
   b. It aims to present people as they actually are.
4. a. Truman fought one war in Korea.
   b. He had to fight another at home against Senator McCarthy.
5. a. President Kennedy was receptive to new ideas.
   b. He did not call up task forces as frequently as did President Eisenhower.

6. a. Kennedy's ideas poured out too fast and went to Congress too fast.
   b. This happened before a public understanding and acceptance had been generated.
7. a. There was a chilliness in Congress.
   b. Kennedy did leave his legislative monuments.
8. a. Kennedy might have lived longer and had time to do more.
   b. Then he would have sought more outside advice.
9. a. I arrived in front of Patton.
   b. Then he whipped out a flask and said I needed a drink.
10. a. The war entered its final stages.
    b. Coincidence brought Patton and me together again.
11. a. Patton was a great general.
    b. His troops often resented him.
12. a. Patton was invariably successful in the field.
    b. He received honor after honor from the High Command.
13. a. We expected an immediate enemy attack.
    b. There was a twenty-four-hour lull.
14. a. Patton might have wanted my help again.
    b. Then he should have shown gratitude for my initial intervention.
15. a. I visited Moscow last fall.
    b. The threat of war seemed to worry the Soviet High Command.

EXERCISE 37. Generating Various Kinds of Complex Sentences

DIRECTIONS: Combine the sentence cores in each of the following sets into one clear, smooth complex sentence. Use any kind of sentence expansions that seem most appropriate to you.

1. a. The urban renewal proponents often have had no experience with slum life.
   b. Most of the urban renewal proponents are well-meaning people.
   c. Slum life has its own peculiar set of mores.
2. a. Not all slum children become delinquent.
   b. The proportion who do is high.
   c. This fact leads sociologists to attribute much delinquency to slum conditions.
3. a. The evidences of maladjustment in Oswald might have led to his being given early treatment.
   b. He might have overcome his instabilities.
   c. He might have overcome them at least sufficiently to lead a nearly normal life.
4. a. It was on that day in April 1963.

   b. The 21st Recon Company was with us.
   c. The 21st Recon Company was a particularly good outfit.
   d. It was largely made up of certain troops.
   e. These were troops who had fought with the Vietminh during the
       Indo-China war.

5. a. Racial discrimination is not virulent in New Mexico.
    b. There exists some prejudice against citizens of Spanish descent.
    c. Many of the citizens of Spanish descent consider themselves the
        elite of the state.
    d. They rightly consider themselves the elite.

EXERCISE 38.   Generating Sentences from Models

DIRECTIONS: Imitating the structure of the following model
sentences, generate a new sentence with any kind of subject
matter you fancy. Do not be concerned with labeling grammatical
constructions, but do try to make your sentences vary no more
than slightly from the models in structure. Two examples are
given to illustrate the procedure.

A. MODEL SENTENCE: To speak critically, I never received more than one
    or two letters—I wrote this some years ago—that were worth the postage.
    —Henry David Thoreau
    IMITATIVE SENTENCE: To be frank, I have never had a love affair—
    I would not have said this last year—that was worth the trouble.
B. MODEL SENTENCE: No matter what language is used—in the jungles of
    Africa or South America, the mountains of Tibet, or the islands of the
    Pacific—it has a complex, versatile, and adaptable structure.—W. Nelson
    Francis
    IMITATIVE SENTENCE: No matter whom I danced with—the homecom-
    ing queen, a chaperone, a wallflower, or a close friend—she complained
    about my awkward, stumbling, unrhythmical way of dancing.

   1. To a philosopher all *news*, as it is called, is gossip, and they who
       edit and read it are old women over their tea.—Henry David Thoreau
   2. The nonchalance of boys who are sure of a dinner, and would dis-
       dain as much as a lord to do or say aught to conciliate one, is the
       healthy attitude of human nature.—Ralph Waldo Emerson
   3. Accept the place the divine providence has found for you, the society
       of your contemporaries, the connection of events.—Ralph Waldo
       Emerson
   4. Some of the ghost towns—there are hundreds of abandoned mining

and ranch communities—are recreating themselves as TV-style Western towns with saloons, clapboard fronts, and arcaded walls.—David Boroff

5. If the economists considered schooling part of the national product (as they should), our economic growth rate would have looked pretty good all through the postwar period.—Peter F. Drucker

SOME PROBLEMS IN SENTENCE CLARITY AND CORRECTNESS

Of all the qualities of expository and persuasive writing that we emphasize in this text, clarity is the most important, for the chief purpose of exposition is to inform and of persuasion to convince, and writing cannot inform or convince unless it is clear. One source of lack of clarity in student writing is the writer's failure to put on paper what he has in his mind. For example, here is a passage that a student left as a complete paragraph without any clarification before or after it:

> Children are probably one of the first things a young couple thinks about. Children should be planned in the future, especially now with the education available, and the population problem.

What does "children should be planned in the future" mean? That at present children are not planned but that they should be from now on? Or that a young couple should wait to plan their children? Or what? And doesn't the phrase about education imply that it is desirable to have children, while the phrase about the population problems implies that it is undesirable to have children? The writer could hardly have been less clear. She was vague, first, because she did not think carefully and, second, because she did not reread her theme *as though she were a stranger to it.* To be clear, a writer must put on paper what is actually in his mind and not expect the reader to read his mind. To be sure that he has done this, he must reread his work carefully as though someone else had written it. Then he is likely to spot passages that do not clearly say what he intended to say.

Other than incomplete thoughts—such as the sample above—one of the most common sources of unclear writing is **faulty sentence structure.** Since most sentences in mature writing are a complex arrangement of several or many parts (including the sentence expansions we have discussed), it is easy for a sentence's structure to become mixed and thus for its clarity to be marred. Literally every writer at times writes a bad sentence, but good writers revise, leaving few if any of their sentences badly formed.

Almost all errors or serious weaknesses in sentence structure involve some improper change of structure after the sentence is underway—in effect, the generating process goes awry. Any language is based on an immense number of rules, and when its rules are followed, proper signals are present to help the reader or listener follow easily what is written or said. For example, when a sentence begins this way:

I was waiting for a _____ ,

the English speaker's mind receives the signal that (usually) either a noun, such as *lady,* is to follow, or an adjective plus a noun, such as *lovely lady,* or an adverb plus an adjective plus a noun, such as *spectacularly lovely lady.* The rules of English call for a structure like one of these (variations are possible). When such an expected structure comes, the mind accepts its signal and understands instantaneously. But if a structure such as *knows something* should fill in the blank in the uncompleted structure above, the reader's mind would reject it and become confused.

Very few such rules of English as the one just illustrated are ever violated by a native speaker more than four or five years old. But some more complicated rules are rather frequently violated by inexperienced writers, thus producing confused sentence structure that interferes with clarity or proper response from the reader. For example, when a structure such as

Having finished the weekly maintenance

begins a sentence, a rule of grammar requires and the reader expects that the next structure will name the person (or thing) that performed the action in the verb *having finished,* such as *we.* When that rule is violated an improper change of sentence structure occurs, eliciting an improper response from the reader. For example:

Having finished the weekly maintenance, the pool was now ready for use.

The reader is not completely confused, but *his attention is called to the faulty structure* (the pool didn't finish the maintenance), and that means the writing is bad. Effective and correct writing does not call the reader's attention to its structure; instead, the reader accepts the proper signals unconsciously.

There are a number of kinds of errors in sentence structure that are so common in student writing as to have specific names. They violate rules of English grammar in such specific ways that students can learn either to avoid them altogether or else to spot them quickly and revise them as they reread their papers. The rest of this chapter will be devoted to an analysis of these common sentence errors.[5]

Mixed Sentence Structure

The structure of a sentence is mixed when the generating process begins with one acceptable kind of structure but then goes awry and shifts to another kind of structure that violates the rules of our English grammar. We will examine four kinds of these mixed sentences; all represent very serious errors in composition.

Garbled Sentences. The term *garbled sentence* is not as specific as are the three terms to follow in this section. Those three represent very specific kinds of errors in sentence structure, the three terms being their specific names. **Garbled sentences** applies to various kinds of mixed sentences with no specific names. In general, however, the term means that a sentence starts out with one kind of structure and somewhere along the way shifts to another kind of structure that will not correctly complete the sentence. *Confused sentence structure* is an equally descriptive term for such errors.

The examples of garbled sentences to follow and most of the sentences in the exercises were written by students. One student began a sentence with this acceptable structure:

The older generation knows that in their younger days . . .

At this point the reader's mind expects a subject (of the noun clause beginning with *that*), probably *they,* followed by a predicate. But the student writer literally forgot what kind of sentence he had started generating, shifted to another kind, and produced this garbled sentence:

The older generation knows that in their younger days how irresponsible and immoral they were.

Instead of the expected subject and predicate to follow *that,* the writer used a second subordinating conjunction (*how*) followed by a subject and predicate. Perhaps the student could be forgiven for writing the bad sentence (every writer occasionally writes a bad sentence), but he could not be forgiven for not revising it for correct structure. He could have written either of these sentences:

The older generation knows that in their younger days they were irresponsible and immoral.

[5] See also the section on the proper placement of modifiers earlier in this chapter. Errors not involving sentence structure but conventional usage will be discussed in Chapter 7.

> The older generation knows how irresponsible and immoral they were in their younger days.

The student did not need a *conscious* understanding of rules of English grammar to compose either of these sentences. As with every native speaker of college age and intelligence, he had an *unconscious* knowledge of the rules of grammar necessary to compose such simple sentences. But for some reason—carelessness, panic, or what?—many students do write many such garbled sentences.

Here is another truly garbled sentence:

> Today it is increasingly hard for teen-agers to stay out of trouble in which our parents never came in contact with.

All is clear through the word *trouble,* but after that word the sentence is so jumbled that no clear signals are present. The student thoughtlessly made present and future trouble the same as past trouble. Just a little thought should have let him compose the sentence he intended:

> Today it is increasingly hard for teen-agers to stay out of a kind of trouble our parents never came in contact with.

That is a rather impressive and insightful idea. It seems strange that a student capable of thinking such a penetrating thought could not manage the simple structure to express it.

As a last example here is the clear beginning of a sentence that was to become garbled:

> In furthering my education here at the college by attending adult classes . . .

This structure demands that the next word be the subject *I* followed by a predicate. But the writer continued with

> . . . has been very interesting.

Apparently the writer forgot that he began his sentence with the preposition *in.* Omit that word and his structure becomes correct. Or he could have written

> In furthering my education here at the college by attending adult classes, I have taken several interesting courses.

His failure to revise his original garbled sentence was inexcusable.

Let us emphasize again that you do not need to consciously understand grammatical analysis to avoid such garbled sentences, for you have an unconscious understanding of the grammar necessary for such simple sentences (conventional usage is another matter, as you will see in Chapter 7).

EXERCISE 39. **Revising Garbled Sentences**

DIRECTIONS: Rewrite a proper version of each of the following garbled sentences and be prepared to explain, if you can, how the writer lost control of his sentence structure.

1. The secret of political success is a good memory for names and willingness to compromise make it easy to achieve.
2. The speaker insisted that the only way to avoid world war, the United Nations must have an independent military force larger than that of any one country.
3. The more I tried to explain my absence, the teacher was not willing to listen to me.
4. By encouraging more and more common people to buy corporation stocks can strengthen the capitalist system.
5. Because his secretary forgot to make a note of the appointment was why Mr. Jones did not appear at the conference.
6. I think the world can only have peace is when disarmament is a completed fact.
7. If the accused was insane at the time of the crime, his punishment is enough by being put into a mental institution.
8. Suburbanites want houses that are reasonably priced, attractively designed, and upkeep should be inexpensive.
9. Freedom must forever be guarded with vigilance is a fact demonstrated by human history.
10. Christmas comes during the yuletide season which many people interpret it as being the yuletide season.
11. By forcing a student to take a science class, the purpose of the class is not fully realized.
12. The fact that the professor had traveled in Europe, this added interest to his course.
13. The unexpectedly large number of students voting in the election took a great deal of time for the tellers to count them.
14. Every letter that we got seemed to be a different person writing it.
15. The opening paragraph is kind of hard to tell what he is driving at.
16. The number of advantages lost by both the strikers and the employers took a matter of years in order to regain them.
17. In establishing a new method of cost accounting has resulted in important savings for the company.
18. Many scientists have admitted that in some of their experiments how they did not understand what they were doing.
19. Every time one world crisis is solved seems to bring a new one.
20. Swimming is a form of exercise that if you do it regularly you will have better health.

Faulty Predication.   The term *predication* has two meanings: **predication** is the grammatical function of fitting a subject to a predicate. This function results in **a predication,** which is a statement, assertion, affirmation, declaration, or the like. Faulty predication results when a subject does not fit its predicate, making the statement weird or nonsensical.

In one sense, many if not most sentences with faulty predication are not ungrammatical. For example, the sentence pattern *something is something else* is extremely common in English. Thus

Television / is a valuable asset to education

is a common kind of grammatical sentence. Similarly,

Television / is a morgy blution of kluppers

would be recognized by literate people as grammatical even though nonsensical, for *television* obviously is being called something else (*morgy* must be an adjective and *blution* and *kluppers* must be nouns). But now consider this sentence from a student paper:

Television / is the best kind of advertisement.

In a sense the predication is grammatical, since one thing is called another thing. Computer analysis of the grammar would not spot the faulty predication, for it is not a grammatical but a **semantic** flaw (semantics is the study of meanings of words). But since *television* is not an *advertisement* the predication is faulty and the sentence illogical, for a subject has not been fitted to a proper predicate.

Here are some similar examples of faulty predication:

The arguments presented in favor of parent-arranged marriages / are financial security and social standing. (Are financial security and social standing arguments?)

The first step in writing / is spelling and sentence structure. (Are spelling and sentence structure a step in writing?)

One example of the courage of a Peace Corps member / is the tractor. (Can a tractor be an example of courage?)

Apparently muddy thinking is the cause of such errors in sentence structure.

Closely related to the *something is something else* kind of faulty predication are the notorious *is when* and *is where* constructions. Examples:

The Dean's List / is when you have a grade-point average of 3.5 or above.

Courage / is when you act brave even though you are scared.

> Sluice mining / is where you use water to wash out the ore-bearing gravel and sand.

The subjects in these sentences do not denote a time or place of occurrence, and thus the predication is faulty.

Faulty predication also occurs with verbs other than forms of *to be*. Examples:

> Unemployed men / constitute the lack of available jobs.
>
> The mass destruction of human life and property / would take a terrible toll.
>
> My first reaction to being in a large English class / seemed a little strange and different.
>
> The price of his election / cost him the respect of his close friends.

In none of these sentences do the subject and predicate properly fit each other, and illogical and absurd constructions result. Such faulty predication is not a rare error and is one of the most serious errors that can be made in composition.

EXERCISE 40.   Revising Faulty Predication

DIRECTIONS: Rewrite the following sentences to eliminate faulty predication. In some cases it may seem as though the predication is satisfactory, but further thought should reveal the flaw to you. For example, the sentence

> Water / is one of America's most pressing problems

may at first glance seem acceptable, but it isn't just *water* but *maintaining an adequate supply of fresh water* that is the problem. Similar constructions occur in this exercise.

1. Too many people working on a good thing may prove faulty.
2. Cheating in school is another area in which I must disagree with my parents.
3. Teaching their children would be another prevention of delinquency.
4. The white lie is not living up to what one believes.
5. For people to break all social and financial relations and move to another part of the world takes a very dedicated person.
6. Twenty-five years ago was quite different from what it is now.
7. An understanding of our country's standing in the world is one of leadership.
8. The best method of deception is the advertisements for a sale.
9. Another way to help preserve wildlife is during the winter months.
10. Sex is another serious controversy.

11. Another example of how people are dishonest is in the schools.
12. One of the reasons restricting the fulfillment of goals may be conformity.
13. Another argument that one may use is the Bill of Rights.
14. Another well-known advertisement is hair oil.
15. An example of not rotating crops is during the time of the great cotton plantations.
16. Franklin's *Autobiography* was written as an old man giving advice to his son.
17. My opinion about the age of drafting young men into the service should stay as it is today.
18. Flagrant infractions of discipline by students, particularly those involving drinking and relations between the sexes, usually demand the participation of the President of the College.
19. Children playing with matches could be prevented if parents were more cautious.
20. Onomatopoeia is when the sound of a word is the same as its meaning.
21. Another undesirable trait of sports is where money is involved.
22. Some misconceptions of the black race are intelligence, responsibilities, and their standard of living.
23. My first reaction to being placed in a large class frightened me.
24. His first trick was a deck of cards.
25. The price of the components for modifying the engine cost me $259.

Faulty Parallelism. In writing, parallelism means the use of any kind of sentence constituent in a series of two or more, usually with a coordinating conjunction between the last two constituents in the series. The constituents are also said to be compounded. Here are two examples:

> That is a story *which I have heard before, which I expect to hear again,* but *which I wish I had never heard the first time.* (three parallel adjective clauses)
> *Expecting his aunt to drop in* but not *relishing the idea of talking to her,* Denny became increasingly nervous. (two parallel present-participial phrases)

Usually parallel constituents are of the same grammatical construction, as in the two examples just given. But sometimes constituents different in structure but identical in function occur in acceptable parallelism. Examples:

> Billy was *hungry* but otherwise *in a good mood.*
> He spoke *rationally* but not *as an authority would speak.*

In the first example, an adjective and a prepositional phrase are in parallel structure, with the phrase functioning exactly as the adjective does. In the second example, an adverb and an adverbial clause are in parallel structure, both functioning the same by modifying *spoke*. This type of acceptable parallelism of nonidentical grammatical structures is not very common.

When two or more constituents different in grammatical structure (with such exceptions as noted above) are compounded, the serious error in sentence structure called **faulty parallelism** occurs. Here are some typical examples of faulty parallelism, with a proper revision of each:

> Several committee members *were at the secret meeting* but not *agreeing to change their votes.* (sentence predicate in faulty parallelism with a present-participial phrase)
> Several committee members *were at the secret meeting* but *did not agree to change their votes.* (two parallel sentence predicates)
>
> I believe *that the United Nations has been fairly effective* but *we can improve it.* (noun clause in faulty parallelism with an independent clause)
> I believe *that the United Nations has been fairly effective* but *that we can improve it.* (two parallel noun clauses)
>
> Mullins of the White Sox had a near-perfect day on the mound, *striking out twelve batters* and *he allowed only two hits.* (present-participial phrase and an independent clause in faulty parallelism)
> Mullins of the White Sox had a near-perfect day on the mound, *striking out twelve batters* and *allowing only two hits.* (two parallel present-participial phrases)

Faulty parallelism almost always disrupts sentence rhythm and vigor; thus a writer with little knowledge of grammar can usually detect and eliminate the error by rereading his sentences and listening with his mind's ear.

EXERCISE 41. Revising Faulty Parallelism

DIRECTIONS: Each of the following sentences has an error in parallelism. Write a correct version of each by placing all constituents in a series in parallel structure.

1. A person may be brilliant in a specific field but he does not have general knowledge.
2. When we turn on our TV sets, radios, or read magazines, we are usually seeking entertainment.
3. A citizen of this country is assured freedom of many things and one of these being freedom of speech.

4. Americans want peace, a high standard of living, to be the best, and they want to be liked.

5. Agricultural areas use water not only for everyday use and crop use, but the wildlife also use it.

6. He would leave his farm idle and may cause erosion.

7. The poem starts out with an ant running into a moth and is so busy that he doesn't notice.

8. Disinfect diapers with boiling, sunshine, or, best of all, use special antiseptic diaper rinse granules.

9. He was like the king who ate and drank poison and he finally became immune to it.

10. These three things can be decided by the young people and do not need any interference from the adults.

11. The flowers are smaller, many having holes in the petals and some petals are discolored.

12. The armed forces offer financial security, opportunity for travel, and to learn of people from different cultures.

13. There are two ways to preserve wildlife: One is be careful with fire, and second have laws to control the hunter.

14. Franklin set up his own code of ethics, not to please God but he thought his ethical system would increase his prosperity.

15. He is the kind of man who is honest but he makes careless mistakes.

Dangling Modifiers.   A rather common kind of sentence pattern is one that opens with a verb phrase that expresses an action or state of being but that does not have in it the thing or person who performed the action or existed in the state of being. Here are three examples of such phrases:

> Having expressed his opinion that the proposal would not work, . . .
> Known as a persistent social climber, . . .
> Being the daughter of a millionaire, . . .

These phrases do not mention the person who did the *expressing,* who *was known,* or who simply *was* (the daughter of a millionaire). Thus when a sentence opens with such a phrase, one of the rules of our grammar calls for, and the reader expects, the next word (which will be the subject of the sentence) to name the person who did the expressing, and so on. For example, in the sentence

> Having expressed his opinion that the proposal would not work, the committee chairman took a quick vote,

the grammatical signals are all in order, for *the committee chairman* fills the sentence position that tells who did the expressing. The long opening phrase **modifies** *the committee chairman,* fulfilling the demand of one of our rules of grammar.

But when such an opening verb phrase is not followed by the doer of the action expressed in the phrase, the phrase does not have a proper word to modify and thus is said to dangle. In such a case, one of our rules of grammar is violated and mixed sentence structure results. The technical name for the error is **dangling modifier.** Here are three sentences with dangling modifiers, based on the three phrases above:

> Having expressed his opinion that the proposal would not work, a quick vote was taken. (Did a quick vote express its opinion?)
> Known as a persistent social climber, few worthwhile invitations were received. (Were the invitations known as a social climber?)
> Being the daughter of a millionaire, the boys pretended great romantic interest in her. (Were the boys the daughter of a millionaire?)

The introductory verb phrases must serve as modifiers, but in these sentences none has a proper word to modify, and hence the sentences contain dangling modifiers. Note that in the last example the pronoun *her* does name the person who was the daughter, but the pronoun is not in the proper (subject) position for the verb phrase to modify it, and thus the phrase still dangles. Though the reader can make out the meaning of the whole sentence, his attention is called to the mixed sentence structure; hence the sentence is a bad one.

Sentences with dangling modifiers can be recast in various ways to produce clarity and correctness. A noun for the verb phrase to modify can be put in the subject position, as in these sentences:

> Known as a persistent social climber, Rory received few worthwhile invitations.
> Being the daughter of a millionaire, Cora was pestered by boys who pretended great romantic interest.

Now the phrases do not dangle, since each has a proper word to modify. The faulty sentences could also be recast in other ways, such as these:

> Since Rory was known as a persistent social climber, he received few worthwhile invitations.
> The boys pretended great romantic interest in Cora, since she was the daughter of a millionaire.

Any pleasingly and correctly formed sentence is a satisfactory revision of a sentence with a dangling modifier.

Most dangling modifiers are verb phrases.[6] But various kinds of

---

[6] Identification of the kind of verb phrase—such as perfect past participle, passive voice—is unimportant.

prepositional-phrase and adjective-phrase modifiers can also dangle. In such nonverb-phrase danglers, the phrase, which usually opens a sentence, describes a person or thing that the reader expects to be the next word (usually the sentence subject) after the phrase. For example, if a sentence begins with

> Without a penny to his name, . . .

the reader expects, and a rule of our grammar calls for, the next word to be the name of the person without a penny, as in this sentence:

> Without a penny to his name, Murdock felt that things were hopeless.

The opening prepositional phrase modifies *Murdock* and thus does not dangle. But observe these sentences:

> As an experienced grifter, many were cheated out of their money.
> Happy over her approaching wedding day, the years of waiting now seemed worthwhile.

The opening phrases do not have suitable words to modify and thus are dangling modifiers, causing a kind of mixed sentence structure. The dangling can be eliminated in this way:

> As an experienced grifter, Carney cheated many out of their money.
> Happy over her approaching wedding day, Miss Bildt felt that her years of waiting were now worthwhile.

Now the grammatical signals are in proper order.

Most authorities on usage will now accept as grammatical a sentence with an opening verb phrase that has only a possessive pronoun or noun to relate to in the main clause of the sentence. Example:

> Being absolutely in the right, my feelings were hurt by the unfair accusation.

Technically, the opening verb phrase modifies the noun *feelings* rather than the possessive pronoun *my* and is therefore a dangler, but this kind of construction is commonly enough used now by educated people not to be considered an error.

Certain set introductory phrases are quite acceptable even though technically they seem to dangle. Examples:

> Considering the scarcity of experienced mechanics, it's easy to understand why so few used cars are in good condition.
> In dealing with the public, the first lesson to learn is that almost everyone is dominated by self-interest.

There is no one in the sentences to do the *considering* or the *dealing,* but the phrases, because they refer to everyone, are not true danglers.

Whenever an introductory phrase seems perfectly clear and not absurd, it need not be considered a dangler even though it has no specific noun to modify.

EXERCISE 42. Revising Dangling Modifiers

DIRECTIONS: Recast each of the following sentences in any way that will eliminate the dangling modifier and produce a clear correct sentence.

1. By doing right all the time, your conscience will feel at ease.
2. Most accidents take place when angry.
3. While investigating the burglary, another house was robbed.
4. Being unused to such attention, the hotel service delighted me.
5. Coming at an inconvenient time, I rather resented my parents-in-law's visit.
6. Although suave and sophisticated, anyone could see that he was an intellectual fraud.
7. Besides offering a great deal of entertainment, people can sometimes improve their educational status by watching TV.
8. By teaching the dangers of communism, our citizens can learn to protect our freedoms better.
9. When in a state of despair, a visit to the church is helpful.
10. The game between the Rams and the 49ers was quite exciting, not having seen a professional football game before.
11. Having numerous dangerous curves, she drove very carefully over that stretch of road.
12. Not having been refilled after the last draining, we just sunbathed around the pool's edge.
13. The rescue team could hardly be seen, having been nearly blinded by the flash of the explosion.
14. Although sometimes exaggerated a bit, anybody can see through most advertisements.
15. Intently searching his underside for parasites, the zoo attendant showed us a rare South American species of monkey.

Miscellaneous Shifted Constructions

In the above sections on mixed sentence structure we have shown that errors in sentence structure are chiefly due to an improper shift within a sentence from one kind of sentence structure to another, incompatible kind (though in faulty predication there may not be an improper grammatical shift). The errors dealt with so far are quite serious because they often destroy sentence clarity. There are several other kinds of shifts in sentence structure that do not seriously disturb clarity but that do annoy educated readers. These shifts all denote inconsistency in grammatical structure, and college students should learn to avoid them. We will examine six of these **miscellaneous shifted constructions.**

In Number.   There are two grammatical **numbers** in English: the **singular** (one) and the **plural** (more than one). The grammatical feature of number in English is expressed in nouns and pronouns and in some verb forms. Quite often a sentence will have two or more nouns or pronouns that, for consistency, should be in the same number. But an inexperienced writer may improperly shift the number of one or more of the nouns or pronouns from singular to plural or from plural to singular, thus producing an inconsistency that irritates, though it does not mislead, the educated reader. Here is a typical example of a **shift in number:**

> A *person* may be a celebrity even when *they* are notorious rather than famous.

The noun *person* is singular but the pronoun *they* referring to it is inconsistently plural. Some authorities on usage call this kind of error **faulty agreement in number between pronoun and antecedent.** Either label for the error is satisfactory, though the true source of the error is an improper shift.

The reason that an improper shift in number can, and frequently does, occur in our language is that we can grammatically refer to people in general in either the singular or the plural. Here are examples:

> A *teacher* must respect the beliefs of *her* pupils even when *she* disagrees with those beliefs.
>
> *Teachers* must respect the beliefs of *their* pupils even when *they* disagree with those beliefs.
>
> *Everyone* stated *his* opinion.
> *All* stated *their* opinions.

These pairs of sentences have identical meanings in referring to people in general, but one is phrased in the singular and the other in the plural. Both modes of phrasing are completely acceptable. But this capacity of our language often leads to a shift in number such as

> *Everyone* stated *their* opinion,

a sentence that has one component in the singular and one with the same reference in the plural.

But at this point in our discussion we must admit that the *everyone . . . their* construction is now so common in the language usage of educated people that it must be accepted as correct, since it is not arbitrary rules but usage in the language of educated people that makes for correctness. Nonetheless, people who take pride in their command of the language still say and write *everyone . . . his,* and some instructors insist that students do so. Other shifts in number, however, many not be condoned as standard usage.

Here are some examples of the most common kind of shift in number—from a singular noun to a plural pronoun:

> If a *person* is ignorant of the law, *they* can still be prosecuted for breaking it.
> A *musician* is probably the most envied of professionals because *they* enjoy *their* work so much.
> A football *player* deserves pay, for *they* work hard.
> *Anyone* who thinks *they* are being cheated should complain to the manager.

In each case the pronoun *they* can be changed to the singular *he* (with proper verb change) to produce consistency. Or in the first three examples the noun (again with proper verb change) could be changed to the plural for consistency.

As we have said, this error is sometimes called faulty agreement in number between pronoun and antecedent, and that label is acceptable. However, the fact that an improper shift in number can occur with only nouns shows that the true source of the error is an improper shift. Here are some examples of the error with no pronoun involved:

> *People* may be a *celebrity* when they should be jailed.
> Football *players* can show they are a good *sport* by accepting a loss gracefully.
> All the *members* raised their *hand.*

The italicized nouns in each sentence have the same reference and therefore for consistency should be in the same number. Sometimes, however, it is hard to maintain consistency in number. For example, if the last example above were written

> All the members raised their *hands,*

would the meaning be that each member raised both of his hands or only one? A little thought shows that the sentence should read

> Each member raised his hand.

A writer can avoid a shift in number only by being intellectually aware that the error exists and by carefully reviewing each of his sentences.

In Person.   In English grammar there are three **persons:** (1) the

first person (the person speaking: *I, me, we, us*); (2) the **second person** (the person being spoken to: *you*); and (3) the **third person** (the person or thing being spoken about: *he, him, they, them, anyone, people,* and so on). Our language allows us to refer to people in general in either the third person or the so-called **indefinite second person.** Example:

> A *person* should not depend on a crutch if *he* doesn't need one.
> *You* should not depend on a crutch if *you* don't need one.

There is no difference in meaning between these two sentences, for the indefinite *you* is commonly used to refer to people in general. Some authorities on usage object to the use of the indefinite *you*, but professional writers in magazines such as *Harper's* and *The Atlantic*, and also authors of books, often use the indefinite *you* without its flawing their styles. Unless a writer wants his style to be especially formal, he can safely use the indefinite *you*, though it is quite reasonable for a composition teacher to ask his students to avoid it.

Since English allows either the third person or the indefinite second person to refer to people in general, careless writers sometimes improperly shift from one to the other, creating inconsistency that annoys knowledgeable readers. Here are two examples:

> A *person* should not depend on a crutch if *he* doesn't need one, for if *you* do *you* will soon find *yourself* unable to be independent.
> When *someone* finds a piece of money, *he* usually keeps it, but sometimes *you* are honest enough to look for its owner.

For consistency such sentences should be wholly in the third person or in the second. The context of the whole piece of writing would dictate which would sound smoothest. This kind of shift is not nearly as common as a shift in number. Again, the error can be called **faulty agreement in person between pronoun and antecedent,** but its true cause is a shift in person.

In Tense.   Since tense in English grammar is very complicated, we will not present a list of labels, for we can talk about improper shifts by using just the terms **past tense** and the so-called **historical present tense.** An improper shift between these can occur because our language lets us refer to the past, as in summarizing the plot of a novel or a book of history, in either the past or the historical present tense. An essay exam answer, for example, might open with either of these sentences:

> PAST TENSE: At the beginning of his reign, King John *was* very suspicious of his nobles and *decided* that he *would* put them to a test before he *trusted* them with policy making.
> PRESENT TENSE: At the beginning of his reign, King John *is* very

suspicious of his nobles and *decides* that he *will* put them to a test before he *trusts* them with policy making.

There is no difference in meaning between these two sentences, for the historical present tense can tell about the past.

Since English provides for either the past or the historical present tense to be used in narrating the past, careless writers often improperly shift from one to the other. In fact, even the best and most experienced writers sometimes have trouble controlling their tenses when describing events of the past or summarizing fiction. Here is an example of a typical shift of this sort:

The setting of the story *is* Padua in pre-Renaissance Italy. Giovanni *has come* to the city to study at the University. He *rents* a suite that *overlooks* the botanical garden of a scientist. He *had been* there only a short time when he *saw* a beautiful girl in the garden.

Is, has come, rents, and *overlooks* are in historical present tenses; *had been* and *saw* are past tenses. Such a shift does nothing to obscure clarity, but its inconsistency is noticeable to the perceptive reader and causes him to think less of the writer.

In Voice.   There are two **voices** in English: (1) the **active voice,** in which the subject of a sentence performs the action (as in *John killed a snake*) and (2) the **passive voice,** in which the subject receives an action (as in *a snake was killed by John*). Again, our grammar gives us two ways to say exactly the same thing. Thus in sentences with two or more clauses—or sometimes from sentence to sentence in a paragraph—careless writers occasionally improperly shift from the active to the passive voice. On pages 144–145 we demonstrated that the active voice usually makes a more vigorous sentence, though on many occasions, and for several reasons, a sentence in the passive voice is fully acceptable or even mandatory.

But when the first clause in a sentence is in the active voice, the next clause usually should also be in the active voice, for frequently the same person will be performing the action in both clauses. Here are examples, with revisions:

SHIFT IN VOICE: When I study hard for a test, it is usually passed with a high grade.
CONSISTENCY IN VOICE: When I study hard for a test, I usually pass it with a high grade.

SHIFT IN VOICE: We refused to admit defeat, and the game was won by us in the last few seconds.
CONSISTENCY IN VOICE: We refused to admit defeat and won the game in the last few seconds.

SHIFT IN VOICE: The Governor called in his lieutenants, and they were lectured by him about press leakage.
CONSISTENCY IN VOICE: The Governor called in his lieutenants and lectured them about press leakage.

Such a shift in voice as illustrated in each first sentence produces awkwardness and weak rhythm. Consistency in voice contributes to economy and vigor in sentence composition. You should try to acquire an intellectual understanding of the nature of the shift in order to avoid it.

In Mood.   The least common kind of shift, but one quite annoying to skilled readers, is a **shift in mood.** There are three **moods** (indicating the attitude of the writer or speaker) in English: (1) the **indicative mood,** which expresses a statement (such as *Baldwin Day is running for Governor*); (2) the **imperative mood,** which issues a request or command (such as *Run for Governor, Baldwin*); and (3) the **subjunctive mood,** which expresses potentiality, possibility, condition contrary to fact, desirability, obligation, and so on (such as *Baldwin Day should run for Governor*).

Careless writers sometimes improperly shift moods, producing poor writing. Here are examples:

SHIFT FROM INDICATIVE TO IMPERATIVE: Benjamin Franklin felt that learning was as good as earning. Spend some time every day with books. Try to progress as the times progress.
CONSISTENCY IN MOOD: Benjamin Franklin felt that learning was as good as earning. He advised his readers to spend some time every day with books and to try to progress as the times progress.

SHIFT FROM IMPERATIVE TO SUBJUNCTIVE: First, set aside a definite period of study time. Then develop study habits suitable for your kind of courses. Next you *should* work to make studying a pleasure rather than a task.
CONSISTENCY IN MOOD: First, set aside a definite period of study time. Then develop study habits suitable for your kind of courses. And next, work to make studying a pleasure rather than a task.

Improper shifts in mood are very annoying to good readers because such shifts force the reader to adjust to unexpected patterns of thought. A writer who is willing to reread his sentences carefully will usually detect an improper shift in mood easily, for the inconsistency produces an abruptness. When the mood is consistent he will experience a smoothness in reading from sentence to sentence.

Of course a shift in mood can be proper and even necessary. Example:

Your success in college will depend on your establishing good habits.
First, set aside a definite period of study time.

The first sentence is in the indicative mood, for it makes a statement. The second is properly in the imperative mood, for the writer now needs to give his reader advice in the form of a command sentence.

In Point of View.   In the first example of shift in mood in the previous section there is also a **shift in point of view.** The first sentence is written from the point of view of Benjamin Franklin. Then the following two sentences in the imperative mood express the point of view of the writer, for a request or command sentence must express the point of view of the speaker or writer. That additional inconsistency only makes the piece of writing worse.

But a shift in point of view can occur even when all the sentences are in the indicative mood (making statements). Here is an example from the writings of a famous philosopher not noted for making his complex thought clear:

> (1) Those who argue that social and moral reform is impossible on the ground that the Old Adam of human nature remains forever the same attribute to native activities the permanence and inertia that in truth belong only to acquired customs. (2) To Aristotle slavery was rooted in aboriginal human nature. (3) Native distinctions of quality exist such that some persons are by nature gifted with power to plan, command, and supervise, and others possess merely capacity to obey and execute. (4) Hence slavery is natural and inevitable. (5) There is error in supposing that, because domestic and chattel slavery has been legally abolished, slavery as conceived by Aristotle has disappeared. (6) But matters have at least progressed to a point where it is clear that slavery is a social state, not a psychological necessity.—John Dewey, *Human Nature and Conduct.*

Sentence (1) of this passage represents the point of view of the author about an idea held by "Those who argue. . . ." Sentence (2) represents the point of view of Aristotle. Sentences (5) and (6) again represent the point of view of the author. But whose point of view is involved in sentences (3) and (4)? It seems to be the author's, but close inspection shows that these sentences continue to express Aristotle's thought. The passage is not immediately clear because of the muddy shifting of point of view.

The author should have made it crystal clear that sentences (3) and (4) were still Aristotle's ideas. He might have done so in this way:

> Those who argue that social and moral reform is impossible on the ground that the Old Adam of human nature remains forever the same attribute to native activities the permanence and inertia that in truth belong only to acquired customs. To Aristotle slavery was rooted in aboriginal human nature. He thought that native distinctions of quality

exist such that some persons are by nature gifted with power to plan, command, and supervise, and that others possess merely capacity to obey and execute. Hence to him slavery was natural and inevitable.

With the use of proper transition for coherence, the various points of view of the passage become clear rather than discernible only through a pause for rereading.

EXERCISE 43. **Eliminating Improper Shifts**

DIRECTIONS: Each of the following sentences or passages contains a faulty shift of some sort. Identify the kind of shift involved in each and compose a revised version. In some cases you will need to recast the sentences completely to achieve clarity.

1. Aristotelian scholars are all a professor in some philosophy department.
2. Aristotle believed in spontaneous generation. Small creatures just come into being in stagnant water.
3. Aristotle taught the golden mean. Always avoid excess. Don't drink too much or too little. Don't be too high tempered or too phlegmatic.
4. Aristotle says that the good life calls for moderation; he suggested ways in which we can avoid the extremes that cause us pain.
5. An epicurean is one who thinks that the good life consists in avoiding pain and cultivating pleasure. But they mean the kind of pleasure that does not cause pain later on.
6. A stoic is one who believes in facing life's harsh realities with fortitude and determination. Don't whimper and complain and don't try to run away.
7. After about A.D. 300 many of the old Greek and Roman philosophies begin to wane, and the Christian philosophy became dominant.
8. In the early 1840s Henry David Thoreau lived in the woods by himself for two years and two months, and the book *Walden* was written by him about his experiences there.
9. In *Walden* Thoreau says that his sojourn in the woods was an experiment in simple living; he did not say that he was trying to escape from civilization.
10. According to Thoreau, one should keep his life as simple as possible, for only in simple living can you realize your full spiritual and intellectual powers.
11. A farmer, says Thoreau, is not the keeper of his herd; instead, it is their keeper.
12. "Superfluous wealth will buy superfluities only," said Thoreau, which means that he thought that a person should pay more attention to their mind than to their material possessions.

13. In the chapter in *Walden* entitled "Economy," Thoreau tells how he built his own cabin and raised his own food; he claimed that his food cost him only about one dollar a month.

14. From reading *Walden*, one can learn a great deal about what is wrong with modern life; but chances are you won't be moved enough to change your own mode of living.

15. All of the professors at Westend College have a doctorate.

16. A student of American literature may not fully agree with all that Thoreau says but they most certainly should be acquainted with his work.

17. Thoreau was a close associate of Ralph Waldo Emerson's; in fact, for a while Emerson's household chores were done for him by Thoreau.

18. At first a reader does not see much similarity between the writings of Thoreau and Emerson, but after some close reading you realize that they thought alike to a considerable degree.

19. Students can become a member of the CQ Club by dating one of the campus queens.

20. A college student should try to learn about the philosophies of the Ancients as well as the Moderns, for you need a wide range of ideas in order to function in the complex modern world.

21. You should not be quick to accept one philosophy of life and to reject all others; be open-minded and form your opinions carefully.

22. A determinist believes that every occurrence is determined by a rigid sequence of cause-and-result and that therefore man does not have any free will. If they are right, then you can't help being quick or slow to make up your mind.

23. The modern physicist, however, does not believe in scientific determinism; they believe in something called Heisenberg's Principle of Uncertainty.

24. College students are often confused by all the conflicting opinions of the experts. Don't be dismayed, however, for you will soon learn that it is mostly a world of gray rather than of black and white.

25. The last three chairmen of the Ways and Means Committee have all been a conservative.

Unclear Reference

In language usage, **reference** is a general term used to indicate that one word gets it meaning from another word (or whole idea, in some cases). The most common kind of reference word is the pronoun, of which there are a variety of kinds, such as personal, demonstrative, and indefinite. The word or construction to which a pronoun refers is called its **antecedent.** Sometimes a pronoun has specific reference (such as

John being the antecedent of *he*), sometimes indefinite reference (such as in *they say* . . .), and sometimes reference to a whole idea (see below). Of course the use of a pronoun without clear reference reduces sentence clarity. Verb auxiliaries are also often used as reference words. For example, the modal auxiliary *could* in the sentence *I could* can have meaning only as it refers to a verb in the previous sentence, such as *can you leave now? Could* gets its meaning from *leave.* Unclear pronoun reference is rather common in student writing. Unclear auxiliary reference to verbs is not very common.

Reference is said to be **ambiguous** when there are two possible antecedents to which a pronoun may refer. Example:

> The Governor and the Attorney General are currently engaged in a bitter political dispute. *He* claims that *he* deceitfully betrayed *him* for a political gain.

As we read or listen to such sentences our minds keep such nouns as *Governor* and *Attorney General* stored in a signal position just in case a following pronoun must get its meaning from one of them. But in the above sentence the same pronouns may refer to either of the nouns, and thus the reference is ambiguous because we don't know which of the nouns to reissue from its signal position so that *he, he,* and *him* can have specific meaning. In such cases a writer often must abandon reference words to avoid ambiguity, as in this sentence:

> The Governor and the Attorney General are currently engaged in a bitter political dispute. The Governor claims that the Attorney General betrayed him for political gain.

The one pronoun *him* can be retained, for it reference is clear. Of course if the dispute had been between the Governor and his wife, pronouns could be used because our pronouns differ with gender. But actually, ambiguity in personal pronouns is not especially common, even in the work of inexperienced writers.

More common is ambiguity—or at least annoying indefiniteness—in the use of the pronoun *this* (and less often *that*) to refer to a whole idea. Reference to whole ideas is not wrong per se. For example, in the sentence

> I had an uncanny feeling that a surprising piece of world news would soon flash on my television screen, and *that* is exactly what happened,

the pronoun *that* (it could be *this*) quite properly refers to the entire idea of the first clause in the sentence. Such **inclusive reference** is very common in our language. It is often misused, however, producing ambiguity or irritating awkwardness. Here is a typical example:

> Parents are asking themselves if they should force their children to go to college. In most cases *this* is wrong.

The reference of *this* is ambiguous, for it can refer to the parents asking or to the forcing of the children. After the reader pauses and thinks, he is sure that the writer means the *this* to refer to forcing children to go to college. But if he has to pause to think out the reference (and gets irritated at the awkwardness), then the writing is bad.

Here are more examples of this annoying kind of use of the pronoun *this*:

> It was once thought that the atom was indivisible, but today this theory has been discarded. The atomic bomb has proved *this*.
> Our era has been called the Age of Anxiety, and perhaps *this* is true.
> There are many people today who feel that the human conscience is a reliable guide to moral conduct. *This statement* is fallacious.

In the first example, the *this* cannot refer to the first clause, and it makes little sense for it to refer to the second clause. What the writer wanted to say is that "the atom bomb has proved that the atom is divisible," but as the sentences are written the *this* simply cannot have that reference. The passage represents the worst kind of muddy, poorly thought-out writing. The second example is almost as bad, for the writer wants to say that our era *is* the Age of Anxiety, and the sentence is not constructed to deliver that meaning without discommoding the reader. And in the third example does *this statement* refer to the whole statement beginning with *There* . . . or just to the noun clause beginning with *that* . . . ? Such misuse of *this* as a reference word is quite common in student writing and represents a serious weakness in style.

Broad or **vague reference** occurs when there is no specific noun for a pronoun to refer to. (Actually, the use of any pronoun to refer to a whole idea, as in the case of *this* in the above discussion, can be called broad reference, but usually authorities use the term to mean faulty reference; thus we have used the term *inclusive reference* to mean the acceptable use of a pronoun to refer to a whole idea.) A common kind of broad or vague reference is the use of a pronoun to refer to an adjective. Examples:

> Maury was quite amorous, but he kept *it* under control.
> If our teen-agers are irresponsible, a great deal of *it* is due to their parents.

The reader's mind has to manufacture the nouns *amorousness* and *irre-sponsibility* for *it* and *it* to refer to. Though such faulty reference does not destroy clarity, it annoys good readers.

Also broad reference occurs when a pronoun refers to an implied noun. Example:

> I was surprised when I visited Hawaii to find that almost all of *them* speak English.

The pronoun *them* is intended to refer to *Hawaiians,* but since that noun does not appear in the sentence, the reference is broad. This kind of error in reference is not serious, but it is common and should be avoided; it shows that the writer has a poor understanding of sentence structure.

The relative pronoun *which* often refers to a whole idea rather than to a specific noun. Example:

> The City Council voted to increase property taxes, *which* enraged the Property Owners Association.

The *which* refers to the whole idea of the first clause. Some authorities have asserted that such use of *which* for broad reference is not good usage, but they are mistaken, for such sentences occur in untold numbers in the work of the best authors. When the meaning is perfectly clear, there is no rational basis for condemning the usage.

But sometimes such a use of *which* may be ambiguous, and then of course the sentence structure should be revised. Here is an example in which *which* may refer to the whole preceding clause or to a specific noun:

> John was thrown by a horse, *which* hurt him.

The sentence could mean that the throwing hurt John, in which case *which* refers to the whole idea in the first clause. Or it could mean that the horse hurt John after he had been thrown, in which case *which* refers to the noun *horse.* Such an ambiguous use of *which* should obviously be avoided.

Ambiguous reference may also occur with the use of verb auxiliaries. Here is an amusing example from an old movie announcement that was flashed on the screen:

> Those that have seen the entire show will please pass out so others may do so.

The *do so* is intended to refer to *have seen* (which it cannot do grammatically) but seems to refer to *pass out.* Here is another example from a book on bridge:

> How many people would fail to play the king in this position? Well, Sam Fry, Jr. didn't.

The auxiliary *didn't* is a reference word, but it is ambiguous here because the reader cannot tell whether it refers to *fail* or *play*.

EXERCISE 44.   Revising Unclear Reference

DIRECTIONS: Each of the following sentences or passages contains one or more errors in reference. Write a clear version of each and be prepared to explain why the reference is faulty.

1. The automobile has become in the space of a few years one of the largest industries in the United States today. This was not done overnight.
2. Although the car struck the palm tree with considerable force, it was not damaged.
3. He was discharged from the Army because of his father's death, but it did not help him improve his financial status.
4. This man was very intelligent, but it did not help him in the kind of work he entered.
5. Unfortunately, our party ignored the warnings of the independents, which turned out to be the right policy.
6. Our chairman told us to ignore the attacks of the extremists. This was difficult.
7. Professor Obon testified that the student had maliciously disrupted his class. That was a despicable thing to do.
8. Will those who have looked at the exhibit please leave so others may do so too?
9. If I can be a volunteer, I hope it will be possible to do so.
10. It is time the country developed some new industry, like the helicopter, for example.
11. The use of *ain't* is considered an error in usage because cultured people do not do so.
12. The conservative position has a lot of merit. Senator Taft was a good example of this.
13. I believe all Christians will be saved because my pastor explains it so clearly.
14. The speaker spent too much time on the introduction to his talk on sex education, which was boring.
15. The professors don't understand the young students' need to rebel. They are really just like they have always been.
16. The audience requested a repetition of his earlier talk, which he did.

17. The Rules Committee objected to the antidiscrimination section of the bill. This was unnecessary.
18. A student who doesn't know how to study properly will probably not pass, which this booklet is designed to prevent.
19. The Dean of Students was informed about our infraction of the rules. This was all too true.
20. Belief in one God meant a rejection of the Trinity, which Tom Paine did.

Run-on Sentences and Comma Splices

Sentences are separated from each other by periods or other end punctuation, and independent clauses in a compound sentence are either joined by coordinating conjunctions (sometimes with and sometimes without a comma) or separated by a semicolon. When two sentences have no punctuation between them, and no capital letter for the second one, the error called **run-on sentences** occurs. When two sentences have only a comma (no conjunction) between them, the error known as a **comma splice** occurs. These errors could be treated in the section on punctuation in Chapter 7 on the conventions of usage, but they are such serious errors and do so much to irritate good readers that we will treat them here under our main heading "Some Problems in Sentence Clarity and Correctness."

Usually these errors occur for one of two reasons: The first is carelessness or haste on the part of the writer. The second is a lack of **sentence sense** on the part of the writer—he doesn't *feel* the pause or break; in other words, he does not have a thorough understanding of the structure of his language. In the first case a careful rereading would reveal the flaw to the writer. In the second, more serious case the writer may be in need of considerable remedial work.

Here is a typical example of a run-on sentence:

> We didn't have anything special planned that night we just thought we'd wait to see what happened.

The fusion at ". . . night we . . ." causes the run-on. Apparently the student did not feel any pause between the sentences or he did not take the time to reread his work. Fortunately, not very many college students write such run-ons, but the error does occur occasionally.

A comma splice, on the other hand, occurs more often in student writing. Sometimes it may be due to carelessness or thoughtlessness. But if it occurs with any frequency in the work of a student, he is obviously in need of help.

Before we look at some typical examples of comma splices, let us make the important point that technical comma splices do appear rather frequently in the work of excellent professional authors. But they appear only when the two sentences (really independent clauses that could form a compound sentence) are quite short, are very closely related, and call for the reader not to pause as though a period or semicolon separated them. Here are examples:

> The bill to increase taxes didn't just fail, it was smothered.
> We weren't honored, we were exploited.

Such acceptable comma splices almost always occur only with short clauses, often with the same subject (that is, with the same meaning) for both clauses, and with a meaning that suggests that the first clause is simply encompassing the second, so to speak. No stigma can be attached to such acceptable comma splices, though a composition teacher may justifiably ask his students not to use such a construction on the grounds that otherwise he can't be sure that the students know what they are doing.

Unacceptable comma splices have none of the qualities specified for the acceptable ones just illustrated. Here are examples of very bad comma splices which show that the writer doesn't have sentence sense:

> We voted that $500 in student-body funds be given to the project, this would give us some say in how it would be carried out.
> We got our student evaluations of teachers published just yesterday, they will be distributed in the Student Union.
> I don't think it was fair for you to give that test, we didn't know we were supposed to know Chapter 5.

Such comma splices as these are serious errors. The subjects *this, they,* and *we* in the second clauses simply demand to be capitalized to begin a new sentence, unless a coordinating conjunction (such as *for* for the last example) is used. Also the clauses in these examples are longer than those in most acceptable comma splices.

The most commonly occurring kind of comma splice (and one not quite as serious a flaw as those just illustrated) is the one in which a comma rather than a semicolon is used between clauses connected by one of the so-called conjunctive adverbs: *however, moreover, therefore, nevertheless, consequently, furthermore,* and a few others. When one of these connectives is used to join two independent clauses, the clauses must be either punctuated as separate sentences or separated by a semicolon rather than a comma. The following sentences have comma splices.

> Senator Foreman was absent when his pork-barrel bill came to a vote, however, his colleagues saw that it passed safely.

The Watch and Ward Society banned *Three on a Honeymoon* from sale in Boston, moreover they announced that the movie based on the book would not be shown in Boston theaters.

English teachers are likely to have personal prejudices about little matters of usage, consequently, students often feel that they have been given conflicting rules.

A good rule of thumb to remember is that a semicolon (or a period) is necessary when the connective word can be shifted to the interior of the second clause.

Senator Foreman was absent when his pork-barrel bill came to a vote; his colleagues, however, saw that it passed safely.

The Watch and Ward Society banned *Three on a Honeymoon* from sale in Boston; they announced, moreover, that the movie based on the book would not be shown in Boston theaters.

English teachers are likely to have personal prejudices about little matters of usage; students, consequently, often feel that they have been given conflicting rules.

A few conjunctive adverbs, chiefly *hence* and *thus,* cannot be shifted to the interior of the second clauses. But for the most part the capacity of the connective to be shifted is a good guide to the punctuation needed. The connective *so* is in reality a conjunctive adverb, but it is treated by all authorities as a coordinating conjunction and does not require a semicolon, but usually a comma.

EXERCISE 45. Identifying and Correcting Comma Splices

DIRECTIONS: Some of the following constructions are comma splices and some are different and correct constructions. A few of the comma splices may be acceptable. List the numbers of the unacceptable comma splices and be prepared to explain how each can best be corrected. Tell why an acceptable comma splice is acceptable.

1. Having only $50,000 for campaign money, Fred Harris decided to withdraw from the race.
2. McCarthy organized a series of testimonial dinners, in this way he raised sufficient money to campaign.
3. They weren't Basques, they were French.
4. Emerson founded the Transcendental Club, it attracted famous people to Concord.
5. The book sale was a failure, since none of the books were pornographic.

6. We finally decided to increase membership dues, this would let us redecorate our meeting hall.

7. The midnight flight having been canceled, we could only wait for the morning flight.

8. We didn't realize that the trip was unnecessary, for we did not receive the telegram from headquarters.

9. My final grade in Calculus was a C, Professor Trembly had been very generous.

10. Old Bookworm Henderson's score on the test was 97, nobody else scored higher than 63.

11. We couldn't move, we were trapped.

12. The Advisory Council expelled all the demonstrators, therefore the attempt to free the school paper from all controls failed.

13. We sneaked back to our dormitory rooms, which was the sensible thing to do.

14. I want the lobster dinner, which do you want?

15. I decided to trade in my old car, its odometer already having turned past 100,000 miles.

16. We never know what the morrow will bring, that's what makes life so interesting.

17. Nature doesn't make men equal, society can try to correct some of the inequalities.

18. Do not lay up treasures on earth, for thieves may steal them.

19. Lay up treasures in Heaven, because thieves can't steal them.

20. We couldn't make it to the political rally, however, we got to the party after it.

21. The police fired warning shots over their heads, that brought them to a halt.

22. He not only agreed to the plan, he contributed a dollar.

23. My father's business went bankrupt, nevertheless I was able to stay in college.

24. Don't spend all your time studying, there's education in things other than books.

25. The Dean canceled all classes with fewer than ten students, furthermore he said that next year every class must have at least fifteen students.

Sentence Fragments

A serious kind of sentence error, at least in the eyes of many authorities on usage, is the **sentence fragment,** that is, a construction that is not a full sentence with a subject and predicate. But a distinction must be made between acceptable and unacceptable fragments. An unacceptable fragment is indeed a serious error; it is usually symptomatic of the writer's lack of understanding of the structure of his language.

In some kinds of professional writing intentional fragments abound and must be considered acceptable. A few newspaper columnists use many fragments with the intention of being lighthearted, "modern," cute, or maybe just different. Here is a small sample of fragmented writing from a well known columnist:

> Sunny days around the scatter. Irises blooming and dogwood budding. *Captain Farragut, the manx, is itching to stray.* No stopping that. More work for the animal warden. Ah, spring.

The italicized sentence is the only nonfragment in this opening paragraph of a column. Some readers get very tired of this kind of fragmentary folksiness. Also, nowadays it is the rule rather than the exception for advertising copy to be fragmentary. For example, these fragments were used in an ad for Bushmills Whiskey:

> Bushmills. Full of character. But not heavy-handed about it. Flavorful. But never overpowering. *Bushmills is unique.* Reflecting the past beguilingly, with a light and lively flavor that is all today.

The only sentence in this ad copy is italicized. All the other constructions are fragments. Many perceptive readers also get tired of this mannered type of advertising. But since the illustrated fragments in these examples were intentionally composed by professionals, they cannot be considered errors.

Acceptable fragments also appear in serious, and high-quality, professional writing. One kind is the answer to a rhetorical question (which is a question that the writer or speaker intends to answer himself). Here is an example:

> Why did the United States enter World War I? *To save democracy, of course.*

Also exclamations are acceptable fragments. Example:

> The White House tells us that agricultural information might be of value to our enemies. *Such scrupulous security officers!*

Such a fragment has a desired stylistic effect. Also transitions of various sorts appear as fragments in good writing. Examples:

> A case in point—Aristotle.
> But to get back to the main argument.
> And now to conclude.

But though fragments of these sorts are fully acceptable, some composition teachers ask their students to use no fragments, on the grounds that they may not be able to tell whether a student is writing a fragment deliberately or in error.

One common kind of unacceptable fragment is the **detached clause** or **phrase** that grammatically needs to be attached to the sentence preceding it. Here are some examples:

> Professor Steinmann wrote an unfavorable review of a colleague's monograph. *Since he found it contained errors in fact.*
>
> Professor McCall was wary of discussing Marxism in class. *Because several students had misquoted his comments on the Counter Reformation.*
>
> Professor Sackett agreed to give the Memorial Lecture on Elizabethan drama. *Having just finished writing a new book on Shakespeare's comedies.*
>
> William Faulkner's *Sanctuary* is a study of good versus evil. *Not just a cheap sensational novel.*

Since a period is a signal for a full pause, a reader at first assumes that he is beginning a new sentence when he comes to such a detached clause or phrase as those italicized in the examples. He stumbles in his reading because the writing is poor.

Another kind of unacceptable fragment is the construction in which a **nonfinite verb form** is used instead of a **finite verb.** A finite verb is one that can be used as the verb of a sentence predicate, such as *spoke, was expressed,* and *will arrive.* A nonfinite verb form is one that cannot be used as the main verb in a sentence, such as *speaking, having been,* and *being expressed.* Such nonfinite verb forms have other functions in sentences. When a nonfinite verb form is used as though it were finite, an unacceptable fragment occurs. Examples:

> The ballots being counted by a nonpartisan committee.
> The committee having been dissolved by executive fiat.
> The student wanting to express a dissenting opinion.

Because such fragments make readers stumble they are serious errors.

Occasionally a jumbled fragment will occur in student writing. Examples:

> Another brand of gun, not too accurate, but when cared for very long lasting.
> A kind of movie I like, though not too often, whether in color or black and white being a western.

Carelessness is the cause of such nonsentences as these. Good writers take care to review and revise their work.

EXERCISE 46.　**Identifying Sentence Fragments**

DIRECTIONS:　Identify by number the unacceptable fragments in the following constructions.

1. Linda had saved $500.
2. A sum large enough to purchase a used car.
3. She decided to shop first at the used-car lot of one of her uncles.
4. A genial crook known as Mournful Morty.
5. Because he was always moaning about his losses.
6. Linda knowing, since he was a crook, to be careful.
7. So she pretended that her father had sent her.
8. In order to find a second car for him, since he occasionally needed a second one.
9. Because Morty was a relative, no reason to trust him.
10. Old Mournful Morty decided to palm off on Linda a worthless clunker.
11. One which he had bought for $25 at a junk auction.
12. Its major parts—engine, body, wheels—all of which did not work very well.
13. However, Morty had fixed the car so that it would run well for two or three hundred miles.
14. Linda, therefore, induced to try out the "beautiful 1950 Kaiser Virginian."
15. A car which had remnants of luxurious upholstery, which seemed to have few squeaks, and which purred like a kitten.
16. Morty offered her the car for $300.
17. Linda, being thrilled at the idea of having cash left over, but had enough presence of mind left to offer only $250.
18. Which Morty took with much moaning, secretly gloating.
19. Linda drove home happily and explained the deal to her father.
20. Who was very doubtful of the wisdom of the purchase.
21. But Linda drove and drove and drove without trouble, which mystified her Uncle Morty, who began to moan about having lost money on that fine car he sold his niece.
22. And Linda's father, who felt that the money he expended on secret repairs for the Kaiser, was well spent.
23. Not to mention that the old car was becoming valuable as a classic.
24. Linda writing, as she had been advised, to the Classic Car Club.
25. With the result that she got $800 for the car, which gave Morty apoplexy.

CHAPTER 6

Diction

CHOSEN WORDS AND STYLE

Sentence structure and diction make style, and just as sentences can be composed instead of issued thoughtlessly from the writer's mind, so words can be **chosen.** In a very real sense, style is choice. True, in almost any sentence many if not most of the words are not really subject to choice. For example, in the preceding sentence no word was consciously chosen over another for stylistic purposes. We may say that most of the words we use in our writing are **mandated:** the idea expressed dictates the choice of most of the words. But because of the richness of our language and the complexity of ideas, a writer can exert considerable control over the words he uses, and his *chosen* words help create his style.

Here are two examples of chosen words nestled among mandated words (italics are supplied). First, a sentence from an anthropologist's defense of making his book humanistic rather than rigidly scientific:

Why is so much anthropological writing so *antiseptic*?

We do not know how long this writer thought before choosing *antiseptic* as his adjective, but it is obviously a chosen word, and it has its stylistic impact. Such a phrase as *carefully scientific* would not have had so rich an effect. Next is a sentence about fossil remains of a remote ancestor of the species *Homo sapiens*:

> At last, and from a *distance* of some 20 million years, could this be the first *faint whisper* of *humanity*?

The word *distance* to refer to time instead of space, the elegant metaphor *faint whisper* to mean "early beginnings," and the soulful word *humanity* instead of *Homo sapiens* overshadow the mandated words of the sentence to create a distinctive stylistic note. Word choice, then, along with sentence structure, fashions style.

LEVELS OF DICTION

Everyone who stops to think about it recognizes that he varies his language usage according to the speaking or writing situation he is in. For example, at the dinner table with his visiting minister, a student will probably take much more care with his language usage than he does when he is strictly among friends of his own age and sex. In writing, too, his language usage in a friendly letter to a peer would vary from that in a letter of application. But if asked to define *language usage,* he would probably falter or be vague. There are four categories of language usage: **pronunciation, spelling, grammar,** and **diction.** Spelling is not involved in conversation and pronunciation is not involved in writing. Since this is a composition text, we can ignore pronunciation. Spelling is simply spelling and is covered in the next chapter. Grammar has to do with such functions as agreement, reference, tense, mood, voice, case, and other aspects of inflection and with sentence structure, which includes punctuation; these matters are considered in Chapters 5 and 7. Diction has to do with individual word choice, and it is the **level of diction** that varies according to speaking and writing situations.

But just what does the word *level* mean in this usage? Perhaps the best definition is that it has to do with "the appropriateness of word choice according to the importance of the speaking or writing situation." This definition implies—and, according to linguists, correctly implies— that no one word is *linguistically* better than any other with the same or approximately the same meaning. For example, as words, *stuck-up* and [a certain four-letter word] are not at all inferior to *egotistical* and *dung.* They just belong in situations of differing importance (the importance depending on the value judgment of the speaker or writer). Linguists take the same view of grammar, too. For example, every linguist of professional standing will agree that *he don't know no better* is as good *grammatically* as *he doesn't know any better,* since the former is the natural grammar of many native speakers. It is only *socially* that the latter construction is better, and linguists agree wholeheartedly with that social (rather than scientific) judgment.

The point of view that we have just expressed (and stand by) has for many years been the cause of arguments, often acrimonious, between linguists and certain professors and authors who think our language is decaying. These guardians of our language think, for example, that *made a mistake* is intrinsically better language than *goofed,* and some of them stay outraged that professional linguists (who are scientists) should deny the superiority of the former. These purists charge that the linguists are contributing to the debasement of our language by sanctioning *any* usage of clear meaning, even *ain't.*

But the linguists have been misunderstood by the purists. When the linguists claim that no one word of clear meaning is linguistically either better or worse than another, they do not at all mean that any word is appropriate for any situation. They recognize that value judgments must come into play in word choice and that in certain situations certain words are very bad indeed. They also are quite aware that *artistically* (that is, in the creation of style in all kinds of literature, including exposition and persuasion) certain word choices are much superior to others, since value judgments again must come into play. The linguists themselves take great care with the diction in their own scholarly writings. The principle they subscribe to is that a word is appropriately used *if it does not call attention to itself as being out of place.* (Of course the phrase *out of place* must include no place at all. For example, some purists still consider the word *finalize* out of place in all writing or speaking.)

But since value judgments are involved in anyone's appraisal of the importance of a writing or speaking situation or of the artistic merit of a piece of writing, there will inevitably be differences of opinion even among the most highly educated as to the proper level of diction in any one particular situation. For example, a word such as *shakedown* might call itself to the attention of one reader as out of place but not to another reader. Or as an extreme example, the great General George S. Patton, Jr. thought [the aforementioned four-letter word] quite appropriate in a highly important speaking situation and did not hesitate to use it instead of *dung* or *feces.* But at that time almost every other speaker of English of moderate education would have thought the General's level of diction too low in that instance. Nowadays, however, even the high-class, intellectual magazines such as *Harper's* and *The Atlantic* occasionally admit some of the four-letter words to their pages, usually as part of a quotation from some person of importance. Language changes, and taste in language changes. But when we speak later of colloquial language and slang, remember that even English teachers will not always agree as to the appropriateness of various words and expressions in particular writing situations.

We should also mention here—though it is perhaps obvious—that many if not most of the words in a piece of writing are not subject to choice, or are subject to little choice, and that therefore *level of appropriateness of diction* cannot be applied to them. Such words include all of our structure words (such as determiners, prepositions, and connectives) and many, many, common nouns, verbs, adjectives, and adverbs, such as *animal, to continue, large,* and *soon.* But many words are subject to choice, and thus there is a place for the study of levels of diction in a composition course.

The phrase *levels of diction* implies that there should be names for various levels, but no generally agreed upon systematic terminology has been established. A favorite system of classification of some decades ago, and one still used by some authorities, is the three-level classification **vulgate, informal** (or **general**), and **formal.** But this classification will not do for levels of diction, for *vulgate* means the whole language usage of unschooled or poorly educated people, and thus includes grammar (*him and me ain't coming*), pronunciation (*this widder's chillun*), and spelling (*wimmin*) but not really word choice to any degree, for those people have very limited vocabularies. And though *informal* and *formal* refer to diction and are useful terms, they do not include the large amount of slang in our language or such diction as jargon. So that classification is flawed. **Standard** and **nonstandard** are useful terms applying to language usage, too, but they by no means can encompass levels of diction. However, terms that are reasonably descriptive and useful are available.

But before we mention the few terms we will use to designate levels of diction (*appropriateness of diction* is just as useful a term), we should mention and briefly comment on **usage labels** as they appear in dictionaries. A **subject label** for a definition in a dictionary specifies the field of learning or occupation that the definition applies to. A **usage label** tells something about the nature of the word (or one of its definitions) so far as its usability is concerned. A number of usage labels commonly appear in the best dictionaries. The label **obsolete** means that a word (or one of its definitions) is no longer in use. For example, *prester,* meaning "priest," is no longer in use. **Archaic** is a label applied to words now obsolete except for special uses, such as in church ritual and poetry. *Thou* for *you* and *silvern* for *silvery* are archaic. The label **dialectal** is used to denote words in good usage only in restricted localities. For example, in Appalachia *to angle* is still used to mean "to walk slowly without purpose." You need not concern yourself with obsolete, archaic, or dialectal diction. It is not likely that you would have use for any obsolete or archaic words; a true dialectal word might charm a composition teacher.

Substandard is a label applied to vulgate forms, such as *drownded* for *drowned*. **Nonstandard** is applied to a few words that have no reason for being, such as *irregardless* for *regardless*. **Vulgar** applies mostly to the notorious four-letter words, one of the least offensive of which is *snot*. Also British, Canadian, and Australian usages are often labeled. And **slang** (which we will discuss later) is a label no one can really define accurately but that applies to racy words and expressions that lie well below what is generally considered standard diction. You should be concerned with, and generally avoid, words to which labels in this paragraph are applied.

One usage label—**colloquial**—is conspicuously absent from the above cataloging. The word has nothing to do with local, as many people think. **Localisms** or **regionalisms** are labeled dialectal. *Colloquial* comes from the Latin *colloquium,* meaning "conversation." Thus a colloquialism originally was a word or expression in good usage (in **any** locality) in spoken language but not in writing. Now *colloquial* just refers to words or expressions suitable only for informal usage, both spoken and written. We omitted this usage label because in 1961 the third edition of Merriam-Webster's *New International Dictionary* abandoned the label on the grounds that people misunderstood it by thinking that a colloquialism was in some way tainted and should be avoided by educated people; actually, colloquialisms are fully acceptable in many writing and speaking situations that confront all of us. This decision on the part of America's best-known dictionary brought howls of rage from purists who were sure that the dictionary was collaborating with linguists to debase our language. In fact the controversy still rages. Two other excellent dictionaries—*The American Heritage Dictionary of the English Language* and *The Random House Dictionary of the English Language*—quietly substituted the label **informal** for **colloquial** in order to stay out of the controversy. Still, the word *colloquial* remains a useful one, and we will consider it again below. Colloquialisms are such words and phrases as *know-how* for *technical skill* and *split up* for *separate* (as man from wife).

But what terms should we use in discussing levels or appropriateness of diction in college writing? The following should suffice: **slang** and **jargon** as nouns and **colloquial** or **informal, general** or **standard, formal,** and **pretentious** as adjectives. Let's consider these terms briefly before we make general statements about desirable levels of diction.

Slang is the kind of diction most likely to interest students and to raise questions in their minds and in instructors' minds as to appropriateness of usage. *Slang* is one of those words that everyone understands but that no one can define adequately. In general, it is a level of diction below the colloquial and one that has a strong (if undeserved) aura of disrespectability about it. It is usually the result of linguistic inventiveness, especially of young and lively persons who want fresh, original, pungent, or racy terms with which they can rename ideas, actions, and objects they feel strongly about. In effect, it is the result of a combination of linguistic irreverence and a reaction against staid, stuffy, pompous, pretentious, or colorless diction.

Most slang terms are derived from, or give new meanings to, standard words. For example, *heller* (a noisy, wild person), *kisser* (mouth or face), and *ripsnorter* (a noisy or violent person or thing) are not completely original creations but are coinages from common words. Similarly, *dirt* (slanderous gossip), *pass* (an amorous overture), *off* (mentally unbalanced), and *railroad* (to rush a decision through a committee quickly) are slang only when used for nonstandard meanings. Other, but much fewer, slang words seem to be new creations or only vaguely connected with established words. Some examples are *zit* for *pimple, floozy* for *low-class female,* and *goop* for *sticky substance.* As new applications for established words or as new creations, slang terms originate as nonstandard diction because they run counter to established, traditional usage. For example, a word coined out of a Greek root to name a new chemical is not slang because it is derived from a respectable tradition and fulfills a new need. But the coinage of a word like *pooped* to mean "fully exhausted" does not follow a tradition of respectable language change and fulfills a demand only for a racy or pungent word to replace an established one and thus is slang. The precise origin of a slang word is almost never known, yet each term must have had a first use by one individual. New slang terms, if they catch on, spread very rapidly.

Slang varies regionally, by class structure, and by occupation. Much New York slang would not be understood in Los Angeles. The slang of ghetto dwellers, college students, middle-class matrons, taxi drivers, merchant seamen, drug pushers, and so on also varies, though there is of course much overlapping in all these categories. The lifetime of most true slang words is short; they either drop from use soon or rise on the scale of respectability to a standard level. For example, it is unlikely that the slang terms *peachy keen* or *zorch* of some years ago are still in use. On the other hand, many people would be surprised to learn that *mob, scoundrel, bored, nice,* and many other such words were once slang. But occasionally a slang term will remain slang for generations or centuries. For example, *gab* was slang before 1400, a woman was called a *broad* or a *piece* in the 1600s, and *high* meaning "drunk" originated in the eighteenth century.

But what about the use of slang in college writing? Is it to be permitted or not? A composition instructor is perfectly justified in asking his students not to use slang in their writing, on the grounds that such use might get them into bad habits. But it is a fact that slang is occasionally used by professional writers publishing in such magazines as *Harper's* and *The Atlantic,* which fact would seem to suggest that slang is not per se out of place in student writing. Here are some examples of the use of slang in intellectual magazines:

> The Globe *dishes up* the fattest menu of canned goods. (Actually, this whole sentence could be called slang.)
> Nikita Khrushchev once again emerged as *top dog* in the Communist orbit.
> They come up with viruses, which eventually, and predictably, become *old hat* when the professional men get going on some new and fascinating diversion like the current cholesterol *kick.*

The articles from which these sentences came were written for the highly educated members of our society.

But a most important point is that the use of slang in such articles is very sparing and is consciously intended to produce a certain effect. The articles from which such sentences come use a high level of diction occasionally flavored with a racy slang word. And only a small percentage of slang words are racy and pungent enough to be so used. It is true that in the past quarter of a century experts in the study of language have become much more tolerant of slang than were their predecessors. For example, the famous editor H.L. Mencken wrote at length and learnedly of the value of such slang creations as *rubberneck, lame-duck, cow-catcher, to gum-shoe,* and *poppycock.* He and other students of language thought, and many still think, that some slang words enliven the language and keep it growing. But also all people knowledgeable about language realize that much if not most slang is limp, uninspired, and unfit for writing of even an informal nature. Such terms as *guys and gals, real cool, icky, out of sight,* and so on are not likely to enliven any piece of writing.

So in general we express the dictum that you should avoid slang except when you think a particularly racy and lively slang term will enrich rather than dampen your style. For example, good use might be made of such terms as *burn artist* (someone who tries to do you out of something), *bull jive* (misinformation), *psyched out* (in an abnormal mental state), *passion pit* (drive-in theater), and so on.

The term **jargon** has several meanings, the most common one being "long words, circumlocutions, and generally hard-to-comprehend language, often connected with a specialized field of learning, such as sociology." Though college students (unless they are graduate students who have been stylistically corrupted) seldom use jargon, we will give a sample of it to show how it obscures clarity. Here is the opening paragraph of a college textbook:

> The proper understanding of the transcultural equivalences of all cultures begins with the sociology of knowledge. The sociology of knowledge is concerned not simply with such forms of deception as false dichotomization, the all-or-nothing mistake, by which binary choices between easy extremes obscure the value of contextual clues in the formulation of rational decisions. It concerns itself also with the situational determinants of binary decisions.

It is quite likely that the student-users of this text were lost forever after this first paragraph. Could the author have written clearly without sacrificing meaning? Or was he expressing ideas so complex that only this kind of jargon could contain them? Undoubtedly he could have written more clearly. He could have begun the paragraph in this way:

> To properly understand that any culture is equal to all other cultures in its capacity to serve the needs of its own cultural system, one must begin with the sociology of knowledge, which may be defined as the study of how knowledge is disseminated in a society.

But evidently this author was just not interested in making himself understood. The dictum is clear: do not mistakenly think that using jargon will cause your readers to be favorably impressed; they may only be confused, or even *turned off*.

Colloquial language is not out of place in college writing, and yet usually your writing will be better if you choose diction on a level higher than colloquial, unless you use a colloquialism for the same purpose you might use a slang word—to enliven your style. But remember that opinions of experts will often differ as to the level of a particular word. For example, *ham* (pretentious or egotistic actor) might be considered slang by one person, colloquial by another, and general or standard by another. But here are samples of colloquial language that you probably should avoid in your writing: *kid* (child), *down in the mouth* (depressed), *go places* (make a quick and easy success), *chew the rag* (engage in a general discussion), *dig* (a calculated insult), *join up* (enlist), and *ride* (to torment or tease). (Some of these might be considered slang by some people.) But we cannot categorically say such terms should be avoided in college writing. *A most important point is* *that level of diction is usually not as important as the use of precise, vigorous, and concrete diction,* as discussed later in this chapter. For example, in writing about the theater a student (or professional, for that matter) might very well prefer the slang or colloquial term *corn* to the standard term *sentimental drama.* Value judgments must enter into choice of diction.

The terms **general** or **standard** as applied to levels of diction refer to words and expressions that no one could consider out of place in any normal writing or speaking situation and that do not smack of pretension or snobbery on the part of the writer or speaker. For example, *boxing skill* as applied to a prize fighter is general or standard diction, whereas *pugilistic artistry* would strike most people as pretentious. Or, for another example, *divided* is certainly standard diction, whereas *divvied up* would strike most people as being out of place in any but the most informal situation. General or standard diction is the level that you should cultivate most. It is the level of diction used in textbooks such as this one.

Formal diction is not easy to define or illustrate. It lies only slightly above what we have called general or standard diction. Diction that rises (perhaps that is the wrong word) conspicuously above the general usually becomes pretentious. Generally, formal diction is that used in situations in which the writer or speaker wants to avoid familiarity between himself and his audience. (For example, in this text I have not at all tried to give an impression of being separated from my readers, and hence the diction cannot be called formal.) Also, formal diction may be said to be on the highest level possible without giving the impression that the writer is pretentious or snobbish. And finally, formal diction does not usually create the ease and naturalness of style that general diction can. Here is a sentence that can fairly be said to typify formal diction:

> Thus I venture to think that the pretensions of our modern Humanists to the possession of the monopoly of culture and to the exclusive inheritance of the spirit of antiquity must be abated, if not abandoned.—Thomas Henry Huxley

As this sentence illustrates, it is not just individual words but a certain stylistic use of them that creates formal diction, for all the words in the above sentence fit into the category of general or standard diction. We recommend that you not try to make your writing especially formal, for in trying to be formal you are likely to end up with a stilted style. **Semiformal** is perhaps a good label for the desirable level of college writing.

Pretentious diction is that which makes use of words too sesquipedalian (or "big") for the situation under discussion. It marks the writer as snobbish and as contemptible in his effort to be impressive. For example, this sentence typifies pretentious diction:

> The sales-potential analyst and the direct-contact representative bifurcated their monetary accumulation.

In general diction the sentence would read

> The canvasser and the salesman divided their earnings.

Needless to say, you should avoid all semblance of pretentious diction.

Now, what general comments can we make about the proper level of diction for college writing? Some students report that they are told to just write as they talk. This is not good advice for beginning writers. Just as sentence structure in good writing is more complex than that in casual conversation, so the level of diction in good writing is higher than that in idle chatter. Writing is different from talking; if it were not, presumably there would be no need for teaching composition. One noted linguist in commenting on the differences between writing and talking said that "a composition style foreign to beginning students— whether foreign because of its elegance, or its technical nature, or its contrast with oral style—must be learned *as a foreign language* is learned."[1] Thus you should be aware that the sentence structure and diction of ordinary talk will not suffice to create effective composition.

Yet it is very desirable that exposition and persuasion have the ease and naturalness of conversation. This kind of writing should not sound strained or stilted, and it should not give the impression that it caused its author great labor (though it usually does). It should sound like high-level conversation even though it isn't conversation. Sentence composition (as discussed in Chapter 5) partly creates the ease and naturalness of a good style. But the use of a high level of diction— that is, words not commonly used in casual conversation—does not diminish the natural, conversational-like quality of good style. In fact, the use of a high level of diction enhances the natural quality of good style because an experienced reader is accustomed to a high-level vocabulary in his reading; low-level diction only irritates him. *Therefore you should use the highest level of diction you have at your command, provided it sounds natural and unpretentious.* Words like *smart, two cents' worth, high-faluting,* and *real useful* usually sound awkward or unnatural, whereas their higher-level counterparts *precocious, contribution, prestigious,* and *invaluable* can contribute to the ease and naturalness of a style.

---

[1] Kenneth Pike, "A Linguistic Contribution to Composition," *College Composition and Communication,* XV (May 1964), page 82. (The italics are the author's.)

But a natural style, unfortunately, does not come naturally. The ease of a good style is really *artful* ease, for the writer must deliberately try to achieve it. It is a truism for experts on style that the more natural and smooth a piece of writing sounds, the more its author worked to make it seem unlabored. It follows that you should make a conscious and sustained effort to increase the range of your writing vocabulary and sentence structure and to utilize this range as you work at making your style fluent, comfortable, at times even a little elegant.

However, let use repeat that level of diction is often a consideration secondary to precision, vigor, and concreteness, and thus at times you may use colloquial or slang terms with desirable effect. But take care not to shift levels indiscriminately within a piece of writing. Suppose you were asked to write a paper on a college dramatic performance; you would not begin with such phrases as "carefully coached stage business," "precise and distinct delivery of lines," "gifted mimicry," and "exotic props" and then suddenly use such phrases as "cut it sharp," "a honey of an entrance," "wowed 'em with his ad-lib cracks at the college brass," and "jazzed-up gimmicks." Such incongruity of phrasing would be quite distracting to perceptive readers. However, an occasional brief drop in level of diction can be effective. For example:

> His carefully measured delivery of the Queen Mab speech was exquis-
> itely lyrical until he *cracked his jaw* on "Her whip, of cricket's bone;
> the lash, of film."

The incongruity of a momentary shift of this sort can be engaging rather than distracting. But such a shift must be consciously made; it will sel-dom be effective if it occurs accidentally. Indeed, our final dictum about choice of level of diction is: *Think about it.*

EXERCISE 47. **Investigating Terms Relating to Diction**

DIRECTIONS: Through consulting two or three good diction-aries, show with examples why the following terms do not belong in the categories of slang or colloquialisms. Discuss whether they have a place in college writing.

1. jargon (definitions other
   than that on page 216)
2. argot
3. cant
4. gibberish
5. idioms

6. lingo
7. shoptalk
8. vernacular
9. vulgate
10. lingua franca

EXERCISE 48.   **Investigating Low-Level Diction in High-Level Writing**

DIRECTIONS: Scan an entire issue of either *Harper's* or *The Atlantic* to see if you can find words that you consider below the general or standard level. Copy the sentences they are in and be prepared to comment on the usage.

EXERCISE 49.   **Comparing Usage Labels**

DIRECTIONS: Choose ten slang terms that you think have been around a long time, such as *hogwash, booze, crummy,* and *chicken.* Check them in at least three collegiate dictionaries and list all inconsistencies in usage labels that you find.

EXERCISE 50.   **Judging Slang**

DIRECTIONS: This exercise has little to do with composition but may be entertaining. Following is a list of slang terms used by college students in Central California in the early '70s. Which do you know? What are their meanings? What is your judgment of the desirability of their use in college writing? Which do you think might rise on the scale of respectability and become colloquial or general words?

flake off	scratch	bug off
kill it	dig it	pole
shag	split	rattle your cage
bummer	bitching	chopper
out of sight	hat up	rip off
zit	sewer wisp	bull jive
hang up	scutter trash	scarf
peel out	bird out	crash
jacked up	train time	good call
boss	clicking	chop
slick	foxie lady	bombed out
dudly	skate	tuff
cat nip	hummer	sacked out
heavy	rap	bag
up tight	plastic	baked
pig	gross out	fuzz
garbage wagon	make out	tracks
burn artist	trainpuller	wolfman Jack

travel agent	hooked	bread
Mexican sweat	switched on	junk
cookie	camp	jam
wheelie	pop	quail

PRECISE AND VIGOROUS DICTION

In our previous section on levels of diction, we were chiefly concerned with the appropriateness—that is, the social respectability—of word choice. For example, though there is no intrinsic inferiority, or even offensiveness, in *the culprit clammed up when the fuzz came,* most people would consider its level of diction inappropriate in most writing— that is, they would think that the writer did not show good manners. But appropriateness is not the only desirable quality in word choice. Equally important, and perhaps at times more important, are **precision** and **vigor of diction.**

A precise word is one that says **exactly** what the writer means. For example, if a candidate for president said, "I pledge to renew our country's role of leadership," what does he mean by *leadership*? Is it a precise word that all listeners would understand the same, or is it a rather vague word that the politician wants each listener to interpret in his own way so that he will approve of the speech? Would the candidate have expressed himself more precisely if he had said, "I pledge that our country will again be the strongest military power in the world," or "I pledge that economically the United States will again dominate world trade and monetary exchange," or other such sentences? The answer is, of course, that he could have chosen more precise diction than *leadership.* Though words like *leadership* have their place in our language and sometimes are quite the proper words to use, in general a writer of exposition or persuasion should be as precise as he can in expressing his meaning.

A vigorous word is one that has **strength of meaning** and **strength of sound.** For example, compare these three sentences:

The man I sat by was offensive.
The man I sat by had body odor.
The man I sat by stank.

First, precision is involved here; the second two sentences are more precise than the first, for *offensive* is a general word that can apply to many different kinds of situations. But vigor also is involved in the diction of these sentences. The word *stank* simply has more strength of meaning and strength of sound than *offensive* or *body odor.* It might offend a reader who wants only delicacy of language, and therefore in certain writing or speaking situations might be intentionally avoided, but it is the most vigorous of the three terms. And for the most part, choice of vigorous as well as precise diction improves style. Following are some principles of word choice that lead to more precise and vigorous diction.

Specific and General Words

The more **specific** a word is, the more precise it is; the more **general,** the less precise. A general word covers many different varieties of whatever the word applies to; a specific word covers only one or a few varieties—there are degrees of specificity. For example, here are three sentences in descending order from the general to the specific:

> An animal hurt a person.
> A dog bit a boy.
> A boxer nipped Freddie Spivak.

Even this simple paradigm illustrates the value of specific diction. It shows that the more clearly a writer specifies the particular variety of whatever he is mentioning, the more exact his meaning becomes. Note that there are degrees of specificity in verbs as well as nouns.

More precision, and often vigor, can be achieved, then, by using specific rather than general words. Here are some illustrative pairs:

> another thing
> another idea, accident, proposal, habit, gambit
>
> another factor
> another cause, detail, point of view, aspect, character trait
>
> a book
> a novel, biography, anthology, textbook of chemistry
>
> bad weather
> a tornado, cyclone, a windstorm, a bitter or foggy day
>
> a game
> bridge, poker, tiddly winks, post office, soccer
>
> illness
> mumps, cancer, respiratory ills, undiagnosed aches and pains
>
> good looks
> trim figure, flawless complexion, regular features, even teeth
>
> a professional man
> doctor, lawyer, dentist, professor, confidence man
>
> made a noise
> rattled, boomed, scratched, thundered, whistled

talked

jabbered, rambled, gossiped, preached, inquired, lectured

misbehaved

stole cookies, broke a chair, teased a cat, refused to wash

Choosing the specific rather than the general word requires thought on the part of the writer. Even the most experienced writers often ponder the choice of a word, and also often change a word for more precision when revising their work. Legend has it that the American poet Emily Dickinson once went through a choice of twenty-six words before she got the exactly right one in one of her poems.

Among the most common offenders in **nonspecific diction** are the adjectives that we use for **general approval** or **disapproval** without specifying a particularity that causes our attitude. Here are the most common ones:

General Approval	*General Disapproval*
swell	lousy
terrific	terrible
nice	awful
fine	wretched
splendid	horrid
grand	foul
marvelous	abysmal
wonderful	horrible

Most of these words once had specific meanings. For example, *wonderful* originally was applied to an event or object that struck wonder or amazement in the viewer, and *terrific* once meant causing great fear. Now these are generalized terms of approval that do not specify just what characteristic the writer or speaker is praising. So with all the words in both columns. They are of little value when used for their generalized meanings.

The nonspecific adjectives in the above lists should be avoided in favor of **specific adjectives** such as the following:

Specific Approval	*Specific Disapproval*
reliable	irritable
valid	false
skillful	untrustworthy
adept	boring
stimulating	awkward
agreeable	repulsive
cheerful	headachy
vivacious	distressing

Specific Approval	Specific Disapproval
sympathetic	insipid
helpful	dull
moving	stereotyped
touching	childish
sweet	malodorous
kind	monotonous
effective	sentimental

Specific words like these are much to be preferred over the indiscriminate terms of blanket approval or disapproval. Remember, to increase the precision of your diction, you need not only to learn new words, such as *stereotyped,* but also to **think** about your word choices so that you can make the best use of the vocabulary you already have.

EXERCISE 51. **Using Specific Diction**

DIRECTIONS: Improve the precision and vigor of the following sentences by replacing general diction with specific.

1. An animal injured my property.
2. A book led to my taking the job.
3. The reading material affected my attitude.
4. The injury was caused by a blunt instrument.
5. The accident resulted in part of his clothes being damaged.
6. The man treated his wife badly.
7. The tree was diseased.
8. The men talked about the issues.
9. A workman damaged a piece of art.
10. Just one thing about the affair bothered me.

Concrete and Abstract Words

As we have seen, specific words are more precise and vigorous than general words. Similarly, **concrete words** tend to be more precise and vigorous than **abstract words.** A concrete word is one that names an object that really exists and can be perceived by the human senses. An abstract word names a quality that an object can have, but that cannot be detached from that object so that it has a separate existence of its own. For example, the word *girl* names something you can see or touch. Therefore it is a concrete word. But the word *beauty* does not name a thing that you can see or touch by itself. It does not have an independent existence; something or someone must be beautiful if beauty is to exist. So *beauty* is an abstract word.

The word *abstract* comes from the Latin *abstrahere,* meaning "to draw from or separate." Thus abstract words are those that express qualities apart from the things that have the qualities. Perhaps this concept can be made clearer with an illustration from *Alice in Wonderland.* Do you remember that Alice saw a Cheshire cat that had the ability gradually to fade away? As Alice looked at the cat, it gradually faded until nothing but its grin was left. The grin was just there without the cat. That grin was abstract—literally separated from the object that owned it. Thus a grinning cat is concrete, but a grin by itself is abstract.

We use abstract words in almost all of our utterances. Here are a few of the common ones we depend upon:

courage	greed
glory	hate
fame	sympathy
goodness	jealousy
patriotism	cowardice
devotion	fear
love	despair
honor	hope
pride	foolishness
humility	wisdom
cunning	ignorance
piety	faith
generosity	anger
pain	remorse
sweetness	pity
kindness	cruelty
joy	snobbishness
contentment	treachery
charm	ambition

The list could be almost endless.

Words like these are indispensable in our language. They are good words and should not necessarily be avoided. However, an overuse of abstractions weakens the precision and vigor of writing because abstractions cannot create mental images for the reader nearly as successfully as concrete words can. As we read, our minds try to picture (to form images of) what we read. Thus if we read that General Trotter is patriotic, we try to visualize what he is, and we have a hard time. The image will at best be vague in our minds. But if we read that he pledges allegiance to the flag each morning and spends one-third of his salary on savings bonds, we have actions we can picture in our minds. Thus writing that names objects and actions is usually more precise and vigorous than writing that names abstractions. The difference lies in the varying capacity of words to form images in our minds.

We do to a certain degree form images in our minds when we read abstract words. We do so by relating the abstraction to some concrete object or action or situation that we have experienced. Suppose we hear the sentence "Boris is very *courageous*" but nothing further about Boris. We then interpret the abstraction *courageous* according to our own experiences and may think that Boris is not afraid to fight. But the speaker may have had in mind that Boris is willing to disagree with his professors in class. Thus the more abstractly one writes, the more he allows his readers to make their own interpretation of his words. For example, when the American poet William Cullen Bryant ended his famous poem *Thanatopsis* with "So live . . . By an unfaltering trust. . . ." he allowed each reader to make his own interpretation as to what he should trust, for the poem makes no mention whatsoever as to what should be trusted. Millions of readers have just assumed that Bryant meant a trust in the Christian God, but at the time he wrote the poem he was something of a Deist (Deism not being orthodox Christianity). Obviously, the more concrete writing is, the more precise it is; and the more precise it is, the more the writer controls his reader's understanding.

To illustrate the value of concrete words in expository writing, a speech by Chief Seattle, one of the great American Indian chiefs, is reproduced below. This speech has considerable literary merit, much of which is due to the use of concrete language. Since the Indians lived close to the earth, it was, perhaps, natural for them to avoid abstractions and to rely on concrete terms to deliver their meaning. As an exercise for this section, point out concrete words in Chief Seattle's speech.

Message to the White Chief

by Chief Seattle

Yonder sky that has wept tears of compassion upon my people for centuries untold, and which to us appears changeless and eternal, may change. Today is fair. Tomorrow may be overcast with clouds. My words are like the stars which never change. Whatever Seattle says the great chief at Washington can rely upon with as much certainty as he can upon the return of the sun or the seasons. The White Chief says that Big Chief at Washington sends us greetings of friendship and good-will. That is kind of him for we know he has little need of our friend-ship in return. His people are many. They are like the grass that covers vast prairies. My people are few. They resemble the scattering trees of a storm-swept plain. The great, and I presume—good, White Chief sends us word that he wishes to buy our lands but is willing to allow us enough to live comfortably. This indeed appears just, even generous, for the Red Man no longer has rights that he need respect, and the offer may be wise also, as we are no longer in need of an extensive country. . . . I will not dwell on, nor mourn over, our untimely decay, nor reproach our paleface brothers with hastening it, as we too may have been somewhat to blame.

Youth is impulsive. When our young men grow angry at some real or imaginary wrong, and disfigure their faces with black paint, it denotes that their hearts are black, and then they are often cruel and relentless, and our old men and old women are unable to restrain them. Thus it has ever been. Thus it was when the white men first began to push our forefathers further westward. But let us hope that the hostilities between us may never return. We would have everything to lose and nothing to gain. Revenge by young men is considered gain, even at the cost of their own lives, but old men who stay at home in times of war, and mothers who have sons to lose, know better.

Our good father at Washington—for I presume he is now our father as well as yours, since King George has moved his boundaries further north—our great good father, I say, sends us word that if we do as he desires he will protect us. His brave warriors will be to us a bristling wall of strength, and his wonderful ships of war will fill our harbors so that our ancient enemies far to the northward—the Hydas and Tsimpsians—will cease to frighten our women, children and old men. Then in reality will he be our father and we his children. But can that ever be? Your God is not our God! Your God loves your people and hates mine. He folds His strong and protecting arms lovingly about the paleface and leads him by the hand as a father leads his infant son—but He has forsaken His red children—if they really are His. Our God, the Great Spirit, seems also to have forsaken us. Your God makes your people wax strong every day. Soon they will fill the land. Our people are ebbing away like a rapidly receding tide that will never return. The white man's God cannot love our people or He would protect them. They seem to be orphans who can look nowhere for help. How then can we be brothers? How can your God become our God and renew our prosperity and awaken in us dreams of returning greatness? If we have a common heavenly father He must be partial—for He came to his paleface children. We never saw Him. He gave you laws but He had no word for His red children whose teeming multitudes once filled this vast continent as stars fill the firmament. No; we are two distinct races with separate origins and separate destinies. There is little in common between us.

To us the ashes of our ancestors are sacred and their resting place is hallowed ground. You wander far from the graves of your ancestors and seemingly without regret. Your religion was written upon tables of stone by the iron finger of your God so that you could not forget. The Red man could never comprehend nor remember it. Our religion is the traditions of our ancestors—the dreams of our old men, given them in solemn hours of night by the Great Spirit; and the visions of our sachems; and it is written in the hearts of our people.

Your dead cease to love you and the land of their nativity as soon as they pass the portals of the tomb and wander way beyond the stars. They are soon forgotten and never return. Our dead never forget the beautiful world that gave them being.

Day and night cannot dwell together. The Red Man has ever fled the approach of the White Man, as the morning mist flees before the morning sun. However, your proposition seems fair and I think that my people will accept it and will retire to the reservation you offer them. Then we will dwell apart in peace, for the words of the Great White Chief seem to be the words of nature speaking to my people out of dense darkness.

It matters little where we pass the remnant of our days. They will not be many. A few more moons; a few more winters—and not one of the descendants of the mighty hosts that once moved over this broad land or lived in happy homes, protected by the Great Spirit, will remain to mourn over the graves of a people once more powerful and hopeful than yours. But why should I mourn at the untimely fate of my people? Tribe follows tribe, and nation follows nation, like the waves of the sea. It is the order of nature, and regret is useless. Your time of decay may be distant, but it will surely come, for even the White Man, whose God walked and talked with him as friend with friend, cannot be exempt from the common destiny. We may be brothers after all. We will see.

We will ponder your proposition, and when we decide we will let you know. But should we accept it, I here and now make this condition that we will not be denied the privilege without molestation of visiting at any time the tombs of our ancestors, friends and children. Every part of this soil is sacred in the estimation of my people. Every hillside, every valley, every plain and grove, has been hallowed by some sad or happy event in days long vanished. . . . The very dust upon which you now stand responds more lovingly to their footsteps than to yours, because it is rich with the blood of our ancestors and our bare feet are conscious of the sympathetic touch. . . . Even the little children who lived here and rejoiced here for a brief season will love these somber solitudes and at eventide they greet shadowy returning spirits. And when the last Red Man shall have perished, and the memory of my tribe shall have become a myth among the White Men, these shores will swarm with the invisible dead of my tribe, and when your children's children think themselves alone in the field, the store, the shop, upon the highway, or in the silence of the pathless woods, they will not be alone. . . . At night when the streets of your cities and villages are silent and you think them deserted, they will throng with the returning hosts that once filled and still love this beautiful land. The White Man will never be alone.

Let him be just and deal kindly with my people, for the dead are not powerless. Dead, did I say? There is no death, only a change of worlds.

Colloquial Phrases and Single-Word Equivalents

More vigor, and sometimes more precision, can be achieved in a sentence through the use of a single word to replace a weak colloquial phrase of two or more words. English is full of **multiple-word collo-quial phrases** that have **single-word equivalents.** In our conversation we tend to use the phrases, but in writing the single-word equivalents are usually superior. Here are some examples:

play a big part in	dominate
do away with	abolish
get a hold of	control
cut down on	decrease
on account of the fact that	because
get a kick out of	enjoy
run into	meet
put up a fuss	quarrel
get down off of	dismount
run rings around	outperform
come up with	suggest
talk a lot about	discuss
make a hit with	impress
come in contact with	encounter
find out	discover
take a lot away from	diminish
leave out	omit
catch up with	overtake

In sentences a reader can feel the greater power of the single-word equivalents in this list. For example, "He dominated the meeting" has more strength and precision than "He played a big part in the meeting."

EXERCISE 52.   Using Single-Word Equivalents for Colloquial Phrases

DIRECTIONS: Improve the precision and vigor of the following sentences by substituting single-word equivalents for colloquial phrases.

1. His attitude took a lot away from our enjoyment of the play.
2. We went down into the canyon and looked closely at its rock walls.
3. We got off of the ship just after it pulled in to the pier.
4. He let go of the rope in order to keep a disaster from happening.
5. I can't put up with Tom's attempts to buy off the policeman.
6. The speaker made fun of pacifist proposals to do away with nuclear weapons.
7. Manski took the place of the first-string quarterback, who did not have the academic right to play.
8. While looking into the treasurer's report, the committee found several discrepancies that needed to be straightened out.
9. The workmen bound themselves into one group to make their cause have more strength.
10. I got a great deal of pleasure out of that novel.

Idiomatic Diction

An **idiom** is an expression peculiar to a language, not readily understandable from the meanings of its component parts, and not literally translatable into another language. *To put up with,* meaning "to tolerate," is a typical English idiom. The total meaning of the phrase is not the sum of the meanings of the different parts. Many idioms in English, like the one just illustrated, are colloquial and might not often appear in semiformal writing. But many are standard or general diction, such as *to turn down a proposal* or *to run across a rare manuscript.* Also the words *idiom* and *idiomatic* are nowadays used in a broader meaning than the specific definition given above. We say that an expression is idiomatic if it is natural, native English and that one is unidiomatic if in some way it is unnatural or un-English. Thus though *listen to me* is not, according to the definition above, an idiom since it is literally translatable into other languages and is not "peculiar," we still say that it is idiomatic English. If writing is to be precise, vigorous, and correct, it must be idiomatic, or natural to the language.

Most expressions in English that are thought of as idioms involve prepositions or words that look like prepositions.[2] Here is a list of expressions that illustrate the wide variety of idioms in English. A main point is that there is often no logical reason for the preposition or particle to be what it is—as in *slow up* and *slow down*.

get out of a car
get away from the scene of a crime
get down from a horse
get up into the attic
get up out of a chair
come up against a problem
come around to a point of view
come across with a blackmail payment
be in the movies
be on television
be in on a good thing
contrary to one's code of morals
in conflict with one's code of morals
a stand on a question
an opinion of a question
advantages of a separate peace treaty
reasons for a separate peace treaty
ways by which a problem can be solved
ways in which a problem can be stated
angry with one's teacher
angry at a delay
happy for one's uncle
pleased with one's wife
opposed to the legislation
in favor of the legislation
grateful for one's advice
appreciative of one's service

[2] Actually, three different kinds of words (though perhaps identical in pronunciation and spelling) occur in our idiomatic expressions. One is the **preposition,** as in *the car turned down the driveway*. Here *down* is a preposition with an object, the two forming a prepositional phrase telling where the car turned. Another kind of word is the **particle,** as in *he turned down my proposal*. Here *down* is not a preposition but a particle; note that *down my proposal* is not a prepositional phrase but that *turned down* is one unit of meaning (a verb) with *proposal* as its direct object. This kind of construction is a **verb-particle composite.** The third kind of word in these idiomatic expressions is the **adverb,** as in *at the end of the walk Jack stepped down*. *Down* here is not a preposition, for it has no object, and it is not a particle since it does not form one unit of meaning with the verb *stepped*. Instead, it is an adverb modifying the verb *stepped,* telling where Jack stepped.

an opinion of a book
an attitude toward a book
reach an agreement on a proposal
reach an agreement with one's neighbor
ashamed of one's behavior
sorry for one's behavior

Idiomatic expressions like these follow no clear linguistic principles. They just are what they are, and we learn them naturally as we learn our native language. But since there is such a variety of idioms in English and since they do not obey simple rules of grammar, writers occasionally get their phrases confused and write unidiomatic—or un-English—sentences. For example, in haste or panic one might write "sorry of my behavior." Such a faulty idiom weakens sentence precision and vigor because it distracts the reader.

English has a number of widely used **colloquial idioms** that some people think are improper for semiformal usage. Here are a few of the most common ones:

Pleased with is standard.
STANDARD: I was pleased with his reply.
COLLOQUIAL: I was pleased at his reply.

Listen to is standard.
STANDARD: I listened intently to his story.
COLLOQUIAL: I listened intently at his story.

Because of is best used as an adverb.
STANDARD: Because of the accident, I was late.
COLLOQUIAL: My tardiness was because of the accident.

Due to is best used as an adjective.
STANDARD: My tardiness was due to an accident.
COLLOQUIAL: Due to an accident, I was tardy.

Different from is considered the proper idiom.
STANDARD: My answer is different from yours.
COLLOQUIAL: My answer is different than yours.
COLLOQUIAL (*chiefly British*):   My answer is different to yours.

Try to do is preferable to *try and do.*
STANDARD: I will try to do my best.
COLLOQUIAL: I will try and do my best.

Within is preferable to *inside of.*
STANDARD: I will call within a week.
COLLOQUIAL: I will call inside of a week.

In regards to is considered nonstandard.

STANDARD: I have nothing to say in regard to his proposal.

Like as a conjunction is colloquial.

STANDARD: It looks as though it may rain.

COLLOQUIAL: It looks like it may rain.

Reason is because is colloquial.

STANDARD: The reason he laughed was that he misunderstood the joke.

COLLOQUIAL: The reason he laughed was because he misunderstood the joke.

Plan to is considered preferable to *plan on*.

STANDARD: We plan to cooperate.

COLLOQUIAL: We plan on cooperating.

Sure and is colloquial.

STANDARD: Be sure to inspect the motor.

COLLOQUIAL: Be sure and inspect the motor.

Had is preferable to *would have* in an *if* clause.

STANDARD: If I had gone, I would have seen him.

COLLOQUIAL: If I would have gone, I would have seen him.

Those who want their writing to be acceptable on all levels try to avoid colloquial idioms, but the use of such an expression cannot be counted a serious error in college writing.

The use of two idioms together with the careless omission of one of the particles or prepositions is a source of faulty idiom. For example:

OMITTED PREPOSITION: When a person has a goal to hope and work toward, he will be happy.

RIGHT: When a person has a goal to *hope for* and *work toward*, he will be happy.

Note that the first sentence has either the faulty idiom "hope a goal" or the equally faulty "hope toward a goal." Here is another example:

OMITTED PREPOSITION: Neither his interest nor concern for his employees' welfare brought him respect.

RIGHT: Neither his *interest in* nor his *concern for* his employees' welfare brought him respect.

Note that "interest for" is not the correct idiom. Errors of this sort are due mostly to carelessness.

The use of a colloquial idiom does not constitute a serious error. The omission of one preposition in using a double idiom is not excusable but, is, after all, a minor error of carelessness. Some errors in idiom, however, are truly serious. They are also hard to deal with, for they may be made only one time by one writer on one paper. That is, a frequently used faulty idiom is almost always a colloquial one and therefore informally acceptable. The true error in idiom is generally not a commonly recurring one. For example, the following sentences, taken from student papers, contain errors in idioms that may never have been made before or since:

> This contradicts with my own opinion.
> Our government should keep things at an equal basis.
> Our economy should grow at the rate for which it has in the past.
> There are several advantages toward federal aid being given to church schools.
> There are different ways into which the problem might be interpreted.
> Poe was a completely different person to which you pictured him.
> My grandfather had many books toward which I was interested.
> I do not know upon what he used as a basis for his statement.

No rules can be given to help writers avoid such errors in idioms, since each error is a separate case. However, you can learn to avoid such errors by paying close attention to what you read in order to know the correct idioms of our language, and by carefully reviewing your own sentences to see that each is phrased naturally.

EXERCISE 53.   Eliminating Faulty Idioms

DIRECTIONS: Improve the precision and vigor of the following sentences by eliminating faulty idioms.

1. People are deceived in many ways of advertising.
2. Delinquents never really look into the situation in which they are faced with.
3. The whole problem must be given time to work out.
4. One important factor to the success of doctors is tactfulness.
5. The student will value from what the film has to offer.
6. They are in their own little shell of living of which a Peace Corps worker must try to bring them out.
7. I have proof to the fact that he took bribes.
8. The American newspaper reader is more intelligent than to read the sports page first.
9. When so much is stressed on education, students get nervous.
10. Since we are rated upon nothing but grades, we try to get high grades.
11. When one reaches the legal age of voting, he should become interested about politics.

12. He found himself in an entirely different situation from that of which he was formerly accustomed.
13. The only reason of any value in dividing classes into different levels is to benefit the brightest students.
14. I believe strongly against birth control.
15. What I do has little or no bearing to others.
16. He wanted to follow the late President's footsteps.
17. All students should keep up on current events.
18. For those who prefer relaxing a bit on edge, there are situation comedies.
19. If he continues his good work, he will accomplish helping the students.
20. Americans take great pride and respect for sports.

Overuse of Modifiers

The **overuse of modifiers** can reduce the vigor, and often the precision, of writing. Some writers seem to think that the more adjectives they can attach to a noun, the more precise their sentence will be. Often the reverse is true. Cluttered writing is weak writing, and nothing clutters up a sentence more than useless modifiers. You should follow this precept: *when a noun or verb by itself says all you want to say, do not add adjectives or adverbs.* The following examples illustrate the improved vigor and precision of sentences stripped of excess modifiers:

The *worthy* minister of the First Methodist Church *magnanimously* assisted the *hard-working* lay committee.
The minister of the First Methodist Church assisted the lay committee.

Our *duly elected* new Speaker opened the legislative session with a *fine* prayer.
Our new Speaker opened the legislative session with a prayer.

The *wonderful* examples set by our *grand* scoutmaster taught the boys *valuable* self-reliance.
The examples set by our scoutmaster taught the boys self-reliance.

The first sentence in each example illustrates a gratuitous use of modifiers—that is, the inclusion of modifiers just for the sake of having them, not because they are needed. The modifiers sound as though they were added by force. Such excessive use of adjectives and adverbs weakens vigor and precision. A good writer makes it a habit to omit all modifiers not specifically needed.

Student writers should be specially warned against the overuse of two particular modifiers: *very* and *definitely*. Though both of these words have legitimate uses, they are among the most overused and misused words in the language. They are intensifiers in that they are used to reinforce or intensify the meaning of other words. But they have been so overused that they have lost their force and so no longer intensify to any noticeable extent. For example, to most people nowadays *very important* carries little more force than *important* and *I definitely believe* little more than *I believe*. These two intensifiers are somewhat like the little shepherd boy's cry of "wolf!" They have been used so much that no one any longer believes them. You would be well advised to use *very* and *definitely* sparingly. Other acceptable intensifiers are *especially, quite, considerably, truly,* and others of this type.

Euphemisms

Euphemisms can detract from sentence precision and vigor. The word comes from Greek roots meaning "to sound good." In English, a euphemism is a word or phrase that is less expressive or direct but also less offensive or distasteful than another. In short, we use euphemisms to avoid shocking the sensitive or to soften the blow for those who have suffered a loss. Here are some euphemistic statements, with more direct and expressive counterparts:

I just learned that you *lost* your son in the war.
I just learned that your son has been killed in the war.

His *remains* will be shipped to Arlington.
His corpse will be shipped to Arlington.

A *portly* matron bought a *foundation garment*.
A fat woman bought a corset.

Paying guests are welcome.
Boarders are welcome.

Fudd's Department Store experienced a *considerable inventory shrinkage*.
A large amount of goods was stolen from Fudd's Department Store.

My seatmate had an *unpleasant odor*.
My seatmate stank.

The play offers *mature entertainment*.
The play is full of illicit sex.

Aivin had a *social disease*.
Alvin had syphilis.

Most such euphemisms run to mild vagueness, as opposed to the blunt precision of their counterparts. Often the blunt precision is preferable. Sometimes euphemisms are downright laughable. For example, the well-bred Victorians (both in England and America) used the euphemism *limbs* for *legs* because the word *legs* was far too suggestive of sex, a taboo topic of conservation for them. Some of the Victorians even avoided the word *arms* for the same reason. In satirizing this absurd delicacy of language, Ambrose Bierce called toes *twigs*.

Disturbing Sound Patterns

A careless handling of sentence sounds can weaken the vigor of diction. **Rhyming words** can be especially distracting in exposition or persuasion. For example:

When you have a choice, always choose the active voice.

Such rhyming is irritating rather than pleasing in prose. Similarly, the **close repetition of words or syllables** can create distracting sound patterns in prose and thus reduce vigor. Examples:

The players played their parts well in the play.
A sentence should make sense, since it is a complete unit.
It's cheaper to ship freight by ship than to ship it by train.
We had a restful rest while the rest of the group worked without rest.

You can avoid such annoying repetition either by recasting a sentence or by substituting synonyms. For example:

The actors played their parts well in the drama.
While we rested comfortably, the remainder of the group continued to work.

But it is only *jarring* repetition of words that you should avoid. Much word repetition from sentence to sentence is necessary for coherence and clarity, as demonstrated in Chapter 4.

Excessive **alliteration** (the close repetition of consonant sounds) is thought by most stylists to be out of place in prose. Examples:

Avoid writing a sequence of similar sentences.
The playful pups pranced proudly in their pen.

In poetry, alliteration can have a pleasing effect; in prose, it usually distracts the reader's attention from the meaning.

The sound of **too many** *tion* **words in a sequence** also is annoying. Examples:

> The celebration of the birth of the nation was an occasion for wild jubilation.
> The approbation of the delegation insured the adoption of the proposition.

Good writers listen carefully with their mind's ear to avoid annoying sound patterns.

EXERCISE 54. **Improving Sentence Precision and Vigor**

DIRECTIONS: Improve the precision and vigor of the following sentences by eliminating excessive modification in the first five, substituting direct expressions for euphemisms in the second five, and recasting the third five to eliminate distracting sound patterns.

1. Our great and glorious leader gave a splendid speech on the absolute necessity of preparedness.
2. This grand occasion is definitely reminiscent of our first great demonstration.
3. This modest and demure young lady has gallant and admiring beaux by the plentiful dozens.
4. Our devoted and well-trained medical doctors most certainly believe that most highly touted patent medicines are absolutely worthless.
5. Our able and hardworking Governor made a very important announcement about our noble youths' eligibility to serve patriotically in the splendidly altruistic Peace Corps.
6. The battle injury left his intestines hanging from his abdomen.
7. Educational programs for exceptional children need to be adjusted to accommodate modern educational theory.
8. The liberating army undertook the task of pacifying the population.
9. The sanitation engineer complained that the extermination engineer left dead bodies for him to collect.
10. Mr. Jones's neighbor made some uncomplimentary remarks about his use of natural fertilizer on his lawns.
11. The students thought the teacher ought to have taught his class from the books they bought.
12. The opposition opposed the contribution of the delegation.
13. The athlete felt that he could not face the race against such a strong pace setter.

14. Television teaches teen-agers to tackle tasks with togetherness.
15. The devotion of the congregation was an inspiration to the visiting Committee for Integration.

Trite Diction

One of the most common enemies of vigor, and consequently of precision, in diction is the **cliché.** This is the trite or hackneyed or overused phrase that the unthinking or unimaginative writer habitually depends upon. Much writing and many speeches consist of little more than strings of phrases that have been used over and over in other such writing or speeches. As we read or listen we pick up the pattern of clichés, and then, unfortunately, tend to use them ourselves when we are faced with thinking of something to say. The less willing we are to phrase our sentences with care, the more likely we are to use clichés. And the more we use them, the more dull, imprecise, and empty our writing is.

Probably no single occasion produces more cliché-ridden language than Fourth of July oratory. The following, for example, is hardly more outrageously trite than actual speeches produced by hundreds of orators on our chief national holiday.

> Fellow Americans,
>
> It gives me great pleasure to stand before you today to remind you of the glorious heritage that is ours. My poor words will not be able to do justice to this occasion. But there above you, in all its glory, hangs the symbol of our freedom, our unsullied flag. There may be some in our midst who do not feel patriotic fervor each time they see it waving in freedom. If so, I address them more in sorrow than in anger, for I would like to think that every heart that beats here belongs to a true American who will be vigilant so that our great flag will ever reign supreme.

The nauseating quality of clichés becomes quite apparent when many are strung together.

Not only Fourth of July oratory but almost every area of human activity has its quota of clichés. This has been wittily demonstrated by Frank Sullivan, one of America's best humorists, who created Dr. Arbuthnot, the cliché expert. In many articles in *The New Yorker,* Sullivan's Dr. Arbuthnot has gathered clichés from fields as diverse as baseball, atomic energy, dramatic criticism, political oratory, and tabloid journalism. Here are a few from baseball journalism; they will certainly ring familiarly in your ears (!) :

towering first baseman
fleet baserunner
scrappy little shortstop
veteran spark plug
sensational newcomer
mound adversary
rival hurler
aging twirler
mound duel
driven off the mound
erratic southpaw
heated argument
relegated to the showers
keystone sack
hot corner
connect with the old apple

Here are a few clichés Dr. Arbuthnot garnered from writings about atomic energy:

usher in the atomic age
tremendous scientific discovery
never be the same world again
prove a boon to mankind
pave the way to a bright new world
spell the doom of civilization as we know it
vast possibilities for good or evil
boggles the imagination
threshold of a new era
world at the crossroads
dire need of control by international authority
terms so simple a layman can understand
spells the doom of large armies

Dr. Arbuthnot also reads the drama critics:

battle-scarred veterans of not a few first nights
powerfully wrought
richly rewarding
wholly convincing
admirably played
poorly contrived
masterly performance
stole the show
brought the house down

captivate the audience
radiated charm
skyrocketed to fame
rare and refreshing talent
elevated to stardom
stellar role
immortal heroine
eternal verities

He listens to political oratory:

Fellow Americans
say with all due modesty
point with pride
view with alarm
four-square
worthy of trust
carry the banner
prophetic view
sterling character
burning questions
forces of reaction
enemies of America
troubled times
eternal vigilance
dedicate ourselves anew
generations yet unborn

And he reads the stories of love and murder in the tabloid newspapers:

bared in court
morals being impaired
striking blonde
stunning brunette
erring mates
pretty ex-model
much-married film star
swank penthouse apartment
love nest
sizzling love missives
cold-blooded slaying
gangland killings
love-crazed suitor
stumbled on the corpse
met with foul play

nabbed the suspect
held incommunicado
wring a confession out of
scene of the crime
morbid curiosity seekers
rain of bullets
refused to name his assailants

Such lists of clichés could be extended to hundreds of phrases and dozens of categories. Indeed, such a list could be prepared about English composition texts themselves. Clichés are so common, in fact, that no writer can avoid them altogether. But excessive use of them means dull, limp, near-meaningless writing. Therefore you should learn the nature of this sort of trite language and should guard against its use in your own writing.

EXERCISE 55. Eliminating Clichés

DIRECTIONS: Recast the following sentences to eliminate clichés.

1. After an uphill climb I realized my dearest ambition.
2. If you will take off your rose-colored glasses, you will see that life is a snare and a delusion.
3. By and large, I have a sneaking suspicion that all is not right with the world.
4. The measure of one's success is how he played the game.
5. At the crack of dawn I beat a hasty retreat to the arms of Morpheus.
6. Tired but happy, we arrived home in the wee small hours and slept the sleep of the just.
7. Poor but honest and pretty as a picture, she seemed none the worse for wear.
8. The fate of the world hung in the balance.
9. Earlier she had been the picture of health but now she was pale as death.
10. We must strike while the iron is hot, for in this broad land of ours time and tide wait for no man.

CORRECT DICTION

There is a difference between vague, imprecise diction and **incorrect diction,** for the imprecise word (such as *discussed* when *argued* more truly expresses the situation) says approximately what the writer means whereas the incorrect word is wrong. Imprecise diction reflects fuzzy thinking; incorrect diction indicates ignorance.

There are two broad kinds of incorrect diction. One is the infrequent or nonrecurring use of a wrong word. Examples:

I am *solicitous* for spring.
John behaved *redundantly*.

Solicitous does mean "anxious for" but not in the sense of the above example. *Redundant* does mean "useless repetition" but only in the use of language. Such misused words are called malapropisms, and no rules can be given for avoiding them. When in doubt, consult your dictionary. But it is better to make such a mistake once in a while in an effort to increase your vocabulary than to avoid all attempts at developing a high level of diction for fear of making a mistake.

The other kind of incorrect diction involves a few dozen frequently **confused pairs of words,** such as *affect* and *effect*. The confusion of some of these pairs represents a real error due to ignorance; the confusion of others involves only a failure to distinguish between colloquial and more formal usage.

Following are two exercises in correct diction based on words from Appendix 3, **A Glossary of Usage.**

EXERCISE 56.   **Revising Incorrect Diction**

DIRECTIONS: There are two parts to this exercise. First there are ten sentences and then there are two paragraphs with errors in diction to be corrected.

1. John inferred that he would vote Republican.
2. Henry is a contemptuous person of low morales.
3. I was all ready on my way when I met my high school principle.
4. I am anxious to date Joan, for I am much effected by her beauty.
5. The members of the city counsel seem disinterested in reform.
6. In fact, I expect the councilmen will except bribes.
7. John wasn't suppose to loose his temper.
8. Therefore he laid down for a while to quite his nerves.
9. It seems incredulous that such a rascal as the Governor would feel a twinge of conscious.
10. A large amount of people wanted less changes than the council seemed prepared to make.

As the time for the election drew near, the incumbent, Ethical Ed, began more boldly to infer that his opponent, Fairminded Fred, was a contemptuous person of low morales. Even though he was all ready rich, Ed was anxious to retain his seat on the counsel, for he was pleasantly effected by the sense of power it gave him. In his last speech he abandoned implication all together and make a direct attack on Fred. He sited Fred's claim of being one of the principles in the Reform Movement and then showed that Fred had proposed less changes in council procedures than he, Ed, had. He claimed that Fred was really disinterested in reform and would except bribes without the least twinge of conscious. Beside that, he continued, Fred was libel to make verbal promises and then break them.

By the end of Ed's speech, Fred, who was setting in front of his TV set listening, was about to loose his temper. But since he had heart trouble, he knew he was not suppose to get excited, and so he laid down for a while to quite his nerves. As he lay on his bed, a large amount of people called to tell him that Ed's attack was incredulous and that they would vote for Fred. They said most all of their friends also felt that Ed went farther in his speech then he should have. So Fred's fit of anger past, and he said he expected Ed had won the election for him.

FIGURES OF SPEECH

The Nature of Figurative Language

Language may be used for communication on a **literal** or on a **figurative** level. Literal language uses words only for their actual, basic meanings. It may be taken at face value; it means just what it says on the surface. Thus in literal use *fire* means a flame-producing oxidation of combustible material; *naked* means unclothed or without artificial covering; a *cloud* is a visible mass of vapor suspended in the atmosphere; *gold* is a metal of high value; *to throw* means to cause an object to fly through the air; *ears* are anatomical organs for registering sound. What, then, do we mean then when we say

> My heart is on *fire* with love for you.
> I was determined to tell the *naked* truth.
> He left town under a *cloud* of suspicion.
> She had a heart of *gold*.
> He *threw* himself on the mercy of the court.
> When her friends gossiped, she was all *ears*.

Obviously, we do not mean the italicized words to be taken literally. To see why, try to visualize the concrete, literal meanings of these sentences.

The italicized words above are used figuratively. **Figurative language,** then, is language wrenched from its literal meaning—that is, it cannot be true literally. It in effect tells a lie on the surface in order to express a truth beneath the surface. For example, since one's heart cannot literally be on fire (at least while he is alive), such a use of the word *fire* is nonliteral or figurative.

In interpreting figurative language, the mind makes a transfer of meaning based on a comparison: in the sentences above, between the feeling of love and the heat of a fire; between the startling quality of a surprising truth and the shocking quality of a naked body; between the dimly understood nature of a suspected wrongdoing and the mistiness of a cloud; between the desirable qualities of a good and kind person and the value of gold; between a body tossed into a position of subjection and one's giving himself up to a court's decision; between one's being composed of nothing but ears and his eager interest in hearing all that is being said. Such comparisons in figurative language are literally false but they nevertheless deliver understandable and expressive meaning.

Much of our language usage is basically figurative without our realizing it. In fact, so many originally concrete words have been given expanded meanings that we can hardly utter two or three sentences together without using figurative language. For illustration, pick out the figuratively used words in the following sentences.

> She is a sweet-tempered girl.
> He is a blackhearted rogue.
> His high position gave weight to his proposal.
> We have only scratched the surface of that market.
> He played a devilish trick on me.
> She maintained a stony silence.
> He's just a green youth with no experience.
> With heavy hearts, we paid for our crimes.

The original, basic, core meanings of the words you picked out have been extended so that, for example, we accept *sweet* as a word to be applied to temperament. But actually such usage must be figurative, for *sweet* literally means having the taste of sugar.

As illustrated, much long-established figurative language fills our speaking and writing. But a writer often creates new figures of speech either to make a point clearer or to add color and freshness to his style. Consciously created figures of speech are not especially common in the exposition and persuasion written by college students (in the so-called Creative Writing courses the use of figurative language is much more emphasized). But as a student of exposition, you should at least be introduced to the use of figures of speech.

The Chief Figures of Speech

Many different kinds of figures of speech have been identified by rhetoricians. Only one of them (*metaphorical*) is of especial value in the study of expository writing, but an explanation of the chief figures of speech may be of interest and may increase your general knowledge of how language delivers meaning.

Personification attributes human qualities to nonhuman objects or entities. For example:

> All nature mourned the death of the King.
> The surf flung its arm around the swimmers and enveloped them with love.
> God frowned with displeasure.

Metonymy is the use of the name of one thing for that of another suggested by it or associated with it. For example:

> The White House (meaning the President) issued a denial of Mr. Appleson's accusation.
> Reading Mark Twain (meaning his works) is always fun.
> The table (meaning the food on the table) looked delicious.
> My transportation (meaning car) broke down.

Synecdoche is a type of metonymy in which a part is used for a whole, or vice versa. For example:

> I'll go with you if you have wheels (meaning a car).
> We hired two extra trombones (meaning trombone players).
> The law (meaning a policeman) arrived.
> Here comes the Navy (meaning one sailor).

Hyperbole is a figure of exaggeration. It tells more than the truth about the size, number, or degree of something without intending to deceive. For example:

> The comedy team had them rolling in the aisles.
> My sweetheart is perfection itself, flawless and divine.
> His dormitory room was filled with books.
> Rivers of tears were flowing as the heroine died.

Litotes is a figure of understatement. It uses terms less strong than is to be expected. For example:

> The Prime Minister explained that war would mean some inconveniences for the home front.

I have a line or two of Cicero to translate for tomorrow's Latin class.
Rockefeller was content to make a dollar here and there.
Haven't you lost a little weight (meaning fifty or more pounds)?

Some other nonliteral uses of language are **analogy, allegory, irony,** and **symbolism.** These represent figurative uses of language, for in grappling with them the reader's mind must make a transfer of meaning in order to understand the author's true intent. An analogy is an extended comparison of two essentially unlike ideas or processes, the intent of which is to make one clear in terms of the other. For example, a writer might try to explain the arcane features of high finance in terms of a child's game. An allegory is a story in which the characters and actions really represent people and events not literally expressed in the story. For example, the conflict between communism and the free world could be told allegorically in a story about rival neighborhood clubs. Verbal irony is language in which the author's intent is in contrast to what his words seem to say on the surface. For example, when you praise someone sarcastically with the true intent of disparaging him you are using irony. Symbolism is a complex term, but basically a symbol in writing is the use of the name of an object to represent a complex and abstract idea. For example, a story writer might use the recurring symbol of a liquor bottle to represent the degradation of one of his characters. Analogies and irony can be highly useful in expository writing, but allegory and symbolism are chiefly used in imaginative writing.

The kind of figurative language that is most commonly used in exposition and persuasion is called **metaphorical.** Two figures of speech are included in this term: **metaphor** and **simile.** A simile is a comparison of two essentially unlike things with the use of *like* or *as*. For example:

His face was like a piece of stone sculpture.
Learning a new language is like building a new window in the mind.

A metaphor is a direct identification of two essentially unlike things. For example:

His face was made of stone.
To learn a new language is to build a new window in the mind.

The technical distinction between metaphors and similes is unimportant. They represent the same kind of figurative use of language: a comparison of two objects, ideas, or situations essentially dissimilar but having points of resemblance that make one clear in terms of the other. Most figurative language is metaphorical.

Use of Figurative Language in Student Writing

Although metaphors and similes occur more often in imaginative writing, unless overused they may be quite useful in exposition and persuasion. They can add both color and clarity to factual writing. They add color because, when successfully created, they form interesting, vivid images and impart the flavor of concreteness. They add clarity by making abstract ideas and concepts more readily accessible to the reader's mind through relating them to concrete objects or actions that he is already familiar with.

Successful metaphors are created for specific purposes. When a writer of exposition has a particular idea or concept that he would like to make clearer or more engaging, he will often create a figure of speech to explain it. If he creates a fresh, original, and appropriate one, his writing will be improved. If he relies on an established, **trite figure,** his writing is likely to be limp and dull. Most clichés are overused figures of speech. For example, not much color or clarity is added to writing with such hackneyed figures as these:

pretty as a picture
tired as a dog
dead as a doornail
sharp as a razor
ugly as sin
brown as a berry
the lap of luxury
fly off the handle
a face that would stop a clock
hitch your wagon to a star
a bonehead
a wet blanket
an ace in the hole

Of course no writer can avoid the occasional use of an established figure, and such occasional use will not weaken writing. But do not depend on established figures to add much color or extra clarity to your composition.

You should avoid not only trite but also **mixed** or **inconsistent figures.** When a metaphor is continued through two or more phases, all the phases should be based on the same kind of comparison, or at least not on clashing comparisons. For example, the following metaphors are mixed:

Mr. Beane headed into the wild blue yonder of stock speculaton, confident that he could keep his feet on the ground and make money as easily as falling off a log.

As his temper was about to boil over, Mr. Bang caught hold of the reins of his passion and locked his anger inside his stormy breast.

In the first example, Mr. Beane is, figuratively, in the air, standing on the ground, and falling off a log at the same time. In the second there is a figure of cooking, one of driving a horse, and one of locking a door, all mixed up together. Such inconsistency in metaphors is distracting; the reader does not know where to focus his attention. In exposition, the single-phase metaphor is the most useful; piled-up metaphors are not often effective.

Successfully used metaphors, then, should be fresh, consistent, and appropriate. In exposition especially, they should contribute to meaning as well as style. Their function is dual: to clarify ideas by establishing meaningful comparisons and to enliven style by adding color, flavor, and vividness. Here are a few original and colorful figures:

as disappointed as a worm on a wax apple
yielded as graciously as a wild horse to bit and reins
as stuffed with knowledge as the New York Public Library
muscle reflexes like a stretched rubber band
as selfless as a ten-year colonel bucking for general
like pouring water into a bucket seat
as pious as the spirit of Christmas at Gimbel's
groomed like an untrimmed poodle
as free of prejudice as a fox in a henhouse
an idea as weightless as a man in orbit
an idea as dangerous as a drunken navigator on a spaceship
an idea as deceptive as a black widow spider at mating time
as carefully planned as a spontaneous Communist demonstration
an idea as sound as the axioms of Euclid

Some of the above figures are ironical; point them out.

EXERCISE 57. **Creating Figures of Speech**

DIRECTIONS: Think of a figurative way to express each of the following ideas or situations.

1. A student sleeping in class
2. A salesman stretching the truth
3. A bashful man proposing
4. Reading a boring book
5. A person being obnoxious at a party
6. A teacher wandering from the subject matter

7. Arguing with an adamant traffic cop
8. Studying while friends talk or listen to TV
9. A poor product highly advertised
10. A politician speaking in meaningless generalities

CONNOTATION AND SLANTED DICTION

So far in this chapter we have discussed the principles of word choice for exposition and rational, objective persuasion. Since the purpose of this kind of writing is to inform or to convince in a reasonable manner, the writer should choose precise words that deliver honest, full, and comprehensible meaning. But much writing is designed not just to make facts and ideas clear or to convince with sound logic but to deceive or hoodwink the reader. Much political, economic, social, and religious writing, and almost all advertising copy, is of this sort. Writers of material intended to deceive or exploit rather than to inform often use principles of word choice different from those proper for exposition and rational persuasion. They use words for their **connotative value,** and in more rapscallion cases they use **slanted diction** or **loaded words.**

Words are said to have **denotative** and **connotative** meanings. The denotative meaning of a word is its basic dictionary definition—what the word means to all who know it. For example, the denotative meaning of *orchid* is "any of a number of related plants having flowers with three petals, two regularly shaped and the third enlarged and irregular in form." This, the denotative meaning, is just a bare, factual definition without emotional suggestions. All nouns, verbs, adjectives, and adverbs have denotative meanings that form the basis of their use for language communication.

Many content words also have connotative meanings. These are the suggested or associated meanings of words beyond their core denotative definitions. These meanings often differ with individuals or groups and so cannot be put into dictionaries. Connotative meanings have emotional overtones because they reflect the attitude of an individual or a group toward a word. Thus if you respond emotionally to a word, it has a connotative meaning for you. The term *associated meaning* is also applied to this language phenomenon because our reason for having an emotional attitude toward a word is that we associate it with some public event or situation or with some private event in our lives. For example, to a young girl the word *orchid* may have an unspoken and favorable connotation if she has just received one to wear to her first formal dance. To her it is not just a three-petaled flower, but a symbol of expected romance and youthful pleasure. If her expectations should be met, the word *orchid* will continue to have strong connotative meaning for her for at least several days.

Consider the different emotional impact that the following words will have on the two different persons mentioned:

The word *funeral* to an undertaker and to a man who has just buried his young son.

The word *teacher* to a disturbed problem child and to a responsive youngster who makes good grades and likes school.

The word *politician* to a dedicated elected public official and to a chronic failure who blames the government for all ills.

The word *poetry* to a badly taught, tough young hoodlum and to a sensitive, well-educated youth.

The word *husband* to a deserted wife with six children and to a young and happy bride.

The word *revolution* to a radical with a cause and to a wealthy, privileged aristocrat.

These examples show that words can vary widely in their connotative value. What a word really means to an individual may depend partly on his point of view, not just on its core definition.

Much connotation is of course public rather than private—that is, the suggested meaning is about the same for all persons who hear or read the word. Therefore writers with prejudices and biases or with commercial aims will often choose a word for its calculated emotional influence rather than for its precision and honesty. Such word choice is notoriously common among advertising coypwriters. Why, for example, has the phrase "the seventy-cent spread" been used? Obviously because the word *butter* has a connotation of richness and luxury that the word *oleomargarine* will probably never have. A copywriter for a wine company has an easier task than one for a beer company because the word *wine* has, for many, a permanent connotation of gracious living and refined taste, whereas the word *beer* has a lowbrow connotation in spite of the fact that many highly cultivated people relish it. The word *country* has for many a connotation of crudeness or lack of sophistication; but add the word *club* to it and you have a compound word with a connotation that helps sell everything from high-priced beauty creams to expensive automobiles. A few truly cultured people may laugh at the phrase "the country-club set" but most Americans will associate it with elegance and wished-for luxury. Like advertising copywriters, the creators of movie titles also work on connotative meanings. Can you, for example, imagine the title "Days of Wine and Roses" being changed to "Days of Beer and Petunias"?

The copywriter's addiction to words with strong connotative values is perhaps annoying, but it is probably not especially harmful or wicked. The same manipulation of language by political, religious, social, and economic propagandists, however, is the cause of much misunderstanding, hatred, and bigotry. For example, one United States Senator always used to refer to another as "the Jewish Senator from New York." He intended the word *Jewish* to carry an unfavorable connotation. But writers and speakers with strong biases usually do not stop with connotative manipulations. They pervert language communication even further by using slanted diction or loaded words.

The use of slanted diction involves more than the choice of a word for its connotative value. Since connotation may vary with individuals or groups, a biased writer must know his audience if he is to produce successful connotative effects. For example, a highly conservative politician speaking to a like-minded group might use the word *liberal* for its unfavorable suggestive meaning to that group. But he could not depend on a common reaction from everyone, for many think of *liberal* as a "good" word.

When a writer uses slanted diction, he expects everybody to react in about the same way. He tries to present an event, situation, or idea from his biased point of view by choosing words that give his own "slant." Thus a situation can be made to appear desirable or undesirable, according to the words used to describe it. For example, both of the sentences in each of the following pairs could easily be written about the same situation.

The good-natured Governor tried to please everyone.
The easily influenced Governor bumbled along.

Coach Fox is a notable competitor.
Coach Fox will use any tactics to win.

The General controlled his troops with firm discipline.
The General behaved like a martinet.

The sweet-tempered teacher let the children have fun.
The lax teacher permitted the children to misbehave.

In its extreme form slanted diction is called *loaded words*. These are highly charged words that are always at the disposal of propagandists or prejudiced writers. Consider such sentences as these:

Left-wing pressure groups threatened the stability of the loyal union members.
The reactionary National Association of Manufacturers is trying to keep workers in sweatshop conditions.

One-hundred-percent Americans will resist this foreign attempt to pervert our principles.

The Communist-dominated Senator from New York ranted and raved as he propagandized for federal aid to education.

The very tone of such slanted diction will, to perceptive readers, reveal the writer's intent to sway rather than to inform.

The more factual and honest writing is, the more it depends on denotative meanings and widely accepted and unprejudiced connotations. The more propagandistic writing is, the more it uses calculated connotations and slanted diction. In college, then, the study of connotation and slanted diction is more a part of training in reading than in writing. College students—and everybody, in fact—need to be taught to protect themselves from editorially slanted writing and propaganda in general, but they do not need to be taught to manipulate language for the purpose of spreading prejudice. The kind of writing done in the beginning composition course should be honest, sound in logic, open-minded, and fair. Those students who become propagandists quickly enough learn their lessons about connotative meanings and slanted diction.

CHAPTER 7

Conventions
of Usage

THE CONVENTIONAL ASPECTS OF WRITING

Chapters 5 and 6 of this book have identified various kinds of errors and weaknesses that affect the logic, clarity, or precision of writing: confused sentence structure; faulty pronoun reference; improper shifts in number, person, voice, tense or mood; faulty parallelism; misplaced modifiers; vague and incorrect word choice; and so forth. These errors and weaknesses range from the very serious, which can obscure meaning altogether, to the minor, which are only mildly confusing. But all have to do with the way sentences deliver **meaning.**

Other errors—such as those in spelling, capitalization, and the use of the apostrophe—have to do with the **social acceptability** rather than with the meaning of writing. When such errors are committed, meaning is really not affected, for the conventional rather than the logical aspects of writing are violated.

The word *convention* comes from the Latin *venire,* meaning "to come," and *con,* meaning "together." So, literally, a convention is a coming together. Figuratively, it is a custom that the members of a particular society have come to accept as proper and right for them.

Thus in writing, conventions are just standard forms that a particular group of writers (for us, educated writers of English) accept as proper and correct for them. For example, signaling a new paragraph by indenting its first line five spaces is just a convention. In business writing nowadays, it is also a common practice not to indent a paragraph at all but to double space between paragraphs. Either convention for signaling a new paragraph is perfectly satisfactory provided those concerned agree on it. Or, for another example, it has been conventional in the past to form the plural of a letter or a numeral with an *'s*: E's, T's, 3's, 7's. But nowadays many professional writers and book publishers form such plurals with an *s* only: Es, Ts, 3s, 7s. Either convention is quite satisfactory for those who accept it. A liberal-minded person will accept both conventions, since both are practiced by educated writers.

All spelling is, of course, conventional. Any method of spelling a word is satisfactory provided those who use the word agree on that spelling. For example, convention dictates that we use such spellings as *cough, bough, rough, though,* and *through,* and so for centuries these odd spellings have been satisfactory for hundreds of millions of writers.

The use of capital letters, apostrophes, and hyphens is also conventional. For example, in German all nouns are capitalized and apostrophes are not used to show possession; but in English most nouns are not capitalized and apostrophes are used to show possession. Such differences are purely conventional and really do not affect meaning.

Punctuation is, of course, a great aid to clarity in writing, and in a few cases it can determine the meaning of a sentence. But for the most part, punctuation is conventional, and fashions in it have changed in English over the centuries. Consider, for example, the following passage:

> I had rather beleeve all the fables in the Legend, and the Talmud, and the Alcoran, then that this universall frame is without a minde. It is true, that a little philosophy inclineth man's minde to Atheisme; but depth in philosophy bringeth men's mindes about to religion.

Will educated people say this passage is unclear, imprecise, or illogical? No, they will understand it perfectly. But some might point out that it has "errors" in spelling, capitalization, and punctuation. The fact is, however, that it was written by Sir Francis Bacon, one of the greatest of all English writers and thinkers. Certain conventions acceptable in his day are not now standard; the change in conventions, however, has not affected the logic, clarity, or precision—in short, the meaning—of the passage.

The word *usage* is applied to our handling of the above-mentioned conventions of writing, and it is also applied to certain aspects of grammar. But *grammar* and *usage* are not synonymous terms. Grammar involves a study of the whole structure of a language. You could not learn everything about English grammar even in an advanced college course. But that is not of especial importance, for every native speaker of English—even an illiterate—has an unconscious knowledge of all the indispensable aspects of English grammar. The "mistakes" made by the uneducated involve only the tiniest fraction of the whole of grammar.

Usage is a term applied not only to spelling and capitalization, but also to certain aspects of grammar in which variations do appear among native users of the language. These variations are largely limited to the different forms or endings that are given verbs, pronouns, and certain modifiers. For example all users of English know how to distinguish between the various tenses, but not all use the same form of a verb for a particular tense. One person may say, "I took the money, but I don't have it now." Another may say, "I taken the money, but I ain't got it now." These sentences are identical in most aspects of their grammar, but vary in the verb forms used for tenses. Both sentences are clear, however, and no one could misunderstand which tenses are meant. But the sentences are not equal in their social acceptability.

The aspects of grammar that have to do with usage may be called conventional, for they do not affect the meaning of a sentence but only its social acceptability. Observing the various conventions of educated usage is analogous to observing social conventions of proper dress, neat grooming, and polite manners. You should observe those conventions suitable for the society you are active in.

The following illustration can help you understand better the distinction between convention and logic in language. It is easily possible that a century or less from now the most highly educated speakers of English may naturally use such expressions as, "I ain't interested in stock speculation." Or, "I don't have no money for real estate investment." Such a shift in conventional usage would not at all affect clarity or meaning. But it is highly unlikely that sentences like the following can ever become standard:

> We found a picture of her swimming with him after he died.
> He described the faults that his wife has clearly.

In these sentences the misplacement of the modifiers *after he died* and *clearly* makes for awkward or humorous ambiguity. The difference between the two sets of sentences is that the first two have only nonstandard grammatical forms which do not interfere with clarity, while the second two have faults of word order which make them difficult to understand.

The difference between matters of sentence structure that affect clarity, precision, and logic and the conventions of grammar that affect only social acceptability can also be illustrated by a close look at the so-called bad grammar of uneducated people:

ain't
he don't have none
had took
him and me have went
them books

Do educated people object to this language because they don't readily understand it? Of course not. They object to it because it is, to them, socially unacceptable, like dirty or rumpled clothing worn to a fashionable banquet. It is clear then that word forms in grammar are conventional. For many people with little or no formal education, certain forms are conventional, while other forms are conventional for those with more formal education.

There is, however, no immutable, fixed system of educated usage, for language is in constant change. Most well-schooled Americans agree on most points of usage, but there are areas of variant practices (for example, capitalization), and therefore you will not be able to please all educated people in all aspects of your usage. You can only hope to be "right" most of the time and to hold criticisms of your usage to a minimum. In fact, a few deviations from so-called standard usage are likely to appear in anybody's writing. It is a mistake to think that observance of a few rules of grammar will make a person's writing good, or that violation of a few will make it bad. Much English teaching in the past has overemphasized a few minor matters of usage that play only the tiniest part in the whole process of writing, such as the distinctions between *shall* and *will, good* and *well, who* and *whom, sure* and *surely, it's me* and *it's I, none is* and *none are,* and *everyone . . . his* and *everyone . . . their.* Such matters are minor; you should not think that points of usage such as these are as important as clarity, precision, and logic in writing. And as for split infinitives, sentences beginning with *and,* and sentences ending with prepositions, no informed person today can reasonably object to such usage.

A nineteenth-century writer, later identified as Mark Twain, once received the following letter:

Dear Mr ——:
Your writings interest me very much; but I cannot help wishing you would not place adverbs between the particle and verb in the Infinitive.

For example: "to *even* realize," "to *mysteriously* disappear" "to *wholly* do away." You should say, *even* to realize; to disappear mysteriously etc. "rose up" is another mistake—tautology, you know. Yours truly

A Boston Girl.

Part of Mark Twain's anonymous comment on this letter was as follows:

. . . . Now I have certain instincts, and I wholly lack certain others. (Is that "wholly" in the right place?) For instance, I am dead to adverbs; they cannot excite me. To misplace an adverb is a thing which I am able to do with frozen indifference; it can never give me a pang. But when my young lady puts no point [period] after "Mr.;" when she begins "adverb," "verb," and "particle" with the small letter, and aggrandizes "Infinitive" with a capital; and when she puts no comma after "to mysteriously disappear," etc., I am troubled; and when she begins a sentence with a small letter I even *suffer*. Or I suffer, *even*,— I do not know which it is; but she will, because the adverb is in her line, whereas only those minor matters are in mine. Mark these pro- phetic words: though this young lady's grammar be as the drifted snow for purity, she will never, never, never learn to punctuate while she lives; this is her demon, the adverb is mine. I thank her, honestly and kindly, for her lesson, but I know thoroughly well that I shall never be able to get it into my head. Mind, I do not say I shall not be able to make it *stay* there! I say and mean that I am not capable of *getting it into* my head. There are subtleties which I cannot master at all,—they confuse me, they mean absolutely nothing to me,—and this adverb plague is one of them.

We all have our limitations in the matter of grammar, I suppose. I have never seen a book which had no grammatical defects in it. This leads me to believe that all people have my infirmity, and are afflicted with an inborn inability to feel or mind certain sorts of grammatical particularities. There are people who were not born to spell; these can never be taught to spell correctly. The enviable ones among them are those who do not take the trouble to care whether they spell well or not,—though in truth these latter are absurdly scarce. I have been a correct speller, always; but it is a low accomplishment, and not a thing to be vain of. Why should one take pride in spelling a word rightly when he knows he is spelling it wrongly? *Though* is the right way to spell "though," but is not *the* right way to spell it. Do I make myself understood?

Some people were not born to punctuate; these cannot learn the art. They can learn only a rude fashion of it; they cannot attain to its niceties, for these must be *felt*; they cannot be reasoned out. Cast-iron rules will not answer, here, any way; what is one man's comma is another man's colon. One man can't punctuate another man's manuscript any more than one person can make the gestures for another person's speech.[1]

These sensible and refreshing statements have a sound lesson for students of language.

SPELLING

Spelling is a convention of writing and therefore does not affect meaning (except in those rare cases in which a word is so badly misspelled that its identity is obscured). It is a mistake to assume that one cannot write with clarity and precision unless he spells properly. One pamphlet of dictionary study, for example, says, "To achieve precision in writing, it is necessary to spell correctly." But this very sentence loses none of its precision when written in this fashion: "To acheeve precision in riting, it is necessary to spel corectly." The two versions are identical in meaning. The second, however, lacks social respectability because of its misspellings. But social respectability and precision are entirely different matters.

Further proof that "correct" spelling is not necessary for precision lies in the history of our language. It was not until the eighteenth century that the movement for standardized English spelling became strong. Prior to that time many variations in spelling occurred in the writings of the most learned men. In fact, the greatest writers— Shakespeare, Bacon, Milton, Dryden, for example—often spelled a word in two or three different ways, sometimes on the same page. Their writings, needless to say, are the essence of precision.

But later generations have come to be very spelling-conscious, mostly because of the establishment of "the dictionary" as an authority. Since 1755 a series of excellent English dictionaries have standardized spelling, and our public schools have fostered the notion that failure to follow dictionary spellings is a positive sign of ignorance. Hence there currently exists a colossal public prejudice against misspellings. (Strangely, this prejudice seems to be strongest among poor spellers.) One result is that students with a natural facility for learning to spell English are thought to be especially bright and those without such a facility are often thought to be dull. Actually, many very bright people just don't have the knack of spelling. (Rumor has it that one of the most

---

[1] The Boston girl's letter and Twain's reply were published anonymously in "The Contributors' Club" of *The Atlantic Monthly*, XLV (June 1880), pp. 849–860.

intelligent United States presidents of this century was quite a poor speller, though an excellent writer.) In school, poor spellers are often punished for what may well be just a minor oversight on the part of the Giver of natural abilities.

But whatever one's theory of spelling may be, it is a social fact in present-day America that misspellings reduce the social acceptability of writing. Hence college writers must hold their spelling mistakes to a reasonable minimum. You should cultivate an attitude toward spelling somewhat like your attitude toward dress or other customs. You may often think it unreasonable and onerous to be required to dress in a certain fashion for certain occasions, but though you may complain you are likely to go along with the conventions. You may even study to follow them accurately if you want to be an acceptable member of a group. You simply have to cultivate a similar attitude toward spelling conventions. But it is well to remember that no one is always perfect in his spelling. The following sections will give you practical advice on how to improve your spelling.

Spelling by Phonemics

Mark Twain, in the article quoted above, says *"Though* is the right way to spell 'though,' but it is not *the* right way to spell it." He meant, of course, that we would spell it *tho* if we spelled it as we pronounce it. In his view, *the* right way to spell is the phonemic way, that is, according to pronunciation.

Human vocal cords produce discrete sounds that are merged together to form speech. Linguists call these separate sounds *phonemes,* and one or more phonemes used as a meaningful unit they call a *morpheme.* In spelling, we speak of letters and syllables. When one letter represents one—and only one—phoneme, spelling is phonemic. For example, *put* is composed of three letters representing three phonemes (one morpheme) and is spelled phonemically provided we think of *p, u,* and *t* as always representing only the three sounds in the word. Thus if we had one letter in our alphabet for each phoneme, our spelling could be phonemic.

But as every student knows, much English spelling is not phonemic. And with our present alphabet English spelling could not be wholly phonemic, for we use at least thirty-three phonemes but have only twenty-six letters in our alphabet, three of which (*c, q,* and *x*) are useless. Obviously, some letters, chiefly the vowels, must do double (or even triple or quadruple) duty. And not only that, sometimes one phoneme is represented by one letter in one spelling and then by another letter in another spelling. For example, the sound *z* is sometimes represented by the letter *z* (*lizard*) and sometimes by the letter *s* (*is, was*). Or, for another example, the sound *k* is sometimes represented by *k,* sometimes by *ck* (*kick*), sometimes by *c* (*car*), sometimes by *ch* (*Christmas*), and sometimes by *que* (*clique*). Many more such examples could be given.

But even though, with our present alphabet, English spelling can never be absolutely phonemic and though it is often quite unphonemic, is is more phonemic than is generally believed. Many of our words are spelled approximately as they are pronounced. And in addition, many phonemic principles operate in words that appear to be senselessly unphonemic. Some of these principles (most are too minor and obscure or too riddled with exceptions to be mentioned here) are explained below.[2] Students unconsciously absorb some of these principles, but a conscious knowledge of the most important ones will give you greater confidence in spelling. The common spelling rules are also based on phomenic principles, but, since they form a traditional body of spelling lore, they will be explained separately in the following section on spelling by rules.

The *tion* and *sion* syllables are often confused in spelling. They are sometimes pronounced *shun* (*nation*) and sometimes *zyun* (*vision*). When the pronunciation is *zyun,* the spelling is always *sion*:

aversion	incision
confusion	invasion
decision	occasion
diversion	persuasion
division	revision
evasion	submersion
explosion	suffusion

When the syllable is pronounced *shun,* the spelling is usually *sion* after *l* and *s*:

commission	expulsion
convulsion	passion
discussion	permission
digression	propulsion
dismission	remission
emulsion	revulsion
expression	submission

There are of course exceptions, but in most other cases the syllable is spelled *tion.*

[2] In linguistic texts, phonemic symbols rather than letters are used to identify phonemes. Here we will just use the letters that you are familiar with.

The *ance* (*ant*) and *ence* (*ent*) endings give a great deal of trouble in spelling. The spelling is *ance* when the syllable is preceded by *nd*:

abundance	*Exceptions:*
ascendance	independence
attendance	tendency
dependant	
pendant	
redundance	

The spelling is *ence* after a *d* preceded by a vowel:

accident	evidence
coincidence	impudence
confidence	residence

The spelling is *ance* after a hard *g* (pronounced *guh*) or a hard *c* (pronounced as a *k*):

applicant	extravagance
elegance	significance

The spelling is *ence* after a soft *g* (pronounced as a *j*) or a soft *c* (pronounced as an *s*):

adolescence	innocence
diligence	intelligence
indigence	munificence

The spelling is *ence* when the syllable is preceded by an *r* in an accented syllable:

abhorrence	interference
coherence	occurrence
concurrence	recurrence
deterrence	transference

The spelling is *ence* when preceded by *i* or *l*:

benevolence	omniscience
convenience	prevalent
conscience	resilience
efficient	sufficient
excellent	*Exceptions:*
expedience	alliance
experience	petulant
insolence	vigilant
lenient	

When a long *a* sound occurs before *ght, gh, ge, gn,* and *n,* it is often spelled *ei* but never *ie:*

beige	neighbor
deign	reign
feign	rein
freight	skein
inveigle	vein
neigh	weight

The *c* in the syllable *ice* is sounded as an *s;* the *s* in the syllable *ise* is sounded as a *z:*

advice	device
advise	devise

Words ending in the *f* sound are sometimes spelled with one *f,* sometimes with *ff,* and sometimes with *gh.* If the sound before the *f* is a short vowel (except short *e*), the *f* is usually doubled:

buff	staff
chaff	tariff
doff	whiff
plaintiff	*Exception:*
sheriff	graph

If the sound before the *f* is a consonant or a long vowel, the *f* is not doubled:

belief	half
brief	leaf
dwarf	proof
golf	surf
grief	waif

When the letters before the final *f* sound are *au* or *ou,* the *f* sound is usually spelled *gh:*

cough	rough
enough	tough
laugh	trough

When a *g* is given a hard (*guh*) sound, it usually ends a word or is followed by a consonant or by *a, o,* or *u:*

analogous	rang
angle	sing
bungle	spangle
haggle	tangle
hung	tingle

When a *g* is given a soft (*j*) sound, it usually is followed by *e, i,* or *y*:

advantageous	mangy
angel	pungent
change	range
courageous	rangy
lunge	singe

Note particularly the *angle-angel, lung-lunge, rang-range,* and *sing-singe* pairs.

Sometimes the *ch* sound is spelled *ch* and sometimes *tch*. It is spelled *tch* in most monosyllabic words with a short vowel before the *tch*:

catch	fetch
crutch	notch
ditch	pitch

Sometimes prefixes or suffixes are added to such words:

bewitch	catching
rehitch	clutched

In polysyllabic words and in words with a long vowel or a consonant before the *ch* sound, the spelling is *ch*:

attach	reach
beach	sandwich
branch	squelch
coach	*Exceptions:*
couch	dispatch
detach	hatchet
ostrich	kitchen

Words ending in *ge* and *dge* cause spelling confusion. Those ending in *dge* are mostly monosyllabic words with a short vowel preceding the *dge*:

badge	judge
bridge	ledge
budge	lodge
dodge	pledge
hedge	trudge

Sometimes prefixes are added to such words:

adjudge	dislodge
begrudge	prejudge

In polysyllabic words and in words with a long vowel sound or a consonant before the *ge* sound, the spelling is *ge*:

allege	privilege
college	sacrilege
décolletage	siege
forage	stooge
huge	*Exception:*
marriage	knowledge

Though they are not phonemic principles, certain facts about prefixes and suffixes will be mentioned here because they pertain to phonemic spelling. The following examples are hyphenated to show phonemic spelling. *None of the words is hyphenated in ordinary writing.*

There is no such prefix as *diss* (though *dis* is often added to words beginning with *s*):

dis-agree	dis-appoint
dis-appear	dis-approve

When the prefix *dis* or *mis* is added to a root beginning with *s*, both *s*'s are retained:

dis-satisfaction	dis-solve
dis-sect	dis-suade
dis-service	mis-sent
dis-similar	mis-spell
dis-social	mis-statement

The prefixes *de, pro,* and *re* are never followed by a double consonant:

de-duction	pro-gram
de-ficient	pro-gress
de-finite	re-collect
de-legate	re-ference
de-pression	re-frain
pro-fessor	re-solution

The prefix *e* is attached to many roots beginning with *l,* and the prefix *el* is added to many roots not beginning with *l.* But only one root beginning with *l* has *el* as a prefix: *ellipse* (several words are formed from it). Therefore extra *l*'s should not be put in words like the following:

e-lastic	e-lide
e-late	el-igible
e-lection	e-liminate
e-lectric	e-lision
el-egant	e-longate
el-egy	e-lope
el-ement	el-oquent
el-ephant	e-lucidate
el-evate	e-lude
e-licit	e-lusive

When *ly* is added to a word ending in *l*, both *l*'s are retained:

accidental-ly	natural-ly
fatal-ly	real-ly
final-ly	total-ly

When the suffix *ly* is added to a word ending in a silent *e,* the *e* should not be dropped:

approximate-ly	like-ly
immediate-ly	rude-ly
lame-ly	*Exception:*
late-ly	truly

Words ending in *able* or *ible* do not follow the above principle:

ably	incredibly
dependably	notably

Though minor, the above phonemic principles will help you spell many difficult words. There is also another principle—a major one—that you must understand if you want to spell English with reasonable accuracy. Most students just absorb an understanding of this principle and apply it subconsciously, but illustration of it here may help you avoid pitfalls in spelling. Though there are exceptions to it, this principle in general holds true: In a vowel-consonant-vowel sequence the first vowel, *if accented*, is long; in a vowel-consonant-consonant sequence or a vowel-consonant-end-of-word sequence, the first vowel is short. Thus the first vowel in words like these is long:

bite	pate
cute	rate
dote	rote

But the first vowel in words like these is short:

bit	dotting
cut	pat
dot	patting

Quite clearly, the silent *e* in the first group is a device for spelling the long-vowel phonemes.[3]

The silent *e* is only a part of the principle. In words like these the first vowel is also long:

dating	roping
dative	total
duty	writing

The vowel-consonant-vowel principle is at work here. In words like these, however, the first vowel is short:

matting	stopping
smitten	toddler
smutty	written

Here the vowel-consonant-consonant principle is working.

There are—predictably in English—exceptions to the above principle. For example, *coming* is not pronounced with a long *o*. But in general the principle holds true and therefore a knowledge of it is essential for good spelling. Anyone who understands the principle will not confuse such pairs as these:

before—befor	quite—quit
campus—campuse	redder—reder
careful—carful	refer—refere
confuse—confus	safely—safly
forecast—forcast	scared—scarred
infer—infere	slur—slure
interfere—interfer	stopping—stoping
interpret—interprete	suppose—suppos
occasion—occassion	therefore—therefor
purely—purly	writing—writting

By keeping in mind these phonemic principles and others that you absorb unconsciously (for example, the various sounds of *c, f, k,* and *s*), you can spell many, many English words phonemically, particularly long words. In so doing, you should sound out each syllable much more

---

[3] Though *e*-consonant-silent *e* is sometimes used to spell the long *e* sound (discr*e*te, prec*e*de), the long *e* sound is most often spelled *ee, ea,* or *ie* rather than *e*-consonant-silent *e*.

separately and emphatically than you normally would in using them in speech. For example, in spelling words like the following, sound each syllable separately and emphatically:

ab-bre-vi-ate   com-pe-ti-tion
ac-ci-den-tal-ly   e-rad-i-cate
ac-com-mo-date   pro-nun-ci-a-tion
ac-com-pa-ny-ing   tem-per-a-ture

If you will follow these suggestions, you will find English spelling much more phonemic than you thought.

Spelling by Rules

The so-called rules of spelling are based on phonemic principles like those just explained and thus might have been included in that section. Five of these rules, however, are of such honorable and ancient standing in English textbooks that they are given separate entry here. These rules cover a large percentage of the most often misspelled English words. If you will **memorize** and **use** these rules, you can eliminate a great many of your spelling problems.

☐   *Rule 1: Place* i *before* e *when pronounced as* ee *except after* c.

This rule covers the troublesome *ie* and *ei* combinations. When the combination is pronounced as a long *e,* it is spelled *ei* after *c*:

ceiling   deceive
conceit   perceive
conceive   receive
deceit   receipt

When the combination is pronounced as a long *e* and follows a consonant other than *c,* it is spelled *ie*:

achieve   priest
believe   relief
brief   relieve
chief   shield
field   siege
grief   thief
niece   wield
piece   yield

Of course, there are a few exceptions. Here is a nonsense sentence that gives most of them: "Neither (either) species seized weird leisure."

You should **memorize** this sentence and call it to mind whenever you want to spell one of the *ie* or *ei* words in it.

When the *ei* combination is pronounced as a long *a* or *i,* it is spelled *ei*:

freight	reign
height	reins
inveigh	vein
inveigle	sleight-of-hand
neighbor	weight

The words of the *ie-ei* kind that give the most trouble are *receive, chief, niece,* and *seize.* You should never misspell these (or any of the others) if you will **memorize** the rule and the sentence of exceptions.

☐ *Rule 2: Drop a final silent* e *when adding a suffix beginning with a vowel:*

believe—believing	imagine—imaginative
condole—condolence	mange—mangy
create—creative	write—writing

In current practice this rule is sometimes ignored when *able* or *age* is added to a word ending in a silent *e*:

blame—blamable—blameable	make—makable—makeable
desire—desirable—desireable	mile—milage—mileage
like—likable—likeable	name—namable—nameable
live—livable—liveable	sale—salable—saleable
love—lovable—loveable	use—usable—useable

Probably there will be a general increase in the number of words that may retain the silent *e* when *able* or *age* is added.

Because of the vowel-consonant-consonant principle explained above, the silent *e* should not be dropped when a suffix beginning with a consonant is added. Note, for example, the different pronunciation (short *i* and *a*) that would be required with these spellings:

like—likness	safe—safty

In such spellings the silent *e* should be retained so that a vowel-consonant-vowel sequence will require a long vowel pronunciation:

fate—fateful	like—likeness
hate—hateful	safe—safety

Four common supposed exceptions to the above rule are these:

argue—argument	true—truly
awe—awful	whole—wholly

But the first three are not really exceptions, for the final *e* is not used in any of the three to produce a long vowel sound. (*Judgment* and *judgement* are both acceptable spellings.)

☐ *Rule 3: When a word ends in a silent* e *preceded by* c *or* g, *retain the* e *when adding a suffix beginning with* a, o, *or* u.

The reason for this rule is that normally *c* is pronounced as a *k* before *a, o, u,* or a consonant and as an *s* before *i, e,* or *y,* and that *g* is normally pronounced *guh* before *a, o, u,* or a consonant and as a *j* before *e, i,* or *y.* The first mentioned pronunciations are called hard and the second soft. The silent *e* is retained to preserve the soft *c* and *g* pronunciations. For example, *noticable* would be pronounced *no-tik-able,* whereas *noticeable* is pronounced *note-is-able.* Here are examples of the rule in action:

advantage—advantageous	manage—manageable
arrange—arrangeable	peace—peaceable
change—changeable	replace—replaceable
courage—courageous	service—serviceable

When a suffix beginning with a vowel is added to a word ending in *c,* a *k* is added to retain the hard *c* sound. For example, *picnicing* would be pronounced *pick-nis-ing.* Examples of the rule:

picnic—picnicking	politic—politicking
panic—panicked	traffic—trafficking

☐ *Rule 4: Change the* y *to* i *when adding a suffix to a word ending in* y *preceded by a consonant:*

busy—business	heavy—heaviest
cry—crier	lonely—loneliness
dry—driest	necessary—necessarily
easy—easily	noisy—noisily
gloomy—gloomiest	ordinary—ordinarily
handy—handily	satisfactory—satisfactorily

This rule also applies in the spelling of the plural form of a noun ending in *y* preceded by a consonant. The *y* is changed to *i* and *es* is added to make the plural:

baby—babies	harpy—harpies
copy—copies	lady—ladies
gravy—gravies	navy—navies

The rule also applies in spelling the third person singular of a verb ending in *y* preceded by a consonant. The *y* is changed to *i* and either *es* or *ed* is added:

deny—denies—denied	pry—pries—pried
envy—envies—envied	reply—replies—replied
fry—fries—fried	try—tries—tried

The rule does not apply when *ing* is added to a word:

deny—denying	reply—replying
envy—envying	study—studying
fry—frying	try—trying

When the final *y* of a word is preceded by a vowel, the *y* is not changed when a suffix is added:

annoy—annoys—annoyed	stay—stays—stayed
convey—conveys—conveyed	turkey—turkeys
employ—employs—employed	valley—valleys
play—plays—played	whey—wheys

There are three common exceptions to this rule:

lay—laid	say—said
pay—paid	

Note: The *y*-to-*i* rule does not apply in the spelling of the plural proper names:

Brady—Bradys	Grady—Gradys
Crowly—Crowlys	Kennedy—Kennedys

☐ *Rule 5: When adding a suffix beginning with a vowel to a word accented on the last syllable and ending in one consonant preceded by one vowel, double the final consonant.*

This rule is due to the principle that in a vowel-consonant-vowel sequence the first vowel, if accented, is long and that in a vowel-consonant-consonant sequence the vowel is short. Thus *rate* has a long *a* sound and *rat* a short *a* sound. *Rating* also has a long *a* sound because of the vowel-consonant-vowel sequence. So if we want to spell *ratting* rather than *rating,* we must double the *t* in *rat* before adding *ing.* Then the vowel-consonant-consonant sequence will maintain the short *a* sound.

To understand the necessity of the rule, pronounce the misspelled words in the right-hand column following:

bid	biding
cut	cuting
pot	poted
tip	tiped

When the rule is applied, words will retain their proper pronunciation:

beg—begging	readmit—readmitted
compel—compelled	refer—referred
concur—concurred	rot—rotting
confer—conferred	scrub—scrubbed
debar—debarred	sip—sipping
occur—occurred	slap—slapped
pin—pinning	snub—snubbing
prefer—preferred	stab—stabbed

If the last syllable of a word is not accented, the consonant is not doubled when a prefix beginning with a vowel is added, nor is the final consonant doubled in any word if the added suffix begins with a consonant.

banter—bantering	honor—honorable
glad—gladness	leaven—leavening
happen—happened	prohibit—prohibited
hinder—hindered	sin—sinful

Spelling by Mnemonic Devices

Psychologists do not fully understand on a theoretical basis just how our memories work. But on a practical basis everyone knows that **association** is a great aid to memory. We can more easily remember something—a telephone number, a person's name, an address—if we associate it with something else that is easy for us to remember. For example, consider the telephone number 7-1165. A gambler might easily remember this number as a sequence of natural passes in a dice game: a seven, an eleven, and another eleven made up of six and five. Once the gambler made that association in his mind, he would never forget that particular telephone number. Clues of this sort that aid our memories are called **mnemonic devices,** from a Greek word meaning memory. Incidentally, you can remember that *mnemonic* begins with an *m* if you remember that its meaning is *memory*; or you can remember that it means *memory* if you remember that it begins with an *m*.

Mnemonic devices can be valuable aids in spelling troublesome words. Quite a number of these associational clues have been invented for particularly troublesome words. Some of these are listed below. You can also invent your own private clues for those words you find difficult to spell.

all right—Pair it off with *all wrong.*

a lot—Think of buying a lot; so avoid *alot.*

amateur—The last syllable is *not* spelled as it sounds; so spell *teur,* not *ture* or *tuer.*

attendance—Think of *attend dance* and so use *ance.*

bargain—There is a *gain* in a bargain.

battalion—Think of a *batt*le against *a lion.*

breakfast—It is literally to break a fast.

bulletin—Who put a *bullet in* a bulletin?

calendar—Think of calend*ar art.*

courtesy—It is a habit with those who *court.*

definite—It comes from *finite.*

dessert—It has two *s*'s, like *s*trawberry *s*hortcake.

disease—The word literally means *dis ease.*

dissipation—It makes you dizzy, so use *dissi,* not *dissa.*

eighth—Remember the *h-t-h* sequence.

embarrass—Remember two *r*'s and two *s*'s.

familiar—Think of a *fami* (whatever that is) *liar.*

forty—It is not pronounced like *four.*

friend—Remember that he's a friend to the *end.*

grammar—The *rammar* part is spelled the same both ways.

handkerchief—You use your *hand* to pull out your kerchief.

holiday—It comes from *holy* and so has only one *l.*

occurrence—It has *rre* as in *current* event.

peculiar—Think of a *pecu* (whatever that is) *liar.*

principal—The principal of a school is a *pal* to you.

principle—The principle meaning a rule ends in *le* as ru*le* does.

rhythm—Remember the *rh-th* sequence.

separate—It's hard to spell; therefore there is *a rat* in it.

stationery—The word meaning pap*er* has an *er* in it; the other has an *ar.*

sugar—Both sug*ar* and s*a*lt have *a*'s.

together—Think of a date: *to get her.*

tragedy—There is a *rage* in tragedy.

until—The word with two syllables has one *l*; the word with one syllable (*till*) has two *l*'s.

Spelling by Practice

Spelling problems can be overcome only through practice, and generally the practice available in college classes is not sufficient for poor spellers. If you need more practice than your instructor can allow time for, you should arrange practice sessions with a friend.

The kind of practice you undertake is important. Spelling individual words from lists will probably not help you much in your actual writing. Instead, you should practice from dictated sentences, for then you will be imitating a real writing situation and thus will be more likely to retain and be able to use what you learn.

A good plan to follow is to start with the twenty sentences below, which contain about one hundred simple spelling problems. Have them dictated to you by a friend. Then have your friend compose another twenty sentences, using the words you missed from the first twenty sentences plus twenty-five or more words from the lists of words that also follow below. Your third practice session should be composed of dictated sentences that include the words you missed on the first and second tests plus another group from the lists. And so on. Before each practice session you should study the words you missed on the two previous tests and the next group from the study list. If you will get your roommate, sweetheart, or mother to help you with such a planned program of practice and if you yourself will work hard at it, you can soon cure most of your spelling ills. That's assuming, of course, that you have spelling problems.

Spelling Test for Individual Practice

1. Always accept a friend's quiet advice.
2. It's all right to believe your principal's description.
3. Today's tragedy occurred as a necessary occasion.
4. The government's laboratory probably owns shining equipment.
5. Who's supposed to receive separate salaries?
6. I'm not coming until this peculiar weather truly changes.
7. James' (James's) puppies meant to disappear with the donkeys.
8. Whose library is therefore losing business?
9. Someone's neighbor is studying grammar.
10. Jane's babies are usually among ninety-eight enemies.
11. The forty priests are beginning their similar duties.
12. A woman is writing recipes for two hundred attorneys.
13. The professor is hoping his speech won't be omitted.
14. Mr. Jones' (Jones's) worries are too definite.
15. Everybody's courtesy doesn't need improving.
16. The bulletin described Betty's surprise marriage.
17. The dog injured itself while wagging its tail.
18. Sitting Bull's niece tries to be a beautiful amateur chief.
19. College is a bargain and a privilege.
20. A lot of desert sand is quite coarse.

Common Words Quite Frequently Misspelled

accommodate	criticize
achieve	dealt
acquaint	decided
acquire	definite
affect	definitely
all right	describe
altogether	description
among	despair
analysis	dining
analyze	disagree
answer	disastrous
apparent	effect
appear	eighth
appearance	embarrass
argument	environment
balance	equipped
before	especially
beginning	exaggerate
believe	excellent
benefit	existence
benefited	experience
breathe	explanation
brilliant	familiar
buried	fascinate
business	foreign
calendar	forty
career	fourth
carrying	friend
category	government
certain	grammar
changeable	height
choose	imagination
chose	immediately
clothes	incidentally
coming	intelligence
comparative	interest
comparison	interpret
conscience	its
conscious	it's
consistent	itself
controlled	knowledge
course	led

literature
loneliness
lonely
lose
losing
marriage
meant
necessary
Negroes
noticeable
occasion
occurred
occurrence
original
paid
passed
past
perform
personnel
piece
pleasant
possess
possible
practical
precede
preferred
prejudice
prevalent
principal
principle
privilege
probably
procedure
proceed
professor
psychology
pursue
quiet

quite
really
realize
receive
recommend
referring
repetition
rhythm
sense
separate
shining
similar
studying
succeed
surprise
than
then
their
there
they're
thorough
tries
truly
to
too
two
until
using
usually
varies
various
weather
• whether
woman
writing
yield
you're
yours

Common Words Often Misspelled

accept
acceptable
accidentally

across
advice
advise

aggressive
article
athlete
attendance
attendant
authority
basically
Britain
careful
careless
challenge
character
characteristic
college
conceive
condemn
considerably
convenience
curious
dependent
difference
disappoint
discipline
dominant
efficient
extremely
finally
fulfil(l)
fundamental
further
guarantee
guidance
happiness
heroes
heroine
hindrance
hopeless
hoping
hopping
hospital
humor
humorous
hundred
hypocrisy

hypocrite
ideally
ignorance
immense
importance
increase
indefinite
independent
indispensable
individual
inevitable
influential
ingenious
intellect
interfered
involve
irrelevant
irreverent
jealousy
laboratory
laborer
later
latter
leisure
length
likely
livelihood
luxury
magnificent
maintenance
maneuver
mathematics
medieval
mere
miniature
ninety
ninth
omitted
operate
opinion
opponent
opportunity
optimism
parallel

particular	speech
peculiar	sponsor
permanent	subtle
permitted	subtly
philosophy	summary
physically	supposed
planned	suppress
propaganda	technique
quantity	temperament
relieve	therefore
religious	tomorrow
resources	tragedy
response	transferred
ridicule	undoubtedly
ridiculous	unusually
satire	villain
schedule	weird
sergeant	who's
significance	whose

CAPITALIZATION

Though capitalization is the most purely conventional of all aspects of writing, there is an elusiveness about its rules that constantly plagues all writers who want to be wholly "correct" in their usage. One of the questions most frequently asked of English teachers is, "Do you capitalize such-and-such a word in such-and-such a case?" There are two main sources of the uncertainty about capitalization. First, the rules often call for capital letters for specific reference and lowercase (small) letters for general reference, as in President-president, Mayor-mayor, and so forth. But frequently a writer is not sure whether he is making a specific or a general reference. For example, are the references in the following sentence specific or general? "One of the duties of the President (president?) is to appoint Supreme Court Justices (justices?)." Second, a capital letter is often used to give emphasis to an important word, as in this sentence: "A study of the Humanities is the only avenue to true education." But again, writers are often uncertain as to when a word warrants capitalization for emphasis. For example, is *Humanities* a more important word in the above sentence than *education?* Or consider this sentence from a business letter from a publishing company: "I am very happy to send you a Complimentary examination copy of this book." Is *Complimentary* important enough to warrant capitalization?

Because of these two sources of uncertainty, and perhaps also because of personal whim, practices in capitalization vary rather widely among professional writers. There is not, even, a discernible trend toward either more or less capitalization among professional writers. Some writers seem to be increasing and others decreasing the number of instances in which they use capital letters. For example, G. M. Trevelyan, one of the greatest English historians (and a great stylist) of this century, capitalized the following words (and many more like them) without specific reference:

Charity Schools	Librarian
Church	Mayor
Churchman	Nineteenth Century
Colonial	the Press
Deistic	Puritanism
Grammar School	Reform
Hell	State
History	Statute
Industrial Revolution	University

On the other hand, Alfred Kazin, a noted American critic, used lowercase letters in these words:

British army colonel	the Presbyterian church
fascism	socialism
hell	

But to complicate matters, in the same article he capitalized these:

Communism	Depression

Obviously, there can be considerable leeway in the practices of capitalization in English.

In spite of the wholly conventional nature of capitalization and in spite of the variant practices found among professional writers, the general public believes that "errors" in capitalization (like errors in spelling) indicate ignorance. For example, anyone who fails to capitalize the pronoun *I* is thought to be severely retarded educationally. Yet that pronoun is capitalized only because long ago someone thought the lowercase *i* was likely to be overlooked in a line of script or type. Or, for another example, the spelling of *English* with a lowercase *e* is particularly offensive to English teachers. Yet in German (a language rather closely related to English) such proper adjectives are conventionally spelled with lowercase letters. But logic aside, convention calls for adherence to the rules of capitalization, and so you should conform as best you can.

As a student, you should learn (if you have not already done so) the cut-and-dried rules adhered to by most writers, but you should be allowed to exercise your own judgment or preference in doubtful cases. Liberal-minded people do not, as a rule, force their preferences on other people because capitalization seldom affects clarity, logic, and precision. *The following words (and other comparable words or phrases), for example, are now widely accepted with either capital or lowercase letters.* Often a writer will make his decision on the basis of context; that is, on one occasion he may want to capitalize one of these words, but not on another occasion.

Army, Navy, Air Force
Archbishop, Bishop, King, Pope
Board of Directors
Church
Civil Service
Communism, Democracy, Fascism, Socialism
Congressman
Deity
Democrat, Republican
Federal Court, Municipal Court
Federal Government
Fraternity Row
Freshman Class
Heaven, Hell
Mayor, Principal, Professor
Presidential Inauguration
School Board
Scripture
Steering Committee
State Government
State Law
Student Body, Student Government
Sunday School

The following rules of capitalization include only those about which there is little or no disagreement among educated writers of English. You should follow these rules because most educated writers do. In doubtful cases, follow your own inclination.

☐   *Rule 1: Capitalize the first word of each sentence, the pronoun I, the interjection O, and the first word in each line of poetry unless the poet himself did not capitalize it:*

Here lies my wife; here let her lie;
Now she's at peace, and so am I.

☐ *Rule 2: Capitalize the first word and all other words except articles, prepositions, and coordinating conjunctions in a title or chapter heading:*

TITLE OF A BOOK: The Rise and Fall of the Third Reich
TITLE OF AN ESSAY: "Marriage Customs through the Ages"
CHAPTER HEADING: Symbolism in the American Short Story

☐ *Rule 3: Capitalize all proper names and adjectives formed from proper names:*

African	French
Alabaman	Hollywoodish
Caucasian	Oriental
Chicagoan	Platonism
English	Swedish

Note: The word *Negro* is now often used with a lowercase *n*. The word *white* or the word *black*, meaning race, is capitalized by only a few writers. Either usage for these three words is acceptable.

☐ *Rule 4: Capitalize references to the Deity, the names of divine books of all religions, and references to specific religions or religious sects:*

Baptist	Koran
Bible	our Lord
Book of Mormon	Mormon
Catholic	New Testament
Christ	Pentateuch
God	Protestant
Holy Ghost	Seventh Day Adventist
Jehovah	the Trinity
Jewish	the Upanishads

Note: An increasing number of writers are using lowercase letters to spell Protestant, Catholic, Baptist, and so forth.

☐ *Rule 5: Capitalize the titles of relatives when used with the person's name and when the person is addressed directly but not when used with the pronoun* my:

Aunt Nellie   Grandfather Scarne
Uncle Josh   Cousin Margie
"Oh, Mother, can you come here?"
"My goodness, Grandfather, did you hurt yourself?"
"My mother is an excellent cellist."

☐ *Rule 6: Capitalize the titles of officials when a specific in-dividual is meant, whether or not the person's name is included:*

Mayor Hartsfield	the Lieutenant
Vice-President Finlinson	the Senator
Colonel Wetzler	the Pastor
Dean Levinson	the Board Chairman
Principal Wallace	the Chairman

☐ *Rule 7: Capitalize the days of the week and the months of the year but not the names of the seasons:*

Monday	spring
January	winter

☐ *Rule 8: Capitalize the names of streets, avenues, parks, rivers, mountains, cities, states, provinces, nations, continents, oceans, lakes, and specific geographical regions:*

Tenth Street	the Strait of Magellan
Gayley Avenue	Africa
Central Park	the Midwest
the Red River	the Northeast
Ghana	the South
the Iberian Peninsula	Asia Minor
the North Pole	the Far East
the Allegheny Mountains	the Western Hemisphere
Bear Mountain	the Central Plains
Alaska	Lake Tahoe
Alberta	the Pacific Ocean
the West Coast	the Black Sea

Note: Do not capitalize the names of directions:

Go west, young man.
The farther south we drove, the hotter it got.

☐ *Rule 9: Capitalize the names of buildings:*

the Palace Theater	the Capitol
the First Methodist Church	the Sill Building
the Humanities Building	the Empire State Building

☐ *Rule 10: Capitalize the names of private organizations:*

Rotary	the Society of Individualists
the Elks Club	the American Legion

☐ *Rule 11: Capitalize the names of governmental organizations:*

the Veterans Administration	the U.S. Department of Agriculture
Congress	the Peace Corps
the House	the United States Navy

☐ *Rule 12: Capitalize the names of historical documents, events, and periods or eras:*

the Declaration of Independence	the Battle of Midway
the Bill of Rights	the Diet of Worms
the Atlantic Charter	the Middle Ages
the Missouri Compromise	the Renaissance
World War I	the Napoleonic Wars

Note: Some writers do not capitalize the names of periods such as the Romantic Age and the Baroque Era.

☐ *Rule 13: Capitalize the names of specific school courses:*

Senior Problems	Introduction to the Study of Poetry
Twentieth-Century Novels	American Literature
History 3A	Freshman Composition
Elementary Algebra	Advanced Organic Chemistry

☐ *Rule 14: Capitalize brand names but not the name of the product:*

a Ford car	Camay soap
Goodyear tires	Jerseymaid ice cream
Norwalk gasoline	Mum deodorant

These rules do not cover all the cases when you should not capitalize, but a satisfactory rule to follow is not to capitalize a word unless you have a specific reason for doing so. The best policy is to use your own judgment in doubtful cases and not to consider the problem important. For example, most writers do not capitalize the names of foods (rice, spaghetti), games (golf, bridge), diseases (cancer, mumps), occupations (engineer, doctor), animals (trout, robin, collie), plants (maple, rose), or musical instruments (piano, violoncello). But occasionally a specific context may call for the capitalization of words like these, and then you should not hesitate to capitalize them.

THE APOSTROPHE AND THE HYPHEN

Both the apostrophe and the hyphen look like marks of punctuation, and both have been defined as such, even in dictionaries. But actually neither is any more a mark of punctuation than is a letter of the alphabet. Marks of punctuation are used to clarify sentence structure in writing, just as pauses and intonation are used in oral language. Apostrophes and hyphens are used to clarify certain kinds of spelling situations; that is the whole extent of their use in English. They cannot be indicated by the voice as marks of punctuation can be.

Since the apostrophe and hyphen are used only in spelling, their use is conventional. We could actually do without them altogether or we could substitute other devices for them. But they are convenient marks and do help clarify English spelling. Therefore you should, if you have not already done so, learn the rules governing their use.

The Use of the Apostrophe in Possessives

In oral English, the same pronunciation is used for the plural form, the singular possessive form, and the plural possessive form of most nouns. Listeners are seldom confused, however, as to which is meant, for context will almost always supply that information. In writing, not only context but also spelling tells the reader the meaning of a noun ending in an *s* sound. For example, the following triplets are pronounced alike, but have different meanings in sentences:

companies—company's—companies'	peoples—people's—peoples'
days—day's—days'	rats—rat's—rats'
ladies—lady's—ladies'	waiters—waiter's—waiters'

Even in writing, context will almost always tell a reader which of the three meanings is intended, but the apostrophe makes the distinctions crystal clear.

At one time the apostrophe was not used to spell possessives in English. Instead, an *es* was added to words ending in *x* and *s*, as in these phrases:

a foxes tail	a lionesses cubs
Jameses book	his mistresses eyes

And an *s* or an *es* was added to words not ending in *x* or *s*, as in these phrases:

a mans wife	a mannes wife
a dogs tail	a dogges tail
a birds wing	a birdes wing

In the sixteenth century writers began to use apostrophes in contractions, and, to make contractions, they often substituted an apostrophe for the *e* in the *es* possessive ending, in this way:

a fox's tail	a lioness's cubs
James's book	his mistress's eyes

Then gradually, through ignorance or carelessness, writers began using the apostrophe even when no *e* had necessarily been omitted, as in:

a bird's wing	a man's wife
two birds' wings	men's wives

The process of adopting the use of the apostrophe for all English possessives took about two centuries. As late as 1725 its use had not become wholly standardized.

Humorously enough, the use of the apostrophe in possessives led some scholars in the late sixteenth and early seventeenth centuries to believe that the possessive form was a contraction of the possessive pronoun *his*—that is, that the apostrophe marked the omission of the *hi,* in this way:

a man's wife = a man his wife
a dog's tail = a dog his tail

One notable writer even entitled a book *Purchas His Pilgrims,* meaning *Purchas's Pilgrims.*

The use of the apostrophe in spelling English possessives, then, is a historical mistake, growing out of the use of the mark to indicate contractions. Even the present pronunciation of the word occurred through ignorance. The four-syllable word *a-pós-tro-phe* means a certain figure of speech. The three-syllable French word *a-po-stróphe* is an entirely different word and is the one that came into English to designate the mark ('). So if early English writers had not made ignorant mistakes, writers nowadays would use a three-syllable apostrophe only to indicate contractions.

But the four-syllable apostrophe is with us now and is conventionally used in possessive spellings. And, as in all matters of spelling and capitalization, the public thinks that failure to use the apostrophe in possessives is a sure sign of ignorance. Even students who habitually fail to put apostrophes in possessives will, when questioned, assert that apostrophes are absolutely necessary. Since the public feels as it does, you must use apostrophes as conventionally dictated if you want your usage to be acceptable in educated circles.

Following are the conventional rules governing the use of the apostrophe in possessive spellings.

☐ *Rule 1: The possessive form of a singular noun not ending in s is spelled with the addition of an 's:*

John's coat   the teacher's temper
a sheep's fleece   the President's power

☐ *Rule 2: The possessive form of a singular noun ending in s is spelled with the addition of either an 's or just an ':*

a waitress' order *or* a waitress's order
a crocus' odor *or* a crocus's odor
James's book *or* James' book

☐ *Rule 3: The possessive form of a plural noun ending in s is spelled with the addition of an ' only:*

several boys' bicycles
the Supreme Court Justices' decision
the Board of Supervisors' tax cut

☐ *Rule 4: The possessive form of a plural noun not ending in s is spelled with the addition of an 's:*

the men's wives   six sheep's fleece
the women's husbands   the children's toys

Note: For those who have trouble with apostrophes, the previous four rules may be reduced to these two: (1) the possessive of a ncun not ending in *s* is formed with an 's, (2) the possessive of a noun ending in *s* may be formed with just an '. (See note following Rule 6 for determining placement of the apostrophe.)

☐ *Rule 5: The possessive forms of the indefinite pronouns are spelled with the addition of an 's:*

one's desire   nobody's business
someone's sweetheart   everybody's mistake
anybody's guess   everybody else's money

☐ *Rule 6: Nouns expressing periods of time and amounts of money are given normal possessive spellings in possessive constructions.*

one hour's time   the year's end
two hours' wait   a moment's delay
one month's salary   your money's worth
six years' delay   three dollars' worth
today's assignment   one nickel's difference

Note: The placement of an apostrophe can always be accurately determined by converting the possessive phrase into a "belonging to" phrase or an "of" phrase in order to get the base noun that will show possession. Examples:

1. James' book = a book belonging to *James.* The base noun is *James;* therefore the correct possessive form is *James'* or *James's*, not *Jame's* or *James'es.*

2. The men's wives = the wives belonging to the *men.* The base noun is *men;* therefore *men's* rather than *mens'* is the proper possessive form.

3. Three teachers' reports = the reports of three *teachers.* The base noun is *teachers;* therefore the proper possessive form is *teachers'* not *teacher's* or *teachers's.*

4. The Joneses' dog = the dog belonging to the *Joneses.* The base noun is *Joneses* (plural of Jones); therefore the correct possessive form is *Joneses'*, not *Jones'* or *Jones'es.*

5. Mr. Jones' dog = the dog belonging to Mr. *Jones.* The base noun is *Jones;* therefore the correct possessive form is *Jones's* or *Jones'*, not *Jone's* or *Joneses'.*

6. Nobody's business = the business belonging to *nobody.* The base word is *nobody;* therefore the proper possessive form is *nobody's*, not *nobodies'.*

7. Your money's worth = the worth of your *money.* The base noun is *money;* therefore the possessive form is *money's.*

8. Three months' vacation = the vacation of three *months.* The base noun is *months;* therefore the possessive form is *months'.*

9. An hour's delay = the delay of an *hour.* The base noun is *hour;* therefore the possessive form is *hour's.*

□   *Rule 7: The personal possessive pronouns are spelled without apostrophes.*

Its paw is injured.	The profit is *ours.*
The book is *hers.*	The debt is *yours.*
The car is *theirs.*	*Whose* lunch is that?

General note: Some stylists maintain that nouns which name inanimate objects should not have their possessive forms spelled with an *'s.* Instead, they recommend "of" phrases like these:

The entrance requirements of the school (*rather than* the school's entrance requirements)
The eraser of the pencil (*rather than* the pencil's eraser)

This precept, however, is not wholly valid. It is true that euphony will sometimes lead a writer to use an "of" phrase instead of a possessive form, as "the roof of the house" rather than "the house's roof." But such phrases as the following are common in the best writing:

the bank's cashier   the tree's roots
the book's frontispiece   the farm's value
the car's brakes   the light's gleam

The Use of the Apostrophe in Contractions

The original use of the apostrophe in English was to show omission of one or more letters in a word. Such an omission is known as a contraction. The most widespread use of the apostrophe for this purpose was first made by poets to help the reader with his pronunciation. For example, in the original writings of Shakespeare the word *walk'd* is to be pronounced as one syllable and the word *walked* as two. Or, for another example, a poet in the earlier days of modern English might have used the phrase *th' apple* as two syllables instead of three. Even nowadays the spelling *o'er* is often used poetically to denote a one-syllable pronunciation.

The use of the apostrophe for poetic contractions has diminished, but we still use apostrophes for contractions in our ordinary writing. The rule is simple: *enter an apostrophe where one of more letters have been omitted.* Examples:

are not = aren't (*not* arn't *or* are'nt)
cannot = can't (*not* cant *or* ca'nt)
it is = it's (*not* its *or* its')
of the clock = o'clock

In speech, Americans often slur syllables. When reporting conversation, a writer may use apostrophes to indicate the intended pronunciation. Example: "Somethin' funny 'uz goin' on at fo' o'clock this mornin'." The apostrophe is also used in contractions of dates. Examples:

He owns a '68 Ford.
The '30s were a period of economic depression.
Some oldtimers still remember '88 as the year of the big blizzard.

Such contractions can be used only when the century involved is obvious. Unless another century has been clearly mentioned, such a contraction will always apply to the last ninety-nine years.

One of America's greatest contemporary authors, William Faulkner, who died in 1962, often spelled the common contractions without apostrophes, like this:

cant	oclock
dont	wont

He also used *ain't* and other vulgate expressions in his own speech. College students, however, had best conform to convention.

The Use of the Apostrophe in Plural Spellings

Apostrophes should not be used in the spelling of ordinary plurals and verbs in the third person singular present tense. Almost every English teacher is far more tolerant of omitted apostrophes in possessive spellings than he is of their misuse in plurals and verbs. All of the apostrophes in the following examples are **misused:**

My brother read's several book's each month.
He tries' to read the monthly fare of all the book club's.
He spend's about thirty dollar's a month just for books'.

When in doubt, always test with a "belonging to" phrase. Also remember that in general it is better to omit an apostrophe than to use one unnecessarily.

Apostrophes are frequently used in spelling the plurals of numerals, letters of the alphabet, and abbreviations consisting only of capital letters. Examples:

There are four *s*'s and four *i*'s in Mississippi.
I made five C's last semester.
I own three old Colt .44's.
His 9's look like 7's.
The 1920's were an era of lawlessness.
All the CPA's in town have gone to a convention.
The FFA's are meeting tonight.

Though the use of apostrophes for these plural spellings has been standard, many professional writers and book publishers do not use them when clarity is not generally affected. Thus most writers and publishers would use apostrophes in spelling the plurals of lowercase letters (*a*'s, *i*'s, *t*'s, *p*'s) because of improved clarity but omit them in the spelling of the plurals of capital letters (Cs, Ps, PDQs) and numerals (3s, 9s, 44s, 1930s).

Sometimes words are used not for their meaning but as words, as in this sentence: "The word *so* is less often misspelled than the word *therefore.*" The most commonly accepted practice in spelling the plural of a word used as a word is to *italicize* (underline in script or typewriting) the word and to add an *'s*. Examples:

> No proposal should be sprinkled with *if*'s.
> His sermon was full of *consequently*'s.

The Use of the Hyphen

Like the apostrophe, the hyphen is a mark used in spelling, not punctuation. Following are the rules governing its use.

☐   *Rule 1: In dividing a word at the end of a line of script, typewriting, or print, divide between syllables and indicate division with a hyphen.*

Careful pronunciation will usually disclose the syllabification of a word. When in doubt, consult a dictionary. Never divide a one-syllable word at the end of a line, such as *tw-elve, len-gth,* and *stop-ped.* Avoid dividing a word so that a one-letter syllable is left by itself, such as *a-void* or *mush-y.* Do not divide a word unless the maintenance of a margin demands it.

☐   *Rule 2: Hyphenate compound numbers and fractions:*

twenty-two	one-half
thirty-four	a half
one hundred and sixty-three	three-fourths
three thousand and forty-one	sixty-three and a third
fifty-fifth	sixty-three and one-third

☐   *Rule 3: Hyphenate compound nouns when hyphenation contributes to clarity.*

This rule is of necessity vaguely stated. Current practice in hyphenation of compound nouns varies widely. The trend is conspicuously toward less hyphenation and more one-word compounding. For example, the following words were once hyphenated but now are usually spelled as single words:

bypass	schoolboy
gamebag	storytelling
Midwest	sunstroke
playgoer	wallpaper
playhouse	weekend
rightwing	workshop

It seems certain that more and more once-hyphenated compound nouns will in the future be spelled as single words. But when clarity is improved by retention of the hypen, it should be retained.

When in doubt, you may, of course, follow the practice of any good dictionary, but failure to follow dictionary practice need not be taken as an error, for convention in the use of hyphens is shifting rapidly. Following are some hyphenated compound nouns found in one issue of *Harper's Magazine.* Some are standard, according to the dictionary; some just represent the preference of the individual author:

close-up	Pacific-minded
job-hunting	counter-paper
tie-ups	by-passing
kow-tow	shadow-boxing
self-interest	cross-country
dry-goods	globe-trotter
well-being	Mr. So-and-so
boss-man	passer-by
son-in-law	by-product
school-bus	opera-goers
word-counting	half-century
speech-sounds	bomb-testing
writing-convention	co-ed
Europe-firsters	half-a-mile

In the writing of other authors, some of the above compounds undoubtedly would have been written as single words and some as two separate words. There is no such thing as absolute standard practice in the hyphenation of compound nouns. Maintenance of clarity should be your chief guide.

□   *Rule 4: Use a hyphen to separate a prefix when the first letter of the root and the last letter of the prefix are the same vowel:*

anti-industrial	re-echo
de-emphasize	semi-independent
pre-existent	ultra-articulate

Even this rule does not hold 100 percent. It is now common practice to omit the hyphen in such words as *cooperate and coordinate.* In all probability, in the future the use of the hyphen will further diminish.

□   *Rule 5: Use a hyphen to separate a prefix from a root that is normally capitalized.*

crypto-Communist	post-Reconstruction
mid-August	pre-Freudian
non-Christian	un-American

Some professional writers now write such words without the hyphen and either with or without the capital letter, as *unChristian* or *unchristian*.

☐   *Rule 6: Use a hyphen to separate a prefix when nonhyphenation might be ambiguous:*

co-op *and* coop	re-sort *and* resort
re-collect *and* recollect	re-cover *and* recover
re-count *and* recount	re-create *and* recreate

Note: Traditionally, words compounded with the prefixes *self, non, pseudo, quasi, ultra, neo, post, anti,* and *infra* have been hyphenated. However, the move is toward elimination of the hyphen, as in such compounds as *nondevelopmental, selfhood, pseudomorphic, ultraconservative, neoclassic, postgraduate, antivivisectionist,* and *infrared.* Since either convention is acceptable, personal preference can be your guide.

☐   *Rule 7: Hyphenate two or more words that serve a single adjective in front of a noun.*

This is the most important single rule of hypenation and the least understood. It is important not because of convention, but because clarity calls for it. There is no ambiguity in this phrase, for example: *a two dollar bill.* But consider this one: *ninety two dollar bills.* If the phrase is mentioning ninety-two bills, then the rule governing compound numbers should be followed. But if it is mentioning ninety bills, then the above rule must be applied: *ninety two-dollar bills.* For complete clarity, the rule should be followed in the phrase *a two-dollar bill.*

Countless ambiguous phrases could be avoided if writers would universally follow this rule. The misuse of it among professional writers is often shocking. For example, in *Harper's Magazine* a company once advertised a stereo with "two-35 watt amplifiers." Obviously, the machine had "two 35-watt amplifiers." Another ad once mentioned "the new embedded in plastic printed wiring circuit" of an automobile. Once you understand the phrase, it is not ambiguous, but few readers could have read it quickly without pausing to ponder the word relationships. It would have been immediately clear to all if written this way: "the new embedded-in-plastic, printed-wiring circuit"—two clear compound modifiers before the noun. One issue of a publication entitled *School Days* spoke of "word analysis-skills." The phrase is gibberish unless converted to "word-analysis skills."

To give you examples of this rule in action, here are a number of phrases from one issue of *Harper's.* Note how the hyphenated words form one clear modifier, not two or more. Also note how quickly the hyphens make the word relationships clear.

    martinis-and-rich-food lunches
    cradle-to-grave needs
    two-fisted gesture
    double-parked automobile
    all-too-human attributes
    long-term outlay
    long-sustained commitment
    state-supported white schools
    law-school faculty
    civil-rights battle
    management-engineering work
    a soft-spoken type
    a cartharsis-giving experience
    cigar-making firm
    sewing-machine manufacturers
    work-measurement studies
    an eight-year-old girl
    dirty-gray water
    high-pressure steam
    the Rather-Red-Than-Dead people
    a fifty-thousand-dollar-a-year man

To understand the clarifying value of the hyphen, read the following phrases as though each word is distinct in itself:

    two fisted gesture
    double parked automobile
    long term outlay
    a soft spoken type
    a cartharsis giving experience
    cigar making firm
    dirty gray water
    high pressure steam

Subrule A: *When a conjunction is entered in the compound adjective so that two or more adjectives are indicated, leave a space before and after the conjunction:*

    all eighth- and ninth-grade pupils
    all first-, second-, third-, and fourth-ranked candidates
    air- or waterproof clothes
    a heavy- but kind-hearted (*or* kindhearted) caress

Subrule B: *Do not hyphenate adjectival words when they follow the noun:*

> a man who makes fifty thousand dollars a year
> water that is dirty gray
> a manufacturer of sewing machines
> a person who is soft spoken
> the faculty of the law school
> a girl who is eight years old

Subrule C: *Do not hyphenate two words before a noun when one of them is an "ly" adverb modifying the adjective itself:*

> an overly tired horse
> a dismally unamusing play
> a rapidly diminishing bankroll

Practice varies among professional writers in hyphenating compound adjectives including the adverb *well:*

> a well-known writer *or* a well known writer
> a well-equipped expedition *or* a well equipped expedition

Subrule D: *Do not use quotation marks to enclose a compound adjective.*

> a never-to-be-forgotten dance *rather than* "a never to be forgotten" dance
> an I-don't-care-what-you-do attitude *rather than* an "I don't care what you do" attitude

☐ *Rule 8: Use hyphens to separate letters in a word that is spelled to emphasize a drawn-out pronunciation:*

> whoo-o-o-pee-e-e   here-e-e-e-e we go-o-o

Important cautionary note: *Do not confuse hyphens with dashes.* The dash is a mark of punctuation. It is used to clarify sentence structure; it is never used as a spelling device. The hyphen, on the other hand, is used only as a spelling device. The dash is twice as long as a hyphen: the mark (—) in contrast with the mark (-). In typewriting, two hyphens (not one) are used to indicate a dash. The result is a break in the dash in this way: (--). But that mark is preferable to the longer unbroken mark used for underlining, for the underlining mark sits below rather than in the middle of the typed line, in this way: (＿＿). (For further information on the dash, see pages 306–308.)

EXERCISE 58. **Using Capital Letters,
Apostrophes, and Hyphens**

DIRECTIONS: Be prepared to explain where and why capital
letters, apostrophes, and hyphens are needed in the following
sentences. Some spellings may need alteration before the proper
possessive spelling can be indicated.

1. We were advised by dean merson to take introduction to political science
    as well as a course in history.
2. An up to date religious philosophy is a part of the pseudo intellectuals
    cultural paraphernalia.
3. The concert was given at the run down olympic theater, which is
    located on tenth street near the veterans administration building.
4. We were relieved by commander lucases damn the torpedoes attitude
    as he tried to maneuver his craft out of the enemys range of fire.
5. After a years service in the peace corps, I decided to enlist in the
    argentine navy for a year.
6. The captain had earned the name blood and guts donovan, but it was
    his mens blood and guts that had been spilled.
7. Jameses mother grew up in utah as a mormon, but after she read the
    koran she became a mohammedan.
8. Plato was so shocked by socrateses being sentenced to death that he
    undertook an as yet unequalled philosophic career.
9. The much reprinted second chapter of *an introduction to ethnology* is
    entitled "the concept of race."
10. A made in japan label no longer connotes inferior merchandise, as it
    did in the 30s.
11. In spring, when the robins return, I like to stroll among my fathers
    peach trees and observe nature.
12. His holier than thou attitude seemed rather unchristian for a bishop.
13. The long debated missouri compromise only postponed the civil war.
14. I like the smiths house better than the joneses, for the smiths has a
    make yourself at home look.
15. Yesterdays avant garde movement is todays commonplace art.
16. When aunt carolyns children had the mumps, her doctor prescribed
    borodin tablets, which are manufactured by the merck company.
17. The poem entitled "to an athlete dying young," which opens with the
    line "the time you won your town the race," appears in a. e. housmans
    a shropshire lad.
18. A water or airborne craft is suitable for rescues at sea.
19. A five or six months delay in delivery doesn't seem to annoy volks-
    wagen buyers.

20. The history of western man is in large part the history of a never won battle for individual freedom.

PUNCTUATION

Punctuation is a conventional aspect of writing, for most perceptive readers can understand passages written without any punctuation at all. Even unnecessary marks of punctuation seldom destroy meaning. For example, probably not more than one case of real misunderstanding due to faulty punctuation occurs for every hundred errors in punctuation marked on freshmen themes. However, the absence or misuse of punctuation in a passage slows down a reader markedly, for then he must pause frequently to think out word relationships and to clear up momentary confusion. Hence, even though conventional, punctuation is a much more important aspect of writing than capitalization and the use of apostrophe. It is a valuable—some would say indispensable—aid to clarity.

Not all rules of punctuation, however, are equally important, and in many cases expert opinion is divided as to proper usage. The existence of divided opinion will be noted in the discussion of the rules below.

End Punctuation

The conventional use of end punctuation for sentences is too elementary for discussion in this book. But a few notations on other uses of the period, question mark, and exclamation point are in order.

Periods should be used after abbreviations unless convention allows omission:

Mr.	C.O.D. *or* COD
Calif.	A.B. *or* AB
N.Y.	U.N. *or* UN
Wash. Sq.	

When there is doubt in your mind, it is best to consult a good dictionary.

A period or a question mark may be used after a simple, routine request:

Will you please meet with the Committee at 3:00 on Thursday.
Will you see me at your earliest convenience?

Three periods with spaces between them (called an ellipsis) are conventionally used to show omission in a direct quotation:

"In this literature . . . the humorous anecdote mingled with white and Negro folklore."

If the omission is at the end of a sentence, a fourth period shows the end of the sentence:

"The transcendental law," Emerson believed, "was the 'moral law,' through which man discovers the nature of God, a living spirit. . . ."

A question mark may be used in parentheses after a word or phrase to indicate the writer's uncertainty or doubt about the information he has written:

Geminianni's six concerti grossi were first published in Leyden (?) in 1718 (?).

A question mark may be used after an "I wonder . . ." sentence because such a sentence clearly denotes interrogation. A period after such a sentence is also correct:

I wonder if you can send me samples of your latest engravings?
I wonder where I put that book on Chinese pottery.

An exclamation point may be used in parentheses after a word or phrase to denote surprise or some other strong emotion:

Our first year's sales of 25,000 copies (!) of *Neo-Gothic Art* has provided us with capital to publish a book on Sumerian art.

The Comma

The comma accounts for more rules of punctuation than all other marks combined, and probably 80 percent of all errors in punctuation are due to the misuse or omission of commas. Some rules involving the comma are highly important; some are minor. All involve the separation of sentence elements that are in some way logically dissociated and between which there is more voice pause than between words in a phrase. For example, there is more logical dissociation as well as voice pause between the first two than between the last two words in this sentence: "Sam, come here." Commas are used where such logical dissociations and voice pauses occur within one sentence. Following are specific rules.

☐ *Rule 1: Use commas to separate three or more sentence elements in a series.*

Sentence elements can be single words, phrases, or clauses. When three or more such elements form a series with a conjunction between the last two, a comma should be placed between each two elements.

The fans threw bottles, flashlights, and girdles at the umpire.

The thoughtful host served beer, Scotch, bourbon, rum, and Coca Cola.

The candidate promised to lower taxes, increase unemployment pay, and rehabilitate all welfare recipients.

At the Fourth of July picnic, the politicians made speeches, the young couples made eyes, and the children made trouble.

Many writers omit the comma before the conjunction in a series, and such usage must be considered correct. But the most careful writers include that comma to avoid any chance of confusion or ambiguity (as in the second example above).

Sometimes a writer will use three or more elements in a series without a conjunction. Then commas are necessary between all elements. "We must strive to inculcate in our students a sense of self-discipline, an appreciation of beauty, a quest for discovery."

Sometimes a writer will also use only two elements in a series without a conjunction. In such cases the two elements must be separated by a comma. "College taught me how to observe without thinking, how to read without appreciating."

☐ *Rule 2: Use a comma between independent clauses joined by a coordinating conjunction,* unless the clauses are short and closely related.

Edgar Allan Poe is popularly thought to have been a high neurotic preoccupied with morbid thoughts, but actually he was a dedicated genius who worked hard to achieve greatness in literature.

The Board Chairman spoke and the yes-men nodded.

Note: Regardless of the length of the clauses, always use a comma to separate independent clauses joined by *for*. Otherwise the *for* might be taken as a preposition and cause momentary confusion: "I ordered a Mercedes-Benz for my wife wanted to keep ahead of the Joneses." If the comma is omitted before the *for* in such a sentence, the reader will momentarily stumble.

☐ *Rule 3: Use a comma to separate coordinate adjectives not joined by a conjunction.*

In a phrase such as "an awkward old man," the two adjectives are not coordinate because "old" is virtually a part of the noun itself (some languages use just one word to mean "old man"). But in a phrase such as "an irascible, malicious man," the two adjectives are coordinate because they are equal in their relationship to the noun. Such coordinate adjectives have a logical dissociation and a voice pause between them and therefore should be separated by a comma. In general, adjectives are coordinate when the conjunction *and* sounds natural between them, but are not coordinate when the conjunction sounds unnatural. For example, "an awkward and old man" sounds unnatural, but "an irascible and malicious man" sounds natural. In essence, a comma is used to replace *and*.

> a beautiful, functional house
> a wasteful, poorly planned public works program
> a sneaky, ill-mannered little boy
> a grotesque red brick house

☐   *Rule 4: Use a comma to set off an introductory sentence element if the element is long or if a comma is necessary to avoid ambiguity.*

This is one of the less important rules of punctuation. For example, some knowledgeable writers would use commas and some would not in sentences like the following:

> As the moon rose, the platoon departed silently on its mission.
> In general, we must agree with our customers even when we know they are wrong.
> As a starter, we filed a petition with the Dean of Instruction.

The more careful a writer is, the more likely he is to use commas to set off initial sentence elements. But when clarity is not affected, you may include or omit such commas according to your own preference.

All careful writers, however, follow the above rule when clarity is at stake. For example, only a careless writer would omit commas in the following sentences:

> As we were about to leave the restaurant manager hastened to apologize to us.
> Above the buzzards circled ominously.
> As I mentioned the rules may occasionally be broken.

Omission of the commas in these sentences results in ambiguity, for without a comma to make him pause, a reader first assumes that *restaurant, buzzards,* and *rules* are objects of the preceding verbs or preposition rather than subjects of the following clauses. You should always reread each of your sentences carefully enough to avoid such ambiguous constructions.

Initial verbal phrases (verb clusters) are usually set off by commas because of the distinct voice pause and logical dissociation between such a phrase and the following clause.

> Not realizing the danger, the platoon crept forward.
> Speaking harshly and with choppy gestures, the candidate attacked his opponent's integrity.
> Failing that, we must resort to force.
> To avoid ambiguity, a writer must punctuate carefully.

Introductory exclamations and introductory words of assent or doubt are also set off by commas. (But such elements are not common in exposition.)

> Why, we were old friends in optometry school.
> Oh darn, I suppose I'll get another demerit.
> Yes, we feel that he is due compensatory damages.
> Well, perhaps he intended no disrespect.
> Maybe, but I'll have to consult an internist.

☐   *Rule 5: Use commas to set off an interrupter or parenthetic element placed within a sentence.*

A parenthetic element (or interrupter) is an additional word, phrase, or clause placed as an explanation or comment within an already complete sentence. Since there is a dissociated logic between such an element and the rest of the sentence, and since there is a distinct pause before and after it, commas (or, in some cases, dashes or parentheses) should be used to set it off from the rest of the sentence. Various kinds of parenthetic elements or interrupters can be identified.

Words in direct address are parenthetic and should be set off by commas. (Such phrases do not, however, appear frequently in exposition.)

> Let me tell you, sir, that your insinuations are insulting.
> Over here, ladies and gentlemen, is a replica of the Venus de Milo.
> Mother, don't be so devious in your plans.
> That's an ingenious device, young fellow.

Words and phrases denoting logical continuity or transition between ideas are usually set off when used parenthetically.

> We can conclude, then, that Rousseau was not the only fountainhead of Romanticism.
> There is, indeed, ample precedent for the judge's decision.
> Senator Stoner, of course, is a Democrat in name only.

Wheat germ, for example, is a valuable food once just discarded by flour mills.

Thus individual human IQ's, according to Becker's findings, cannot be accurately ascertained.

The words and phrases set off in these examples denote a continuation of thought from the previous sentences and thus are used parenthetically as transitions between ideas.

The so-called *conjunctive adverbs* are often used parenthetically to show logical continuity. When used in the middle of sentences, such connectives (*however, nevertheless, consequently, therefore, accordingly, furthermore, moreover,* and so on) should be set off by commas on both sides.

Atomic energy, however, has not yet produced economical electric power for home consumption.

The judge's decision, moreover, broke a hundred-years-old precedent.

His net income for the year, consequently, was less than his secretary's.

Opinion is divided about the use of a comma after such words when they come at the beginning of a clause. If you feel a distinct pause after such a word, you should use a comma: "However, proof of his guilt was not adduced." If you do not feel a pause, you need not insert a comma: "Therefore the committee decided to implement their plan." But a comma after *therefore* in that sentence would not be wrong.

Appositive phrases are parenthetic identifications and should be set off by commas (or, in some cases, dashes).

The prophecies of Nostradamus, a sixteenth-century French astrologer, enjoyed a new burst of popularity in the 1930s.

Anticholinergics, drugs that reduce muscle spasm, were used by ancient physicians.

Vivisection, an indispensable aid to medical science, is strongly condemned by many fuzzy-minded reformers.

Note: Some appositives are restrictive—that is, are necessary to identify the nouns to which they are in apposition. Such restrictive appositives are not set off by commas.

The movie "Cleopatra" was filmed in Italy.

The color black is becoming to a young woman.

If the appositives *"Cleopatra"* and *black* are removed from these sentences, the nouns *movie* and *color* are left completely unidentified.

When given parenthetic status, *phrases of addition, contrast, and alternative choice* should be set off by commas.

A study of rhetoric, and of grammar too, can increase one's appreciation of literature.

Tom Paine's religious ideas, but not his literary style, have gone out of fashion.

One result of Sade's genius, or else of his psychoticism, was the introduction of new modes of psychological inquiry.

Phrases of personal opinion are set off by commas when they take parenthetic form.

Your estimate, I'm sure, is accurate enough for preliminary studies.

It was Mark Twain, I think, who said "Heaven for climate; hell for company."

My Uncle Jurgen, it seems, left me only a notebook full of good advice.

Dean Etheridge, if I understood him correctly, implied that the Administration will not bend to the pressure of extremists.

Note: A very common error in punctuation is the omission of the second comma needed to set off a parenthetic element. Commas are **erroneously** omitted after the phrases in these examples.

Madison, Hamilton, and Jay, the authors of the Federalist Papers signed their essays "Publius."

Henry David Thoreau, a member of the Transcendentalist movement said, "My mind is my church."

Inconsistency, as Emerson pointed out does not invalidate philosophic thought.

Absence of the second comma in such sentences will momentarily confuse the reader.

☐   *Rule 6: Use a comma to set off a terminal clause or phrase used in contrast with the main clause of the sentence.*

The State Department White Paper dealt with resurgent Fascism, not Communism.

Our students must learn to understand language, not just facts about it.

He is not just a man who will try his best, but who will deliver what he promises.

☐   *Rule 7: In dates, use commas to separate the name of a day from the date of the month and the date of the month from the year.*

If the sentence continues, place a comma after the date of the month and after the year.

The revolution began on Monday, July 26.
The proclamation was issued on October 22, 1962.
On Tuesday, August 13, began our long march into the jungle.
On January 14, 1859, Darwin published his *Origin of Species.*
On Tuesday, February 3, 1888, the Great Blizzard struck the Plains.

Actually, commas in all of these positions are largely ornamental, and it is likely that the future will see a gradual decrease in their use. Even now it is common practice to omit the comma between month and year when no day date is given: May 1973.

☐   *Rule 8: In addresses, use commas to separate the name of a person or an establishment from the street address, the street address from the city, and the city from the state.*

Opinion is divided about the use of a comma after the state.

The rioting occurred in front of the Hamburger Haven, 223 Main Street.
The assignation occurred at 345 Bourbon Street, New Orleans.
Twenty-two bomb-frightened families moved to Chico, California.
The culprit was finally located in the Palace Theater, 413 Michigan Boulevard, Chicago, Illinois, on St. Valentine's Day.
Residents of Los Angeles, California get most of their water from the Colorado River.

There is a definite trend toward omitting the comma after the state, as in the last example. In fact, even a comma between city and state is a functionless ornament. The name of city and state is like the first and last names of a person, between which no one would use a comma. Notice how cluttered the first example following is compared to the second:

The Frelighs moved from Topeka, Kansas, to Gunnison, Colorado, and on to Needles, California.
The Frelighs moved from Topeka Kansas to Gunnison Colorado and on to Needles California.

But since convention has called for a comma between city and state, you should obey the rule. It is, of course, permissible to omit a comma after the name of the state.

☐   *Rule 9: Use commas to set off a nonrestrictive (or nonessential) adjective clause or phrase.*

This is one of the most important rules governing the use of the comma. Adjective clauses (usually introduced by *who, whom, whose, which,* or *that*) and adjective phrases usually modify nouns. If a clause or phrase gives additional information about a noun that is already fully identified, it is nonrestrictive and should be set off by commas.

> President Franklin D. Roosevelt, who defied tradition and ran for a third and a fourth term, died shortly after his fourth inauguration.
> "The Convergence of the Twain," written by Thomas Hardy in his old age, is a powerful lyric poem about the sinking of the Titanic.
> Heisenberg's Principle of Indeterminacy, which asserts that there is no strict operation of cause and effect on a subatomic level, is used by modern philosophers to refute scientific determinism.
> The philosopher's stone, sought by all medieval alchemists, has in a sense been found by modern nuclear physicists.
> School teachers, who are thought by many to be underpaid and over-subjected to community pressures, are not generally vociferous in their complaints.
> School teachers who join unions are sometimes harassed by their administrative superiors.

The adjective clauses and phrases in the first five sentences above are nonrestrictive because they give additional information about nouns that are already fully identified. Since their removal would still leave fully meaningful sentences, they are set off by commas. Note that since example five is talking about all school teachers, its adjective clause is nonrestrictive. Example six, however, is not talking about all school teachers, but only about those identified by the adjective clause. Since the clause is needed to identify the noun it modifies, it is restrictive and therefore not set off by commas.

☐ *Rule 10: Use commas to set off an internal or terminal adverbial clause when a clear logical dissociation and a voice pause are apparent between it and the main clause of the sentence.*

Do not set off an adverbial clause when such logical dissociation and voice pause are not apparent.

> The President's first act after he took his oath of office was to send an ultimatum to Russia.
> The President, after he had sent the ultimatum, ordered a call-up of 100,000 reserve troops.
> The weather report was delayed because the meteorological equipment did not function properly.

The weather report must be broadcast soon, because if it isn't the farmers will suffer losses.

Adverbial clauses cannot be clearly divided into restrictive and non-restrictive categories as can adjective clauses. Note that even without their adverbial clauses the first and third examples above are fully understandable sentences. In fact, the adverbial clause in the last example seems more essential than those in the first three examples, and yet the comma to set it off is distinctly necessary. There simply is no explicit rule to guide you in punctuating internal and terminal adverbial clauses; you must rely on your ear.

☐ *Rule 11: Use a comma to set off a terminal clause or phrase which in tone seems to be an afterthought.*

Grammar can be an exciting intellectual adventure, and that from a fairly early age.

Grammar and rhetoric interact mutually, and in ways that we do not understand clearly.

A real study of grammar is enlightening, and not at all stuffy as most students believe.

Grammar and rhetoric are but two sides of one coin, and inseparable.

☐ *Rule 12: Do not add useless or obstructive commas to any sentence.*

Adding an unnecessary comma usually results in a worse error than omitting a needed one. You should make it a rule of thumb not to use a comma unless you have a specific, known reason for using it. Commas are **misused** in all the following examples.

Do **not** separate a subject from its predicate or a verb from its complement with a single comma (parenthetic elements are, of course, set off on both sides).

The main cause of the friction between the new African nations, is due to tribal jealousies.

Senator Tushure's solution to the impasse with Russia was, to eliminate our bases in the Near East.

Do **not** set off a noun clause used as a subject or a complement.

That scientists will ever reach a final truth, seems doubtful.

The President's second White Paper stated, that the United States would not surrender overseas bases in order to avoid war.

Do **not** set off a restrictive noun clause used as an appositive.

> The belief, that war is inevitable, seems to be widespread.

Do not set off a restrictive adjective clause or phrase. Violation of this rule results in one of the most serious errors in punctuation.

> Nurses, who work night shift, are more likely to administer wrong drugs.
>
> The first book, written by William Faulkner, was *The Marble Faun.*
>
> The novel of William Faulkner's, which earned him the most money, was *Sanctuary.*
>
> The book, most sought after in college libraries, is *God's Little Acre.*

Do not separate noncoordinate modifiers.

> Mr. Gunn is a spirited, public servant.
>
> I found a rare, old, vulgate Bible in our attic.

Do not set off nonparenthetic elements.

> The manager, of the supermarket, decided to poke every woman who poked his tomatoes.
>
> The canned music, supplied by Muzak, should never be let out of the can.

Do not separate two sentence elements in a series joined by a conjunction.

> The patrol's duties were to locate enemy gun emplacements, and to cut enemy telephone lines.
>
> The Lieutenant sent out a second patrol, and radioed headquarters to send more mortar ammunition.

Again note that all the commas in the above examples are *misused.*

The Dash

The dash is perhaps the most misunderstood of all marks of punctuation. Many people use it as a sort of elegant or personalized period; the more personal or exciting their writing becomes, the more they substitute dashes for periods, as though such an ordinary mark as a period would diminish the charm of their self-expression. In intimate letters and *billets doux,* dashes may be used at will. But in exposition a dash should never be used as end punctuation.

Other writers (or perhaps the same ones) use dashes as an excuse for writing in fragments, as in the following passage from an essay exam:

> Emerson represented the optimistic school of Romantic thought—self-reliance, individualism and all that stuff—"hitch your wagon to a star."

He believed that each person is directly in contact with the Divine—has a personal pipeline to God—so to speak. No need for clergymen—you can reach divine truth by yourself. So you should rely on yourself completely—ignore social convention—be a nonconformist.

If the writer of this passage had not been such a dash addict—had not, indeed, "dashed" off his answer—doubtless he would have written in more complete and coherent sentences. There seems to be something about the dash that leads the careless writer into fragmented discourse. Such a mode of writing makes for very weak exposition.

The dash, then, is not a mark of end punctuation and does not justify fragmented discourse. Instead, it is a mark of internal punctuation with specific uses, as illustrated in the rules below.

Conventionally, no space is left before or after a dash. On the typewriter, two hyphens (--) make a dash.

☐   *Rule 1: Use dashes to set off a parenthetic element (1) that is especially emphatic or (2) that has several commas of its own or (3) that is a sentence construction by itself.*

Our minister—even our beloved, incorruptible minister—succumbed to the pressures of the Society for the Advancement of True and Sacred Democratic Principles.

The threatening mob—thrill-seekers, bums, criminals, extremists, dupes —was dispersed with tear gas.

Professor Witter—he was the leader of the faculty group that successfully resisted Midwestern University's Program for Patriotic Education—has been made Chairman of the President's new Commission on Academic Freedom.

☐   *Rule 2: Use a dash to set off a terminal construction that has the tone of a delayed afterthought.*

In the popular mind, astronomy and astrology are still often confused— like religion and occultism.

After extensive research, Professor Sackett reported that the lower a family's income, the larger percentage of it they spend on food— hardly a novel discovery.

☐   *Rule 3: A dash may be used to introduce an explanation or explanatory series.*

Normally, a colon is used in this structural position; a dash represents a more informal usage.

One alternative to war is uncomplex—surrender.

The first moon colony was plagued with difficulties—mechanical break-downs, sudden psychological aberrations, showers of meteorites, interruption of radio communication with earth.

☐   *Rule 4: Use a dash to set off a long series from a pronoun or nominal referring to the series.*

Course work, desultory reading, social contacts, extracurricular activities, friendly conversations with professors—all of these are important in the education of a college student.

Honesty is the best policy, virtue is its own reward, innocence is its own protection, deceit destroys the deceiver—these are precepts to remember.

☐   *Rule 5: Use a dash to indicate an abrupt structural shift.*

This use of the dash is rare in exposition and appears only occasionally in narrative writing: "And then as the traveling salesman—but wait, I forgot to mention the farmer's wife."

Parentheses

The word *parentheses* is plural, for it designates both of the curved marks that go by that name; the singular is *parenthesis.* Spaces are maintained on the outside but not the inside of parentheses.

☐   *Rule 1: Use parentheses to set off an internal or terminal parenthetic element that has a tone of isolation or that is intended as an aside rather than an emphatic addition to the sentence.*

In such cases the first word of the parenthetic element is not capitalized and a period is not placed within the parentheses.

In 1921 Trinity College (later to become Duke University) moved its campus to Durham, North Carolina.

Atomic fission was first demonstrated in 1938 (a year before World War II began).

☐   *Rule 2: Use parentheses to set off a whole sentence or group of sentences parenthetically inserted into a longer passage.*

In such cases, the sentences begin with capital letters and the end punctuation is put inside the parentheses.

In 1929, the stock market collapsed and the Great Depression began. (That was also the year that saw the publication of Hemingway's *A Farewell to Arms,* Wolfe's *Look Homeward, Angel,* and Faulkner's *The Sound and the Fury.* Though economic catastrophe loomed, literature seemed to be entering a period of greatness.) Neither President Hoover, who had been in office only a few months, nor the leaders in Congress seemed to understand the economic forces at work. . . .

☐ *Rule 3: Use parentheses to enclose numerals or letters used to number items in a series.*

Use dashes to set off a parenthetic element (1) that is especially emphatic or (2) that has several commas of its own or (3) that is a sentence construction by itself.

☐ *Rule 4: Use parentheses to enclose cross references and other such interpolated material.*

Epicureanism is the system of moderate and refined hedonism (see axiology) taught by Epicurus (342–270 B.C.).

Brackets

Square brackets should not be confused with parentheses.

☐ *Rule 1: Use brackets to enclose a word or phrase inserted into a direct quotation to replace an otherwise unintelligible reference.*

When such a word or phrase is the antecedent of a pronoun, the pronoun may be included or omitted, according to personal preference.

"He [Professor Billwiller] was granted NSF funds in the amount of $15,000 to continue his researches into the 'Seasonal Changes in Blood Components of Wild Rodents.' "
"[Professor Chapman] denied that he had supplied the editor of the *University Daily* with the literate and well-informed editorials that were reprinted in the *New York Times.*"
"For centuries the study of the sky has been conducted under [the names of astronomy and astrology]."

☐ *Rule 2: Use brackets to enclose the word* sic *or other interpolated comments inserted into a direct quotation.*

Sic, meaning *thus* in Latin, is used to indicate that erroneous or startling material actually appeared in the original source itself. In the first example below the name *Dickinson* is misspelled.

"The poems of Emily Dickenson [sic] are the most exquisite lyrics in American poetry."

"Physicists estimate that ten billion neutrinos [weightless, chargeless particles] pass through each square centimeter on earth every second."

The Semicolon

The basic condition governing the use of the semicolon is that the mark is used only between parallel or coordinate elements, that is, elements that are similar in construction.

☐ *Rule 1: Use a semicolon to separate independent clauses in a compound sentence that has no connective word between the clauses.*

An espousal of leftist causes ruined the political career of Herman Dougfield; he was even defeated recently in his race for state senator.

Even the closest stars appear only as points of light through the most powerful telescopes; astronomers must use spectroscopes to deduce information about their surfaces.

☐ *Rule 2: Use a semicolon to separate independent clauses joined by a connective other than a coordinating conjunction.*

The use of a comma rather than a semicolon in this structural position results in the comma splice.

In California there are over one million more registered Democrats that Republicans; nevertheless, the state often elects Republican officials.

Candidate Cooke felt that integrity and honesty are more important than political victory; therefore he refused to stoop to slander and mud-slinging in his campaigning.

The power of the press is perhaps overrated; for example, Democratic presidents are elected even though more than two-thirds of our newspapers and magazines are Republican.

☐ *Rule 3: Use semicolons rather than commas to separate elements in a series when the elements are long or have internal punctuation of their own.*

Note that, since such elements are coordinate, the semicolons are being used between elements of equal rank.

We sent appeals to three foundations: The Coe Fund for Academic Freedom, 925 Melrose, DeKalb, Illinois; The McCall Foundation for

Anthropological Studies, 483 Main Street, Umatilla, Oregon; and the Libermann Associates Foundation, 896 Beverley Lane, Philadelphia. Professor Reifsnyder's researches disclosed that students with IQ's over 140 have a dropout rate greater than those with IQ's of 120 to 125; that students with IQ's of 110 to 120 make better grades in the humanities than in science; and that grades assigned in science classes correspond more closely with student IQ's than grades assigned in humanities classes.

☐ *Rule 4: Do **not** use a semicolon to separate a dependent clause or phrase from an independent clause.*

The following examples represent an **erroneous** use of semicolons; each semicolon should be replaced by a comma.

Having confronted the Soviet Ambassador with the facts of the case; the U.S. Ambassador to the United Nations waited for his answer to the charges.

Experimental proof of Einstein's theory of relativity is difficult to establish; though almost all scientists assume the validity of the theory.

The categorical imperative; which is the key term in Kant's ethical thought; denotes the supreme moral law. It is unconditional and absolute; admitting of no exceptions since it is in no way relative to some further end.

The Colon

The colon is a mark of punctuation used exclusively to introduce a sentence element, sentence, or longer discourse that follows immediately.

☐ *Rule 1: Use a colon after the salutation in a formal letter.*

When you want your letter to have a more friendly and informal tone, use a comma after the salutation.

Dear Professor Bierman: (formal)
Dear Professor Bierman, (indication of friendly acquaintance)

☐ *Rule 2: Use a colon after introductory labels.*

COLLOQUIAL: It's me.
STANDARD: It's I.

☐ *Rule 3: Use a colon to introduce a series following a noun that establishes the series.*

> Professor Whitehead made three important points: that religion, like science, must be prepared to change and grow; that the idea of the brotherhood of man rather than of the chosen people must underlie all sound religion; and that a balance must be drawn between the need for a learned clergy and the need for each individual to find his own faith.

> Joyce was eclectic in her choice of college subjects: literature, anthropology, physics, comparative religions, ancient history, wine making, and typing.

☐ *Rule 4: Use a colon to introduce a sentence that acts as an explanation of, rather than a continuation of, the preceding sentence.*

The sentence following the colon may be started with a capital letter or not, according to preference.

> Teaching is not a 9:00 to 3:00, nine-months-a-year job: every good teacher spends hours a day every day of the year preparing himself for his work.

> Enlightened school boards and administrations should insist that every teacher take a sabbatical leave every seventh year: no teacher can stave off staleness unless he undergoes massive intellectual refreshment every few years.

☐ *Rule 5: A colon may be used to introduce a direct quotation, especially a formal or long one.*

> In protesting the Puritan emphasis on continual busyness, Thoreau said: "Why should we live with such hurry and waste of life? We are determined to be starved before we are hungry. We say that a stitch in time saves nine, and so they take a thousand stitches to-day to save nine to-morrow. As for *work,* we haven't any of any consequence."

Quotation Marks

Quotation marks are used to enclose not only direct quotations but also certain other kinds of units that appear within written discourse. In general these units, explained in the rules below, are not parenthetic but are integral parts of the sentence structure.

A mark of punctuation that belongs to an enclosed unit is placed within the quotation marks, as in this example: "Mary Ellen asked,

'Where have you been?' " Note that a period is not used in addition to the question mark even though the whole sentence is a statement rather than a question.

A comma or period is placed within quotation marks even when it is not a part of the enclosed unit, as in this example: " 'Let sleeping dogs lie,' a proverb from *Poor Richard's Almanac,* should have been 'let sleeping babies lie.' " The second version of the proverb could also begin with a capital letter, according to preference.

Other marks of punctuation are put outside the quotation marks when they do not belong to the enclosed unit, as in these examples. Note that the quoted units are not themselves questions.

> Do you really think "the better part of valor is discretion"?
> Why did she say she "wasn't interested"?

☐ *Rule 1: Use quotation marks to enclose direct quotations.*

Regardless of the length of a direct quotation, quotation marks are used only at the beginning and end unless there is an unbracketed interruption or unless the quoted material consists of more than one paragraph, in which case marks are not used at the end of a paragraph (except of course the last) but are used at the beginning of each new paragraph. In term papers and other such written discourse, quoted passages of six or fewer lines are usually incorporated with quotation marks directly into the text and those of more than six lines are usually entered as insets, that is, are single-spaced and indented five spaces on the left margin. Inset quotations are **not** enclosed in quotation marks.

When a single-sentence direct quotation is not reported dialogue, it may or may not, according to preference, be capitalized when it comes in the middle of a sentence. Also in such cases a comma is not necessary after the phrase identifying the author. "Thoreau said 'most men live lives of quiet desperation.' " When there is an unbracketed interruption (such as *and* in the following examples), quotation marks are placed before and after the interruption to separate it from the enclosed units.

> Professor Graybo found the book "disarmingly ingenuous" and "subtly provocative."
> We learned from Chairman Cole to "listen well' and "learn fast."

☐ *Rule 2: Use quotation marks to enclose titles of short or minor literary works:* short stories, short poems, short plays, chapters from books, articles, essays, songs, and speeches.

The normal convention is to enclose in quotation marks titles that form a part of a larger collection, and to italicize (underline in script or typewriting) titles of works published as, or long enough to be published as, separate entities. Thus the title *Paradise Lost* is always italicized whether the poem is published separately or as a part of Milton's works, but the title of a sonnet or other short poem from a collection is enclosed in quotation marks.

> "The Fall of the House of Usher," perhaps Poe's best story, is thought by many critics to have a significant theme.
> Have you read Melville's "Bartleby the Scrivener"?
> "Where Are the Snows of Yesteryear?" is a sonnet by Villon.
> The forty-second chapter of *Moby-Dick* is entitled "The Whiteness of the Whale."

☐ *Rule 3: Words used as words may be enclosed in quotation marks,* or they may be italicized, according to preference.

> The word "jabberwocky," meaning nonsensical but grammatical phrasing, comes from the poem "Jabberwocky" by Lewis Carroll.
> A word like "scuttlebutt" often gains respectability after a career as slang.
> The word *larruping* is sometimes heard in the Southeast.

☐ *Rule 4: Use quotation marks to enclose a word used in an unusual or ironical sense.*

> Hollywood stars feel they must belong to the "right set."
> "Correct" spelling has the sanction of the dictionary, but not of all language sophisticates.

In the first example, the writer indicates that the stars' conception of the right set is not his conception. In the second, the writer means that in his opinion the traditional unphonemic spelling of English as given in dictionaries is really incorrect, that correct spelling is phonemic spelling.

☐ *Rule 5: Avoid enclosing slang words and phrases in quotation marks* as an apology for their use.

> Questionable usage:
>
> The heroine of the novel is a "floozy" who likes to "paint the town red."

If you feel a word is worth using, use it without apology. Note the difference between this questionable use of quotation marks and their legitimate use in Rule 4 above.

☐ *Rule 6: Use single quotation marks to enclose a unit within a unit.*

This has been done in many examples in this chapter.

Professor Doner's review calls the story "an ingenious adaptation of Poe's 'Cask of Amontillado.' "
The librarian screamed, "Bring me the book containing 'The Gift of the Magi' right now."

☐ *Rule 7: Use quotation marks to enclose reported dialogue.*

If the phrase naming the speaker comes first, place a comma after it and capitalize the first word of the dialogue. Note the difference between this rule and Rule 1 relating to direct quotations not in the form of reported dialogue.

Professor Connoly said, "Prepare to write on *Finnegan's Wake.*"
Maurice had cried, "Do not borrow my slide rule, please."

If the phrase naming the speaker comes last, place a comma after the dialogue unless a question mark or exclamation point is called for. Do not use both a comma and a question mark or exclamation point.

"Turn to page 79," said Professor Cebull.
"Where did we leave off?" asked Professor Hunter.
"Keep your eyes on your own paper!" shouted Professor Lowers.

Note that in the second example the whole statement is not a question and that in the third the whole statement is not an exclamation.

If the phrase naming the speaker comes in the middle of a sentence, use commas before and after it and do not capitalize the beginning of the second part.

" 'In the second chapter of the text,' said Professor Monteverde, 'the authors have entered erroneous information.' "

If the phrase naming the speaker comes between two sentences of dialogue, use a period after the phrase and start the second sentence with a capital letter.

" 'Don't overlook the footnote on page 72,' said Professor Hernandez. 'It is more important than the textual material itself.' "

☐ *Rule 8: Do not use quotation marks to enclose a title used as a title.*

When the title of an essay is mentioned within written discourse, it is enclosed in quotation marks, but when it is used as a heading it is not so enclosed. Of course a title may have within it a unit enclosed in quotation marks. Note also that a period is not placed after a title used as a heading.

TITLE AS HEADING: Loopholes in the Usury Laws
TITLE AS HEADING: A Study of Milton's "On His Blindness"

In spite of the rather well defined rules of punctuating written discourse, there remains, as explained above, considerable latitude for you to exercise your own preference. Always, however, clarity should be your goal. Since punctuation for all structural positions cannot be covered by set rules, you should be prepared to use (or omit) any mark of punctuation in any position when the clarity of your sentence will be improved. Punctuation is mostly a science, but it is also partly an art. The more you come to understand the complexities of English sentence structure, the more you will be able to punctuate according to personal design rather than set rules.

Note, for example, the punctuation of the opening sentence of Thoreau's *Walden*:

When I wrote the following pages, or rather the bulk of them, I lived alone, in the woods, a mile from any neighbor, in a house which I had built myself, on the shore of Walden Pond, in Concord, Massachusetts, and earned my living by the labor of my hands only.

Now it's true that standard punctuation today is different from that of 125 years ago. But Thoreau's sentence is most artfully punctuated, even with its nine commas; not one of them (except perhaps the one after *Concord*) could be omitted without altering the emphasis somewhat. Only great skill can permit a writer to chop a sentence up into so many short phrases. But by paying close attention to sentence structure, you too can develop a more artful sense of punctuation.

EXERCISE 59. **Identifying Restrictive and Nonrestrictive Constituents**

DIRECTIONS: Some of the adjective clauses and phrases in the following sentences are restrictive and some are nonrestrictive. Identify each and explain why the nonrestrictive elements need to be set off by commas and why the restrictive elements should not be set off.

1. Authoritarianism is a philosophic point of view which says that the ultimate or most valid source of knowledge is authority of some kind.

2. Philosophers who reject authoritarianism are called relativists.
3. Some philosophers who are relativists in politics are authoritarian in ethics.
4. David Hume who was the most notable English philosopher of the later eighteenth century espoused a philosophy of complete skepticism.
5. Idealist philosophers are those who maintain that the ultimate reality is mind or spirit, not matter.
6. Plato who developed the philosophy of forms is generally regarded as the fountainhead of the philosophy of idealism.
7. Transcendentalism which is a religious philosophy developed in America in the 1830s by Emerson and others is a variety of idealism.
8. Another religion based on the philosophy of idealism is Christian Science which many scholars think was an outgrowth of Transcendentalism.
9. Hawthorne who was a friend of Emerson's rejected Transcendentalism which he felt ignored the problem of evil in man's life.
10. The Book of Job written about 1500 B.C. is a literary discourse on the nature of evil in man's life.
11. Theologians who support the Calvinist doctrines believe that evil in man's life is due to the original sin of Adam and Eve.
12. No religious or philosophic doctrine that is acceptable to all has ever been devised.
13. A question often asked by psychologists is whether a particular behavior pattern manifested in an individual is due to heredity or environment.
14. Professor Newman's point of view which seems logical is that all behavior patterns are due to both heredity and environment.
15. He maintains that no event can happen to you that is not due to both heredity and environment which is to say that nothing can happen to you which your heredity did not provide for and that nothing can happen to you in a nonenvironment.
16. Biochemists and geneticists both of whom work with the chemical determinants of heredity have been carrying on experiments which show that the mechanism of heredity can be altered.
17. It is expected that scientists will soon actually create life in a test tube, an event which will have profound religious and philosophic significance.
18. Even now scientists find a borderline between life and nonlife which suggests that there is no really clear-cut distinction between the living and the nonliving.
19. Some viruslike particles seem to be living material but incapable of reproduction which suggests that the difference between life and nonlife is chemical.
20. The code that is stored chemically in the genes in a human cell is said to contain enough information to fill ten thousand encyclopedic volumes.

EXERCISE 60. Modernizing the Conventions of Usage in Seventeenth-Century Writing

DIRECTIONS: As best you can, modernize the punctuation, capitalization, spelling, and use of the apostrophe in the following passages from seventeenth-century English writers. Do not alter the diction or word order.

1. "Nature hath made men so equall, in the faculties of body, and mind; as that though there bee found one man sometimes manifestly stronger in body, or of quicker mind then another; yet when all is reckoned together, the difference between man, and man, is not so considerable, as that one man can thereupon claim himselfe any benefit, to which another may not pretend, as well as he."—Thomas Hobbes, *Leviathan.*

2. "Poor intricated soule! Riddling, perplexed, labyrinthicall soule! Thou couldest not say, that thou beleevest not in God, if there were no God; Thou couldst not not beleeve in God, if there were no God; if there were no God, thou couldest not speake, thou couldest not blaspheme the Name of God, thou couldest not sweare, if there were no God: For, all thy faculties, how ever depraved, and perverted by thee, are from him; and except thou canst seriously beleeve, that thou art nothing, thou canst not beleeve that there is no God."—John Donne, *Sermon for the Feast of the Conversion of St. Paul.*

3. "I think it is beyond Question, that *Man has a clear Perception of his own Being;* he knows certainly, that he exists, and that he is something. He that can doubt, whether he be any thing, or no, I speak not to, no more than I would argue with pure nothing, or endeavor to convince Non-entity that it were something. If any one pretend to be so sceptical, as to deny his own Existence, (for really to doubt of it, is manifestly impossible,) let him for me enjoy his beloved Happiness of being nothing, until Hunger, or some other Pain convince him of the contrary. This then, I think, I may take for a Truth, which every ones certain Knowledge assures him of, beyond the liberty of doubting, *viz.* that he is something that actually exists."—John Locke, *An Essay Concerning Humane Understanding.*

4. "The immoderate use of, and indulgence to *Sea-coale* alone in the City of *London,* exposes it to one of the fowlest inconveniences and reproches, than can possibly befall so noble, and otherwise incomparable City: and that, not from the *Culinary* fires, which for being weak, and lesse often fed below, is with such ease dispell'd and scatter'd above, as it is hardly at all discernible, but from some few particular Tunnells

and Issues, belonging only to *Brewers, Diers, Lime-burners, Salt,* and
Sope-boylers, and some other private Trades, *one* of whose *Spiracles*
alone, does manifestly infect the *Aer* more than all the Chimnies of
London put together besides."—John Evelyn, *Fumifugium.*

EXERCISE 61. Analyzing the Uses of Marks of Punctuation

DIRECTIONS: Explain the use of each mark of punctuation in
the following passages. Indicate structural positions where commas are optionally used or could be optionally used.

1.   " 'I couldn't find nobody there.' This sentence, as anybody who
will read this probably knows, contains a double negative, a construction with a fascinating history. Today in all parts of the English-
speaking world, its use or avoidance is one of the clearest marks of
differentiation between social groups. Among those who have had
little formal schooling and whose social and occupational status is
relatively low, the construction is extremely common. Among the well-
educated and more 'privileged,' it is rare almost to the point of non-
existence. In many circles, in fact, a double negative uttered by a presumably educated person would cause the same embarrassed silence as
a loud belch in church.

"In earlier English, the doubling, tripling, or even quadrupling
of negatives was frequent even in the most formal literary styles. King
Alfred, for example, in a translation made late in the ninth century,
writes a sentence which in modern form would read: 'No man had
never yet heard of no ship-army.' A little later, in the oldest English
version of the Gospels, we read: 'The five foolish maidens took lamps,
but didn't take no oil with them.' In the fourteenth century, Chaucer
writes of his 'gentle knight' that 'in all his life he hasn't never yet said
nothing discourteous to no sort of person' (four negatives!). As late
as Shakespeare's time, the construction was still possible in Standard
English, particularly in speech. Thus, in *Romeo and Juliet,* when
Mercutio is confronted by Tybalt he cries out, 'I will not budge for no
man's pleasure.' "—Allan F. Hubbell, "Multiple Negation."

2.   "The one phenomenon which has invariably accompanied [writing]
is the formation of cities and empires: the integration into a political
system, that is to say, of a considerable number of individuals, and the
distribution of these individuals into a hierarchy of castes and classes.
Such is, at any rate, the type of development which we find, from
Egypt right across to China, at the moment when writing makes its
debut; it seems to favour rather the exploitation than the enlightenment

of mankind. This exploitation made it possible to assemble work-people by the thousand and set them tasks that taxed them to the limits of their strength: to this, surely, we must attribute the beginnings of architecture as we know it. If my hypothesis is correct, the primary function of writing, as a means of communication, is to facilitate the enslavement of other human beings. The use of writing for disinterested ends, and with a view to satisfactions of the mind in the fields either of science or the arts, is a secondary result of its invention—and may even be no more than a way of reinforcing, justifying, or dissimulating its primary function."—John Russell, tr., Claude Levi-Strauss, *Tristes Tropiques*.

3.   "Everyone knows that our sun is a star, that it has a group of planets circling around, relatively close to it—ranging from the planet Mercury nearest the sun, out to tiny Pluto, the most distant planet. Suppose we go beyond Pluto and off toward the next star which is the nearest neighbor to the sun, the star called by the astronomers Alpha Centauri. How long would it take us to reach that star and explore its vicinity for other planets? Well, the time required, of course, would depend upon how fast we could travel. I might point out, however, that if we could get away from the gravitational pull of both earth and sun, and still have a speed of twenty miles per second, then to reach Alpha Centauri would take forty thousand years. Even if we could speed up our spacecraft, after getting away from the sun, to the unimaginable speed of two hundred miles per second, it would take four thousand years to reach the very nearest star. Other stars—even the relatively nearer ones in our own Milky Way—would require millions or hundreds of millions of years of travel time. I suggest that we cross off our list of near-term objectives any journeys to the vicinity of other stars."—L. A. DuBridge, "A Scientist Calls for Common Sense."

4.   "At this late hour of the world's history, books are to be found in almost every room in the house—in the nursery, in the drawing room, in the dining room, in the kitchen. But in some houses they have become such a company that they have to be accommodated with a room of their own—a reading room, a library, a study. Let us imagine that we are now in such a room; that it is a sunny room, with windows opening on a garden, so that we can hear the trees rustling, the gardener talking, the donkey braying, the old women gossiping at the pump—and all the ordinary processes of life pursuing the casual irregular way which they have pursued these many hundreds of years. As casually, as persistently, books have been coming together on the shelves. Novels, poems, histories, memoirs, dictionaries, maps, directories; black-letter books and

brand new books; books in French and Greek and Latin; of all shapes and sizes and values, bought for purposes of research, bought to amuse a railway journey, bought by miscellaneous beings, of one temperament and another, serious and frivolous, men of action and men of letters."—Virginia Woolf, *The Second Common Reader.*

5.   "Charles Darwin was born in Shrewsbury, England, in 1809, the year in which Lamarck published his theory of evolution through the transmission of acquired characters. At the age of nine, like most English boys in families of considerable means, Darwin was sent to a near-by private boarding school. There he did nothing to suggest that he would grow up to be the prime mover in a major scientific revolution. 'Nothing could have been worse for my mind than Dr. Butler's school,' he later wrote. . . . 'Much attention was paid to learning by heart; this I could effect with great facility, learning forty or fifty lines of Virgil or Homer whilst I was in morning chapel; but this exercise was utterly useless for every verse was forgotten in forty-eight hours.'

"Darwin was not a loafer, however, and he studied even those subjects that he disliked. In the meantime he developed strong interests in extracurricular matters. He became an avid collector of shells, coins, minerals, and insects, especially beetles. He was specially fond of bird shooting and of long hikes through the beautiful English countryside. Through application to his studies, rather than an interest in them, Darwin qualified for admission to university work and spent three years at Edinburgh studying medicine and then another three at Cambridge studying theology. His spare time he devoted to learning everything he could about the subjects he really loved—botany, zoology, and geology. 'Although . . . there were some redeeming features in my life at Cambridge,' he writes in his autobiography, 'my time was sadly wasted there, and worse than wasted. From my passion for shooting and for hunting, and, when this failed, for riding across country, I got into a sporting set, some dissipated and low-minded young men. We often used to dine together in the evening, though these dinners often included men of a higher stamp . . . with jolly singing and playing at cards afterwards. . . . I know I ought to feel ashamed of days and evenings thus spent, but as some of my friends were very pleasant, and we were all in the highest spirits, I cannot help looking back to these times with much pleasure.' Actually, while cultivating these extracurricular interests, Darwin did not neglect to pass his examinations creditably, and he had 'many other friends of a widely different nature' who interested him in music and art, subjects in which, to his regret, he later lost interest almost entirely."—Thomas S. Hall and Florence Moog, *Life Science.*

EXERCISE 62.   **Punctuating Written Discourse**

DIRECTIONS: All marks of punctuation except end punctuation have been omitted from the following passages. Indicate the structural positions where punctuation is needed and suggest a suitable mark of punctuation for each position.

1.   "When we distinguished between the various kinds of general statements we noted that there are some statements which can be confirmed by observation or experimentation or both. Other sweeping assertions seem to resist being confirmed by these means. Even though a substantial body of evidence may appear to support such truths that evidence often is capable of different interpretations depending on who does the interpreting. One man will believe a certain truth because his personal background his tastes and temperament everything that makes him an individual distinct from other men incline him to do so. Another man will reject the same assumption because he has a different background different tastes and a different temperament. In trying to understand the judgment of a person therefore we must always be aware of the way that individual differences affect the understanding and interpreting of human experience.

"If someone were to assert that Beethoven was born in the eighteenth century and someone else were to maintain that he was born in the nineteenth the two could settle the argument by consulting certain historical record which they agreed would tell the truth of the matter. But a similar disagreement over whether Beethoven was a greater composer than Brahms that is composed finer music cannot be settled so definitely. Nor indeed would the two parties be likely even to agree on a way by which they could come to a meeting of minds. It is a question of taste and a meeting of minds may be impossible."—Richard D. Altick, *Preface to Critical Reading.*

2.   "There have been at different times and among different people many varying conceptions of the good life. To some extent the differences were amenable to argument this was when men differed as to the means to achieve a given end. Some think that prison is a good way of preventing crime others hold that education would be better. A difference of this sort can be decided by sufficient evidence. But some differences cannot be tested in this way. Tolstoy condemned all war others have held the life of a soldier doing battle for the right to be very noble. Here there was probably involved a real difference as to ends. Those who praised the soldier usually consider the punishment of sinners a good thing in itself Tolstoy did not think so. On such a matter no argument is possible. I cannot therefore prove that my view of the

good life is right I can only state my views and hope that as many as possible will agree. My view is this The good life is one inspired by love and guided by knowledge."—Bertrand Russell, *Why I Am Not a Christian.*

3.   "The overseas libraries are plagued by problems similar to those which beset libraries in the United States they are perpetually short of money manpower and space. In addition they are faced with other difficulties owing to their location abroad and their relationship to Congress. Because their relatively small collections must retain balance the libraries are never able to stock enough books on any one subject to satisfy specialists. Visiting Americans including historians educators musicians artists religionists economists sociologists and experts in other fields frequently complain about the lack of books and magazines representing their specialties. Liberals tend to find a preponderance of material on the conservative side while conservatives see the opposite. This is particularly true of religious groups some of which go through our catalogues with great care and complain loudly if they think we lean toward Catholic or Protestant authors. Congressmen apart from expressing their own preferences are obliged to serve as outlets for opinions expressed often in strong language by their constituents. Selection of books requires a combination of common sense and courage. It is not an easy task."—George V. Allen, "Books and the American Image."

VERB FORMS

One of the most obvious distinctions between the language usage of those with and those without formal education is the verb forms that each group uses. The pattern of verb usage in standard English is rather rigidly established, while that in vulgate (or nonstandard) is variable. For example, standard usage allows only the forms in the left-hand column below, whereas vulgate usage does not distinguish between the forms in the right-hand column.

I saw	I saw, I seen
I have seen	I have saw, I have seen
I took	I took, I taken
I have taken	I have took, I have taken
I knew	I knew, I knowed
I have known	I have knew, I have knowed, I have known
they were	they was, they were

An individual unaffected, or only slightly affected, by formal education may use the variant forms above indiscriminately, without being aware that in one sentence he has said "I saw" and in another "I seen."

The reason for the considerable rigidity in standard and the variability in nonstandard usage is that educated people adhere to the usage patterns established and maintained traditionally in schools, whereas the uneducated absorb variable forms from their nonschool environment and use them unconsciously. A few variable forms exist in standard usage because textbooks and teachers since the eighteenth century, when grammarians began crystallizing formal English usage, have not been able to establish unanimous opinion in all cases and also because at any given point in time some language forms will be in the process of change, so that for a while two forms may exist side by side. For example, standard usage still allows these variant forms:

I dived, I dove
I have showed, I have shown
I lighted, I lit (the cigaret)
I have proved, I have proven
I waked, I woke

The problem of verb form is strictly one of grammar, not of diction. It is grammatical form and not word choice that varies in the above examples, for the lexical (dictionary) meaning of *know, knew, known, knowed, have known, should have known,* and so forth is the same. The various forms indicate differences in time of occurrence (tenses), in number involved (number), and in attitude of speaker (mood), but they do not indicate differences in word definition.

The problem is not only one of grammar rather than diction, but also of social acceptability rather than clarity, for none of the forms used in vulgate language is ever ambiguous to educated ears unless it is also ambiguous to vulgate speakers. For example, the use of *was* instead of *were* for plural meaning never results in ambiguity, for the plurality is also indicated in another way, such as *"they* was." The sentence "he knowed I taken his money" is just as clear and meaningful as "he knew I took his money." Verb form in English, then, is a matter of conventional usage. Educated Americans simply tacitly agree to accept some forms, but not others accepted by the uneducated.

Social prejudice against vulgate usage does not extend to its appearance in literature. In fact, in that context the prejudice may even be transformed into admiration. Almost everyone would agree that the following passage from "Two Soldiers" by William Faulkner is beautiful and that the short story itself is great literature:

I seen all the towns. I seen all of them. When the bus got to going good, I found out I was jest about wore out for sleep. But there was too much I hadn't never saw before. We run out of Jefferson and run past fields and woods, then we would run into another town and out of that un and past stores and gins and water tanks, and we run along by the railroad for a spell and I seen the signal arm move, and then I seen the train and then some more towns, and I was jest about plumb wore out for sleep, but I couldn't resk it. Then Memphis begun. It seemed like, to me, it went on for miles. We would pass a patch of stores and I would think that was sholy it and the bus would even stop. But it wouldn't be Memphis yet and we would go on again past water tanks and smokestacks on top of mills, and if they was gins and saw-mills, I never knowed there was that many and I never seen any that big, and where they got enough cotton and logs to run um I don't know.

The language usage in this passage is perfectly acceptable to educated ears when used in literature, but not when used naturally by real human beings. Of course Faulkner transformed the vulgate usage into literary art.

The social prejudice against vulgate verb forms carries with it a suspicion that a user of such forms is not likely to know what he is talking about, since he is obviously uneducated. However, this suspicion is shown to be more social than intellectual, for whenever a sophisticated American encounters a true vulgate document that clearly is sound in subject matter—such as a diary of a common soldier or a moun-taineer's account of moonshining—he is quite willing to ignore the vulgate usage (or even find it charming) in his eagerness to read the material itself.

Another interesting corollary of this social prejudice is that many highly educated Americans love to play around with vulgate usage when there is no danger of their play being mistaken for ignorance. For example, many English teachers, in the presence of their social peers, like to use such expressions as "I brung it," "have you thunk it over," "who dolt the cards," "she clang to him tightly," and "he squoze her tenderly." In a situation that doesn't permit such social freedom, most educated Americans would be as likely to belch at a formal banquet as to use vulgate forms. Language usage is perhaps more subject to social prejudice than any other noncriminal aspect of human behavior.

Verb Forms in Tense, Mood, and Voice

All finite verbs have tense, mood, and voice. *Tense* is a grammatical term having to do (chiefly) with time of occurrence. The three simple tenses are of course the past, the present, and the future, but English tenses become complicated because of such forms as past perfect, present progressive, future perfect progressive, and so forth. *Mood* is a grammatical term having to do with the attitude of the speaker. The three moods are the indicative (which makes a statement), the imperative (which issues a request or command), and the subjunctive (which indicates an obligation or a condition). *Voice* has to do with whether the subject performs the action (the verb is then in the active voice) or whether it receives the action (the verb is then in the passive voice). The forms required by tense, voice, and mood make the grammar of English verbs frightening. Consider these forms: *go, went, have gone, will go, is going, was going, will be going, will have been going, will have been gone, shall go, shall be going, shall have been going, shall have been gone, shall be gone, was gone, were gone, should go, should have gone, should have been gone, should have been going, could go, could have gone, could have been gone, could have been going, might go, might have gone, might have been gone, might be gone, might be going, ought to go, ought to have gone, ought to be going, ought to have been going, may go, may have gone, may have been gone, may have been going, can go, can be gone, can be going, can have been going, was to go, was to have gone, was to have been gone, do go, did go,* and so on.

An organization of such verb forms into coherent groups is known as *conjugation*. In years past, school children had to memorize the various perfect and progressive as well as simple tenses, and also the indicative, imperative, and subjunctive mood forms and active and passive voice forms for each of the tenses. It was enough to terrify the conscientious and to make hardened linguistic criminals of the rebellious. Fortunately, such a study of tense and mood is now abandoned. Probably not one English teacher in twenty could now give a full scheme of conjugation of any one verb, with proper terminology, without checking in an old, traditional grammar book. *The truth is that even for standard usage, verbs take care of themselves except for confusion of the simple past and the past participle forms of a few verbs.* A study of tense, mood, and voice is interesting to those who want to know grammar just for the sake of knowing it, but such a study has little value in improving the correctness of one's usage. The range of mistakes made in verb forms is really very narrow.

The so-called principal parts of verbs are the present (infinitive form without the *to*), the simple past, the past participle, and the present participle (both of these last two being used with an auxiliary, such as *have* or *are*). The forms of **regular** verbs are as follows:

Present	Past	Past Participle	Present Participle
walk	walked	(have) walked	(are) walking
explain	explained	(have) explained	(are) explaining

Regular verbs give no trouble to anyone.

The principal parts of **irregular** verbs involve more complexity and do give trouble to those who have vestiges of vulgate forms in their speech but who are trying to learn standard grammatical usage. The present participle of irregular verbs has the regular *ing* ending, and thus gives no trouble. The other principle parts are sometimes confused, as *saw* for *seen,* *run* for *ran,* *swum* for *swam,* and so forth, and this limited confusion accounts for most nonstandard verb usage. Occasionally, mistakes are also made in mood, as *if I was king* for *if I were king.* On a regular college level, however, few students make mistakes in tense and mood forms of verbs, and the whole matter may be ignored for our purposes. The following list of the principal parts of the most troublesome verbs is given here for reference, not for textual study. (Since all present participles are regular, they are not included here.)

Present	Past	Past Participle
begin	began	(have) begun
blow	blew	(have) blown
break	broke	(have) broken
bring	brought	(have) brought
choose	chose	(have) chosen
climb	climbed	(have) climbed
come	came	(have) come
deal	dealt	(have) dealt
do	did	(have) done
draw	drew	(have) drawn
drink	drank	(have) drunk
drive	drove	(have) driven
eat	ate	(have) eaten
fall	fell	(have) fallen
flee	fled	(have) fled
fly	flew	(have) flown
freeze	froze	(have) frozen
give	gave	(have) given
go	went	(have) gone
grow	grew	(have) grown
know	knew	(have) known
lead	led	(have) led
ride	rode	(have) ridden
ring	rang	(have) rung
run	ran	(have) run
see	saw	(have) seen
send	sent	(have) sent
shake	shook	(have) shaken

sing	sang	(have) sung
speak	spoke	(have) spoken
swim	swam	(have) swum
take	took	(have) taken
throw	threw	(have) thrown
wear	wore	(have) worn
write	wrote	(have) written

One distinction needs to be made between certain verb forms used in the subjunctive mood in an *if* clause.

STANDARD: If the Governor *had* been re-elected, he would have commuted the Ripper's sentence to life imprisonment.

COLLOQUIAL AT BEST: If the Governor *would have* been re-elected, he would have commuted the Ripper's sentence to life imprisonment.

STANDARD: If I *had* had an MA degree, I would have got the job.

COLLOQUIAL AT BEST: If I *would have* had an MA degree, I would have got the job.

The verb usage in the second (colloquial) examples seems to be on the increase, and it may some day be standard usage. At this time, it should be avoided.

Verb Forms in Subject-Verb Agreement

Verb forms vary not only in tense, mood, and voice, but also, in a few cases, in number.[4] *Number* is a grammatical term having to do with, obviously, the number of units involved. In English grammar there are only two numbers: singular (one) and plural (more than one). (Some languages have more than two numbers.) Nouns and pronouns[5] in English have number: *man-men, it-they, this-these.* When a noun or pronoun is used as the subject of a verb, the verb agrees in number with the subject. Fortunately, however, the singular and the plural of most English verb forms are identical, thus precluding mistakes in subject-verb agreement.

The use in English of the same form of a verb for both singular and plural usage creates very little ambiguity, for there is almost always some other aspect of the sentence that also shows number. For example, there can be no ambiguity in the following, though the same verb form is used:

The man walked.   The men walked.

[4] Only one case of variation in verb form according to *person* remains in English: *I am.*

[5] In the new grammar many of the words formerly called *pronouns* or *possessive adjectives* are now called *markers* or *determiners*.

Similarly, there would be no ambiguity in these forms if both were standard:

He has money.   They has money.

The reason there can be so many variant verb forms in vulgate language is that in structure English is so redundant that the necessary information is often entered in a sentence in several different ways. Hence such forms as *we was, they was,* and *he were* offer no ambiguity in number.

On rare occasions the failure to make a distinction in number in verb form can lead to ambiguity. For example, the following sentence is ambiguous because the verb form *can be* is both singular and plural: "Bathing beauties can be fun." Rewrite the sentence with a verb form that does change with number and the ambiguity vanishes:

Bathing beauties are fun.   Bathing beauties is fun.

In actual practice, however, such ambiguity seldom occurs. And in fact, stress in oral language would remove the ambiguity from the first example above.

Except for the verb *to be,* verb forms in English vary in number only in the present tense, indicative mood. One form is used for the third person singular present tense:

Subject	Verb Form
he	walks
she	eats
it	runs
one	sneers
everybody	speaks
everyone	knows
person	flies
thing	brings
nothing	has

Another form is used for all other subjects:

Subject	Verb Form
I	walk
you	eat
they	run
all	sneer
persons	speak
things	fly
many	have

A distinction in number is made in both the present and simple past of the verb *to be*:

Subject	Verb form
you	are, were
they, things	are, were
he, thing	is, was

In all other past and all future tenses and in all forms involving imperative and subjunctive moods, the verb form is the same for both the singular and the plural.

The following rules cover all common structural patterns that cause trouble in subject-verb agreement. These rules are based on what actually happens in the writing of educated Americans, not on pre-established grammatical dicta.

☐   *Rule 1: A prepositional phrase intervening between subject and verb does not affect the verb form.*

A list of banned books was (not *were*) posted in the library.

The scoutmaster together with six members of his troop is (not *are*) representing Council 8 in Washington.

The Mayor as well as the Councilmen refuses (not *refuse*) to endorse Measure A.

If a noun phrase begins with *and* but is separated from the subject and verb by commas, it also has no effect on the verb.

Finite Mathematics, and other courses similar to it, has (not *have*) been widely adopted throughout the country.

If the commas were removed from this sentence, the subject would then be compound and the proper verb form would be *have*.

☐   *Rule 2: The indefinite pronouns* one, each, either, neither, everyone, everybody, *and so on are singular and require singular verbs.*

Each of the buses is (not *are*) supposed to carry forty students.

Either of the answers happens (not *happen*) to be acceptable.

The indefinite pronouns *none* and *any* may take either a singular or a plural verb form.

None of you is (or *are*) qualified.

Has (or *have*) any of you read Maritain's *The Range of Reason?*

☐ *Rule 3: The indefinite pronouns* few, several, many, *and* some *take plural verb forms.*

Several were (not *was*) accepted for membership.
A few are (not *is*) sufficient for this experiment.

☐ *Rule 4: A compound subject (two or more elements joined by* and*) is plural and requires a plural verb form.* (See exceptions in Rule 6 following.)

One Republican and one Democrat were (not *was*) appointed to the committee.
A book of instructions and a pad for taking notes have (not *has*) been provided for each member.
Both a letter and a telegram have (not *has*) been sent.

☐ *Rule 5: In the constructions* either (neither) . . . or (nor) *and* not only . . . but also, *the verb agrees with the element of the subject closest to the verb.*

The conjunction *or* by itself sometimes functions as *either . . . or.*

Either the Mayor or the members of the Council are responsible for Measure A.
Either the members of the Council or the Mayor is (not *are*) responsible for Measure A.

Not only the Mayor but also the members of the Council defend Proposition B.
Not only the members of the Council but also the Mayor defends (not *defend*) Proposition B.

The maid or my parents are at home.
My parents or the maid is (not *are*) at home.

☐ *Rule 6: Subjects that are compound in appearance but that function as singular units may take singular verbs.*

Some gas and dust actually shows up in photography.—*Scientific American.*
Disparate clatter and chatter has fascinated linguists.—*Time.*
Your rattling and banging is giving me a headache.
A woman's sweetness and gentleness is a civilizing force.
Sighing and swooning is the way to attract the sentimental man.
Cussing and growling is no way to fix a flat.

When a plural verb form sounds natural, it may also be used with such a construction:

Grousing and growling are no way to curry favor with the sergeant.

☐ *Rule 7: When a form of the verb* to be *connects a subject of one number with a subject complement of another number, the verb agrees in number with the subject.*

Cars are Detroit's chief product.
Detroit's chief product is cars.

The stars were the cause of my proposal.
The cause of my proposal was the stars.

☐ *Rule 8: The so-called collective nouns—*family, crew, team, series, crowd, group, number, *and so on—may take either singular or plural verb forms, depending on which form sounds most natural to the user.*

Often either form sounds natural, and then either form must be considered correct. A singular verb form is always correct with these words unless a plural form is needed to keep the sentence from being nonsense.

A number of spectators were (or *was*) hurt in the crash.
A number of students has (or *have*) been expelled.
My family are taking separate vacations.
The crew are on their way to their battle stations.
The team is (or *are*) in good physical shape.
A series of coincidences has (or *have*) disrupted our program.

☐ *Rule 9: Nouns that are plural in form but singular in meaning* —civics, economics, mathematics, politics, physics, mechanics, acoustics, statistics, athletics, mumps, measles, checkers, *and so on—normally take singular verb forms.*

When a plural verb form sounds natural, however, it may be used with such a noun.

Economics is (not *are*) a difficult course for me.
Athletics is (or *are*) good for character building.
Measles is (or *are*) preventable with a new vaccine.

☐ *Rule 10: A plural noun that establishes a weight, measurement, period of time, or amount of money normally takes a singular verb form.*

When such a noun clearly indicates a plurality of units, however, it takes a plural verb form. When either a singular or plural verb form sounds natural with such a plural noun, then either must be considered correct.

> One hundred and fifteen pounds is (not *are*) a good weight for an eighteen-year-old girl.
>
> Thirty-six inches is (not *are*) not only a yard but also an ideal in beauty contests.
>
> In the nineteenth century two years was (or *were*) not considered too long for an engagement.
>
> Ten dollars is (not *are*) too much for a parking fine.
>
> Three cents is (not *are*) the correct price.
>
> Three cents were (or *was*) lying on the piano.
>
> Three dollar bills were (not *was*) stolen from my wallet.
>
> Two gallons of gasoline is (or *are*) all I can afford.

☐ *Rule 11: In the* there . . . *and* here . . . *constructions, the verb agrees in number with the subject, which follows the verb.*

> There is one important reason why I believe in metempsychosis.
> There are (not *is*) two reasons for his defection.
> Here comes an expert in verbal gymnastics.
> Here come (not *comes*) two petty officers properly ranked.

☐ *Rule 12: In inverted sentence order, the verb agrees in number with the subject, which follows the verb.*

> Lined against the wall were (not *was*) six spies awaiting execution.
> Behind the rose bushes sits (not *sit*) the complacent gardener.

☐ *Rule 13: A verb phrase used as a subject always takes a singular verb form.*

> Hiring someone because he is related to you *is* called nepotism.
> To expedite relief for those damaged by natural disasters *is* a primary function of the Red Cross.
> Denying others the right to their opinions *makes* you a slave to your own.

☐ *Rule 14: In a subordinate clause with a relative pronoun— who, which, that—as the subject, the verb agrees in number with the antecedent of the relative pronoun.*

> The *theory that was* most strongly supported was that advertising is the chief stimulant of the American desire to improve social status.
> The *theories that were* most quickly discredited had already been advanced two decades earlier.

Professor Profant is one of those *critics who are* (not *is*) trying to revive certain elements of eighteenth-century esthetic theory.

Professor Nichols is one of the *supporters* of the BTAC *who urge* (not *urges*) a campaign of letter-writing to Congressmen.

Professor Freligh is the *one who seems* most reluctant to establish a precedent in promotion by seniority.

EXERCISE 63. **Subject-Verb Agreement**

DIRECTIONS: Comment on the verb forms—present tense, indicative mood, or past tense of *to be*—that can be used in the blanks in the following sentences.

1. He is one professor who _____ willing to listen to students.
2. He is one of those professors who _____ dogmatic and narrow-minded.
3. Baby-sitting for the Joneses _____ an onerous task.
4. Lining the top shelf _____ twenty-odd volumes of Shakespeare's plays.
5. There _____ six Shakespeare festivals in England each year.
6. Thirteen dollars _____ a rather exorbitant price for a theater ticket.
7. Economics _____ one of my most difficult college subjects.
8. A series of fire drills _____ held yesterday.
9. Florida's chief agricultural product _____ oranges.
10. Singing and cheering _____ a habit with our football fans.
11. Not only the Joneses but also my father _____ taking the 3:30 flight.
12. Either Jackie or the twins _____ supposed to stay at home.
13. One junior and one senior _____ appointed to the Advisory Council.
14. Few if any freshmen _____ allowed to sit in the Student Council.
15. Each of the runners-up _____ given a $500 scholarship.
16. The professor as well as his students _____ happy to have a holiday.
17. A crowd of hungry orphans _____ patiently waiting for the CARE official to finish his speech.
18. The quarterback together with three others of the backfield _____ to quit before Saturday's game.
19. The Pleiades and one other constellation in the area of Andromeda _____ selected for close study during the semester.
20. The frug as well as other suggestive dance routines _____ banned from half-time shows.
21. A number of honor students _____ selected to attend a Chamber of Commerce meeting.
22. The soil in the three large plots _____ different from that in the two small ones.
23. The acoustics in our theater _____ perfect.

24. Two gallons of grape-ade _____ consumed at Billy's birthday party.
25. Lining both sides of the street _____ a stand of ancient live oaks.
26. There _____ many who will take exception to that assumption.
27. Running counter to Professor Wicklund's theory _____ the findings of Professor Frenz.
28. Hiring unreliable thugs _____ Professor Wattrous's downfall.
29. Checkers _____ more strategic skill than chess.
30. Two acres _____ a large residential lot.
31. Thirteen dollars _____ the sale price.
32. Calendars _____ a chief advertising medium for patent medicines.
33. An important local source of power _____ earth-filled dams.
34. The whole group _____ democratic.
35. A group of professors _____ interviewed on "People Are Funny."

PRONOUN FORMS

The two basic divisions of grammar are word order (syntax) and word form (morphology). To deliver meaning in any language, words must be put in proper grammatical (syntactical) arrangement and in proper grammatical (morphological) form. In delivering meaning, languages vary in their relative dependence on word order and word form. English grammar depends more on word order and less on word form than the grammar of most other languages. For example, the following two sentences, though composed of identical word forms, have different meanings:

The goat butted the sergeant.
The sergeant butted the goat.

In English, rearrangement of the words without alteration of their forms results in different meaning, for word order rather than word form determines which noun is the subject and which the object.

In many languages, such rearrangement of word order does not alter meaning. For example, the following Spanish sentences have identical meaning even though their word order varies:

La cabra pegó al sargento.
Al sargento pegó la cabra.

These two German sentences, with different word order, also have the same meaning:

Der Kater frass den Vogel.
Den Vogel frass der Kater.

These pairs of sentences in Spanish and German, though different in word order, can have identical meanings because in those languages word form rather than word order can determine whether a noun is a subject or object.

Inflection (an aspect of morphology) is the general grammatical term applied to the change of word form for different sentence functions. Inflection changes only word form, not lexical meaning. For example, the words *is, are, was, were, has been, may be,* and so forth do not vary in lexical meaning; they are all inflected forms of the verb *to be.* Tense, mood, and voice are phases of verb inflection.

The grammatical term *case* is applied to the phase of inflection that has to do with the change in form of nouns and pronouns. For example, in the previous German sentences *den Vogel* is a noun in the objective case and therefore is the object of the verb *frass* in both sentences. For that noun to be the subject of the verb, its form would have to be *der Vogel.* Similarly, the article *al* in the Spanish sentences makes *sargento* an object, regardless of its position in the sentence. Only the form *el sargento* can serve as a subject. In English, of course, the form *the sergeant* can be either a subject or an object, depending on word order.

Languages vary in their number of case forms. Classical Greek and Latin have five cases, plus vestiges of two others. Some primitive languages have more than a dozen. In English, cases have been reduced to three: (1) the subject (or nominative), in which the noun or pronoun acts as a subject; (2) the objective (or accusative), in which the noun or pronoun acts as an indirect object or object of a verb, verbal, or preposition; and (3) the possessive (genitive), in which the noun or pronoun shows ownership.

The possessive case of English nouns calls for proper use of an ' or *'s*, as explained earlier. In the subjective and objective cases, all English nouns have exactly the same form. Thus a mistake in noun form due to confusion of the two cases is not possible, as it would be in many other languages. It is the important role of word order in modern English that allows English nouns to have identical subjective- and objective-case forms. Less than a thousand years ago, English was still a highly inflected language and depended less on word order and more on word form for meaning.

Unfortunately, all English pronouns do not, like English nouns, have identical subjective- and objective-case forms. Some do: *you* (compare the old *thou* and *thee* forms), *it, which, this, that, these,* and *those.* And the distinction between *who* and *whom* is slowly being eroded. But several English pronouns still have different subjective and objective case forms: *I-me, we-us, he-him, she-her,* and *they-them.* In theory, it may seem illogical to use the singular form *it* for both cases, while distinguishing between the plural forms *they* and *them*; but grammar, though always functional, is not necessarily logical.

So far as clarity and logic are concerned, pronoun-case forms (ex-cept for the possessive) are obsolete in English. A mistake in pronoun form almost never obscures meaning; it only reduces the social accepta-bility of a spoken or written utterance. Thus proper choice of pronoun form is a matter of conventional usage. We are often amused to hear small children wrestle with pronoun forms, as in such sentences as "my don't like she" and "she's wagging she's tail." But when used by adults, such constructions as "just between you and I" and "John and him volunteered" may bring raised eyebrows, if not covert sneers. Pronoun usage, like verb usage, is one of the obvious yardsticks of social and educational attainment. The following words of caution, stated as rules, cover the main structural positions that cause confusion of pronoun forms.

☐ *Rule 1: Compound elements do not affect pronoun-case form.*

Perhaps the most common source of error in pronoun form is due to the confusion that may arise when pronouns are used in compound elements. The most illiterate native speaker of English never uses con-structions such as these:

Me received a draft notice.
Her wants to marry I.
My father bought a watch for I.

Yet constructions like these are common in vulgate English:

John and me received draft notices.
Her and me want to get married.

And even highly educated Americans are often heard to use such constructions as these:

My father bought watches for John and I.
Between you and I, I am glad to join the Army.

There is something about compound elements that makes the wrong pronoun form sound correct, when a single wrong pronoun in the same construction would not sound correct.

When in doubt, you may test for the proper pronoun form in a compound element by dropping one part of the element and listening to the sound of one pronoun by itself. For example, your ear will not approve of these constructions:

You shouldn't be seen with I.
Him is an undercover agent.

Therefore you should also reject these constructions:

You shouldn't be seen with Peggy and I.
Professor Verhine and him are undercover agents.

Dropping one part of the compound element will almost always make the proper pronoun form apparent.

Mistakes in pronoun form in compound elements usually come after the prepositions *between* and *for*. Be careful always to use the objective-case form of pronouns after those two prepositions, as in these examples:

> between you and me
> between him and her
> between her and them
> between us and them
> between Phil and me
> for Phil and me
> for him and us
> for her and them
> for you and me

Note: When *for* is used as a coordinating conjunction, pronouns in the subjective case may follow it: "John stopped for a chat, for he and I were to work on the nominating committee." The second *for* in this sentence is not a preposition and thus does not require pronouns in the objective case.

☐ *Rule 2: In semiformal or formal writing, the subjective-case form is used after a form of the verb* to be.

The verb *to be* is a linking verb, not an action verb, and therefore does not take an object. The word is literally the same as an equals mark in mathematics; what is on one side is equal to what is on the other side. Consequently a subject form of a pronoun is used on both sides of a *to be* verb.

> It is I.
> That was she.
> Can it be he?
> Was it they who called?
> The chairman is she.
> The guilty ones were we.
> You must be he.

The subjective pronoun forms are always correct after a form of the verb *to be*. But in colloquial langauge, objective forms must also be considered correct. In casual conversation, even well-educated people are likely to use such forms as these:

It's me.
I do believe it's her.
Are you sure it was them?

No stigma should be attached to such colloquial usage.

☐ *Rule 3: In semiformal or formal writing,* who (whoever) *is the subjective form and* whom (whomever) *the objective form.*

In colloquial language *who* (*whoever*) may be used for both cases. *Whom* (*whomever*) should never be used as a subject.

The distinction between *who* and *whom* is disappearing; within two or three generations *who* is likely to be the only nonpossessive form (as is now the case with *you*). Currently, however, correct written language calls for proper use of the two forms.

Several structural positions cause confusion between the two forms. One of these positions occurs in questions that open with the interrogative pronoun *who* or *whom*. In conversation most educated speakers use *who* to open all such questions, because *who* sounds natural at the beginning of a question:

Who were you talking to?
Who did they choose?
Who did the Dean expell?
Who did the professor say made an A?

Actually, only the fourth example here is grammatically correct, for in the other three *who* is an object, which means that the grammatical form should be *whom*. In colloquial language, however, *who* is fully acceptable in all such questions.

In a formal situation, a distinction should be made between *who* and *whom*. You may choose the correct form by testing. First change the question into an indicative construction:

_____ were you talking to?
You were talking to _____.
_____ did they choose?
They did choose _____.
_____ did the professor say made an A?
The professor did say _____ made an A.

With such a change in structure, the subjective or objective form of the pronoun becomes clear. If with such a change in structure, however, you still are not sure of which form to use, you may test further by substituting *he* or *him* for *who* or *whom*:

_____ were you talking to?
You were talking to <u>him</u>. (So use *whom*.)

_____ did they choose?
They did choose <u>him</u>. (So use *whom*.)
_____ did the professor say made an A?
The professor did say <u>he</u> made an A. (So use *who*.)

Such simple questions occur infrequently in expository writing. Therefore, since *who* as an object is acceptable in colloquial language, the distinction between *who* and *whom* in the interrogative position is a minor matter.

The structural position that causes most confusion between *who* and *whom* occurs in sentences in which such parenthetic expressions as *I think, do you think, I'm sure, he feels,* and *it seems* come between the pronoun and its verb. In such sentences the pronoun may appear to be the object of the verb in the parenthetic expression when it is really the subject of another verb in the sentence. For example, one of America's foremost publishers of English textbooks issued a pamphlet to its authors with these opening sentences:

> Every author tries to discover who among the many publishers can best assure the success of his text. He should, naturally, contract with that publisher <u>whom</u> he feels can most tastefully and appropriately produce and thoroughly and effectively promote his text.

In the first sentence, the writer clearly saw *who* as the subject of *can assure.* But in the second sentence, he apparently thought that *whom* was the object of *feels.* Actually, *he feels* is just a parenthetic expression that can be removed from the sentence. The writer incorrectly used *whom* as the subject of *can produce.*

In such sentences as the following, *who* is the correct form; the parenthetic expressions (which, incidentally, are usually not set off by commas) do not affect the case form of the pronoun:

> Professor Sherman is the man who everyone feels is best qualified to represent the faculty.
> Professor Beal, who I am sure takes a disinterested position, has been chosen to arbitrate the dispute.
> Who do you think is a suitable replacement for Professor Ryan?
> Professor Lubbe is the applicant who it seems will receive the first-place award.

Sometimes, however, the pronoun is the object rather than the subject of another verb (or preposition) in a sentence that has such a parenthetic expression. For example:

> Professor Aspiz, whom I am sure we all rely on frequently, will present our grievance to President Peterson. (We rely on *him.*)

Professor Rosenberg, whom I think the Academic Council intends to promote, is considering an offer from Mideastern Theological Seminary. (The Academic Council intends to promote *him*).

In conversation, you may find it difficult to think of the correct form of *who* and *whom* quickly enough to feel secure. The best practice is always to use *who* (except perhaps directly after a preposition), for in colloquial usage that form is now fully acceptable both as a subject and an object. When writing, you have time to test for the correct form. The simple test is to use *who* when *he* (*she, they*) also fits and *whom* when *him* (*her, them*) fits. Examples:

Professor Dodge is the candidate _____ it seems will be elected.
It seems that he will be elected. (So use *who*).

_____ do you think will replace Professors Marcus and Stone?
They will replace Professors Marcus and Stone. (So use *who*).

Professor Adjoka, _____ I believe the President will select for the award, is also the favorite of the faculty.
The President will select him for the award. (So use *whom*.)

Professor Walters, _____ everyone says the Board treated unjustly, has received an excellent offer from Brookline Institute.
Everyone says the Board treated her unjustly. (So use *whom*).

This simple test can also be applied when no parenthetic expression causes confusion. Examples:

We should be friendly with those _____ we dislike.
We dislike them. (So use *whom*).

I wonder _____ I can recommend for the job.
I can recommend him. (So use *whom*.)

It's impossible to predict _____ will be elected.
He will be elected. (So use *who*.)

The pronouns *whoever* and *whomever* should be selected on the same bases as *who* and *whom*, and the same kind of testing for the correct form can be applied. In colloquial usage, of course, *whoever* is acceptable as both subject and object. There is, however, one structural position involving these forms that can cause confusion in semiformal or formal writing. When an entire dependent clause is the object of a preposition (*to, for, with*, and so on), the preposition itself does not affect the case of a pronoun in the dependent clause. Examples:

The award will be given to whomever the Mayor selects.
The job will go to whoever is gullible enough to take it.

In each of these sentences the dependent clause is the object of the preposition *to,* which has no effect on the pronoun form. You can test for the correct form as explained above. Examples:

> I am keeping the prize money for _____ makes the first valid claim for it.
> He makes the first valid claim for it. (So use *whoever.*)

> Mary goes out with _____ her mother selects.
> Her mother selects him. (So use *whomever.*)

☐   *Rule 4: The case form following the comparative words* than *and* as *is the same as the case form of the first-element of the comparison.*

When nouns form both elements of the comparison, no mistake can be made, for noun forms do not vary. For example:

> The Dean of Instruction is more likely to favor the proposal than the President.

But pronouns often complete the comparison, with a consequent opportunity for a mistake in grammar. For example:

> The President is rather conservative. The Dean of Instruction is more likely to favor the proposal than (*he* or *him*?).

In such a sentence the pronoun should be in the same case as the first element of the comparison. In this sentence *he* is the proper form, for *Dean of Instruction* (the first element of the comparison) is a subject. The construction *as . . . as* also shows comparison:

> Professor Lewis did not praise John as highly as (*I* or *me*?).

If this sentence intends to draw a comparison between John and me, *me* is the correct form, for *John* is an object. But if the comparison is between Professor Lewis and me, the correct pronoun is *I,* for *Professor Lewis* is a subject. Note how the two different meanings can be illustrated:

> Professor Lewis did not praise John as highly as (he praised) me.
> Professor Lewis did not praise John as highly as I (praised John).

Apparently, these sentences show that pronoun form can govern meaning, but actually such an ambiguous construction is extremely rare in writing and speaking.

The simple test to use in selecting the proper pronoun form to follow *than* and *as* is to complete the unstated part of the comparison. Note how the correct pronoun is made obvious in the following examples:

> Professor Chapman is more likely to become Dean of Instruction than he (is likely to become Dean).
>
> Professor Ludwig gave Sue more individual help than (he gave) me.
>
> Professor Saunders is as well known in scholarly circles as I (am well known).
>
> Professor Dickey tolerates Ambrose as readily as (he tolerates) me.

☐ *Rule 5: The possessive form of a noun or pronoun is used to modify a gerund or gerund phrase.*

A gerund is the *ing* form of a verb used as a noun and therefore denotes an action or state of being: *walking, gambling, becoming, appearing,* and so forth. When the action or state of being belongs to someone, that ownership is shown by use of the possessive case. Examples:

> Professor Steele objected to my talking.
>
> I objected to Professor Steele's reprimanding me.

Note that we did not object to each other *in toto.* Professor Steele objected just to the talking, and the talking was *mine.* I objected just to the reprimanding, and the reprimanding was *his.*

When referring just to **one** of the person's actions, use the possessive-case form, as in these examples:

> The judge was annoyed by their (not *them*) resorting to the Fifth Amendment.
>
> Professor Cerveney was surprised at Sue's (not *Sue*) showing up in a swimsuit.
>
> Professor Cox was taken aback by our (not *us*) agreeing to write an extra term paper.
>
> Professor Freeman sympathized with your (not *you*) voting against Proposition 24.

When referring to the whole person as well as one of his actions, use the subjective- or objective-case form, as in these examples:

> I saw him giving a bribe to Professor Stone.
>
> It was they lying in ambush.
>
> Was that Jane leaving with Professor Ranald?

In these sentences the *ing* verbals (called participles) are modifying *him, they,* and *Jane,* not vice versa.

☐ *Rule 6: The objective-case form* them *should never be substituted for the demonstrative pronoun* those.

The demonstrative pronouns *this, that, these,* and *those* are used to point out an object or objects: *this book, that car, those people, these categories.* Often the noun that is being pointed out is not stated but understood:

I'll take six of those (meaning whatever objects are being referred to).

Even in vulgate usage the only confusion of demonstrative pronoun forms is the use of *them* for *those.* You should never use *them* to modify a noun either stated or understood. Examples:

Professor Carey asked us to read those (not *them*) books.
Professor Carey asked us to read those (not *them,* if a pointing action, and thus a noun, is understood).
Professor Carey mentioned six books and asked us to read them. (No pointed action indicated.)
Do you see those girls (pointing action)? I want to talk to them (no pointing action).

The confusion of *them* and *those* is generally accounted an especially gross error in usage.

☐ *Rule 7: In the* we men-us men *constructions, the case of the pronoun should be the same as it would be if no noun were present.*

If the noun part of the construction is mentally omitted, the correct pronoun form will be obvious. Examples:

We (Americans) must learn to be less provincial.
Many foreigners resent the provincial snobbishness of us (Americans).
Many professors think we (students) take the world too seriously.
Give us (students) an inch and we'll convert it into centimeters.

☐ *Rule 8: Pronouns in apposition should be in the same case form as they would be if no nouns were present.*

The simple test for this construction is to substitute the pronouns for the nouns they are in apposition to. Examples:

Two students—Cheri and (*I* or *me?*)—were sent to the conference.
Cheri and I were sent to the conference.

Dean Levinson threatened to expel two students—Cheri and (*I* or *me?*).
Dean Levinson threatened to expel Cheri and me.

☐   *Rule 9: The proper forms of the reflexive pronouns are* myself,
    yourself, himself, herself, itself, oneself, ourselves, your-
    selves, *and* themselves.

Note that these pronoun forms are single words; thus *its self* and
one's self are improper forms. Also note that the plural form is *selves*
rather than *selfs*.

The grossest error in reflexive pronoun usage is the confusion of
hisself for *himself* and of *theirselves* for *themselves*. That these forms
should be considered vulgar is illogical. If the possessive forms *my, your,*
and *our* are properly combined with *self* and *selves* to make reflexives,
why should not the possessive forms *his* and *their* also be so combined?
The situation is made further ironical in that *his own self, one's own self,*
and *their own selves* are correct forms. But grammar, as has been pointed
out, is more functional than logical.

A reflexive pronoun form may be used as a subject or an object in
colloquial usage. Examples:

John and myself were the only members present.
The invitation was for both my father and myself.
Barbara and yourself may be interested.

But such usage should be avoided in semiformal and formal writing.

☐   *Rule 10: The personal possessive pronouns are never spelled
    with apostrophes:* its, hers, his, ours, yours, theirs. *The in-
    definite possessive pronouns are spelled with apostrophes:*
    one's, anyone's, anybody's, everyone's, everybody's, anyone
    else's, *and so forth.*

Examples:

The purse is hers.
The car is ours.
The mistake is yours.
The book is theirs.
Its cover is soiled.
One's religion is important.
Anyone's idea is worth consideration.
Everybody's business is nobody's business.
Do you have anyone else's book?

EXERCISE 64.   **Correct Pronoun Usage**

DIRECTIONS: Discuss the proper choice of pronoun in the following sentences. Indicate in which ones colloquial and semiformal usages diverge.

1. Our dog Snoopy was asking for (its, it's) supper bowl.
2. Mr. Jones (himself, hisself) agreed to escort Cherie and (I, me) to the dance.
3. Two football players—Tom Jones and (I, me)—were assigned to the Sports Council.
4. It is clear that (we, us) students were to blame for the riots.
5. Professor Fleenor pointed to a stack of books and said, "Read one of (them, those) by Wednesday."
6. (We, Us) students objected to (his, him) acting like a martinet.
7. Tom has as high an IQ as (I, me).
8. Professor Williams graded Tom as harshly as (I, me).
9. We were supposed to send the money to (whoever, whomever) we felt needed it most.
10. He is the student (who, whom) I think Professor Palitz recommended for a Fellowship.
11. The two who received the largest vote were Tom and (I, me).
12. There was a telephone call for both John and (I, me).
13. It is true that both Marie and (I, me) failed the exam.
14. If it had been (he, him) at the door, I wouldn't have known (who, whom) to call for help.
15. The accident didn't injure John and (I, me) as much as (she, her).
16. Sue enjoyed (he, him, his) staring at her until she discovered (who, whom) he was.
17. The trust fund established for my brother and (I, me) is administered by one(who, whom) we both trust.
18. No matter (who, whom) the voters elect, he will not be as qualified for the job as (I, me).
19. (No ones, No one's, No ones') report was more appreciated than (hers, her's, hers').
20. Don't subject (yourself, your self) to such a strain, for your health is as important as (theirs, their's, theirs').
21. As a cat washes (its self, it's self, itself), it gets vitamin D from (its, it's) hair.
22. There is no excuse for (we, us, our) missing the surprise party given for Jane and (she, her).
23. Professor Williams appointed only two students—Janice and (I, me)—to the Central Council, and it was (we, us) two (who, whom) Dean Clark favored.

24. It is appropriate for (we, us) students to give books as Christmas presents.
25. Just between you and (I, me), I think (those, them) are of better quality than the first ones he showed us.
26. The cook resigned because of (they, them, their) continual complaining about her lack of sanitary precautions.
27. The star of the play is not as attractive as (she, her).
28. It may have been (he, him) (who, whom) the Dean was referring to.
29. The jest's prosperity lies in the mouth of (he, him) (who, whom) utters it.
30. It must have been (he, him) (who, whom) Professor Plunkett said was to parse the opening sentence of the Declaration of Independence.

MODIFIER FORMS

In grammar, a modifier is a word, phrase, or clause that qualifies, limits, describes, or restricts another word. Traditional grammar identifies two kinds of single-word modifiers: adjectives, which modify nouns and pronouns, and adverbs, which modify verbs, adjectives, and other adverbs. Actually, modification in English grammar is not nearly so simple. For example, in such a phrase as "very funny," *very* is not a true adverb, but an *intensifier*. In "this book," *this* is not an adjective, but a *demonstrative*. In "both sexes," *both* is not an adjective, but a *determiner* (or *marker* or *indefinite*). In "consolation prize," *consolation* is not an adjective, but a *noun*. In "barking dog," *barking* is not an adjective, but a *verbal*. Modification in English grammar is, indeed, very complex—even more complex than these few examples suggest. But so far as conventional usage (that is, correctness) is concerned, the range of mistakes in modifier forms is narrow, and standard usage is not difficult to master.

The following words of caution, stated as rules, cover the few common structural positions in which errors in modifier forms may occur. These rules are intended to be only a practical guide to standard usage, not an exhaustive analysis of modification in English grammar. The many phases of modification that are not a source of errors in conventional usage are not discussed here.[6]

[6] For illustration, however, a few examples may be illuminating. Some adverbs have two forms:
"to climb *high*" and "to value *highly*"
"to sit *close*" and "to look *closely*"
"to fly *direct*" and "to go *directly*"
Many adjective and adverb forms are identical:
"an *early* riser" and "to rise *early*"
"a *fast* walker" and "to walk *fast*"
"a *far* distance" and "to travel *far*"

☐   *Rule 1: Do not use an adjective form in an adverbial pattern.*

Most true adjectives and adverbs are inflectional forms of the same word. Normally the suffix *ly* is added to an adjective form to convert it into an adverb. Examples:

Adjectives	*Adverbs*
rapid	rapidly
smooth	smoothly
angry	angrily
happy	happily
quiet	quietly

The adjective form fits this sentence pattern: "He is a *quiet* man." When a modifier is in that position, it is a true adjective provided the sentence structure can be altered to this pattern: "He is a man who is *quiet.*" And provided the word can be compared: *quieter, quietest;* "He is a *quieter* man than I."

The adverb form fits this sentence pattern: "He spoke *quietly.*" Like the adjective form, it can be compared: *more quietly, most quietly;* "He spoke *more quietly* than I."

Note how modifiers other than adjectives and adverbs will not fit these patterns.[7] Example of a supposed adjective:

He is a circus performer.
He is a performer who is circus (?).
He is more circus (?) than other performers.

Example of a supposed adverb:

He spoke very (?).
He spoke more very (?) than I.

Some adjectives may normally be used only in the predicate of a sentence:
　　The boy is *afraid.*
　　I was *aghast* at his crime.
Some *ly* words can be used either as adjectives or adverbs:
　　"a *leisurely* walk" and "to walk *leisurely*"
　　"a *kindly* word" and "to speak *kindly*"
Following the direct object of the verb *call,* adjective and adverb forms deliver different meanings:
　　He called her *sweet.*
　　He called her *sweetly.*
Since not even illiterate native speakers of English make mistakes in using such modifiers—and many more oddities, irregularities, and anomalies could be cited—they are of interest only in a study of grammar, not of conventional usage.
　　[7] There are some true adjectives (for example, *mere*) that do not fit this theoretical pattern and many adverbs (for example, *again, still*) and a few adjectives that cannot be compared. Such forms, however, are not a source of errors in conventional usage.

These grammatical complexities of modification, however, are not a source of errors in modifier forms. For the most part, errors result from confusion of true adjectives and adverbs.

No native speaker of English ever uses an adverb form to modify a noun. Such sentences as the following would sound absurd even to illiterates:

He is a quietly man.
I have a happily dog.

But in vulgate usage, adjective forms are often used to modify verbs. Such usage is nonstandard and should be avoided in all writing except dialogue. Examples of conventional errors in modifier form:

He talks <u>careless</u> about his wife.
He certainly spoke <u>courteous</u>.
Can't you talk <u>pleasant</u>?
He is breathing <u>normal</u> again.
He mixes <u>easy</u> in a group.
When he returned, he seemed to talk <u>different</u>.
He performed his tasks <u>satisfactory</u>.
You don't come as <u>frequent</u> as you used to.
The faucet is leaking <u>bad</u> again.
The train ran <u>smooth</u>.
He ate <u>considerable</u> more than I.
He didn't eat <u>near</u> as much as I.

All of the underscored modifiers in these examples are adjective forms and should be used to modify only **nouns** or **pronouns.** Examples:

He has a <u>careless</u> wife.
He is a <u>courteous</u> speaker.
We had a <u>pleasant</u> talk.
His breathing is <u>normal</u> again.

And so on. Addition of the inflectional ending *ly* changes such adjectives into adverbs, which should be used to modify **verbs, adjectives,** and **adverbs.** In all of the previous twelve examples, the underscored modifiers should be adverbs ending in *ly*.

Confusion of adjectives and adverbs also occurs occasionally because a number of common *ly* modifiers can be used only as adjectives. Examples:

"a friendly chat" but not "to chat friendly"
"a lively dance" but not "to dance lively"
"a manly stance" but not "to stand manly"

"a lonely girl" but not "to sit lonely"
"a lovely girl" but not "to kiss lovely"
"a holy man" but not "to behave holy"
"a deadly blow" but not "to strike deadly"
"an unsightly appearance" but not "to dress unsightly"
"a surly man" but not "to talk surly"

For the most part, native speakers of English have a natural feel for adjective and adverb forms, and therefore errors due to confusion of these forms are not especially common and are rather easily guarded against. When in doubt, ask yourself whether a noun or the action of a verb is being described, and choose the adjective or adverb form accordingly.

☐   *Rule 2: Use adjective forms with linking verbs.*

A number of verbs—*to be, to become, to grow, to seem, to appear, to remain, to act, to prove, to stay, to look, to sound, to smell, to feel,* and *to taste*—are called linking verbs because they may link the subject of a sentence with either a noun that is the same as the subject (*he became Mayor*) or an adjective that describes the subject (*he became angry*). Such adjectives are called *predicate adjectives* because they appear in the sentence predicate but modify the sentence subject. In the following sentences each adjective modifies the sentence subject, not the verb. Note that substituting the verb *was* for the actual verb in each sentence makes the modification unmistakably adjectival.

He grew restive.
He seemed contented.
He appeared calm.
He remained quiet.
He acted silly.
He proved reliable.
He stayed angry.
He looked cautious.
He sounded odd.
He smelled rank.
He felt greasy.
He tasted gamey (to the cannibals).

Many of these verbs, however, may also be used as action verbs, in which case they may be modified by adverbs rather than followed by predicate adjectives. Entirely different meanings result from the two types of modification. Example:

He looked curious.
He looked curiously.

The first sentence means that to others he had a curious appearance, whereas the second means that he himself gazed at something in a curious manner. Obviously, choosing the proper modifier form to accompany a linking verb is necessary for clear meaning. Here are other examples of adverbial modification of the above verbs:

> The tree grew rapidly.
> The waiter appeared quickly.
> He proved constantly on the alert.
> He smelled the concoction cautiously.
> He felt her sprained ankle gently.
> He tasted the wine eagerly.

Each of these adverbs modifies the verb rather than the subject of the sentence; thus here the verbs are used as action rather than linking verbs.

In actual practice, few errors in modifier form occur because of confusion of linking and action verbs. Students often make mistakes in choosing proper forms for sentences in textbook exercises, chiefly because such sentences are artificial, but they rarely make such errors in their own writing or speaking. The most conspicuous and most common error is the use of *badly* and other adverb forms with the linking verb *feel*. When the subject of the verb *feel* is being described, a predicate adjective rather than an adverb should be used, as in these examples:

> I felt bad (not *badly*) about his stock market losses.
> She feels bad (not *badly*) when her children disobey her.
> I feel sad (not *sadly*) every time I read "That Evening Sun."
> He felt bold (not *boldly*) enough to ask her for a date.

If you will remember always to use the phrase *feel bad* instead of *feel badly,* you will probably eliminate 80 percent or more of your errors (if any) due to improper modification of linking verbs.

Occasionally, adverb forms are misused with the "sense" verbs *taste* and *smell*. Examples:

> The milk tasted sour (not *sourly*).
> The rose smelled sweet (not *sweetly*).

But for the most part, the problem of modification with linking verbs is academic, not practical—important in a study of grammar, but not of conventional usage.

☐   *Rule 3: In semiformal and formal writing or speech, distinguish between the adjective and adverb forms of* good *and* well.

The inflection of a few common modifiers in English is irregular. For example, the comparative forms of *little* may be *less* and *least* and those of *ill* (as well as *bad*) may be *worse* and *worst*. Most such grammatical irregularities simply take care of themselves in usage. Some problems arise, however, in the use of *good* and *well*.

Good is a basic adjective form. If its inflection were regular, *goodly* would be an adverb; but because of an inflectional irregularity, *well* is the adverb form of *good*. However, both have the same comparative forms: *better* and *best*. Thus, according to the modification patterns of true adjectives and adverbs mentioned in Rule 1 above, *good* and *well* should be used as in these examples:

> He is a good worker.
> He is a worker who is good (at his work).
> He is a better worker than I.
> He is the best worker of all.
> He works well.
> He works better than I.
> He works best of all the workers.

The grammar of these modifiers is further complicated in that *well* is the adjective form for the meaning "in good health." Thus *I feel good* refers to a generalized feeling of physical and mental well being, whereas *I feel well* refers to a specific feeling of physical health. Or, for another example, *a well person* (as contrasted with *a good person*) means specifically "a person in good health."

So far as proper conventional usage is concerned, the main problem is to avoid using *good* to modify a verb, for in traditional usage, *good* is an adjective only. Here, however, a distinction must be made between colloquial and formal usage. On a colloquial level, *good* is commonly used as an adverb even by well-educated people. And perhaps within another generation or two, the distinction between *good* and *well* will be of no more concern than the distinction between *shall* and *will* is now. In college-level exposition, however, you should avoid using *good* as an adverb. Examples:

> I did well (not *good*) in organic chemistry.
> After taking Nasaldrin, I can breath well (not *good*) again.
> Everything is going well (not *good*) for the family business this year.
> My Citroen runs well (not *good*) on regular gas.
> Acting pays well (not *good*) if you can get a job.
> My twelve-year-old sister plays bridge quite well (not *good*).

In your eagerness to use *well* as an adverb, however, you should not make the mistake of using it as a predicate adjective. *Good* is the proper form to use with linking verbs. Examples:

> A massage feels good (not *well*) to tired muscles.
> Even the PX food tasted good (not *well*) to the weary G.I.'s.

A change of climate is often good (not *well*) for a sick person.
Adversity can be good (not *well*) for the soul.

☐   *Rule 4: Distinguish between colloquial and formal intensifiers.*

Intensifiers are modifiers (usually called *adverbs* in traditional grammar) that increase the force of other modifiers; they never (as intensifiers) modify nouns or verbs. *Very* is a typical, and the most common, and overused, intensifier. It is used to add strength to adjectives and adverbs (*very rapid, very rapidly*), but can never modify a noun or verb directly (*a very man* [?], *to talk very* [?]).

In colloquial usage, the intensifiers *real, awful, awfully, pretty, mighty,* and *plenty* are acceptable, but in college-level exposition more appropriate intensifiers are *especially, fairly, extremely, quite, fully, wholly, rather, really,* and *somewhat.* Examples:

"especially intelligent" rather than "mighty intelligent"
"quite appropriate" rather than "real appropriate"
"fairly well trained" rather than "pretty well trained"
"extremely alert" rather than "plenty alert"
"really surprising" rather than "awfully surprising"

☐   *Rule 5: Avoid double negatives.*

Negation is expressed in English both in nouns and pronouns (*none, nothing, nobody, no one*) and in modification (*no, not, never, hardly, scarcely*). Two negatives in the same statement make, of course, the notorious double negative. Probably no other vulgate expression has been so diligently combatted in public schools, with the result that a once-useful intensive is now virtually eliminated from the speech of those with as much as a high school education.

The double negative is, of course, an intensive, for it is not true that "two negatives make an affirmative," as many grammarians have said. No one in the history of English has ever interpreted a double negative as an affirmative. To everyone, the statement "I don't have no money" means that I have no money—and it will always mean that. Therefore, from a linguistic point of view a double negative is never an affirmative—just an intensive. It once was a useful intensive, but prejudice against it is so strong now that you should not use it even colloquially (except for the special constructions noted below).

The only unacceptable double negatives likely to appear in college writing are those involving the modifiers *scarcely* and *hardly.* Since these words are themselves negatives, an additional negative should not be used with them. Examples:

I have scarcely (not *haven't scarcely*) any work done yet.
He knows scarcely anyone (not *scarcely no one*) at camp.

I have hardly any (not *haven't hardly* or *have hardly no*) grades below a B.

A grammatically interesting double negative occurs in this construction:

He *won't* be eligible next semester, I *don't* think.

In colloquial conversation, such a construction is acceptable. It should be avoided in writing, but then it virtually never appears in writing, anyway.

Another fully standard double negative involves the word *but,* which, when not a conjunction or preposition, expresses negation. Examples:

There is *no* doubt *but* that political pressures caused his resignation.
I *can't* help *but* feel that we should negotiate disarmament.

These constructions are fully acceptable, but note that the negative *but* can be removed without change of meaning (in the second example *feel* must be altered to *feeling*).

☐ **Rule 6: Make a distinction between colloquial and formal adverb forms.**

Slow, quick, loud, and *sure* are adjective forms; the inflectional *ly* ending converts them into adverbs. But all four adjective forms are commonly used as adverbs in colloquial language. Examples:

Drive *slow* through this neighborhood.
Finish as *quick* as you can.
Don't talk so *loud.*
He *sure* is an expert malingerer.

Such colloquial usage is fully acceptable, and even in semiformal usage *slow, quick,* and *loud* are acceptable adverb forms. *Sure* as an adverb is colloquial at best. In formal usage, *slowly, quickly,* and *loudly* are more appropriately used as adverbs.

☐ **Rule 7: Avoid awkward comparative forms of adjectives and adverbs.**

Examples:

"more famous" rather than "famouser"
"more quickly" rather than "quicklier"
"most consistent" rather than "consistentest"
"most admirably" rather than "admirabliest"

☐   *Rule 8: Avoid awkward use of nouns as modifiers.*

In English, nouns are frequently used to modify other nouns (in which case they may be called *adjectivals*). When an awkward construction results from such modification, a revision for smoothness is advisable. Examples:

"The Dean of the University of Minnesota Law School" rather than "The University of Minnesota Law School Dean"

"Instruction in architecture" rather than "architecture instruction"

"An interruption in construction" rather than "a construction interruption"

"An appeal to the State Supreme Court" rather than "a State Supreme Court appeal"

"A death from pneumonia" rather than "a pneumonia death"

EXERCISE 65. Choosing Proper Modifier Forms

DIRECTIONS: In the following sentences, identify modifier forms improper for college exposition and explain in grammatical terms why a different form is needed. Some sentences may be correct.

1. Information regulation by the press is considered undemocratic.
2. She was the beautifullest girl in the pageant.
3. The Senator sure did talk loud.
4. I hadn't hardly begun the experiment when my assistant said she felt badly.
5. Professor Benston gave an awfully difficult final exam.
6. Nevertheless I did good on the exam.
7. He sounded oddly on the telephone, but he spoke clear.
8. Professor Willard doesn't give tests now as frequent as he used to.
9. When you become a homeowner, you will think different about property taxes.
10. We talked friendly for a while, but then he spoke abusive about my Alma Mater.
11. When you eat is not near as important as what you eat.
12. Your Alfa-Romeo runs smoother than my Sunbeam Alpine.
13. Schoenberg's music sounds oddly to my ears.
14. Professor Duax felt uneasily about taking over Professor Lefevre's classes.
15. Professor Liberman stepped cautiously into the Yucatan jungle.
16. Mayor Sullivan felt safely enough to accuse the commissioner openly of bribery.

17. Professor Eley stared angrily at the innocent-looking student.
18. There are scarcely no old-fashioned classicists left even in the big universities.
19. The freshman defended his thesis well against the criticism of Professor Fleishcher.
20. After a night in the open desert, we all felt miserably.

COMPARISONS

Logically, a comparison must involve two elements: more *money* than *brains; books* are better than *movies;* clearer *now* than *before*. A comparison is incomplete when one of the two elements is neither stated nor clearly implied.

Incomplete comparisons are commonly used in advertising slogans: *Green's beer is lighter; Cornsilks smoke smoother; Flimsey's underwear costs less; Butterfinger's service saves you more; Polkadot toothpaste is different; Slurry Cola is so refreshing*. The general implication of such incomplete comparisons is clear, and therefore the slogans, though perhaps not truthful, are conventionally acceptable. In expository writing, however, such generalized comparisons are not conventionally acceptable. The second part of the comparison must be specifically clear, either through unmistakable reference to a preceding sentence or completeness of the comparison within the sentence. Examples:

INCOMPLETE: Cultural Anthropology is so interesting.

COMPLETE: Cultural Anthropology is interesting.

COMPLETE: Cultural Anthropology is so interesting that I advise all my friends to take it.

INCOMPLETE: Attending a community college is different.

COMPLETE: Attending a community college is different from leaving home to go to school.

INCOMPLETE: Professor Gorrell tells more funny jokes.

COMPLETE: Professor Gorrell tells many funny jokes.

COMPLETE: Professor Gorrell tells more funny jokes than any other professor I have.

Not only should the second element of a comparison be stated, but a necessary part of a comparative structure should not be omitted. The structure words *other* and *as* are the ones most frequently omitted. Examples:

INCOMPLETE: Theodore Roosevelt was younger than any President.

COMPLETE: Theodore Roosevelt was younger than any other President.

INCOMPLETE: Professor Wicklund is as learned or perhaps more learned than Professor Frenz.

COMPLETE· Professor Wicklund is as learned as or perhaps more learned than Professor Frenz.

Conventions of usage call for complete comparisons in expository writing even when colloquial usage may condone the incomplete structure.

ABBREVIATIONS, CONTRACTIONS, ITALICS, NUMBERS, MECHANICS

Abbreviations

Many abbreviations are standard in all levels of writing. Abbreviations designating individuals:

Mr.	St. (Saint)
Mrs.	Sr.
Messrs.	Jr.
Mmes.	Esq.
Ms. (meaning either Mrs. or Miss)	

Abbreviations indicating degrees and honors:

A.B. *or* AB *or* BA	LL.D. *or* LLD
M.A. *or* MA	D.H.L. *or* DHL
M.D. *or* MD	O.M.
Ph.D. or PhD	D.S.C. *or* DSC
D.D. *or* DD	

Abbreviations in designating time:

2100 B.C.	9:00 A.M. *or* 9:00 a.m.
A.D. 1688	2:10 P.M. *or* 2:10 p.m.

Abbreviations of governmental agencies and certain organizations and foundations:

UNESCO	WAVES
NRA	CARE
CAB	FOUR
CIA	ILGWU

The abbreviations *no.* and *$* with numerals:

no. 324821	$612.86

In technical writing many abbreviations are common. Consult a good dictionary when in doubt. Examples:

oz.	BTU
gr.	MPH
cc	MPG
cm	RPM

The abbreviation *etc.* may be used in exposition when the writer's intent is to give representative samples from what could easily be a long list. *Etc.* should not be used as a cover-up when the writer can think of no more examples.

Most other abbreviations should be avoided in college-level exposition. Avoid abbreviations of titles, such as *Pres., Prof.,* and *Rev.;* of first names, such as *Benj., Jas.,* and *Geo.;* of the names of states and countries, such as *Ala.* and *Can.;* of months and days of the week, such as *Jan.* and *Tues.;* of streets and avenues, such as *Main St.* and *First Ave.;* of the word *company,* as in *Standard Oil Co.;* of Christmas, as in *Xmas;* of weights and measurements, such as *oz., lbs., in.,* and *yds.;* and of common words, such as *yrs.* and *gov't.* Avoid the ampersand (&) unless it is, in fact, a part of a business name.

The use of full words rather than abbreviations (except for standard usage given above) is desirable not only because of increased clarity, but also because the use of full words adds an aura of politeness to writing. Where politeness is of no consequence, clearly used abbreviations are fully acceptable.

The capitalization of abbreviations should follow that of the full words.

Italics

In print, italics are used to distinguish certain kinds of written units from the main body of discourse. In longhand or typing, italics are designated by underlining.

Words, phrases, and whole sentences may be italicized for emphasis. This use of italics is often thought to have such a personal or sensational tone that it is out of place in high-level exposition. But it is a technique commonly used in good exposition, as a glance through almost any issue of, say, *Harper's* or *The Atlantic* will disclose. Examples:

> Given all this, I still do not think that the demand by the Soviet Union to liquidate *all troops and bases on foreign soil* in the first stage of disarmament is a plausible first step.—P. M. S. Blackett, *Harper's Magazine.*

Hence our anxiety to picture Eichmann as a monster. It is easier than believing him guilty *while accepting his defense.*—A. Alvarez, *The Atlantic.*

Slightly more responsible is the writer who tries to convey opinion *to* the reader rather than express it *from* himself.—John F. Huntley, *CCC.*

Capitalization for additional emphasis may also be used. Example:

I have *hung this fantasy on the Bureau of Internal Revenue precisely because it does NOT operate in this way.*—Bernard de Voto, *Harper's Magazine.*

Proper use of italics for emphasis calls for intelligent judgment. An indiscriminate, false-alarm use of them greatly weakens exposition.

Italics for emphasis may be supplied in direct quotations when the writer using the quotation wants especially to call attention to a particular part of the quotation. The fact that the italics have been added must then be noted in brackets. Example:

The board shall have the power and authority to elect heads of various institutions of higher learning and to contract with all deans, professors, and other members of the teaching staff and all administrative employees of said institutions *for a term of not exceeding four years* [emphasis supplied].—E. Philip Trapp, *AAUP Bulletin.*

The titles of books, plays, long poems, magazines, newspapers, musical compositions, works of art, and names of ships and aircraft are commonly italicized in exposition, though in journalism and casual writing such italicization is often omitted. The whole title, not just individual words, should be underlined. Examples:

Faulkner's last novel was <u>The Reivers</u>.
W. Somerset Maugham's most famous play is <u>The Circle</u>.
More people talk about <u>Paradise Lost</u> than read it.
<u>The New Yorker</u> is America's most sophisticated magazine.
<u>The Portland Oregonian</u> is noted for its crusading editorials.
Handel's most popular oratorio is <u>The Messiah</u>.
<u>The Mona Lisa</u> was brought to the United States for public display.
<u>The Titanic</u> sank on its maiden voyage.

Foreign words and phrases which have not been fully anglicized are usually italicized in exposition. Examples:

The *sine qua non* of astrological forecasts is ambiguity.
The *raison d'être* of many education courses seems to be to provide employment for professors of education.

Do not italicize foreign words and phrases which are well established in English usage, such as *bona fide, et cetera, gratis, tour de force,* and *verbatim.* Examples:

> James Jones's first novel was a tour de force.
> Many foreign jokes cannot be translated verbatim.

There are too many words and phrases of both types to be listed here. Any good collegiate or unabridged dictionary is a reliable guide.

Words used as words should be italicized in exposition, but the more casual the writing, the less need for such italicization. Examples:

> The word *autointoxication* was once important in medical terminology.
> Was his use of *tomato* slang?

Sometimes such italicization is necessary for clarity in any writing, as in this oddity: "James, where John had had *had had,* had had *had; had had* had had the teacher's approval." The italicized *had's* are words used as words; the others are normally used verbs.

Numbers

In exposition, it is customary to spell out numbers from zero to ten. Usage varies in handling numbers from eleven to ninety-nine and round numbers: some writers spell them out and some use figures. Figures should be used for numbers that require more than two words in spelling. Examples:

> Casey won election by nine (not *9*) votes, and would have lost if 39 (or *thirty-nine*) absentee ballots had not been disqualified. He can usually depend on a margin of at least 200 (or *two hundred*) votes, and once he won by 423 (not *four hundred and twenty-three*) votes.

Whichever method you choose, be consistent within any one paper. Figures should not be used to start a sentence. Example:

> Eight hundred and thirty-three (not *833*) Democrats registered.

Always use figures for dates, street and room numbers, pages of a book, percentages and decimals, hours of the day when used with A.M. or P.M., numbers involving dollars and cents, and a series of numbers. Examples:

> I live in room no. 6 (not *six*) at the Mariners' Boarding House at 322 (not *three hundred and twenty-two*) Westlake Street.
> The quotation appears on page 9 (not *nine*) of *Fox's Martyrs.*
> Only 43 (not *forty-three*) percent of the voters voted.

According to my figures, you should get a remainder of .0432 (not *four hundred and thirty-two ten-thousandths*).

The countdown began at 9:00 A.M. (not *nine o'clock* A.M.).

The net cost is $4.23 (not *four dollars and twenty-three cents*).

The daily results for a week were 66, 9, 101, 2, 6, 13, and 10 (not *66, nine, 101, two, six, 13, and ten*).

There is no need to use figures in parentheses with spelled-out numbers. In technical and mathematical writing, figures may be used exclusively.

Mechanics

When writing longhand, use blue or black ink and write on one side of the paper only. Use wide-spaced, 8½-by-11-inch notepaper and do not skip every other line; avoid narrow-spaced paper that might, for legibility, require skipping alternate lines. Make corrections neatly; do not leave errors enclosed in parentheses, for parentheses may be used to enclose pertinent parts of the discourse itself.

When possible, type papers prepared outside of class, in which case use unruled, 8½-by-11-inch typing paper. Typed papers should be double spaced, except for inset quotations and footnotes. Two spaces should be used after all end punctuation and colons, but one space after commas and semicolons. No spacing should precede or follow dashes. In typing, two hyphens (--)—not the underlining mark (_____)—make a dash and the small letter l—not a capital I—makes the figure 1. Capital letters are used for roman numerals, except for numbering the pages of a preface or table of contents, for which lowercase roman numerals may be used. Arabic rather than roman numerals are used to number the pages of a paper other than the prefatory matter; the first page need not be numbered. All typed papers should be carefully proofread for typographical errors.

No quotation marks, underlining (italics), or punctuation should be used in a title unless other rules call for them. Examples of titles:

A New Approach to Disarmament
The Dual Theme of "Richard Cory"
Visual Imagery in *Paradise Lost*
Where Are the Snows of *This* Year?

Always skip a line or double space between your title and the first line of your paper. Maintain at least a one-inch, but no more than a 1½-inch, margin on all four sides of each page.

The Research Paper

THE PURPOSE OF THE RESEARCH PAPER

In everyday usage, the term **research** has two common meanings. First, it means the discovery through investigation or experimentation of new knowledge—something that people now living have not known before. For example, a researcher in literary history might find evidence to show that Shakespeare wrote a play never before attributed to him. Or a researcher in American history might discover documents that prove that a great Confederate general sold military information to the Union forces (or vice versa). Such research discoveries would add to our available store of knowledge. The term **original research** can be applied to this first meaning. Very little original research goes on in school work below the advanced graduate level, for (though there are rare exceptions) one must have considerable training before he is competent to discover really new and important knowledge.

The term **research** is also commonly used to mean the process of seeking out information known by some but not by the person seeking it. Such research is not the discovery of new knowledge, but of established information new to the person seeking it. For example, a student in American literature might ask his professor whether William Faulkner really fought in the Canadian Air Force in France during World War I. The professor might in turn say, "Why don't you do some research and find out?" The actual information is already known to some people and is recorded in reliable reference works in any good library. Looking up the information in the library, then, would constitute a minor piece of research in the second meaning of the word. The term **practical research** can be applied to this meaning of the word. Practical research is quite important in college work, for one of the most distinguishing skills of the college-educated person is his ability to find out information—complicated, involved information, not just isolated facts—that he does not have readily available in his memory. A considerable amount of originality may be involved in practical research, as will be explained below.

Term papers are common assignments in college work. Of the two broad kinds of term papers, one, the so-called **critical paper,** usually requires little research. The purpose of such a paper is to present the student's own evaluation and interpretation of a book or an issue. The writer may gather some information through practical research, but mostly he evaluates on the basis of his current knowledge and set of values. Such a paper is usually more subjective than objective. It may not even send the student to the library.

The second kind of term paper is called the **research** or **reference** or **library paper.** (The name *reference* means that the paper refers to the sources of its information; the name *library* means that the materials for the paper are gathered in the library.) This kind of term paper is based mostly on practical research; it relies more on objective presentation of discovered information and less on subjective interpretation than does the critical paper. A critical paper may be based on the reading of only one book or article; a research paper usually sends the student to a dozen or more sources.

The research paper assigned in freshman composition is often used as a training device designed to prepare students to write term papers in such content courses as history, anthropology, sociology, economics, philosophy, and literature. *The techniques of preparing this kind of paper are rather well standardized. The better you learn how to follow these techniques step by step, the more successful (and easier) your work in academic courses will be.* The composition-course term paper is intended to train you to (1) find source materials in the library; (2) take usable notes from them; (3) evaluate their soundness and reliability; (4) digest and assimilate the source materials rather than let them by-pass your mind in their transference to your own paper; (5) draw sound conclusions from the evidence found in the source materials; (6) organize your findings into a coherent whole; (7) present your evidence and conclusions in an effective expository style; and (8) give credit to your sources and to distinguish between your own original work and your source materials.

SELECTING A RESEARCH PAPER TOPIC

In such fields as history and anthropology, term-paper topics are often assigned by the professor, and in any case they must pertain to the subject matter of the course. But term papers in freshman composition can hardly be written on the subject matter of the course itself, for not much research can be undertaken in the simple principles of expository writing.[1] Thus term-paper topics in freshman composition may come from any subject-matter field. If your professor assumes the burden of providing you with a topic, you can relax and handle it as best you can. If you are asked to choose your own topic, you must exercise careful judgment.

Limiting the Topic

The first criterion of a good term-paper topic is that it be limited enough so that it can be adequately handled in the 2000 to 4000 words accorded it. Even 4000 words are not very many (and the length commonly suggested is about 2500). Only a closely limited topic can be thoroughly developed in so short a paper. Topics such as "The Napoleonic Wars," "The Development of Democracy," "The Life of Beethoven," and "Space Exploration" are hopelessly broad and general. A good topic must be quite narrowly limited.

The process of limiting a topic involves the principle of subdividing. The first topic you think of will undoubtedly be too general; your task is to investigate the possibilities of limiting it. You do this by seeing if you can isolate just one coherent aspect of the general topic that first entered your mind; and then you continue the process of isolating coherent aspects until you feel your topic would vanish if it were further reduced. Then you *may* have a sufficiently limited topic.

Here is an example of such a process of subdividing: General topic: "Slum Problems in the United States." First reduction: "Slum Problems in Washington State." Second reduction: "Slum Problems in King Country, Washington." Third reduction: "Slum Problems in Seattle." Final reduction: "Slum Clearance Projects in Seattle from 1968 to 1971."

---

[1] In advanced work in language and literature, there is much opportunity for research.

Here is another example: General topic: "Integration Problems Outside the South." First reduction: "Integration Problems in the West." Second reduction: "Integration Problems in California." Third reduction: "Integration Problems in San Francisco." Final reduction: "Controversies over *de facto* segregation in San Francisco High Schools in the Early 1970s."

Though you may jump from a general to a sufficiently limited topic in one leap, the need for such a process of subdividing a topic cannot be overstressed. The choice of too broad a topic will invariably result in a poor paper. Always ask yourself if your topic can be further subdivided. Overlimited topics are almost unheard of in term-paper writing, whereas overbroad ones are in the majority.

One of the best ways to test your topic for proper limitation and to understand just what information you want to put into your paper is to *turn your topic into a few specific questions*. Once you can do this successfully, you will know whether your topic is sufficiently limited and will also know much more clearly what you are to look for in your source materials. For example, suppose you decide to write on "President Truman's Administration." What kind of questions can you turn that topic into? Obviously it is a wholly worthless topic for a term paper. Through a process of subdivision, however, you might arrive at this topic: "The Reasons for President Truman's Dismissal of General MacArthur." Then you could formulates these questions: "When and under what conditions did the dismissal occur? What reasons did President Truman and his spokesmen give for the dismissal? What reasons did Republicans or opposition leaders give? What reasons did various news analysts give? Did highly placed military leaders venture opinions? From the evidence, which spokesmen do I think expressed the real reasons for the dismissal?" Actually, such a topic as this is fairly broad and could command many times 4000 words. But freshmen research papers must be allowed some license in dealing with generalities because of the limited knowledge of young students. Any topic that you can convert into four or five such specific questions is likely to be sufficiently limited for a term paper.

If you know precisely the few specific questions for which you are seeking answers, you will not only feel secure in having a limited topic, but will also be able to work rapidly in gathering material for your paper. If you are hazy about the answers you are seeking, or if your questions are too broad or numerous, you will waste time on irrelevant material and will probably turn in a paper that is weak because it is too general. Occasionally, of course, you may want to revise your questions as your work progresses.

Detective Work in Research Papers

A second important criterion of a good research paper topic is that it require you to select information from several sources. A topic for which all the material can be found in one source is not satisfactory for a research paper. Ideally, even a freshman research project should result in the presentation of a body of material that has never before been presented in that form. Thus, though millions of words have been written about President Truman's dismissal of General MacArthur, perhaps no one has yet prepared a paper that presents the basic views of Truman's spokesmen, of his enemies, and of reasonably objective news analysts. If you took this topic, then, you would not engage in original research in that you would be discovering actually new knowledge, but you could show originality in putting together known information that had never before been put into that exact arrangement.

A good research-paper topic requires a certain amount of detective work. If you can find all the evidence you need for your paper in one encyclopedia article, you don't have a research-paper topic. Your topic should require you to seek different pieces of information from various sources. Then you prepare your paper by merging these pieces of information together into one coherent whole—ideally, a kind of whole work that has never before been created. Success in this task will give you great intellectual pleasure and will markedly improve your college work.

Factual and Controversial Topics

Research-paper topics fall into two broad classifications: those that call for an orderly presentation of factual or hypothetical material about which there is little if any controversy and those on controversial issues. Some examples of the first type are "Seventeenth-Century Theories of Tidal Action," "The Critical Reception of Faulkner's *The Sound and the Fury* in 1929," and "The Growth in United Nations Membership from 1950 to 1960." In writing on a factual topic, you are not called upon to take sides but simply to present—and comment intelligently on—the information that you discover. In preparing a paper on the second topic, for example, you would read all the contemporary reviews of the book you could find and would report the varying critical opinions. You would mention that critics now are virtually unanimous in their praise of the book, and you might explain the biases that brought unfavorable reviews in 1929, but it would not be your task to take sides in any controversy that raged in 1929. You would not evaluate evidence in order to reach a debatable conclusion.

Other research-paper topics are of an argumentative or controversial nature. Some examples are "The Therapeutic Value of Vitamin

C," "The Value of Required Foreign Language Study in Elementary Schools," and "The Deterrent Value of Capital Punishment." There is no general agreement among experts on these issues. In writing a paper on one of them, you would seek out and present the established evidence for both sides and then either present a conclusion of your own or express the opinion that not enough evidence is yet available for a sound conclusion to be reached. This kind of topic puts considerable demand on the writer's ability to evaluate the evidence he seeks out, about which more will be explained below.

Topics that simply call for factual reporting may be highly informative and interesting. Controversial topics are likely to be more exciting and to give the writer a greater sense of his own worth as a thinking human being.

Following are a variety of possible research-paper topics for freshman composition:

1. Abraham Lincoln's Religious Views (Questions: What general definition of religion will I use in this paper? What comments have been made by historians and biographers about Lincoln's religious views? From his own words what do I think his views were? Do his writings indicate that he changed his views during his adult life?)

2. The Use of Hypnotism as an Anesthetic (Questions: How do doctors describe the anesthetic effects of hypnotism? In what kinds of medical treatment has it been used as an anesthetic? Do medical doctors and dentists disagree about its value as an anesthetic? What seems to be the majority opinion?)

3. Analysis of Instances of Passive Resistance in the Civil Rights Movements, 1955–1970 (Questions: What were the major instances of the use of passive resistance? What groups led the resistance? What tactics were used? What retaliations were used by opponents? What were the notable successes of passive resistance? Do the successes appear to be lasting ones?)

4. Legislation and Social Work Pertaining to "The Battered Child"

5. Recent Controversy over Sex Education in Public Schools

6. Pollution in Our Cities in 1900 and Prior

7. Current Federal Attempts to Control and Reduce Pollution

8. Henry David Thoreau's Social Criticism

9. Themes in the Works of Any One or Two Notable Black Writers

10. The Work of Some Notably Successful Negroes of the Nineteenth Century

11. Current Opinions as to the Harmful Effects, If Any, of Using Marijuana

12. The Origin and Early History of Detective Stories
13. An Investigation of Devil-Worshiping Cults
14. Arguments in Favor of the Direct Election of the President of the United States
15. Arguments in Favor of the Abolishment of the Jury System of Trial
16. Naturalism in American Fiction in the 1890s
17. The Main Characteristics of the "Theater of the Absurd"
18. The New Science of Cryonics
19. An Argument against (or in Favor of) the Validity of Astrology
20. Current Proposals for Improving Prison Conditions and Rehabilitation of Prisoners
21. Nature Poetry in English before the Romantic Age
22. The Critical Reception of a Few Great American Novels Published in 1929
23. The Controversy over Prayer in Public Schools
24. The Origin of Transcendentalism as Established by Ralph Waldo Emerson
25. The Religious Revival among Youth in the Early 1970s
26. The Present Status of Public Education in the Soviet Union
27. The Contribution of Religious Music to Jazz
28. The "Big Bang" Theory *vs* the "Steady State" Theory of the Origin of the Universe
29. Current Controversy over Birth Control and Legal Abortion
30. Therapeutic Uses of Music
31. Some Aspects of Psychic Phenomena
32. Mark Twain's Philosophic Outlook in the Last Ten Years of His Life
33. Possible New Uses of Computers in the Future
34. Ezra Pound and the Imagist Poets
35. An Analysis of the Social and Racial Philosophy of the Black Muslims
36. The Achievements (or Lack of Them) of Compensatory Education
37. Contrasts between the Poetry of Walt Whitman and That of Emily Dickinson
38. A Study of Contemporary Slang
39. The American Sex Revolution of the '60s and early '70s
40. Legislative Successes of Nader's Raiders

After the selection of a properly limited topic, the procedure in preparing a research paper follows rather rigidly a set pattern of steps. The kind of brilliance that can produce a prize-winning critical paper may increase your success in following these steps, but it cannot be substituted for them. You should learn and patiently adhere to the disciplined routine explained below. Once you have mastered the pattern, you will find term-paper writing both easy and rewarding. And the basic procedure presented here is the foundation of the highest-level scholarly research.

SOURCE MATERIALS FOR RESEARCH PAPERS

Whether your research-paper topic is of a factual or controversial nature, you will gather information for it from library sources. Practical research calls for a systematic use of materials that are given standard arrangement and accessibility in all good libraries. An orderly approach in using these materials is essential for good term-paper work.

The General Encyclopedias

The most available and reliable source of established factual information is a good general encyclopedia. The three most notable ones are the *Britannica,* the *Americana,* and the *New International.* They are available on the open shelves in the library's reference room.

Though they are monumental works, the general encyclopedias have a limited use in research-paper work and are not usable at all for many topics. *Any topic for which you can gather most of your material from a general encyclopedia is not a satisfactory term-paper topic.* For example, if you decided to write on "The Origin of Language" and simply used the material you found in the *Britannica,* you would produce an unacceptable paper. Furthermore, many of the best topics pertain to issues or events of such recent occurrence that no encyclopedia has material on them.

But when a general encyclopedia can contribute some minor pieces of information that will help you build your paper, you should not hesitate to use it. Suppose, for example, you decided to write on "The Use of the Sinking of the *Titanic* in Imaginative Literature." You could certainly use a general encyclopedia to obtain factual information about the sinking of the *Titanic.* General encyclopedias, then, are not a major source of research-paper materials, but they need not be avoided just because they contain established factual information on alphabetically arranged topics.

Special Encyclopedias and Reference Books

On the open shelves of the library are also many special encyclopedias and reference books. These works, like the general encyclopedias, are limited in their usefulness for term-paper work. They may occasionally contribute specific bits of factual information, but, since they are themselves the product of research, they cannot by themselves provide complete materials for a good term-paper topic. When you need to verify or establish a fact, use any appropriate reference work, but do not consider these works a prime source of materials for term papers. Following is a list of some of the most useful reference works.

Biography

American Men of Science
Contemporary American Authors
Current Biography
Dictionary of American Biography
Dictionary of National Biography (British)
International Who's Who
Twentieth Century Authors
Who's Who (mostly British)
Who's Who in America
World Biography

Business

Encyclopedia of Banking and Finance

Education

Cyclopedia of Education
Encyclopedia of Educational Research

History, Political Science, and Social Science

Cambridge Ancient History
Cambridge Medieval History
Cambridge Modern History
Cyclopedia of American Government
Dictionary of American History
Dictionary of Philosophy and Psychology
Dictionary of Political Economy
Encyclopedia of Psychology
Encyclopedia of the Social Sciences
Encyclopedia of World History

Literature and the Arts

A History of Architecture
Cambridge History of American Literature
Cambridge History of English Literature
Columbia Dictionary of Modern European Literature
Dictionary of Music and Musicians

Dictionary of Painters and Engravers
Dictionary of World Literature
Harper's Encyclopedia of Art
International Cyclopedia of Music and Musicians
Oxford Classical Dictionary
Oxford Companion to American Literature
Oxford Companion to Classical Literature
Oxford Companion to English Literature

Religion
Catholic Encyclopedia
Dictionary of the Bible
Encyclopedia of Religion and Ethics
Jewish Encyclopedia
New Schaff-Herzog Encyclopedia of Religious Knowledge

Science and Agriculture
Cyclopedia of American Agriculture
Dictionary of Applied Chemistry
Scientific Encyclopedia
Technical and Scientific Encyclopedia

Yearbooks
The American Yearbook
The Americana Annual
The Britannica Book of the Year
The New International Yearbook
Social Work Yearbook
Statesman's Yearbook
United Nations Yearbook
World Almanac

Not all libraries have all of these reference works, but any college library will have several for most subject-matter fields. All such books are available on the open shelves in the reference room. When you cannot find a potentially useful reference book, consult the card catalogue or ask the reference librarian for help.

Though the general and special reference works may make minor contributions to your term papers, they are not major source materials. Most of your information you must collect from books, pamphlets, newspapers, and articles from magazines and learned journals. These materials are also given standard arrangement and accessibility in all libraries.

The Card Catalogue

The library card catalogue guides you in finding books and pamphlets that may provide source materials for your term papers. Most books are entered three times in the card catalogue: once under the name of the author, once under the title, and once by subject heading. (All the cards are arranged alphabetically.) Occasionally you will know the name of an author who has written on your subject or the title of a possibly useful book, in which case it is a simple matter to discover whether your library has the book.

Here is a sample card that lists a book alphabetically by author's name; it was found under the N's.

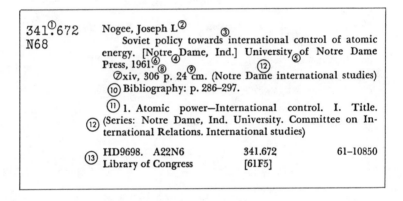

The small numbered circles do not appear on the card; they correspond to the following explanations:

1. Library call number
2. Author
3. Title
4. Place of publication
5. Publisher
6. Date of publication
7. Number of pages in prefatory material
8. Number of pages in text of book
9. Height of book in centimeters
10. Indication that the book contains a 12-page bibliography
11. Subject heading
12. Indication that the book is one of series
13. Information for librarians only

Here is a sample card that lists the same book alphabetically by title; it was found under the S's.

```
341.672    Soviet  policy  towards  international  control  of  atomic
N68            energy
           Nogee, Joseph L. [Notre Dame, Ind.] University of
           Notre Dame Press, 1961.
               xiv, 306 p. 24 cm. (Notre Dame international studies)
               Bibliography: pp. 286–297.

               1. Atomic  power—International  control.  I.  Title.
           (Series: Notre Dame, Ind. University. Committee on In-
           ternational Relations. International studies)

           HD9698.   A22N6              341.672          61–10850
           Library of Congress          [61F5]
```

With knowledge of either the author's last name or of the title of the book, you can quickly see if it is in your library's holdings.

In gathering materials through the card catalogue, however, your main reliance must be placed on subject-heading cards, for you will seldom know many authors or titles to investigate. For example, suppose you chose the topic "Methods of Inspection in International Control of Atomic Weapons." What useful titles or authors would you already know about? Probably few, if any. Therefore you would need to look for books and pamphlets by subject-heading cards. Here is a sample card that lists the same book by subject heading; it was found under the A's.

```
341.672    Atomic power—International control
N68        Nogee, Joseph L
               Soviet policy towards international control of atomic
           energy. [Notre Dame, Ind.] University of Notre Dame
           Press, 1961.
               xiv, 306 p. 24 cm. (Notre Dame international studies)
               Bibliography: p. 286–297.

               1. Atomic  power—International  control.  I.  Title.
           (Series: Notre Dame, Ind. University. Committee on In-
           ternational Relations. International studies)

           HD9698.   A22N6              341.672          61–10850
           Library of Congress          [61F5]
```

Since subject headings are so important in term paper research, most libraries type subject headings in red for quick identification.

Cross Reference

In using the card catalogue for practical research, you will frequently be plagued with the question "What subject heading should I look under?" For example, if you were to choose the topic mentioned in the preceding paragraph, which subject heading would you look for: atomic energy, atomic weapons, international control, inspection, or some other? All too frequently you will feel baffled. But **cross-reference** subject-heading cards will give you good guidance. Often in front of the first book listed under any subject heading, you will find a cross-reference card that suggests other headings that may be fruitfully investigated. For example, before the first book listed under the subject heading "Astronomy," which usually appears in red above the author and title of the book, you will find several cross-reference cards suggesting the following as possible alternatives for investigation:

Astronomy
See also

Calendar	Cosmography
Comets	Earth
Constellations	Geodesy
Mechanics, celestial	Planets, and names of planets
Meteorites	Seasons
Meteors	Solar system
Milky Way	Spectrum analysis
Moon	Stars
Nautical almanacs	Sun
Nautical astronomy	Also headings beginning with
Orbits	the word Astronomical

Of course not all subject headings will have such extensive cross references, but most will have a few, and you will find it absolutely essential to investigate cross-reference subject headings if you are to do successful term-paper research.

The Periodical Indexes

Most research-paper topics require some source materials from articles in magazines, learned journals, and newspapers; and topics on recent issues or events often draw on those sources only. The periodical indexes list articles just as the card catalogue lists books and pamphlets.

In fact, there are only two essential differences between the indexes and the card catalogue: the indexes print many entries on a single page rather than one entry per card, and most of them list articles only by author and subject heading, not also by title. As with the card catalogue, you will find most use for the subject headings in the indexes.

Since articles appear by the millions (it is estimated that about one million articles on science alone appear each year), not all articles can be listed in one periodical index. Hence there is a periodical index for each major subject-matter field. There is, however, one important general index: *The Readers' Guide to Periodical Literature*. This is the index you will find most useful in seeking source materials for your term papers. *The Readers' Guide* lists articles from about 200 general, wide-circulation magazines, but not from the thousands of small-circulation learned journals. However, it may often be the only index you need to consult for term-paper work—that is, until you undertake advanced work, at which time you will probably not use *The Readers' Guide* at all.

Issues of *The Readers' Guide* appear in pamphlet form about every month, and these in turn are incorporated into volumes that list articles for one or more years. The inclusive dates are clearly imprinted on the spine of each cumulative volume. *The Readers' Guide* lists articles since 1900 (first volume published in 1905).

Following is a sample selection of entries from *The Readers' Guide:*

PARKER, William Riley
Refocusing the English program. NEA J 50:
38–40 N '61

PARKES, A. S. and Bruce, H. M.
Olfactory stimuli in mammalian reproduction.
bibliog Science 134: 1049–54 O 13 '61

PARKING, automobile. *See* Automobile parking

PARKING lots. *See* Automobile parking

PARKING meters
Fast figuring of parking charges. il Am City
76: 120 Jl '61
Newport Beach's parking policy. T. H.
Childs. il Am City 76: 119+ Mr '61
This hitching post makes a profit for many
communities! Sat Eve Post 234: 10 Ap 1 '61
Tight parking enforcement: Huntington,
W.Va. E. F. Duff. il Am City 76: 96–7 Mr
'61

PARKINSON, Cyril Northcote
Art of being no. 2. Fortune 64: 123–6+ S '61
Mr Upton-Cumming, of the establishment.
   NY Times Mag p 43+ Ag 20 '61
On the ball. New Yorker 37: 22–3 Ja 20 '62
Parkinson's lore. il pors Arch Forum 114:
   92–5 Mr '61

PARKINSON, Margaret B.
And from now on, no hooky. Mlle 53: 154–5+
   S '61

PARKINSONS disease. *See* Paralysis

In this sample, items 1, 2, 6, and 7 are entries by name of author; item 5 includes four entries under one subject heading; the other entries are cross references. As in the card catalogue, cross references in the periodical indexes are often extensive. For example, the cross references for "Astronomy" in one volume of *The Readers' Guide* are as follows:

ASTRONOMY
   See also
   Comets
   Constellations
   Cosmography
   Earth
   Galactic systems
   Meteorites
   Nebulae
   Radar in astronomy
   Radio astronomy
   Stars
   Telescope
   Television in astronomy

In other volumes, even more cross references might be listed. In seeking source materials for your research paper, you must depend heavily on cross references both in the card catalogue and the periodical indexes.

The entries in *The Readers' Guide* include many abbreviations, which are explained in prefatory material for each volume. For example, in the first entry reproduced, NEA J means that the article appeared in the *NEA Journal;* the figure *50: 38–40* means volume 50, pages 38 to 40; and N '61 means the November issue of 1961. In the fourth entry under C. N. Parkinson, the *il* means that the magazine *Architectural Forum* is illustrated and the *pors* means that it has portraits. You consult the prefatory material in *The Readers' Guide* for abbreviations that you don't understand.

There are several other general periodical indexes that are often useful in term-paper research:

> *International Index* (covers American and foreign periodicals in the humanities, from 1907)
>
> *Poole's Index to Periodical Literature* (covers American and English periodicals, many now defunct, from 1802 to 1906)
>
> *Public Affairs Information Service* (covers books, periodicals, and pamphlets in economics, government, and public affairs, from 1915)
>
> *United States Government Publications* (covers all government publications, from 1895)

Periodical indexes for special subject fields are the following:

> *Agriculture Index* (includes books, pamphlets, and articles, from 1916)
>
> *Art Index* (from 1929)
>
> *Biography Index* (from 1946)
>
> *Book Review Digest* (lists book reviews by author, title, and subject, from 1905)
>
> *Dramatic Index* (American and English, from 1909)
>
> *Education Index* (includes books, pamphlets, and articles, from 1929)
>
> *Engineering Index* (from 1906)
>
> *Index to Legal Periodicals* (from 1926)
>
> *Industrial Arts Index* (from 1913)
>
> *Quarterly Cumulative Index Medicus* (covers medical literature from many countries, from 1927)

The chief index to newspaper articles is *The New York Times Index,* which is published monthly and has annual volumes dating from 1913. Most libraries have files of *The New York Times,* but even when that newspaper is not available, the *Index* can be useful, for it will indicate the approximate date news items were published in other newspapers.

The Periodical Card File

Since many hundreds of magazines and journals are covered in the periodical indexes, many libraries will not have copies of all of them. Every library, however, has a card file listing the magazines and journals that it does have, with the inclusive dates of its holdings. Small libraries often file these periodical cards in the regular card catalogue; larger libraries usually have a separate card catalogue for periodicals only. In either case, it is easy for you to determine whether your library has the magazines in which you are interested.

Many aids to research other than those listed are available, but few undergraduate term papers require research beyond the sources listed here.

THE WORKING BIBLIOGRAPHY

Once you have selected a suitable research-paper topic, your next step is to prepare a working bibliography by canvassing the library sources discussed above. A **bibliography** is a list of books, articles, and other source materials on any particular topic. At the end of your research paper you will have a bibliography that lists all the sources from which you gathered information for your paper. But of course you must have a list of these sources before you can begin work on your paper, and so you compile a working bibliography.

You can compile a complete working bibliography before you read a single item of your list; and it is wise to compile as full a bibliography as you can before you begin intensive work on your paper. However, if you know little about your topic, you should first read some general material pertaining to it in order to be certain of its suitability. Also you should be prepared to add to your working bibliography after you begin intensive work, for one piece of source material will sometimes lead you to others that you did not discover originally.

Be systematic is compiling your working bibliography. First, come to as full an understanding of your topic as you can by converting it into a few specific questions. For example, suppose you chose the topic "The Scandals that Destroyed the Pacific Coast Conference in the Late 1950s." Your questions might be these: "What was the constitution of the Pacific Coast Conference? What charges of irregularities in sports activities were made against which universities and who made the charges? How did the defendant universities try to refute the charges? What punishments were inflicted on the supposedly guilty schools? How and when did the disintegration of the Conference occur?"

After converting your topic into a few such specific questions you should then make a list of key terms that might be used as subject headings in the periodical indexes (including *The New York Times Index*) and the card catalogue. For the above topic you might list these possible headings:

1. Pacific Coast Conference
2. Football
3. The names of the universities in the Conference
4. Sports
5. Recruiting in sports
6. Sports scandals
7. The name of any university official prominent in the controversy

After compiling a list of possible subject headings (and of course any specific authors and titles you may know that are pertinent to your topic), you should begin canvassing the library sources for items to put in your working bibliography. If you think the general and special encyclopedias and reference works may have usable information for you, investigate them first. Then try the card catalogue, making sure that you exhaust all cross references. Finally you canvass *The Readers' Guide* and, if necessary, other periodical indexes, also being sure to examine every cross reference.

As you follow this ordered process, fill out a separate bibliography card for each item you think may provide you with information; never list two items on the same card. Use 3-by-5-inch note cards and number each card sequentially in the upper right-hand corner. (You will need these numbers later in your note-taking.) Be sure to list on each card full information about the item: (1) the library call number of a book or periodical; (2) the full name of the author; (3) the exact title of the book or article; (4) the exact name of a magazine, journal, or reference work; (5) the date, place of publication, and publisher of a book; (6) the date and volume number of a magazine; (7) the page numbers of the article in a magazine; (8) the volume and page numbers of an article in a reference work; and (9) a notation on whether the item has a bibliography of its own or any other feature that might be of additional help to you. All of this information can be secured from the card catalogue or a periodical index; you do not check out an item in order to prepare a working bibliography card for it.

Here is a sample bibliography card:

Explanation of the encircled numbers on the bibliography card:

1. The number of the bibliography card
2. The call number of the book
3. The author
4. The title
5. Publication data: place, publisher, date
6. Informational note

Here is a sample bibliography card for a magazine article:

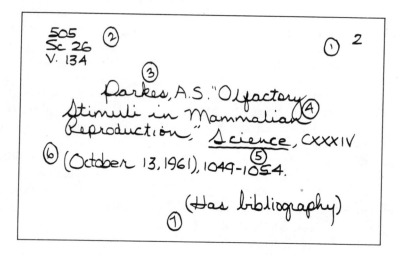

Explanation of the encircled numbers on the bibliography card:

1. The number of the bibliography card
2. The call number of the periodical (This information is obtained from the periodical card file or the card catalogue rather than from the periodical index. In smaller libraries, periodicals may not be given call numbers, in which case they are placed in the stacks alphabetically and thus are easily found.)
3. The author
4. The title of the article
5. The name of the magazine
6. Publication information
7. Informational note

For two reasons it is very important to enter all of the above in-formation on each bibliography card: (1) so that you can check out a book or periodical without returning to the card catalogue or periodical index and (2) so that you can write footnotes and bibliographic entries for your paper without checking out the item a second time. If you omit any of the information, you will be forced to spend time rechecking later on.

In preparing your working bibliography, you will often have to judge from titles, subject headings, or other scant information whether a particular item will be useful. Since you will not be preparing an exhaustive paper for publication, you need list only those items that seem to have a reasonable chance of furnishing you information. After you begin reading the articles and books on your working bibliography, you should watch for references to other works that may have pertinent information for your paper. Often you will discover your most important source materials in this way.

Different topics will of course require various quantities of source materials, and thus there can be wide variation in the number of items on working bibliographies. With almost any topic you should feel unsafe with fewer than ten items as a starter; not many topics should require more than thirty.

PRELIMINARY OUTLINING

As you gather material for your paper, you should keep in mind the need for organizing it into a coherent whole. Your paper is not to be a mere compilation of facts selected at random; it is to be a new, organic whole of its own. It should not read like a series of excerpts, but should have a clear beginning, middle, and end. It must be organized, and this means that its parts must fit together clearly and logically and in the proper sequence.

An outline is concrete evidence of organization. You will present a formal outline with your finished paper (see Appendix 2), but that kind of outline is best prepared after the paper is written. You need a working (scratch) outline to help you write your paper. How much you already know about your topic will determine how much of a scratch outline you can prepare before you actually begin taking notes from your source materials. *You should, however, make as much of an outline as you can as soon as you can and then revise or add to it periodically as you do more reading and note-taking.*

Turning your topic into a few specific questions will help you prepare a general scratch outline before you do much reading. For example, suppose you should choose the topic "Communist Brainwashing of American Prisoners in the Korean War." You might formulate these questions: "What was the aim of the brainwashing attempt? What techniques were used? How many American prisoners were involved and what were some of the notable cases? What success did American officials think the Communists had in their brainwashing? What official judgment was passed on those who were brainwashed?" From these questions you might decide, tentatively, that your paper could take this form:

I. A definition and explanation of the aims of brainwashing

II. The techniques of brainwashing practiced by the Communists in Korea, with examples

III. The results of their program as officially admitted by American government officials

IV. Governmental action toward American soldiers who were brainwashed

With a preliminary scratch outline like this to begin with, your actual work on a paper will be greatly simplified. As soon as you can, you should list in scratch form the three, four, or five main parts around which your paper will be organized. Then you should revise and amplify your outline as your work progresses. Preparing a preliminary outline, however scant, will make your task of note-taking much easier.

NOTE-TAKING

After you have a working bibliography compiled and, if possible, a scratch outline prepared, your next step is to begin taking notes from your sources, notes from which you will develop your finished paper. Since your materials are gathered from sources and not created out of your imagination, note-taking is perhaps the most important part of your research-paper work. The accuracy and skill with which you can take usable notes will in large part determine the success of your paper.

Evaluating Source Materials

If your topic is of a factual nature, such as "Current Theories about the Neutrino," your chief task is to be accurate and complete in taking notes. But if your topic is controversial, such as "The Role of General Walker in the University of Mississippi Riots of 1962," then you must use in your note-taking all your powers of evaluating the reliability and soundness of your sources.

One of the most important aspects of your college education is learning to pass valid judgment on what you read. You can't rely on the truthfulness of a statement just because it is in print; in fact, probably more untruth than truth is in print. Evaluating source materials, then, is a very important part of research-paper writing, particularly if the topic is controversial.

Evaluating source materials does not mean just determining whether they pertain to your topic, but whether they are sound, reliable, and truthful. For example, if you were writing on "The Controversy over Bombing in the Vietnam War," you would need to distinguish between Republican and Democratic propaganda and objective and truthful materials. Making such a distinction is very difficult (often impossible, for truth can be very hard to find or recognize), but as a researcher you must do your best to be objective and honest and you must be willing to take pains in trying to find the truth. In evaluating source materials, you must take into consideration (1) the reliability of the author, (2) the recency of the material, (3) the completeness of the material, and (4) the distinction between verifiable facts and opinions. Complete success in evaluation is, of course, impossible; you can only do your best.

Digesting Source Materials

As you take notes, you must use your mind as well as your pen and paper. Many students try to escape work by merely transferring information from the source material to the finished paper without letting it register in their minds. Consequently, many research papers are no more than compilations of sentences and paragraphs taken at random from various sources and put together in a haphazard fashion. Such work can by no means receive a passing grade as a research paper. You must not only seek out source materials, but you must assimilate them into your mind. You should make yourself a bona fide expert on your topic by reading your materials carefully and retaining the essence of what you read. If your paper is to be really good, you must come to know a great deal more about your topic than you put in your paper. You must digest your materials, not merely transfer them from the original sources to the typewritten page.

Techniques in Note-Taking

Note-taking is, in a large degree, an individual matter. Some people can successfully take notes in an apparently disordered fashion, and some have excellent memories which enable them to take only sketchy notes. But most students need to take notes systematically. You should follow these suggestions closely:

1. As best you can, arrange your bibliography cards in a sequence of general importance to your paper and take notes on the various sources in that sequence. Be prepared, of course, to add new bibliography cards.

2. For your note cards, use half-sheets of notebook or typing paper. You may also use 3-by-5-inch or 4-by-6-inch cards, but half-sheets give more flexibility in space, are cheaper, and are just as handy to arrange for use in writing the paper.

3. Identify the source of the information on a note card by entering in the upper right-hand corner the number of the bibliography card which lists that source. (Remember, your bibliography cards should be numbered in sequence.) This short method of identification will eliminate a lot of tedious recopying.

4. In addition to the number of the bibliography card, be sure to put on each note card the exact page numbers from which you take the information. Failure to enter page numbers can only result in tedious rechecking.

5. Do not put on one note card information from two distinct parts of your paper, even though both pieces of information come from the same source. Instead, use two note cards.

6. Do not put information from two different sources on one note card, even though both pieces of information belong to the same part of the paper. Each note card should be identified with only one bibliography card. This simplifies the writing of footnotes.

7. Take most of your notes in a condensed, summarized form so that you can re-expand them later in your own words. However, you will want to take some notes verbatim, and then you must take care to be absolutely accurate. (The section following on paraphrasing and the use of direct quotations will further explain this aspect of note-taking.)

8. As you develop your working outline, try to identify on each note card just to which part of your outline the information belongs. This will simplify your task when you begin to convert your notes into your finished paper, for you can then arrange your note cards to correspond with your outline headings.

9. Learn to skim through source materials so that you will not waste time in concentrated reading of useless material. Having turned your topic into a few specific questions or having a good working outline will help you examine materials rapidly

without overlooking pertinent information. As soon as you find useful material, slow down and be thorough and accurate in your reading and note-taking. After you begin systematically examining the items listed on your bibliography cards, you will find that some of them are of no use to you at all. Such minor frustrations are just a part of research and investigation. Consider the research chemist. Can he always discover a useful product on his first experiment? Research means separating the usable from the useless.

10. Be as neat and legible in your note-taking as your own abilities require. Don't be too hasty for your own good and don't crowd too much material on one note card. Be sure to get everything accurate the first time: bibliography card reference, page numbers, direct quotations (if any), and the information itself.

Following is a sample of note-taking. Topic: "Controversy over the Existence of Extrasensory Perception." Questions: "What is a definition of extrasensory perception? On what bases do some notable scholars claim that it exists? What are a few specific experiments that they have conducted? On what bases do other scholars refute these claims? What is my objective conclusion on the basis of the evidence?"

Let us examine this passage from a source listed on a hypothetical bibliography card:

> . . . Whether or not there is enough material left to sustain Dr. Rhine's case, one comes away from his account with the feeling that, much as he believes in the necessity for rigor, he is not always willing to insist upon it.
>
> Dissatisfaction with the controls is increased by the long list of conditions with which he finds it necessary to surround his experiments. Extrasensory perception is a "delicate and subtle capacity" something like the creation of poetry in its instability. The experimenter must be "friendly, almost fraternal" and the experiments "casual and informal." The situation must appeal to the subject; he must not be reluctant or feel hurried. There must be a spirit of play; a monetary reward is destructive. Strong emotions, illness, fatigue, over-intellectual analysis, or pre-formed beliefs may interfere. And so on.—B. F. Skinner, "Is Sense Necessary?"

A note card based on this source would look as follows:

② Refutation of Claims   ① 4

④ Author says Dr. Rhine believes in rigor
in experimentation but doesn't always
insist upon it. Author feels Rhine does
not control experimentation suficiently
and That he has too many conditions
attached to Them. E.g., claims Rhine puts
his experiments in realm of something
Like creation of poetry rather than
something with scientific rigor, such
as being "friendly, almost fraternal"
③ PP. with the subject and "casual
5-6 and informal" in the experimentation.

Explanations of encircled numbers on the note card:

1. The number of the corresponding bibliography card, which will contain all the informatoin about the source: call number, author, title, facts of publication
2. Heading that identifies where the information fits in the paper
3. Actual page numbers that the information is taken from
4. A condensed summary of the information

If the information from this source had seemed usable as a direct quotation, the note-taker would have copied it verbatim and would have indicated on his note card that it was a direct quotation.

DIRECT QUOTATIONS; PARAPHRASING; PLAGIARISM

Paraphrasing

A direct quotation is, of course, an *exact* reproduction of the words of another writer. A paraphrase is the statement in your own words of information or ideas you have taken from source materials. It is most important in term-paper work for you to distinguish between direct quotations and paraphrasing. Using someone else's words as your own is **plagiarism**—literary theft—which alone justifies a grade of F. Your professor can easily distinguish between professional writing and your own, and he will not tolerate plagiarism. The best way to guard against it is to take condensed, summarized notes (except when you take verbatim notes for probable use as a direct quotation). Then when you use your notes you will expand them in your own words.

Look again at the condensed notes on the sample note card. In preparing his paper, a writer might use these notes to compose this passage for his paper:

> In addition to maintaining that Dr. Rhine does not practice the rigor in experimentation that he says he believes in, this reviewer feels that Rhine fails to control his experiments sufficiently because he attaches too many conditions to them. For example, he believes that Rhine loses scientific rigor when he insists on the experimenter being "friendly" and "casual and informal" with the subject of the experiment. He also believes that Rhine attributes too many of his failures to such causes as payment for services, illness, fatigue, and prejudice or emotionalism on the part of the subject.

A comparison of this finished passage for inclusion in a term paper with the original source quoted above will illustrate proper paraphrasing: remaining true to the spirit and facts of the source material, but using one's own style of writing. *The process is from source material to condensed notes to re-expression in one's own style.* Of course beginners in academic research must be allowed some freedom in imitating the style of their sources, but deliberate plagiarism cannot be tolerated.

Uses of Direct Quotations

Direct quotations have two minor and two major roles in research papers. One minor role, which usually calls for a short quotation, is to emphasize a point or fact; quoted material is naturally emphasized by virtue of being quoted. Another minor role is to share with the reader material that is striking and original in its phrasing; this is an esthetic use of direct quotations. These uses should not be overworked.

The two major, and important, uses of direct quotations are (1) to make use of the direct words of an authority to sanction a point of view and (2) to present original evidence for a conclusion you draw. These two uses differ. For example, suppose you wrote a paper on "Natural Control of Insect Pests." You might quote a famous entomologist to the effect that natural control eliminates many of the dangers of pesticides. His eminence in his field would lend weight to this point of view. Now suppose you wrote on "Jeffersonian Ideas in the Speeches of Franklin D. Roosevelt." You would, of course, first become acquainted with Jeffersonian ideas and then would read the speeches of Roosevelt to discover Jeffersonian overtones. In writing your paper you would quote from the Roosevelt speeches simply to give evidence for your conclusion that he expressed Jeffersonian ideas. You would not be quoting Roosevelt because he was an expert on Jeffersonian ideas, but as evidence of the fact that he used the ideas.

When a direct quotation appears in a research paper, it must fulfill one of these definite purposes. *It must not be aimlessly tossed into the paper.* The paper is your creation; the direct quotations in it must be used creatively. Do not quote commonly known information such as can be found in several sources. For example, you should not quote birth and death dates, statistics that can be found in various good reference works, or scientific information that any good teacher might be expected to know. Few practices give as gauche an appearance to a term paper as a direct quotation of this sort: "Beethoven was born in Bonn, Germany, on December 16, 1770, and died there on March 26, 1827." (accompanying footnote) Also be wary of using a direct quotation to open a term paper, for such a practice is usually awkward.

There are two methods of entering a direct quotation into a paper. When it will take up five or fewer normal lines of your text, you should enclose it in quotation marks and incorporate it directly into the text of your paper.

Some times you will want to leave out part of the original in using a direct quotation. You indicate such an omission by putting three spaced periods (. . .) in place of the omitted material. If you omit the last part of a sentence, or a whole sentence, use four periods. If you enter words not actually in the original quotation, such as a name for clear reference, enclose them in square brackets [like this].

> The second method--called the inset or block method of quotation--is illustrated here. You should use it when a quotation will take up six or more lines of your paper. You do not enclose an inset in quotation marks, for the inset form itself indicates a direct quotation. Indent each line of the inset five spaces. Give the first line additional paragraph indentation only if a paragraph actually began there in the source material. Single space the inset (the rest of the paper, except footnotes, to be double spaced); in longhand, skip a line before and after it. An inset need not be--usually is not--a separate paragraph.

When using a direct quotation as evidence for a conclusion you draw or to establish authority for a point of view, use an *introductory phrase or sentence* that will make the quotation an integral part of the paper. Even such a short, simple phrase as "according to the well-known geneticist So-and-so" will tie a quotation in with the rest of the paper and provide coherence. You should never just abruptly enter an important quotation without announcing its purpose. Such a practice makes a paper appear disjointed.

Always be absolutely accurate in using direct quotations. Get the habit of checking carefully as you take verbatim notes for possible use as direct quotations. Be sure to paraphrase when you do not quote material directly.

DOCUMENTATION

In a research paper, documentation means the acknowledgment of the sources used. One aspect of documentation is the appendage of a bibliography of items used in preparing the paper; another is footnoting.

Uses of Footnotes

There are three main uses of footnotes. The first is to acknowledge the source of direct quotations. Every direct quotation must be absolutely accurate and either enclosed in quotation marks or identified as an inset. The footnote tells the reader exactly where he can find the quotation. Well-known quotations (such as from Shakespeare or the Bible) and common dictionary definitions should not be footnoted when they are used for embellishment rather than as evidence.

The second use of footnotes is to acknowledge the source of evidence or important information even when it is not quoted directly. Here you must distinguish between important information or evidence that builds your paper and relatively unimportant information or easily ascertained facts. Obviously the source of every single fact in a paper should not be acknowledged, else the paper would be cluttered with excessive footnotes. But the source of evidence and information of central importance must be cited. In general, it is difficult to learn when and when not to footnote unquoted (paraphrased) material. *The crux is to avoid footnoting material that will pass without question*—that is, that a critical reader will accept without doubt or suspicion. Information that is central to the paper or that a critical reader might question or that can be found in just one source should usually be footnoted.

The third use is to put in the paper explanatory material that would be out of place in the text of the paper. An explanatory footnote is likely to begin with such a phrase as "an interesting sidelight in this connection . . ." or " a consequent result that had no bearing on cancer research itself. . . ." Explanatory footnotes are not common in term papers. Using them to be impressive is not a recommended practice.

Location of Footnotes

There are three ways of entering footnotes in a research paper, though one of the methods doesn't actually involve footnote forms. The traditional method, most frequently used in freshman composition because the term paper in that course is often a training device, is to place the footnote at the bottom of the page on which appears the source material being acknowledged. Under this method a two- or three-inch line should separate the text from the footnotes on any one page, and a one-inch margin should be maintained at the bottom of each page.

Typing footnotes at the bottom of a page presents difficulties, for even the most careful typist will often forget to leave enough space for the footnotes of any particular page. A good way to prevent this trouble is to insert a guide sheet under your sheet of typing paper. On an 8½-by-11-inch sheet of typing paper you can prepare for yourself a guide sheet like the one illustrated here. The numbers and lines of the guide sheet will show through and will guide you in leaving enough space for your footnotes. If you are also typing a carbon copy, be sure to place the guide sheet on the inert side of the carbon paper.

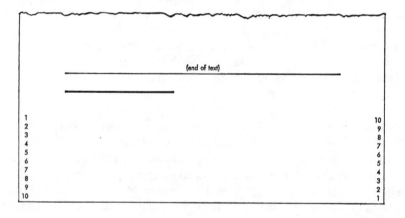

The second method is to place all footnotes at the end of the paper. This method makes the typing of a paper much easier.

In both of these methods (a necessity in the second) footnotes should be numbered consecutively throughout the paper (1, 2, 3, and so on). Each footnote should be single spaced, with double spacing between footnotes. Raised numbers (without periods) should be used both in the text immediately **after** the material being acknowledged and with the footnote itself. Each footnote should be indented as a paragraph—that is, the first line indented five spaces and successive lines flush with the established margin.

The third method of acknowledging source materials is the simplest, but the least used in term papers. In using this method, you number the items in your bibliography, and then in place of a footnote number in the text of your paper you place in parentheses the number of the bibliographic entry that is the source of the material and the page numbers on which the material appears. For example, (4, pp. 21–22) after a quotation would indicate that it appears on pages 21 and 22 of the bibliographic entry number 4. A variation of this method is to use the name of the author rather than the number of the bibliographic entry— for example, (Morton, p. 14). Under this variation, the bibliographic entries are not numbered, the full name of the author is given if two in the bibliography have the same last name, and both the author's name and the title are given if that author is represented more than once in the bibliography.

Which of these methods of footnoting you use will depend on your professor's preference.

Footnote Forms

Various footnote forms are in common use, and any standard form, if consistently used, is satisfactory. The forms recommended here emphasize simplicity. You should not make a special effort to memorize the forms, though if such memorization comes easy for you, you can certainly profit from your talent. Even experienced writers of term papers usually just check the proper guide form each time they write a footnote. Since there are so many commas, periods, quotation marks, underlinings, and parentheses in footnotes, you can ensure accuracy best by patiently copying a guide form. Accuracy in form has the same importance that conventions of usage have in writing.

Guide to Footnote Forms

Though you will refer to these forms as you write footnotes, you should first study them all carefully so that you will know how to use them as guides. Remember that the use of italics here is equal to underlining in a typed paper.

Form for a Book
[1] John F. Bateson, *A New Look at Vocational Education* (New York, 1968), p. 106.

Form for a Magazine Article
[2] Jasper S. Jackson, "Education in the Atomic Age," *The Atlantic,* CII (June 1959), p. 97.

Form for an Encyclopedia Article (Anonymous)
[3] "Education," *Encyclopaedia Britannica* (12th ed.), IV, 642.

Form for a Newspaper Article

[4] *Portland Oregonian,* 17 August 1960, sect. G, p. 7.

Note: If the name of the newspaper does not clearly identify its city, put the city and state in parentheses after the name of the newspaper. If the paper consists of only one section or part, give only the page number. If the reference is to a newspaper article with a by-line, put the author's name and the name of his column before the name of the newspaper, as in the form for a magazine article.

Form for a Later Edition of a Book

[5] Herbert Schwimp, *The Philosophy of Education* (New York, 1956; 2d ed.), pp. 18–21.

Form for an Edited Book

[6] Helen Fogle (ed.), *Tributes to John Dewey* (New York, 1940), p. xiv.

Form for a Component Part of an Edited Book

[7] E. Z. Morales, "Wealth and Education," in *Essays in Philosophy,* edited by P. G. Wall (Caldwell, Idaho, 1968), p. 275.

Form for a Work in Several Volumes

[8] Harry Speigle, *A History of Education* (Chicago, 1955), III, p. 90.

Form for a Work by Two Authors

[9] Thomas Jones and Alfred Hill, *Perspectives in Education* (New York, 1964), p. 66.

Form for a Work by Three or More Authors

[10] Mary Blake and others, *Educational Studies* (New York, 1968), p. 48.

Form for a Translated Book

[11] Julio Petrillo, *Education and Class Structure,* trans. by John Moon (New York, 1962), p. 290.

Form for a Pamphlet

[12] *Higher Education for Democracy,* Report of the President's Commission on Higher Education (Washington, 1957), p. 26.

Short Forms

Once a work has been referred to, any subsequent footnote for it should be of a **short form.**

If the footnote is the same (except for page number) as the immediately preceding footnote, the abbreviation *ibid.* (meaning "in the same place") should be used as the short form. *Ibid.* may be used any number of times in succession, and intervening pages without footnotes do not limit its use. Practice is now divided on underlining *ibid.;* it is always capitalized as a footnote; it always has a period after it. Note that a comma separates *ibid.* from a new page number.

[13] Norman Harris, *Education and Technology* (London, 1964), p. 98.
[14] *Ibid.,* p. 119.
[15] *Ibid.*

When there has been an intervening footnote, *ibid.* cannot be used. In such a case the **short form** can be just the author's last name, plus a page number.

¹⁶Speigle, p. 39.

The short form can be a title (if anonymous) plus a page number.

¹⁷ "Education and Earnings," p. 43.

If the paper has footnotes referring to two authors with the same last name, then the short form should list the author's whole name, plus the page number.

¹⁸ Bertrand Smith, p. 42.

If the paper has referred to two words by the same author, then the short form should give the author's last name and the title, plus the page number.

¹⁹ Harris, *Industrial Education,* p. 346.

Always use *ibid.* as a short form when the footnote is the same as the immediately preceding one. Use the author's name as a short form when there has been an intervening footnote. The abbreviation *op. cit.* (work cited) is totally unnecessary in a short-form footnote.

In the form for a magazine article, the roman numeral refers to the volume number of the magazine. Most good magazines have volume numbers. However, if you use a magazine that does not have a volume number, just refer to it by date.

²⁰ Jerry Bildt, "Be Educated and Healthy," *Modern Health,* June 1962, pp. 54–55.

Bibliography

At the end of your research paper you will place a bibliography, a list of all the sources you have used in preparing your paper. You need not necessarily have referred to a work in a footnote to place it in your bibliography, but you should have found definite use for it in preparing your paper. Enter your bibliography on a separate sheet or sheets of paper and center it for neatness. Number the entries in it *only* if you are to use the numbers as explained above in the third method of foot-noting. Do not separate entries into categories, such as books and magazine articles. Alphabetize the entries according to last name of author or, if the work is anonymous, the first word of the title (except *a, an,* or *the*); do not use the word *anonymous* in the bibliography. If you have two or more entries by the same author, you may substitute a long dash (————) for the author's name after its first use. Indent the bibliographic entries just the opposite of footnotes; begin the first line with the established margin and indent all succeeding lines five spaces. Single space each entry but double space between entries.

As with footnotes, you should not try to memorize the bibliographic forms. Just refer to the guide as you write each entry. All the information needed should be on your working bibliography cards.

Guide to Bibliographic Forms

Form for a Book
Jackson, James Thomas. *Tank Warfare in Africa.* New York: The Macmillan Company, 1968.

Form for a Magazine Article
Bates, Thomas H. "The American Army in Africa," *Harper's Magazine,* CCXXV (April 1964), 89–101.

Form for a Newspaper Article
Spokesman Review (Spokane, Washington), 14 July 1963, part A, p. 6.
    Note: See note under form for a newspaper article in the section on footnote forms.

Form for an Encyclopedia Article (Anonymous)
"Tank Warfare," *Encyclopaedia Britannica,* 13th ed., XXI, 906–13.

Form for a Later Edition of a Book
Mosely, Ivan. *Tanks and Men.* 2d ed. Chicago: Claxton Press, 1968.

Form for an Edited Book
Hill, James T. (ed.). *Stories of Tank Warfare.* New York: Home Press, 1958.

Form for a Component Part of an Edited Book
Ruiz, Richard. "Panzer Units," in *Essays on Warfare,* ed. by Harley S. Jones. Chicago: Mobile Press, 1954.

Form for a Work in Several Volumes (All Used)
Jones, Harley S. *A History of Tank Warfare.* New York: S. S. Filtch, Inc., 1956. 3 vols.

Form for a Work in Several Volumes (One Used)
Jones, Harley S. *A History of Tank Warfare.* New York: S. S. Filtch, Inc., 1956. Vol. I.

Form for a Translated Book
Gerhardt, Erich. *Blitzkrieg.* Trans. by Abner Porter. New York: The Dial Press, Inc., 1943.

Form for a Work by Two Authors
Field, Robert, and Charles Foreman. *Ancient Tanks.* Ann Arbor, Mich.: Adoption Press, 1962.

Form for a Work by Three or More Authors
Filed, Robert, and others. *Modern Tanks.* New York: World Press & Co., Inc., 1963.

Form for a Pamphlet

American Preparedness and International Tension. Washington: National
Association of Pacifism, 1968.

In research-paper work, follow your professor's directions (1) in
preparing a title page; (2) in entering a table of contents or prefatory
material; (3) in providing an outline (see Appendix 2); (4) in entering
appendixes, charts, graphs, and so on; and (5) in method of submitting
paper.

The following specimen paper is an actual, undoctored freshman
research project prepared by a good college student. It is intended to
represent the real work of a college freshman, not an ideal product that
ordinary students cannot hope to emulate. Its defects might be found in
the work of the best college freshmen; its virtues are worth study.

THE SCIENTIFIC AMERICAN PSYCHICAL INVESTIGATION:

A CASE AGAINST SPIRITUALISM

by

William Wolfe

English 1A -- Section 12

Professor Willis

January 1968

OUTLINE

I.   The <u>Scientific American</u> Psychic Investigation was well organized.

   A.   Its committee was composed of five open-minded, level-headed men, who were sincerely interested in psychic research.

   B.   It offered a $2500 prize to the medium who produced a genuine psychic phenomenon under laboratory conditions.

   C.   It used scientific techniques in detecting fraud.

II. The majority of America's mediums did not cooperate with the committee.

   A.   Only five mediums presented themselves before the committee during its two years of work.

   B.   The mediums who entered were not among the nation's best or best known.

   C.   The remainder of the mediums refused to enter or ignored the psychic competition.

III. The committee's findings were well founded.

   A.   All five mediums investigated were declared to be fraudulent.

   B.   The findings were borne out, in two instances, by subsequent developments.

      1.   Peroraro confessed to being a fraud seven years later.

      2.   Margery was exposed by two subsequent investigatory committees.

   C.   In two years, the <u>Scientific American</u> Psychic Investigation Committee saw no genuine phenomena and found no actual medium.

ii

THE SCIENTIFIC AMERICAN PSYCHICAL INVESTIGATION:

A CASE AGAINST SPIRITUALISM

Perhaps the Scientific American Psychical Investigation Committee
was doomed to frustration from the very beginning. Before the investigation was over, friction developed between several members, and as a
result, one person resigned and later left his job with Scientific American. The drama behind the findings, however, in no way lessens their
validity. In two years of investigation into psychic phenomena, the
committee saw no manifestation that they considered to be genuine. Their
$2500 prize was not awarded. They found no real medium.

Spiritualism, as it is known today, began in 1848 with the famous
fraud rappings of the Fox Sisters. From that time spiritualism snow-
balled until, as America roared into the twenties, it had attained
stupendous proportions.[1]

By this time the leading magazines could no longer ignore it, and in
January of 1922 Scientific American began a series of articles dealing

---

[1] Harry Houdini, Houdini on Magic, ed. by William B. Gibson and
Morris N. Young (New York, 1953), pp. 122-123.

1

with spiritualism. The first article was authored by Hereward
Carrington, a noted psychical researcher. His article, citing mysterious
facets of the human body,[2] started the magazine's own snowball that was
to produce an article a month for the following two-and-a-half years.
Other articles were by Walter Franklin Prince who explained the problems
of the psychic investigator.[3]

Harry Houdini, the magician and escape artist who had become quite
a psychic exposer, was asked to write some of the articles in the series.
He had to refuse because he could not spare the time necessary. He did,
however, suggest to the magazine that they form an investigatory commit-
tee on which he would serve without pay.[4] The magazine accepted
Houdini's suggestion and in December 1922 it was announced in <u>Scientific
American</u>. The committee consisted of Dr. William McDougall, of Harvard
University; Dr. Daniel F. Comstock, formerly of the Massachusetts
Institute of Technology; Dr. William Franklin Prince, of the Society of
Psychical Research; Hereward Carrington, a psychic investigator; and
Houdini. J. Malcolm Bird, an associate editor of the magazine,was
appointed secretary. <u>Scientific American</u> offered $2500 to the first
medium who could produce psychic phenomena under laboratory conditions
to the satisfaction of four out of five of the committee members.

---

[2]Hereward Carrington, "The Mechanism of the Psychic," <u>Scientific
American</u>, CXXVI (January 1922), p. 60.

[3]Walter Franklin Prince, "The Psychic Detective," <u>Scientific
American</u>, CXXVII (July 1922), p. 6.

[4]Houdini, pp. 134-135.

The mediums were given two years--until December 1924--to decide if they wanted to enter.[5] Shortly afterward, Houdini offered $5000 of his own money, to go to the medium who could produce a psychic manifestation that he could not duplicate by normal means.[6]

The following month Sir Arthur Conan Doyle, who could always be counted upon to have something to say about psychic matters, had a letter published in the Scientific American in which he stated his objections to the committee's organization. He disagreed with the offer of the large sum of money, because, as he said, it would bring out "every rascal in the country."[7] There was probably little disagreement with this statement, but the money had to be offered to give weight and importance to the committee's findings. With such a large amount of money at stake, the decisions would not be hasty. Sir Arthur also disagreed with the make up of the committee. He disliked the skeptical, probing scientist type, and stated that the committee should have been composed of "gentle, quiet, courteous, sympathetic" men who are the most "useful" at a seance.[8] But again the magazine made a good choice. If the committee had been composed of just quiet gentlemen off the street it would not have been taken seriously. All the men on the committee were open-minded and interested in an accurate appraisal of phenomena and, in addition,

---

[5]J. Malcolm Bird, "Square Deal for Psychics," Scientific American, CXXVII (December 1922), p. 375.

[6]William Lindsay Gresham, Houdini: The Man Who Walked Through Walls (New York, 1959), p. 234.

[7]Sir Arthur Conan Doyle, "Answer to Psychic Competition," Scientific American, CXXVIII (January 1923), p. 57.

[8]Ibid.

3

were distinguished enough in their own field to make their decisions
acceptable to the public.

The committee's policy of investigation was that no "rough house"
tactics would be used. They felt that if the medium was a fraud, they
could prove him so by honorable means. It was agreed that the lights
would not be flashed on suddenly during the dark seance, nor would any
member attempt to tackle a spirit in an editorial. In 1923 the Scientific
American said, "...Our investigation is a matter of science, not of
assault and battery; and...any medium may come before us with the expec-
tation of proper and courteous treatment."[9] In addition, the committee
decided to provide conditions under which the medium could produce. As
they stated, "The last thing we want is to be obliged to report that no
phenomena were produced. If the medium is a fraud, our task is to make
him think that it is safe for him to do his stuff, while at the same
time providing means for detecting him."[10]

In all, five psychics entered the competition, the first seances
being held nearly six months after the committee's organization. The
mediums, Valiantine, Josie K. Stewart, Mrs. Tomson, Nino Pecoraro, and
Margery, were each met with different receptions; but all failed to win
the $2500.[11]

---

[9]"Our Psychic Investigation," Scientific American, CXXIX
(August 1923), p. 84.

[10]J. Malcolm Bird, "Another Mediumistic Failure," Scientific
American, CXXIX (December 1923), p. 391.

[11]Harry Price, Fifty Years of Psychical Research (London, 1939),
p. 112.

4

The first seances were held in May, 1923, with a medium referred
to as Mr. X,[12] but later revealed to be Valiantine.[13] The phenomena
produced--voices and touches in total darkness--did not particularly
impress anyone concerned. The only good thing to come from these sittings was the chance for the investigators to test various fraud detection
devices. Because they believed that the medium moved from his chair, they
designed a system using a luminous button, between books on the wall
shelves, directly opposite a member of the committee. The button was invisible to anyone slightly to the left or right of this committeeman. If
the medium left his chair, this button would be eclipsed. On the night
of the second seance, the person observing the button found he could
easily predict when a phenomenon would occur by merely waiting for the
button to be eclipsed.[14]

The most conclusive evidence came from a diabolical device introduced secretly at the third sitting. It was a pressure plate under the
medium's chair that would light a lamp in the adjoining room if the medium
stood up. In addition a microphone in the seance room sent the proceed-
ings to a stenographer in the same adjacent room. The events taking
place in the seance room along with the blinkings of the light were recorded in a single transcript. When the committee members studied the
record, they found that every phenomena had been produced while the

---

[12]J. Malcolm Bird, "Our First Test Seances," Scientific American,
CXXIX (July 1923), p. 14.

[13]Price, p. 112.

[14]Bird, "Our First Test Seances," p. 56.

medium was out of his chair.[15] The first seances were disappointments, but they proved that the committee could work together and function effectively.[16]

In October, 1922, another medium, Mrs. Y[17] (Josie K. Stewart[18]), was tested; and another disappointment was had. Mrs. Stewart came before the committee to produce independent writings under laboratory conditions on cards supplied by the committee. She failed miserably. The messages (described as "platitudinous atrocities") were all produced on cards brought into the seance by her and substituted for the committee's cards. She produced no genuine phenomena and was ruled a fraud by the committee.[19] Even Sir Arthur Conan Doyle was inclined to agree. In a letter to The New York Times, Doyle stated that although he was bound to act in defense of the mediums, he found the case of Mrs. Stewart indefensible. Mrs. Stewart was, however, adamant. She demanded more sittings and even threatened to sue for libel. The magazine stated that the only way that she could obtain her sittings was for her to sue them. She did not.[20]

The investigation of the next medium turned into a comedy of errors and never progressed to a formal sitting. Mrs. Elisabeth Tomson was the first medium to reply to the magazine's offer and the most reluctant to

---

[15]Ibid., p. 14.

[16]Ibid., p. 69.

[17]Bird, "Another Mediumistic Failure," p. 390.

[18]Price, p. 112.

[19]Bird, "Another Mediumistic Failure," p. 445.

[20]J. Malcolm Bird, "Our Psychic Investigations," Scientific American, CXXX (April 1925), p. 236

perform under laboratory conditions. When Mr. Tomson began proposing
conditions under which his wife would appear (which included replacing
several members of the committee with personal friends of the medium), the
magazine withdrew and officially stated that Mrs. Tomson had not permitted a proper investigation and had no claim to the $2500 prize.[21] Of
course Mrs. Tomson still had her followers, and she even ran ads in a
Philadelphia newspaper saying that the seances for the American were
triumphs and that the published accounts were "false stories of jealous
people."[22]

In the February, 1924, issue of Scientific American, the bold subheading of the investigation article proclaimed, "We Find a Medium Whom We
Cannot Characterize as a Conscious Fraud." The medium was Nino Pecoraro,
a 24-year-old Italian who was supposedly controlled by the spirit of the
long dead table-tipper Palladino. Pecoraro was discovered and managed by
Dr. Anselmo Vecchio, who also acted as interpreter. Pecoraro did his
tricks while tied in a chair in semidarkness. When Houdini tied Nino at
the second seance, no phenomena were observed. At the end of three sittings the committee had not prepared a formal statement and said that they
could not be sure until further sittings were held.[23]

The sittings were never held. Dr. Vecchio did not realize the importance of scientific conditions, and he wrote to the magazine only of
conditions under which he would allow further sittings. So, like the

---

[21]J. Malcolm Bird, "Psychic Adventures at Home," Scientific American,
CXXX (January 1924), pp. 20-21.

[22]Bird, "Our Psychic Investigations," p. 291.

[23]J. Malcolm Bird, "Our Psychic Investigation Advances," Scientific
American, CXXX (February 1924), pp. 86, 115, 133.

case of Mrs. Tomson, the matter was formally dropped.[24] In 1931, Nino

Pecoraro made a full confession that he had faked all of his seances

under the direction of Dr. Vecchio. By then Nino had had enough and

announced, "I am sick and tired of giving seances and having others reap

the profits."[25] They found out just seven years too late.

By this time (April 1924) the committee and the magazine were

thoroughly disgusted with the quality of mediums that had entered the

contest. With less than seven months remaining they made an appeal to

the major mediums of the country. The magazine agreed to pay passage to

and from New York and living expenses, if some big name medium would

kindly present himself. None did. The appeal concluded, "It applies

specifically to an American lady of very large mediumistic repute who

sincerely seeks anonymity."[26] This lady was known as Margery,[27] one of

the most versatile mediums in history, whose phenomena included just about

everything that had ever been reported.[28] She was not only quite a

medium, but also quite a woman, and quite a match for a committee accus-

tomed to Mrs. X's and Mrs. Y's.

Margery was the pseudonym of Mrs. Le Roi G. Grandon, wife of a noted

Boston surgeon. She could not be called a professional medium because

she never accepted money for her seances, and she announced that if she

---

[24]Bird, "Our Psychic Investigations," p. 292.

[25]"Truth Will Out," Scientific American, CXLIV (June 1931), p. 374.

[26]Ibid., p. 295.

[27]Price, pp. 110-111.

[28]Gresham, p. 238.

won the Scientific American award she would not accept it but rather
disperse it in psychic research.[29] She and her husband were always extremely generous--to the believers, that is. Mr. Bird, the secretary of
the committee, wrote favorable articles and was their house guest for
months.[30]

The committee's investigation began in April of 1924. By mid-June,
Bird began releasing news stories that the committee had found a genuine
medium. Houdini was angered to find that there had been over fifty
seances held, and that Bird had not notified him of one.[31] Houdini
stormed to the editorial offices to confer with Bird and Mr. O. D. Munn,
publisher of Scientific American. When asked bluntly if Margery was
genuine, Bird replied that she was at least fifty or sixty percent genuine.[32] Houdini then and there declared to Mr. Munn that if he could not
prove Margery a fraud, he would forfeit $1000. Accordingly, Munn and
Houdini set off for Boston on the 22nd of July.[33]

The conditions of the sittings were much less strict. Instead of
holding the seances in their office in New York, as with Valiantine,
Mrs. Stewart, and Pecoraro, the Margery sittings were held in her home
in Boston.[34] The procedures at the sittings were rigidly controlled by

---

[29]G. H. Estabrooks, Spiritism (New York, 1947), p. 201.

[30]Houdini, p. 146.

[31]Gresham, p. 245.

[32]Houdini, p. 137-138.

[33]Gresham, p. 245.

[34]William McDougall, "The Margery Mediumship," Scientific American,
CXXXII (May 1925), p. 339.

Margery's very autocratic spirit control "Walter."[35] In fact his rules were so strict that Dr. McDougall later stated that they hampered the investigator's freedom because he was under the constant threat of exclusion from further sittings. Dr. Crandon always sat immediately to his wife's right, so that he, as well as his wife, had to be controlled.[36]

When Houdini and Munn arrived in Boston, they were invited to join Mr. Bird and Hereward Carrington as house guests of the Crandons. They refused, stating that it would be impossible to retain their objectivity if they did.[37] The seances commenced on July 23rd with, as Long John Nebel describes them, ". . . Margery conducting, Houdini debunking, and a group from the Scientific American refereeing."[38]

During the three seances of July, Houdini was able to detect Margery ringing bells with her feet and lifting tables with her head. It was decided during a committee conference that nothing would be said to the Crandons while Houdini and Munn returned to New York to prepare further tests. Munn stopped the presses already printing the September issue and killed an article by Bird in praise of the Medium.[39]

Already with his publisher angry at him, Bird risked a storm by releasing more statements to newspapers. One was published under the headline: "Experts Vainly Seek Trickery in Spiritualist Demonstration,

---

[35]Houdini, p. 144.

[36]McDougall, p. 339.

[37]Gresham, p. 247.

[38]Long John Nebel, The Way Out World (New York, 1962), p. 147.

[39]Houdini, pp. 144-147.

Houdini the Magician Stumped."[40]   For Houdini this was the last straw.
He called a meeting of the committee that forced Bird's resignation as
secretary. At the same meeting the proposition was put forth by Comstock
and Prince that Houdini design some kind of foolproof, humane confinement
for the medium. Houdini put his assistant Jim Collins to work on it, and
in late August the piano-box-like contraption that completely enclosed
the medium except for her head and hands was ready.[41]

   At the first seance, the medium forced the lid open with her shoul-
ders and was able to ring the bell on the table in front of her with her
head. At the end of the evening she stated that "Walter" had forced the
box open.[42] The second night the box was reinforced with brass strips
which made it impossible to force open. Before the seance, Houdini had
cautioned the committee to keep careful watch that the medium had nothing
with her in the cabinet. Shortly after the seance opened, "Walter"
snarled that Houdini had placed a carpenter's folding rule in the cabinet
to discredit the medium. After Houdini swore that he knew nothing about
it, and after Jim Collins produced his own rule and swore he knew nothing
about a rule in the box, the seance continued; but it was a blank.
Shortly the box was unlocked, and under the cushion for medium's feet
was found a two-foot rule folded to the easily concealed size of six
inches.[43] Houdini later wrote, "I accuse Mrs. Crandon of having smug-
gled it in with her. Mrs. Crandon, knowing that she had been caught,

---

[40]Gresham, p. 250.

[41]Houdini, pp. 149-152.

[42]Ibid.

[43]Ibid., p. 156.

11

made the accusation to clear herself."[44]

In November, 1924, Houdini and Dr. Comstock published formal statements refuting Mrs. Crandon's mediumship. Finally in April, 1925, Drs.
Prince and McDougall issued statements. This constituted a four-to-one
vote against the medium. Mr. Carrington was convinced of supernormal
production. Mr. Bird, the secretary of the committee, left his job as
editor with Scientific American and wrote an entire book supporting
Margery's mediumship; but since he was not a voting member of the committee, his opinion made no difference. She was not awarded the prize.[45]

Margery was later examined by a group from Harvard, which was unanimous in its verdict of fraud,[46] and a group from the American Society of
Psychical Research.[47] In 1933 Dr. Prince published Margery's "box score."
In all she had been examined by twenty-three competent persons. Twenty-
one voted in favor of fraud while only two were convinced that they had
witnessed genuine psychic phenomena.[48]

In two years of investigation with a distinguished committee,
Scientific American could not find a genuine medium. They sincerely tried
to give away their $2500. The only problem was that there was no one who
could earn it. The Scientific American's investigation occurred many

---

[44]Ibid., p. 157.

[45]Walter Franklin Prince and William McDougall, "The Psychic
Investigations," Scientific American, CXXXII (April 1925), p. 229.

[46]Hudson Hoagland, "Science and the Medium," Atlantic Monthly,
CXXXVI (November 1925), pp. 666-678.

[47]Walter Franklin Prince, "The Case Against Margery," Scientific
American, CXLVIII (May 1933), p. 261.

[48]Prince, "The Case Against Margery," p. 261.

years ago and there have been many other investigations since, but not one has been able to prove spirit communication. The <u>American</u>'s was but one of many that have convinced Americans that mediums and spiritualism are frauds.

BIBLIOGRAPHY

Bird, J. Malcolm. "Another Mediumistic Failure," <u>Scientific American</u>,
     CXXIX (December 1923), 390-391, 441-445.

_____. "Our First Test Seances," <u>Scientific American</u>, CXXIX (July 1923),
     14, 56, 64-69.

_____. "Our Psychic Investigation Advances," <u>Scientific American</u>, CXXX
     (February 1924), 86, 115, 133-139.

_____. "Our Psychic Investigations," <u>Scientific American</u>, CXXX (April
     1924), 236, 291-295.

_____. "Psychic Adventures at Home," <u>Scientific American</u>, CXXX (January
     1924), 20-21.

_____. "Square Deal for Psychics," <u>Scientific American</u>, CXXVII (December
     1922), 375.

Carrington, Hereward. "The Mechanics of the Psychic," <u>Scientific American</u>,
     CXXVI (January 1922), 60, 80.

Crandon, L. R. G. "The Psychic Investigation," <u>Scientific American</u>,
     CXXXII (January 1925), 29, 62, 65.

Doyle, Sir Arthur Conan. "Answer to Psychic Competition," <u>Scientific
     American</u>, CXXVIII (January 1923), 57.

Estabrooks, G. H. <u>Spiritism</u>. New York: E. P. Dutton and Co., Inc., 1947.

Gresham, William Lindsay. <u>Houdini: The Man Who Walked Through Walls</u>.
     New York: Henry Holt and Co., 1959.

Hoagland, Hudson. "Science and the Medium," <u>Atlantic Monthly</u>, CXXXVI
     (November 1925), 666-678.

Houdini, Harry. <u>Houdini on Magic</u>, ed. by Walter B. Gibson and Morris N.
     Young. New York: Dover Publications, Inc., 1953.

McDougall, William. "The 'Margery Mediumship'," <u>Scientific American</u>,
     CXXXII (May 1925), 339-341.

_____. "The Psychic Investigation: Formal Statement by Dr. McDougall,"
     <u>Scientific American</u>, CXXXII (April 1925), 229.

Nebel, Long John. <u>The Way Out World</u>. New York: Lancer Books, 1962.

"Our Psychic Investigation," <u>Scientific American</u>, CXXIX (August 1923), 84.

14

Price, Harry. Fifty Years of Psychical Research. London: Longmans,
    Green and Co., 1939.

Prince, Walter Franklin. "The Case Against Margery," Scientific American,
    CXLVIII (May 1933), 261-263.

_____. "The Psychic Detective," Scientific American, CXXVII (July 1922),
    6-7, 71.

_____. "The Psychic Investigation," Scientific American, CXXXII
    (February 1925), 93.

_____. "The Psychic Investigation: Formal Statement by Dr. Prince,"
    Scientific American, CXXXII (April 1925), 229.

"Truth Will Out," Scientific American, CXLIV (June 1931), 374.

Formal
Outlining

A **working** or **scratch outline** is the record of a writer's thought processes as he plans the organization of a paper before he begins writing. The purpose of such an outline is to guide the writer as he composes paragraphs and sentences; it need not conform to conventional patterns. A **formal outline** is for the reader. It summarizes for him in heading form the central points of a finished paper; it is a record of a completed rather than a proposed organization. Since it is intended for public consumption, a formal outline is best prepared after the paper is written, and it must conform to conventional patterns.

There are two kinds of formal outlines. In a **topic outline** the headings are expressed in phrases; in a **sentence outline** they are expressed as complete sentences. The chief advantage of a topic outline is that it is more direct and pithy and less cumbersome than a sentence outline. The chief advantage of a sentence outline is that it compels the writer to express points fully and prevents him from composing vague or indefinite headings that may be virtually meaningless to a reader. Personal preference (yours or your professor's) must dictate which kind of outline you compose. Both kinds should observe the following six principles of good outlining, which are illustrated in topic outline form. Remember: This appendix illustrates how to prepare an outline of a paper or essay *already written*. It does not illustrate how to prepare a scratch or working outline; for material on that kind of outlining see Chapter 3 on preparing a basic organization for a paper.

Principle 1: Balanced Development of Outline

The purpose of a formal outline is to give the reader a quick understanding of the main points of a paper and the order of their development. It must not be so sparse or general in its headings that it omits or obscures main points, and it must not be so detailed in its headings that it goes beyond a presentation of main points. It should present the full essence of the paper, but not its individual details. A properly developed outline will adequately fit the subject matter of its paper.

Here is an example of an outline so sparse and general in its headings that it fails to express the essence of the paper; it is virtually useless to a reader.

Portuguese Oppression of Natives
in Angola in the 1950s

 I. Portuguese military rule
 II. Slave labor
 III. Censorship

Here is an example of an outline so detailed in its development that it goes far beyond the purpose of outlining.

Portuguese Oppression of Natives
in Angola in the 1950s

 I. Portuguese military rule as the force behind oppression
   A. The organization of military forces in Angola
      1. Soldiers organized in a classic system of command
         a. Squad
         b. Platoon
         c. Company
         d. Battalion
         e. Brigade
      2. A three-year tour of duty required of soldiers
      3. Supplies shipped from home bases
      4. Promotions passed on by local commanders

   B. The power of the military force in Angola
      1. The permanence of military law
         a. Presence of soldier-police squads in every village
         b. Curfew for all natives at sundown
         c. Right of any officer to act as judge at any time
           (1) In disputes between natives
           (2) In disputes between Portuguese civilians and natives
           (3) In disputes between Portuguese soldiers and natives
      2. The use of soldiers as straw bosses
         a. To work gangs on plantations
         b. To work road gangs
         c. To work gangs for personal profit
      3. The power of the individual soldier
         a. Is always armed
         b. Can recruit native work force on his own authority
         c. Can enter any native dwelling for any purpose
         d. Can take produce from any native market

An so on. Such excessive detail defeats the purpose of a formal outline, which is to present to the reader in capsule form the central points of a paper. If the above outline were continued, it would be as long as the paper itself.

Here is an example of an outline properly balanced in development.

Portuguese Oppression of Natives in Angola in the 1950s

    I. Portuguese military rule as the force behind oppression
       A. The organization of the military force
       B. The power of the military force
          1. The presence of permanent military law
          2. The use of soldiers as straw bosses
          3. The oppressive power given to individual soldiers
   II. The reduction of the native population to slave labor
       A. Complete absence of civil rights for natives
       B. Governmental expropriation of native economic production
       C. Physical abuses resulting from slave status of natives
  III. The government's use of police-state tactics to prevent world protest
       A. Supervision and restriction of travel by foreigners
       B. Censorship of all news releases
       C. Intimidation of businessmen who might express protest

In a properly developed outline, each heading is a capsule summary of—a sort of title for—a part of the accompanying paper. It is a generality derived from the paper's organization. Headings should not be mere details that occupy as much space in the outline as they do in the paper itself.

Principle 2: Meaningful Headings

Since the purpose of a formal outline is to give the reader a quick summary of a paper before he reads it, each heading must be meaningful. An outline heading that is understandable only to one who has read the accompanying paper is useless.

Here is an outline composed of near-meaningless headings.

The Development of the First Nuclear Submarine

    I. Introduction
   II. Rickover's fight
  III. The Navy's capitulation
  IV. Troubles
   V. Conclusion

First note that the headings *Introduction* and *Conclusion* are worthless in an outline. If a central point is made in the introduction or conclusion, then it should be given meaningful summary in a real heading. It is unnecessary for an outline to tell the reader that the paper opens and closes; only main points should be given outline headings. The other headings in the outline are far too vague and indefinite to be useful to a reader. Here is a more meaningful version.

The Development of the First Nuclear Submarine

    I. Admiral Rickover's demonstration of the feasibility of nuclear submarines
   II. Rickover's controversies with the Navy over his proposal to build a nuclear submarine
  III. The capitulation of the Navy because of Eisenhower's intervention
  IV. The technical difficulties that Rickover encountered in building the submarine
   V. The completion of the first nuclear submarine and demonstration of its capabilities

The purpose of outline writing is not to reduce a heading to the fewest possible words, but to express in compact, meaningful form a central idea of the paper. Meaningfulness in an outline heading is much more important than brevity.

Principle 3: Parallelism of Content

An outline is composed of **levels,** and the headings in any one level represent a division of a previous level. Thus the title of a paper is the point of origin of its outline. A division of the title produces the roman-numeral headings, which are the **first level** of the outline. For example, in the discussion of meaningful headings above, the title "The Development of the First Nuclear Submarine" is divided into five roman-numeral headings. As presented there, the outline has only one level—the five equal headings derived from the title.

When a roman-numeral heading has subheadings, they represent a division of the roman-numeral heading and are thus on the **second level.** For example:

The Development of the First
Nuclear Submarine

    I. Admiral Rickover's demonstration of the feasibility of nuclear submarines
        A. His pilot nuclear-reactor power plant
        B. His demonstration of the practicality of power transmission from the reactor
        C. His solutions to the problems of sustained underwater cruising

Headings A, B, and C here are divisions of roman numeral I and represent the second level of the outline.

A division of any of these headings would represent the **third level** of the outline. For example:

        C. His solutions to the problems of sustained underwater cruising
            1. Provisions for a continuous supply of oxygen
            2. Provisions for physical comfort of the crew
            3. Provisions for psychological adjustment of the crew

Headings 1, 2, and 3, being divisions of a second-level heading, represent the third level of the outline. And so on. Generally, only the outline of a very long paper needs to be taken to more than three levels, and two levels are usually sufficient for most college papers.

In writing, the word *parallelism* means equality in rank. In an outline, all the headings on any one level should be parallel in content—that is, the parts of the paper that the headings summarize should be equal in importance. Thus all the roman-numeral headings, being divisions of the title, should be equal in rank, and all the subheadings under any one roman-numeral heading should similarly be equal in rank. And so on.

Faulty parallelism of content occurs when the headings placed on one level are not really equal in rank. For example:

The Practical Value of a Liberal Arts Education

I. Its development of one's flexibility in adapting to new business or industrial techniques
II. Through providing an understanding of historical perspectives and the evolution of human knowledge
III. Through providing a mastery of theory rather than of just specific techniques

Parallelism of content is violated here because headings II and III are not two more divisions of the title but are really divisions of heading I. They should be headings A and B under I.

Thus when an outline heading is out of place, faulty parallelism of content occurs. You can keep headings properly parallel only by thinking clearly enough to see how the roman-numeral headings derive from the title, how second-level headings derive from roman-numeral headings, how third-level headings derive from those on the second level, and so on.

You should not think, however, that headings parallel in content must necessarily represent parts of the paper that are equal in length. For example, in a paper on "Methods of Soil Analysis" the part represented by roman-numeral I (the first method) might cover only two pages, whereas the part represented by roman-numeral II (the second method) might cover five pages. The two roman-numeral headings, nevertheless, would be equal in importance (parallel in content), for each would pertain to one whole method of soil analysis.

Balanced development, meaningful headings, and parallelism of content are the three most important principles of outlining, for they pertain to the subject matter of the outline. The following three principles are of lesser importance, for they pertain to the mechanical rather than the logical aspects of outlining. They bear the same relationship to outlining that conventions of usage bear to writing, and you should observe them in outlining for the same reasons you maintain correctness in writing.

Principle 4: Parallelism of Structure

An outline maintains parallelism of structure when all the headings of **any one level and division** are in the same grammatical structure. One of the advantages of the sentence outline is that parallelism of structure is no problem since all the headings are sentences. In topic outlines, faulty parallelism of structure occurs when two or more different kinds of phrases are used for one level and division.

There are several kinds of phrases that may be used as headings in a topic outline. When the headword of a phrase (the key word around which the phrase is built) is a noun, verb, adjective, adverb, participle, infinitive, or gerund, the phrase is named after the headword. The prepositional phrase is another kind that may be used as a topic heading. The writer's problem is to use only one kind of phrase for the headings in any one level and division.

In the following outline, phrase names are substituted for actual headings to illustrate how parallelism of structure is maintained.

I. Noun phrase
   A. Participial phrase
      1. Prepositional phrase
      2. Prepositional phrase
   B. Participial phrase
II. Noun phrase
   A. Adjective phrase
      1. Infinitive phrase
      2. Infinitive phrase
   B. Adjective phrase

Headings I and II are on the same level and in the same division (of the title) and thus are parallel. Headings A and B under I are on the same level and in the same division (of heading I) and thus are parallel. Headings A and B under II are on the same level as A and B under I, but they are in a different division (of heading II) and thus, though they are parallel to each other, they do not need to be parallel to headings in another division. And so on.

The following outline violates parallelism of structure.

Methods of Rehabilitating Delinquents

I. The use of psychiatric therapy to rehabilitate delinquents
   A. In out-patient clinics
   B. Institutionalization

    II. Giving delinquents vocational rehabilitation
        A. Through on-the-job training
        B. Putting them in a vocational school
        C. Use of the armed services
   III. To remedy defects in delinquents' homelife
        A. By economic rehabilitation of parents
        B. Marriage counseling of parents
        C. To relocate delinquents in new homes

Headings I, II, and III are not in parallel structure, for I is a noun phrase (the noun *use* is the headword), II is a participial phrase (*giving* is the headword), and III is an infinitive phrase (*to remedy* is the headword). Identify the kinds of phrases in the subheadings, and suggest ways of establishing parallel structure for the whole outline.

Principle 5: Avoidance of Single Subheadings

    Mechanically, the process of outlining is subdividing. The title of a paper is divided into first-level (roman-numeral) headings; a first-level heading is divided into second-level headings; and so on. The principle of division, then, says that a single subheading in an outline is illogical, since if you divide a heading at all, you must divide it into at least two parts.

    For example, an outline with only one roman-numeral heading is faulty:

Public Recreational Facilities in My Home Town

    I. What my home town does to provide public recreation
        A. A senior-citizens recreational center
        B. A summer camp program
        C. A winter sports program
        D. A system of well-equipped parks

Heading I of this outline does not divide the title, but merely repeats it in different words. Headings A, B, C, and D are proper divisions of the title and therefore should form four first-level (roman-numeral) headings under the title.

    Sometimes an outline writer will use a single subheading that is really just a part of the heading it is placed under. Example:

    II. A summer camp program
        A. In conjunction with the YMCA Camp

Heading A is not a division of II, but a continuation of it. The faulty single subheading can be eliminated in this way:

II. A summer camp program in conjunction with the YMCA Camp

Normally, you must divide a heading into at least two subheadings or not divide it at all.

A single subheading may be logically acceptable when it presents a single example to illustrate the heading it is placed under. Example:

Urban Renewal

    I. The economic success of central malls in big cities
       A. Example: Detroit, Michigan's central mall

Heading A indicates that in the general discussion of the economic success of central malls one extended example will be given. Such a legitimate single subheading should be labeled with the word *example*.

Principle 6: Consistency of Form

An outline should be consistent in its numbering system, its capitalization, and its punctuation. Any clear, consistent system is satisfactory. The most common numbering system uses roman numerals (I, II) for the first level; capital letters (A, B) for the second level; arabic numerals (1, 2) for the third level; and lowercase letters (a, b) for the fourth level. Normally in a topic outline only the first word of a heading is capitalized. In a sentence outline end punctuation is of course used, but the most commonly used system in topic outlines omits end punctuation.

A Glossary
of Usage

accept, except   *Accept* is a verb meaning "to receive"; *except* is a preposition indicating that something is excluded; *except* can be used as a verb meaning "to leave out or exclude."

> *right:* I cannot accept your gift.
> *right:* Everyone except me came to the party.
> *right:* (though rare): The professor excepted those who had perfect attendance.

accidentally   The spelling *accidently* is substandard.

affect, effect   *Affect* is a verb meaning "to influence"; *effect* is a noun meaning "the influence exerted on something"; *effect* is also a verb meaning "to bring about."

> *right:* The bad weather affected my morale.
> *right:* The bad weather had an effect on my morale.
> *right:* The prisoner effected an escape.

agree to, agree with   We *agree to* a plan but *agree with* a person.

a lot, lots   *A lot* is less colloquial than *lots.* Some authorities think *a lot* is colloquial, but most accept it as standard.

all ready, already   *All ready* is an adjectival idiom meaning "everyone or everything is prepared"; *already* is an adverb meaning "at this time or before this time."

all right, alright   The spelling *alright* is now accepted by dictionaries, but careful writers still use only *all right.*

all together, altogether   *All together* is an adverbial idiom meaning that "everyone acts in unison"; *altogether* is an adverb meaning "wholly or completely."

> *right:* Let's sing all together now.
> *right:* That solution is altogether unsatisfactory.

allude, refer   *Allude* is a verb meaning "to mention indirectly"; *refer* is a verb meaning "to mention specifically and directly."

> *right:* He alluded to his drinking problem when he spoke of Alcoholics Anonymous.
> *right:* He referred to *Hamlet,* act IV, scene II.

allusion, delusion, illusion   *Allusion* is a noun meaning "an indirect reference"; *delusion* is a noun meaning "a false belief"; *illusion* is a noun meaning "a deceptive appearance." Don't confuse *delusion* and *illusion.*

> *right:* His allusion to *Das Kapital* made him suspect.
> *right:* He is under the delusion that he will be a great baseball player.
> *right:* Her apparent beauty was a mere illusion.
> *wrong:* His illusion that he was another FDR irritated the political pros.

almost, most   *Almost* means "nearly"; *most* means "to the greatest extent." *Most* is colloquially used for *almost.*

> *colloquial at best:* Most all the players were declared ineligible.

among, between   Use *among* when three or more items are designated; use *between* for two items. Occasionally *between* is used colloquially for *among.*

amount, number   *Amount* designates a quantity that cannot be numbered; *number* designates a quantity that is divisible into units.

> *right:* an amount of sugar
> *right:* a number of books
> *colloquial at best:* a large amount of nails

and etc.   Do not use the redundant *and* with *etc.*

and, but   It is not wrong to begin a sentence with *and* or *but.*

and/or   Many authorities advise against the usage "All swimmers and/or waders must obey the lifeguard." Other authorities accept the usage, and there seems to be no sound reason for avoiding it.

anecdote, antidote   An *anecdote* is a little story. An *antidote* counteracts a poison.

anxious, eager   *Anxious* means "uneasy or apprehensive"; *eager* means "strongly desirous of."

> *colloquial at best:* I was anxious to go to the party.

anyway, any way   *Anyway* is an adverb meaning "in any case"; *any way* is a noun phrase.

> *right:* I was broke, anyway.
> *right:* I couldn't find any way to solve the problem.

around   Avoid using *around* (or *round*) to mean "about."

as, as if, like   Some authorities think *like* as a conjunction is colloquial.

> *colloquial to some:* It looks like it may rain.
> *standard:* It looks as if it may rain.
> *colloquial to some:* Do like I do.
> *standard:* Do as I do.

average, median   An *average* is the total sum of the scores on a number of tests or other items divided by the number of tests. The *median* is the score exactly in the middle of a number of tests or other such items.

awful, awfully   Both *awful* and *awfully* should be avoided as intensifiers.

> *low colloquial:* I'm awful (awfully) sorry about your accident.

bad, badly   *Bad* is an adjective, *badly* an adverb.

> *right:* I feel bad.
> *right:* My car runs badly.

because clause as subject   *Because* normally introduces an adverb, not a noun, clause.

> *colloquial:* Just because you're intelligent is no reason for you to be conceited.
> *standard:* Your being intelligent is no reason for you to be conceited.

because of, due to   Many authorities prefer *because of* as an adverb and *due to* as an adjective.

> *preferred:* Because of the rain I was late.
> *preferred:* My failure was due to my poor study habits.

being as, being that   Avoid these low-level constructions. Use *since* instead.

beside, besides   *Beside* is a preposition meaning "at the side of"; *besides* is a preposition or adverb meaning "in addition to."

> *wrong:* We brought everything beside beer.

between   See *among*. Never use "between you and I," "between you and he," and so on. The object form of a pronoun must be used after *between*.

born, borne   *Borne* is the past participle of *bear* when it is in the active voice; *born* is the past participle in the passive voice.

> *right:* She has borne six children.
> *right:* She has borne her poverty with elegance.
> *right:* He was born in France.

burst, bust   *Burst* is the standard usage; *bust* is at best low colloquial. The principal parts of *burst* are *burst, burst, burst*. There is no such word as *bursted*.

but that, but what

> *colloquial:* I don't know but what I'd avoid that store.
> *standard:* I don't know but that I'd avoid that store.

can't help but

> *colloquial:* I can't help but feel sorry for Tom.
> *more formal:* I can't help feeling sorry for Tom.

censor, censure   *Censor* is a verb meaning "to suppress or restrict publication of supposedly objectionable material." It is also a noun meaning "one who censors." *Censure* is a verb meaning "to find fault with or condemn as wrong." It is also a noun meaning "the expression of disapproval or blame."

> *right:* The government should not censor novels.
> *right:* Such behavior is subject to censure.

cite, site, sight   *Cite* is a verb meaning "to indicate or mention"; *site* is a noun meaning "a place where something is, was, or is to be"; *sight* is a noun or verb having to do with vision.

right: He cited a chapter from the Bible as proof.

right: The site for the new building was poorly chosen.

colloquialism, localism, regionalism   A *colloquialism* is "a word or phrase suitable for informal usage"; a *localism* or *regionalism* is "a word or phrase used only in one locality."

wrong: I heard many colloquialisms (meaning localisms) in the hills of North Carolina.

complement, compliment   *Complement* means "something that completes or a number or amount that makes a whole"; *compliment* means "to give praise." Each can be used as a verb or a noun.

right: He complimented her on her dress.

right: The fourth Division had a full complement of troops.

conscience, conscious   *Conscience* is a noun meaning "a knowledge or feeling of right and wrong"; *conscious* is an adjective meaning "aware or alert."

contemptible, contemptuous   *Contemptible* means "deserving contempt"; *contemptuous* means "showing contempt."

right: He is a contemptible person because of his bad habits.

right: I was contemptuous of his pomposity.

continual, continuous   *Continual* means "occurring at close intervals"; *continuous* means "without interruption or cessation."

could of, would of   Illiterate misspellings for *could have* and *would have.*

council, counsel   *Council* is a noun meaning "an official group"; *counsel* is a verb meaning "to give advice" or a noun meaning "advice or adviser." *Counselor* comes from counsel.

right: The city council voted new taxes.

right: I asked my teacher to counsel me.

right: He gave me good counsel.

credible, creditable, credulous   *Credible* means "believable"; *creditable* means "worthy of praise"; *credulous* means "willing to believe readily or easily imposed upon."

right: Your story is credible.

right: His kind actions were creditable.

right: A credulous person is an easy mark for a con man.

data   *Data* is a plural and most writers use a plural verb with it.

right: The data support his conclusion.

delusion   See *allusion*.

different from, different than   *Different from* is the preferred usage; *different than* is colloquial.

> *preferred:* John's book is different from mine.

disinterested, uninterested   *Disinterested* means "impartial"; *uninterested* means "having no interest in."

> *right:* The judge was disinterested.
> *wrong:* John was disinterested in his studies.

double negative   See *hardly*.

due to   See *because of*.

eager   See *anxious*.

effect   See *affect*.

enthuse   Many authorities prefer *be enthusiastic*.

everyday, every day   The single word is normally used as a modifier. The two words are a noun with a determiner.

> *right:* That's an everyday affair.
> *right:* I go to the movies every day.

everyone, every one   The single word is an indefinite pronoun meaning "everybody." The two words are a noun (cardinal number) with a determiner.

> *right:* Everyone should follow his conscience.
> *right:* Every one of the members contributed.

everyone . . . their   Though commonly used, this phrase is not as acceptable as *everyone . . . his*.

except   See *accept*.

expect, suspect   *Expect* means "to look forward to or anticipate"; *suspect* means "to think probable or likely."

> *right:* I suspect he will fail.
> *colloquial:* I expect he will fail.

farther, further   *Farther* relates to physical distance; *further* refers to degree and quantity. More and more, *further* is being used as synonymous with *farther*.

> *right:* I cannot walk any farther.
> *right:* Do you have anything further to say?

fewer, less   *Fewer* refers to separate items; *less* refers to a quantity that cannot be divided into separate items. *Less* is used colloquially for *fewer*.

> *right:* I have fewer marbles than you.
> *right:* I have less sugar than you.
> *colloquial:* I have less marbles than you.

fiancé, fiancée The *fiancé* is the male and the *fiancée* the female.

folk, folks *Folk* is mostly used as a modifier, as in "folk music." *Folks* refers to the members of a family or to a group.

fortuitous, fortunate *Fortuitous* means "occurring by chance rather than design." *Fortunate* means "happening by a favorable chance" or "favored with good fortune."

fulsome *Fulsome* means "offensive," as in "fulsome praise." The word is not related to *full*.

get, got, gotten These words are used in many colloquial idioms, such as "Get going with your project." But they need not be avoided in semiformal writing.

good, well These words are difficult to separate, for both are adjectives and *well* is also an adverb. But most usages are acceptable now. You should, however, avoid using *good* for *well* in such examples as these:

> *right:* The car runs well.
> *right:* John did well in algebra.
> *right:* John carried the joke off well.

hadn't ought to The phrase is low colloquial. *Should not* or *shouldn't* is the standard expression.

hanged, hung Use *hanged* in referring to persons being suspended in a noose. Use *hung* for other uses.

> *right:* The criminal was hanged.

hardly Never use the double negative *can't hardly, won't hardly,* and so forth.

he, she Use *he* when the sex is indefinite. Avoid using "he or she."

healthful, healthy *Healthful* means "giving health." *Healthy* means "having health."

height, heighth The preferred spelling and pronunciation is *height*.

himself, hisself Only *himself* is standard. *Hisself* is vulgate.

human, humane *Human* as an adjective means "having the attributes of man." *Humane* means "characterized by kindness and sympathy."

if, whether Use *whether* to introduce a noun clause.

> *right:* I don't know whether I can come.
> *colloquial:* I don't know if I can come.

illusion See *allusion*.

imply, infer   *Imply* means "to suggest or hint"; *infer* means "to draw a conclusion about."

> *right:* As he talked, he implied I was a fool.
> *right:* From the conversation I could infer that John was displeased with Joan.
> *wrong:* As he talked, he inferred I was a fool.

in, into   *In* shows location; *into* shows direction.

> *right:* He was in the house.
> *right:* He walked into the house.

incidentally   Avoid the spelling *incidently.*

incredible, incredulous   The negative of *credible* and *credulous.* See *credible.*

indefinite you   Some composition teachers prefer their students to avoid the indefinite *you.*

> *not acceptable to some teachers:* To succeed in the business world, you must first of all be tenacious.
> *acceptable to all:* To succeed in the business world, one must first of all be tenacious.

infer   See *imply.*

inside of   Colloquial for *within.*

> *preferred:* I will see you within a week.

invite   Do not use as a noun.

> *substandard:* I received an invite.
> *right:* I received an invitation.

irregardless   Avoid altogether. Use *regardless.*

its, it's   *Its* is possessive; *it's* is a contraction of *it is* or *it has.* Never use the illiterate misspelling *its'*

> *right:* Its waterbowl is empty.
> *right:* It's raining.

it's me, it's I   *It's me* is colloquial. In formal situations use *it's I.*

kind of, sort of   Colloquial. Prefer *rather* or *somewhat.*

later, latter   *Later* is an adjective or adverb meaning "at a time after a specified time"; *latter* is an adjective or noun meaning "nearer the end or the last mentioned."

> *right:* He came later than you.
> *right:* Of the three methods described, I chose the latter.

lay, lie   *Lay* is a transitive verb meaning "to place an object some-where"; *lie* is an intransitive verb meaning "to be in or take a reclining position." The principal parts of *lay* are *lay, laid, laid;* the principal parts of *lie* are *lie, lay, lain. Lay* is used *colloquially* for *lie,* but most teachers oppose such usage.

> *right:* I will lay the book on the table.
> *right:* Yesterday I laid the book on the table.
> *right:* I have laid the book down many times.
> *right:* The book is lying on the table.
> *right:* I will lie down this afternoon.
> *right:* Yesterday I lay down.
> *right:* I have lain down every day this week.

lead, led   *Lead* is not the proper spelling of the past tense of the verb. The pronunciation of the metal *lead* confuses some people.

learn, teach   The use of *learn* for the meaning of *teach* is vulgate and should be avoided altogether.

leave, let   *Leave* in the sense of *let* is vulgate.

> *nonstandard:* I have the habit of leaving nature take its course.

less   See *fewer.*

liable, libel   *Liable* is an adjective meaning "responsible or legally bound or likely to have"; *libel* is a noun meaning "slanderous references" or a verb meaning "to slander."

> *right:* A man is liable for debts contracted by his wife.
> *right:* The gossip columnist was sued for libel.

lie   See *lay.*

lightening, lightning   *Lightning* is the noun meaning "a flash of elec-tricity in the sky." *Lightening* is a verb meaning "making lighter."

like   See *as.*

localism   See *colloquialism.*

loose, lose   *Loose* is an adjective meaning "unfastened"; *lose* is a verb meaning "to mislay or to be deprived of."

loud, loudly   As an adverb, *loud* is colloquial.

> *colloquial:* Don't talk so loud.
> *standard:* Don't talk so loudly.

majority, plurality   In an election, *majority* means "more than half the votes." *Plurality* means "the largest number of votes among three or more candidates, with none having a majority."

maybe, may be   *Maybe* is an adverb meaning "perhaps or possibly"; *may be* is a form of the verb *to be.*

moral, morale   *Moral* is an adjective meaning "right or ethical"; *morale* is a noun meaning "a mental attitude or condition."

> *right:* All moral acts are recorded in Heaven.
> *right:* The troops' morale was high.

most   See *almost.*

nohow   A vulgate term. Avoid in all writing except dialogue.

nowhere near   Low colloquial. Avoid in semiformal writing.

nowheres   A vulgate term. Avoid in all writing except dialogue.

number   See *amount.*

old-fashioned, old-fashion   *Old-fashion* is sometimes used now colloquially, but *old-fashioned* is the standard adjective.

on account of the fact that   Just use *because.*

onto, on to   *Onto* is a preposition. *On to* is an adverb plus a preposition.

> *right:* The dog trotted onto the playing field.
> *right:* We went on to our destination.

oral, verbal   *Oral* means "spoken"; *verbal* means "pertaining to written or oral language." *Verbal* is now much used for *oral.*

passed, past   *Passed* is the past tense and past participle of the verb *pass; past* is an adjective and a noun meaning "of a former time."

> *right:* I passed calculus.
> *right:* The time for reconciliation is past.

plan on, plan to   *Plan on doing* is colloquial. *Plan to do* is standard.

prepositions   It is not wrong to end a sentence with a preposition.

principal, principle   *Principal* is an adjective meaning "chief" and a noun meaning "the head of a school or money used as capital"; *principle* is a noun meaning "rule, law, or doctrine."

> *right:* Stockholm is the principal city of Sweden.
> *right:* Algebraic principles are not difficult to learn.

proved, proven   Both are now standard as the past participle of *prove.*

quick, quickly   As an adverb, *quick* is colloquial.

> *colloquial:* Come quick.
> *standard:* Come quickly.

quiet, quite   *Quiet* is an adjective meaning "not noisy, calm"; *quite* is an adverb meaning "entirely." The words are pronounced differently, *quiet* having two syllables.

> *wrong:* Children, keep quite.

raise, rise   *Raise* is a transitive verb (takes an object) meaning "to put something in a higher position"; its principal parts are *raise, raised, raised. Rise* is an intransitive verb meaning "to go to a higher position"; its principal parts are *rise, rose, risen.*

> *right:* Will you raise my salary?
> *right:* Smoke does not always rise.

real, really   As an adverb, *real* is low colloquial, but it is standard as an adjective.

> *colloquial:* I had a real good time.
> *standard:* I had a really (very) good time.
> *standard:* The real facts of the case never came out.

reason is because, reason is that   Both expressions are now acceptable, but *reason is that* is more suitable for semiformal writing.

reckon   *Reckon* is colloquially and regionally used to mean "suppose." It should not be used for this meaning in semiformal writing.

refer   See *allude.*

regionalism   See *colloquialism.*

rhyme, rime   Either spelling is correct.

scarcely   Avoid the double negative *can't scarcely.* Use *can scarcely.*

set, sit   *Set* is a transitive verb (takes an object) meaning "to place something in a position"; its principal parts are *set, set, set. Sit* is an intransitive verb meaning "to occupy a seat or to be in a sitting position"; its principal parts are *sit, sat, sat.*

> *right:* Yesterday I set the phonograph on the floor.
> *right:* Will you sit in this chair?
> *right:* I have sat here all day.
> *wrong:* He set down
> *wrong:* He has set here all day.

shall, will   Formal rules for the use of these modal auxiliaries no longer hold. Whichever sounds natural is acceptable.

site   See *cite.*

slow, slowly   Both have been adverbs in English for over a thousand years. *Go slow* and *go slowly* are equally correct.

so   As a conjunction, *so* is generally considered colloquial, but many professional writers now use it as standard.

> *colloquial to some:* The rain didn't let up, so we abandoned the game.
> *preferred by many:* Since the rain didn't let up, we abandoned the game.

sometime, sometimes, some time   *Sometime* is an adverb meaning "at some future time." *Sometimes* is an adverb meaning "at times" or "occasionally." *Some time* is a noun with a determiner.

>   *right:* Sometime I'll get my degree
>   *right:* It snows here sometimes.
>   *right:* We spent some time with Susan.

sort of   See *kind of.*

split infinitive   Some stylists oppose the placing of a modifier between the *to* and the verb of an infinitive, such as "to better understand." They prefer "better to understand." Nevertheless, split infinitives are not errors. But usually the style will sound better if the modifier is placed before the *to* or after the verb.

>   *awkard:* I want to learn to better play the game.
>   *smoother:* I want to learn to play the game better.

such as   Do not use a mark of punctuation after this connective.

>   *right:* Bring comfortable clothes, such as slacks, sport shirts, and
>   loafers.

suppose, supposed   To omit the "d" of the past participle is a serious error. When the "d" is needed, the word will normally be preceded by a form of the verb *to be* and will be followed by an infinitive. The same distinction is to be made for *use* and *used.*

>   *right:* I was supposed to vote today.
>   *wrong:* Was he suppose to come?

suspect   See *expect.*

than, then   *Than* is a conjunction used in comparisons; *then* is an adverb of time.

>   *right:* John has a higher IQ than Shirley.
>   *right:* First we ate; then went to the opera.

themselves, theirselves   *Theirselves* is strictly vulgate and should always be avoided.

these kinds, these sorts   These are the correct forms. *These kind* and *these sort* are nonstandard.

toward, towards   There is no essential distinction between these words.

try and, try to   *Try to* is preferable.

uninterested   See *disinterested.*

used to   See *suppose.*

well   See *good.*

where . . . at   Avoid the *at* if it is unnecessary.

> *right:* Where is he?
> *colloquial at best:* Where is he at?

whether   See *if*.

who, whom   Colloquially, *who* is now commonly used as an object except directly after a preposition. In semiformal writing, only *whom* should be used as an object.

> *colloquial:* Who did you mention?
> *standard:* Whom did you mention?
> *unacceptable:* To who should I give the receipts?

whose, who's   *Whose* is a possessive pronoun; *who's* is a contraction for *who is* or *who has*.

> *wrong:* Who's book do you have?

would have   Avoid using for *had*.

> *right:* If he had studied, he would have passed the exam.
> *colloquial at best:* If he would have studied, he would have passed
> the exam.

would of   An illiteracy. Use *would have*.

you   See *indefinite you*.

your, you're   *Your* is a possessive pronoun; *you're* is a contraction for *you are*.

> *wrong:* Your supposed to come at eight.

Index

CORRECTION CHART AND THEME REVISION GUIDE

The page numbers to the right of each of the correction symbols refer to the part of the text where each error or weakness is fully explained. When necessary, consult the text materials for aid in revising your writing.